"We are pleased to witness publication of the
Ancient Christian Commentary on Scripture. It is most beneficial for us to learn
how the ancient Christians, especially the saints of the church
who proved through their lives their devotion to God and his Word, interpreted
Scripture. Let us heed the witness of those who have gone before us in the faith."

METROPOLITAN THEODOSIUS
Primate, Orthodox Church in America

"Across Christendom there has emerged a widespread interest
in early Christianity, both at the popular and scholarly level. . . .
Christians of all traditions stand to benefit from this project, especially clergy
and those who study the Bible. Moreover, it will allow us to see how our traditions are
both rooted in the scriptural interpretations of the church fathers while at
the same time seeing how we have developed new perspectives."

ALBERTO FERREIRO
Professor of History, Seattle Pacific University

"The Ancient Christian Commentary on Scripture fills a long overdue need for scholars and
students of the church fathers. . . . Such information will be of immeasurable
worth to those of us who have felt inundated by contemporary interpreters and novel theories
of the biblical text. We welcome some 'new' insight from the
ancient authors in the early centuries of the church."

H. WAYNE HOUSE
Professor of Theology and Law
Trinity University School of Law

"Chronological snobbery—the assumption that our ancestors working without benefit of
computers have nothing to teach us—is exposed as nonsense by this magnificent
new series. Surfeited with knowledge but starved of wisdom, many of us are
more than ready to sit at table with our ancestors and listen to their holy
conversations on Scripture. I know I am."

EUGENE H. PETERSON
Professor Emeritus of Spiritual Theology
Regent College

"Few publishing projects have encouraged me as much as the recently announced Ancient Christian Commentary on Scripture with Dr. Thomas Oden serving as general editor. . . . How is it that so many of us who are dedicated to serve the Lord received seminary educations which omitted familiarity with such incredible students of the Scriptures as St. John Chrysostom, St. Athanasius the Great and St. John of Damascus? I am greatly anticipating the publication of this Commentary."

FR. PETER E. GILLQUIST
Director, Department of Missions and Evangelism
Antiochian Orthodox Christian Archdiocese of North America

"The Scriptures have been read with love and attention for nearly two thousand years, and listening to the voice of believers from previous centuries opens us to unexpected insight and deepened faith. Those who studied Scripture in the centuries closest to its writing, the centuries during and following persecution and martyrdom, speak with particular authority. The Ancient Christian Commentary on Scripture will bring to life the truth that we are invisibly surrounded by a 'great cloud of witnesses.'"

FREDERICA MATHEWES-GREEN
Commentator, National Public Radio

"For those who think that church history began around 1941 when their pastor was born, this Commentary will be a great surprise. Christians throughout the centuries have read the biblical text, nursed their spirits with it and then applied it to their lives. These commentaries reflect that the witness of the Holy Spirit was present in his church throughout the centuries. As a result, we can profit by allowing the ancient Christians to speak to us today."

HADDON ROBINSON
Harold John Ockenga Distinguished Professor of Preaching
Gordon-Conwell Theological Seminary

"All who are interested in the interpretation of the Bible will welcome the forthcoming multivolume series Ancient Christian Commentary on Scripture. Here the insights of scores of early church fathers will be assembled and made readily available for significant passages throughout the Bible and the Apocrypha. It is hard to think of a more worthy ecumenical project to be undertaken by the publisher."

BRUCE M. METZGER
Professor of New Testament, Emeritus
Princeton Theological Seminary

ANCIENT CHRISTIAN
COMMENTARY ON SCRIPTURE

OLD TESTAMENT
VI

JOB

EDITED BY

MANLIO SIMONETTI AND
MARCO CONTI

GENERAL EDITOR
THOMAS C. ODEN

InterVarsity Press
Downers Grove, Illinois

InterVarsity Press
P.O. Box 1400, Downers Grove, IL 60515-1426
Internet: www.ivpress.com
E-mail: mail@ivpress.com

©2006 by the Institute of Classical Christian Studies (ICCS), Thomas C. Oden, Manlio Simonetti and Marco Conti.

InterVarsity Press® is the book-publishing division of InterVarsity Christian Fellowship/USA®, a student movement active on campus at hundreds of universities, colleges and schools of nursing in the United States of America, and a member movement of the International Fellowship of Evangelical Students. For information about local and regional activities, write Public Relations Dept., InterVarsity Christian Fellowship/USA, 6400 Schroeder Rd., P.O. Box 7895, Madison, WI 53707-7895, or visit the IVCF website at <www.intervarsity.org>.

Scripture quotations, unless otherwise noted, are from the Revised Standard Version of the Bible, *copyright 1946, 1952, 1971 by the Division of Christian Education of the National Council of the Churches of Christ in the U.S.A., and are used by permission.*

Cover photograph: Scala/Art Resource, New York. View of the apse. S. Vitale, Ravenna, Italy.

Spine photograph: Byzantine Collection, Dumbarton Oaks, Washington D.C. Pendant cross (gold and enamel). Constantinople, late sixth century.

ISBN-10 0-8308-1476-0
ISBN-13 978-0-8308-1476-3

Printed in the United States of America ∞

Library of Congress Cataloging-in-Publication Data

Job/edited by Manilio Simonetti and Marco Conti; general editor,
Thomas C. Oden.
   p. cm.—(Ancient Christian commentary on Scripture. Old
   Testament; 6)
  Includes bibliographical references and indexes.
  ISBN-13: 978-0-8308-1476-3 (cloth: alk. paper)
  ISBN-10: 0-8308-1476-0 (cloth: alk. paper)
  1. Bible. O.T. Job—Commentaries. I. Simonetti, Manlio. II. Conti,
Marco. III. Oden, Thomas C. IV. Series.
  223'.107709—dc22
                                                   2006003976

R
220.7
A541
O.T.
v. 6

P	25	24	23	22	21	20	19	18	17	16	15	14	13	12	11	10	9	8	7	6	5	4	3	2	1
Y	28	27	26	25	24	23	22	21	20	19	18	17	16	15	14	13	12	11	10	09	08	07	06		

ANCIENT CHRISTIAN COMMENTARY PROJECT RESEARCH TEAM

GENERAL EDITOR
Thomas C. Oden

ASSOCIATE EDITOR
Christopher A. Hall

OPERATIONS MANAGER AND TRANSLATIONS PROJECT COORDINATOR
Joel Elowsky

RESEARCH AND ACQUISITIONS DIRECTOR
Michael Glerup

EDITORIAL SERVICES DIRECTOR
Warren Calhoun Robertson

ORIGINAL LANGUAGE VERSION DIRECTOR
Konstantin Gavrilkin

GRADUATE RESEARCH ASSISTANTS

Steve Finlan   *Vladimir Kharlamov*
Grant Gieseke   *Kevin M. Lowe*
Patricia Ireland   *Baek-Yong Sung*
Jeffery Wittung

ADMINISTRATIVE ASSISTANT
Judy Cincotta

CONTENTS

GENERAL INTRODUCTION

The Ancient Christian Commentary on Scripture has as its goal the revitalization of Christian teaching based on classical Christian exegesis, the intensified study of Scripture by lay persons who wish to think with the early church about the canonical text, and the stimulation of Christian historical, biblical, theological and pastoral scholars toward further inquiry into scriptural interpretation by ancient Christian writers.

The time frame of these documents spans seven centuries of exegesis, from Clement of Rome to John of Damascus, from the end of the New Testament era to A.D. 750, including the Venerable Bede.

Lay readers are asking how they might study sacred texts under the instruction of the great minds of the ancient church. This commentary has been intentionally prepared for a general lay audience of nonprofessionals who study the Bible regularly and who earnestly wish to have classic Christian observation on the text readily available to them. The series is targeted to anyone who wants to reflect and meditate with the early church about the plain sense, theological wisdom and moral meaning of particular Scripture texts.

A commentary dedicated to allowing ancient Christian exegetes to speak for themselves will refrain from the temptation to fixate endlessly upon contemporary criticism. Rather, it will stand ready to provide textual resources from a distinguished history of exegesis that has remained massively inaccessible and shockingly disregarded during the last century. We seek to make available to our present-day audiences the multicultural, multilingual, transgenerational resources of the early ecumenical Christian tradition.

Preaching at the end of the first millennium focused primarily on the text of Scripture as understood by the earlier esteemed tradition of comment, largely converging on those writers that best reflected classic Christian consensual thinking. Preaching at the end of the second millennium has reversed that pattern. It has so forgotten most of these classic comments that they are vexing to find anywhere, and even when located they are often available only in archaic editions and inadequate translations. The preached word in our time has remained largely bereft of previously influential patristic inspiration. Recent scholarship has so focused attention upon post-Enlightenment historical and literary methods that it has left this longing largely unattended and unserviced.

This series provides the pastor, exegete, student and lay reader with convenient means to see what Athanasius or John Chrysostom or the desert fathers and mothers had to say about a particular text for preaching, for study and for meditation. There is an emerging awareness among Catholic, Protestant and Orthodox laity that vital biblical preaching and spiritual formation need deeper grounding beyond the scope of the historical-critical orientations that have governed biblical studies in our day.

Hence this work is directed toward a much broader audience than the highly technical and specialized scholarly field of patristic studies. The audience is not limited to the university scholar concentrating on the study of the history of the transmission of the text or to those with highly focused philological interests in textual morphology or historical-critical issues. Though these are crucial concerns for specialists, they are not the paramount interests of this series.

This work is a Christian Talmud. The Talmud is a Jewish collection of rabbinic arguments and comments on the Mishnah, which epitomized the laws of the Torah. The Talmud originated in approximately the same period that the patristic writers were commenting on texts of the Christian tradition. Christians from the late patristic age through the medieval period had documents analogous to the Jewish Talmud and Midrash (Jewish commentaries) available to them in the *glossa ordinaria* and catena traditions, two forms of compiling extracts of patristic exegesis. In Talmudic fashion the sacred text of Christian Scripture was thus clarified and interpreted by the classic commentators.

The Ancient Christian Commentary on Scripture has venerable antecedents in medieval exegesis of both eastern and western traditions, as well as in the Reformation tradition. It offers for the first time in this century the earliest Christian comments and reflections on the Old and New Testaments to a modern audience. Intrinsically an ecumenical project, this series is designed to serve Protestant, Catholic and Orthodox lay, pastoral and scholarly audiences.

In cases where Greek, Latin, Syriac and Coptic texts have remained untranslated into English, we provide new translations. Wherever current English translations are already well rendered, they will be utilized, but if necessary their language will be brought up to date. We seek to present fresh dynamic equivalency translations of long-neglected texts which historically have been regarded as authoritative models of biblical interpretation.

These foundational sources are finding their way into many public libraries and into the core book collections of many pastors and lay persons. It is our intent and the publisher's commitment to keep the whole series in print for many years to come.

Thomas C. Oden
General Editor

A Guide to Using This Commentary

Several features have been incorporated into the design of this commentary. The following comments are intended to assist readers in making full use of this volume.

Pericopes of Scripture

The scriptural text has been divided into pericopes, or passages, usually several verses in length. Each of these pericopes is given a heading, which appears at the beginning of the pericope. For example, the first pericope in the commentary on Job is "1:1-5 The Holiness, Fatherly Love and Wealth of Job." This heading is followed by the Scripture passage quoted in the Revised Standard Version (RSV) across the full width of the page. The Scripture passage is provided for the convenience of readers, but it is also in keeping with medieval patristic commentaries, in which the citations of the Fathers were arranged around the text of Scripture.

Overviews

Following each pericope of text is an overview of the patristic comments on that pericope. The format of this overview varies within the volumes of this series, depending on the requirements of the specific book of Scripture. The function of the overview is to provide a brief summary of all the comments to follow. It tracks a reasonably cohesive thread of argument among patristic comments, even though they are derived from diverse sources and generations. Thus the summaries do not proceed chronologically or by verse sequence. Rather they seek to rehearse the overall course of the patristic comment on that pericope.

We do not assume that the commentators themselves anticipated or expressed a formally received cohesive argument but rather that the various arguments tend to flow in a plausible, recognizable pattern. Modern readers can thus glimpse aspects of continuity in the flow of diverse exegetical traditions representing various generations and geographical locations.

Topical Headings

An abundance of varied patristic comment is available for each pericope of these letters. For this reason we have broken the pericopes into two levels. First is the verse with its topical heading. The patristic comments are then focused on aspects of each verse, with topical headings summarizing the essence of the patristic comment by evoking a key phrase, metaphor or idea. This feature provides a bridge by which modern readers can enter into the heart of the patristic comment.

Identifying the Patristic Texts

Following the topical heading of each section of comment, the name of the patristic commentator is given. An English translation of the patristic comment is then provided. This is immediately followed by the title of the patristic work and the textual reference—either by book, section and subsection or by book-and-verse references.

The Footnotes

Readers who wish to pursue a deeper investigation of the patristic works cited in this commentary will find the footnotes especially valuable. A footnote number directs the reader to the notes at the bottom of the right-hand column, where in addition to other notations (clarifications or biblical cross references) one will find information on English translations (where available) and standard original-language editions of the work cited. An abbreviated citation (normally citing the book, volume and page number) of the work is provided. A key to the abbreviations is provided on page xv. Where there is any serious ambiguity or textual problem in the selection, we have tried to reflect the best available textual tradition.

Where original language texts have remained untranslated into English, we provide new translations. Wherever current English translations are already well rendered, they are utilized, but where necessary they are stylistically updated. A single asterisk (*) indicates that a previous English translation has been updated to modern English or amended for easier reading. The double asterisk (**) indicates either that a new translation has been provided or that some extant translation has been significantly amended. We have standardized spellings and made grammatical variables uniform so that our English references will not reflect the odd spelling variables of the older English translations. For ease of reading we have in some cases edited out superfluous conjunctions.

For the convenience of computer database users the digital database references are provided to either the Thesaurus Linguae Graecae (Greek texts) or to the Cetedoc (Latin texts) in the appendix found on pages 223-24.

ABBREVIATIONS

ANF	A. Roberts and J. Donaldson, eds. Ante-Nicene Fathers. 10 vols. Buffalo, N.Y.: Christian Literature, 1885-1896. Reprint, Grand Rapids, Mich.: Eerdmans, 1951-1956; Reprint, Peabody, Mass.: Hendrickson, 1994.
CCL	Corpus Christianorum. Series Latina. Turnhout, Belgium: Brepols, 1953-.
CSCO	Corpus Scriptorum Christianorum Orientalium. Louvain, Belgium, 1903-.
CSEL	Corpus Scriptorum Ecclesiasticorum Latinorum. Vienna, 1866-.
ESOO	J. S. Assemani, ed. *Sancti Patris Nostri Ephraem Syri Opera Omnia.* Rome, 1737.
LF	A Library of Fathers of the Holy Catholic Church Anterior to the Division of the East and West. Translated by members of the English Church. 44 vols. Oxford: John Henry Parker, 1800-1881.
NPNF	P. Schaff et al., eds. A Select Library of the Nicene and Post-Nicene Fathers of the Christian Church. 2 series (14 vols. each). Buffalo, N.Y.: Christian Literature, 1887-1894; Reprint, Grand Rapids, Mich.: Eerdmans, 1952-1956; Reprint, Peabody, Mass.: Hendrickson, 1994.
PG	J.-P. Migne, ed. Patrologiae cursus completus. Series Graeca. 166 vols. Paris: Migne, 1857-1886.
PL	J.-P. Migne, ed. Patrologiae cursus completus. Series Latina. 221 vols. Paris: Migne, 1844-1864.
PO	Patrologia Orientalis. Turnhout, Belgium: Brepols, 1903-.
PTA	Dieter Hagedorn, Rudolf Kassel, Ludwig Koenen and Reinhold Merkelbach, eds. Papyrologische Texte und Abhandlungen. Bonn: Habelt, 1968-.
PTS	Patristische Texte und Studien. New York: de Gruyter, 1964-.
SC	H. de Lubac, J. Daniélou et al., eds. Sources Chrétiennes. Paris: Editions du Cerf, 1941-.

INTRODUCTION TO JOB

The book of Job presents the drama of a righteous man who, after being struck by calamity, is conscious of the fact that he did not deserve it. Even though Job does not lose his hope and does not curse God, he wonders why he had to suffer such calamity. Job does not receive an answer. In fact, according to the legendary plot of the story, the devil obtains from God the permission to tempt Job so that the righteous man after successfully passing through his trials is abundantly rewarded by God. In spite of the book's happy ending, God does not ever answer Job's question. God, who intervenes by speaking directly, extols the magnificence of his creation and his immeasurable superiority to humanity, even to the righteous man, and in this manner avoids clarifying his reasons for the actions that Job had not been able to understand. This is the problem of the incommensurable relationship between God and humankind when it is considered from the point of view of simple reciprocity. The unknown author of the book of Job cannot offer any other answer but the invitation to others to accept humbly and bravely all that God decides even if the reason for God's behavior appears incomprehensible. Scholars suggest that the book dates from a period extending from the fifth to the third century B.C. and regard it as a sign of a period of uncertainty and disorientation in the history of the Jews. In fact, after they had lost the concept of the collective responsibility of the entire people in the relationship with God, there appeared in their culture the prevalence (already from the time of Isaiah and Ezekiel) of a concept of individual responsibility. Each person was called to give reason for only his or her actions. This certainly created a series of difficulties deriving from this new concept of the relationship between the individual human being and God. From this point of view, the questions proposed by the book of Job are addressed, without distinction, to men and women from any time and any place. This also explains, even today, the reason for the great interest raised by this work in moments of tension in the religious context and the culture of western civilization.

The interest in the book of Job, however, was not strong in the first Christian generations that experienced the privileged relationship between them and God in a different way through the redeeming mediation of Christ. Therefore, we find only a few isolated allusions to Job in the books of the New Testament. When they are found, they are concerned with the maxims that abound in this work. For example, the words of Jesus, "With men this is impossible, but with God all things are possible" (Mt 19:26) follow the model of Job 42:2; "He has put down the mighty from their thrones, and exalted those of low degree" (Lk 1:52) contains an echo of Job 12:19. First Corinthians 3:19 plainly quotes Job 5:13, "He catches the wise in their craftiness." Around the end of the first century, we find several hints of Job in the letter of Clement of Rome to the Christians of Corinth, where in 17:3-4, Job is defined as a model of the righteous and blameless man, who nevertheless confesses that nobody is clean from impurity if he has lived a single day (Job

14:4-5). This quotation was often cited, especially by Origen. Job, together with Noah, Abraham, Isaac and Jacob, is mentioned in Justin Martyr as a righteous man.[1] This Christian image of Job's righteousness is in perfect harmony with the presentation of the character of Job in the holy Scriptures, and remains predominant in the whole arena of Christian exegesis. Clement of Alexandria in *Stromateis* 3.100.4 makes reference to the already mentioned passage Job 14:4-5 and presents him in another passage as a model of the perfect Christian, whom he usually defines as "Gnostic." Job, who in his extraordinary temperance and celebrated faith became poor from rich, despised from illustrious, ugly from attractive, ill from healthy, is proposed to us as a model of patient faith. "He caused the tempter to blush, blessed the Creator, acted in his calamities as he had done before, and in so doing taught us in the best way how the 'Gnostic' is able to adjust easily to any circumstance."[2] In the reference to Job made by Cyprian in *De Opere et Eleemosynis* 18, the quotation (Job 14:4-5) is organically connected to the presentation of the righteous conduct of Job, who is also proposed here as a model for rich Christians. Job was aware of the fact that it is impossible not to sin *cotidie*[3] before God, and he was diligent in offering *sacrificia cotidiana*[4] to him.

The first author for whom we have evidence of a systematic interpretation of the book of Job is Origen, who wrote a cycle of twenty-two homilies.[5] As we learn from Jerome, Hilary of Poitiers translated these homilies into Latin.[6] Both the original text and the translation are lost. Only an extremely small amount of Hilary's text has been transmitted to us through indirect tradition. We have a larger quantity of the original text of Origen preserved in the catenae. Yet, even in this case we possess only fragments. Each of them is important for the exegetical detail they give us, but in general they are not sufficient to inform us about the principles of interpretation followed by Origen. In addition, the fragments are not uniformly distributed along the entire book of Job but are gathered in groups. For instance, after an isolated fragment on Job 1, there is a jump to fragments concerning Job 19—22, then to Job 27, and so on. For this reason, it can be conjectured that the *excerptor*[7] who selected the passages from the twenty-two homilies of Origen to be included in the catena had only a few of them at his disposal. From the scarce material transmitted to us, we gather that Origen considered Job to be a prototype of the Christian martyr and symbol of the righteous person who submitted to tribulations. It seems that his exegesis, also in this case, was open to an allegorical interpretation but not in a systematic way. Indeed the content of this biblical book was suitable for a moral, present-day interpretation without exceeding the literal sense of the text.

For a long time, Origen had no followers in his interest in the book of Job. Only in the second half of the fourth century do we find the already mentioned translations of his homilies by Hilary of Poitiers. After a few more years, between the end of the fourth century and the beginning of the fifth, we see a sudden and intense rise of interest in Job both in the east and in the west. We also notice a real flourishing of works that take the experience of Job as a model and comment on his book extensively. This flourishing cannot be con-

---

[1]Justin Martyr *Dialogue with Trypho* 46.3.
[2]Clement of Alexandria *Stromateis* 4.19.2.
[3]Everyday.
[4]Daily sacrifices.
[5]Jerome *Ep.* 33.
[6]Hilary of Poitiers *Lives of Illustrious Men* 100.
[7]The ancient author who selected passages for a catena.

sidered without cause. The Roman Empire at that time, especially in its western part, but also to a lesser extent in the eastern part,[8] faced many difficulties. In times of profound crisis and intense religiosity, a human being inevitably speculates about the judgment of God on the world, on humankind, and on oneself. In such circumstances the book of Job could appear to be particularly suitable for promoting and expanding reflections on this subject, since it presents a righteous man struck by calamities and afflictions. He cannot find a reason for his destiny and wonders why misfortune has tried him so unremittingly.

In addition, and more particularly, it must be noticed that Arian exegetes compiled two of the commentaries on Job that were preserved and have reached us. If we consider the scarcity of the extant Arian exegetical literature, the interest in Job appears to be significant. Therefore, it is not illogical to assume that such interest was due to the fact that the situation of these heretics was quite difficult at the end of the fourth century, for they had become the target of many harsh legal measures against them. In such a situation, the figure of Job was most suitable to be proposed as a model of firmness and resignation amid different calamities. We begin to see in these post-Origen sources a hint of the direction that exegesis would take.

In general, we notice that all the works on Job were composed when there existed a contrast between the Alexandrian trend, which interpreted the texts of the Bible by making a large use of allegory, and the Antiochian trend, which gave preference to a literal interpretation. The book of Job, on which a wholesome lecture on morals could be based, favored the literalist trend. This trend dominates even though, as we will see more fully in the next sections of this introduction, the allegorical interpretation is not completely absent. The text raised difficult questions for the exegetes especially in those passages where the tormented Job bursts into assertions that may appear to be sacrilegious or even blasphemous, as when he curses the day of his birth (Job 3:3). All the exegetes whom we will introduce were extremely careful in interpreting these kinds of passages by adjusting them to their current Christian theodicy so that they might moderate those aspects that could cause scandal.

Of the two Arian commentaries that we mentioned, the first is in Greek and has been recently attributed to an Arian author named Julian.[9] His Arian faith, even though it is disclosed discreetly, is undoubted, and the author who is unknown for the rest must be identified with the Arian author of the *Constitutiones Apostolorum*. The date of the commentary is uncertain but should be later than the middle of the fourth century, probably later for reasons we have explained. Julian, who attributed the authorship of the book of Job to Moses, notices, in the first place, the value that can be derived from its literal interpretation, for the book shows us God's providence which is for all human beings and presents Job as a model of virtue to be imitated. Consequently, Julian's commentary is rigorously literal and like all the other commentaries in Greek follows the official biblical translation of the church, namely, the so-called Septuagint (LXX). The commentary is concise and explains the entire book of Job with a well-measured amount of exegesis. The author is very careful in conveniently explaining the scenes that present the dialogue between God and the devil in a decidedly anthropomorphic form that might be read as sacrilegious expressions. This generally concise text contains a large digression that criticizes the use of astrology,[10] demonstrates the author's knowledge of

---

[8]See W. Geerlings, "Hiob und Paulus: Theodizee und Paulinismus in der lateinische Thelogie am Ausgang des vierten Jahrhunderts," *Jahrbuch für Antike und Christentum* 24 (1981): 56-66.

[9]See D. Hagedorn, *Der Hiobkommentar des arianers Julian*, PTS 14.

[10]PTS 14:252-62.

pagan literature and is rife with quotations from pagan poets.

The second commentary of Arian tendency that has been transmitted to us and was misattributed to Origen is in Latin, and its author is conventionally indicated as *Anonymus in Job*. Unlike the previous commentary, this one is extremely verbose and largely incomplete. In 150 columns of the seventeenth volume of the *Patrologia Graeca*, the unknown author has commented on the book only up to Job 3:19. Job is interpreted as a figure of Christ and his sufferings as types of Christ's passion, an interpretation that cannot be easily applied to all the details of the text. However, the unknown author, being absolutely interested in long digressions of moral character, does not take care to develop systematically this typology and is content to mention it only now and then. He also adds another more obvious interpretation where Job is a figure of the exemplary Christian, who does not give evil for evil but applies the precept to love one's enemies. In particular, this example is demonstrated by the martyr. The interpretation is mostly literal. The Arian faith of the author, which is not openly professed, is shown clearly in certain details. The composition of this writing must be roughly dated from the period between the end of the fourth century and the beginning of the fifth.

Of a commentary on Job by Evagrius, we only have a few fragments transmitted in catenae. The papyri of Tura have preserved, with a small number of lacunae, the commentary on Job by Didymus the Blind, the last great representative of the Alexandrian school and the faithful follower of the doctrine and exegesis of Origen. The papyrus abruptly ends at the beginning of the interpretation of Job 17. In the catenae, the commentary by Didymus stops just after this chapter and suggests that his original work did not amply extend beyond Job 17.[11] In accordance with Origen, Didymus also takes Job as the symbol of the righteous person who is exposed to temptation and trials. Thus he presents him to his readers as a model of courage, persistence and submission to divine will and as a laudable exemplar of the exercise of free will. Consequently, the interpretation of the book is developed in a moral and hortatory sense and therefore presents frequent present-day references of a general character. In order to draw a moral sense from the text, Didymus is often obliged to interpret it tendentiously and in a forced manner. The daily, common banquets of Job's children (Job 1:4) are presented as an example of concord and brotherly love. Job's regret that he had not died in his mother's womb (Job 3:4) signifies a request for an explanation of God's judgments. This regret only seeks to cause an explanation that may be profitably used by others.[12] In his comment on the passage, in which Job curses the day of his birth (Job 3:3), Didymus does not admit any possible literal interpretation and, by making use of allegory, introduces the Origenian theme of the preexistence of the soul where souls are placed into bodies as a punishment for a previous fault. Therefore Job, who does not speak for himself only but for the entire human race, wishes that day (that is, that fault) had never occurred.[13] Didymus's allegorical interpretation is certainly not limited to this passage and is evident in many others, but it is generally less frequent than in his other commentaries. The most natural explanation may be that, because of

---

[11]The text of the papyrus has been published with a facing German translation in Didymus der Blinde, *Kommentar zu Hiob* I (cc. 1-4), edited by A. Henrichs, Papyrologische Texte und Abhandlungen 1 (Bonn: R. Habelt, 1969); II (cc. 5-6), edited by A. Henrichs, Papyrologische Texte und Abhandlungen 2 (Bonn: R. Habelt, 1968); III (cc. 7-11), edited by U. D. Hagedorn, Papyrologische Texte und Abhandlungen 3 (Bonn: R. Habelt, 1968); IV 1 (cc. 12-15), edited by U. D. Hagedorn, Papyrologische Texte und Abhandlungen 33,1 (Bonn: R. Habelt, 1985).

[12]Cf. PTA 1:54-56, 202-8.

[13]Cf. PTA 1:170-84.

the character of this specific text, Didymus was able to draw a moral lesson from it without the need to go beyond its literal sense, so that he limited the allegorical interpretation to particular passages, which, after all, are not all that rare. However, as we will soon see, the contents of the book of Job were extremely suitable for an allegorical interpretation. Nevertheless, we cannot help being fairly amazed at the fact that an exegete who usually made an ample use of allegory in this case significantly limited his typically allegorical method of interpretation. Perhaps this anomaly can be explained in the context of the entire Didymian exegesis that takes into account the fact that Didymus was active in the historical period when the Antiochian reaction against the Alexandrian allegorical method had reached its climax. He might have preferred on some occasions to make a few concessions to his adversaries in the case of texts whose contents were suitable for a tropological, moral interpretation without going far beyond the literal sense. We notice a similar policy in the commentary by Didymus on *Ecclesiastes*. The fact that it is not possible to indicate a precise chronology for this work, but only that it dates from the end of the fourth century, does not allow us to give a more precise explanation.[14]

The commentary by John Chrysostom on Job (late fourth-early fifth century) is slightly later than that by Didymus. It has been directly transmitted in two manuscripts and indirectly in catenae with a large number of fragments that include, as usually happens with this author, abundant spurious interpolated material.[15] There were doubts concerning the genuineness of the entire commentary, but recent studies have proven its authenticity with reasonable certainty. Although not as extensive as his other exegetical works, which were mostly derived from his activity as a preacher, the commentary on Job (as well as that on the prophet Isaiah) does not appear as a development of previous preaching. Rather, this commentary on Job may be a preliminary draft that came to be expanded into a series of homilies to be preached to the congregation. The main structural feature of this commentary is the irregularity in the proportion between the scriptural quotations and their explanation. In some cases, a brief quotation is followed by an extended explanation, while in many other cases an entire series of biblical verses receives only an extremely cursory explanation or is even presented without any explanation. Scholars have suggested the possible loss of material in the course of the manuscript tradition. However, it is preferable to think, on the basis of some clarifications provided by the author, that he intended to offer only a cursory and basic explanation, neglecting many passages in order to focus only on those that he considered to be most significant. The kind of interpretation in this commentary is rigorously moral and literal, as is usual for this exegete of the Antiochian school. If we consider, in addition, his predominant moral interest due to his pastoral activity, we see how the contents of the book of Job were suitable in the highest degree to this purpose without any need to resort to allegory. The author had only to be careful in interpreting conveniently the most desecrating passages. For instance, when Job curses the day of his birth, Chrysostom solves this difficult point by observing that these words derived from despair and not from wickedness or a protest against the Creator.[16] Chrysostom's interpretation of Job in general sees in him a righteous man who resists temptation. Job is a model of the wise man.

---

[14]See Manlio Simonetti, *Origene esegeta e la sua tradizione* (Brescia: Morcelliana, 2004), 357-92.
[15]See H. Sorlin, in SC 346:11-12.
[16]See SC 345:198-202.

A contemporary of Chrysostom was Polycronius, bishop of Apamea and brother of Theodore of Mopsuestia. Like his brother (but without reaching his fame), he produced a large number of exegetical writings in which he faithfully followed the literalism of the Antiochian school. However, only fragments of his numerous commentaries have reached us through catenae. As a result, we can now read only a few short texts concerning the book of Job.

Olympiodorus, a deacon from Alexandria, was active in the sixth century and produced various commentaries on the Old Testament, including one on Jeremiah, one on Ecclesiastes and one on Job.[17] He used the commentary by Polycronius as a source and more sporadically that by Chrysostom. Like the commentary by Chrysostom, Olympiodorus's work was transmitted to us directly through two manuscripts and indirectly through quotations in catenae. The book of Job is divided, in Olympiodorus's commentary, not into the traditional forty-two chapters but into thirty-three. The explanation of each chapter is preceded by an introduction that summarizes its main contents. The author then makes comments on progressive, short pericopes of the entire text of each chapter. Like the three commentaries in Greek that we have mentioned, Olympiodorus's text is based on the biblical text of the Septuagint. This author also refers, unlike the others, to the Greek translations known through the *Hexapla* of Origen, especially to that by Symmachus, and rarely to those by Aquila and Theodotion. At the time of Olympiodorus, the exegetical traditions of Alexandria and Antioch were finished or at least receding. It is not surprising if our deacon produced a mostly literal commentary that uses allegory only occasionally. This author often refers to interpretations proposed by other unidentified exegetes which he relates without arguing. Olympiodorus was active in an age in which the vitality of patristic exegesis in the east was over, so that he appears to be not an original exegete but the last representative of a tradition that had by now become sedimentary and was based on the interpretation of Job as a model of a righteous and wise man.

If we move to the Latin West, after regretting the loss of the commentary on Job by Hilary of Poitiers, which was translated, according to Jerome, from the homilies of Origen,[18] we find around the eighties of the fourth century the *De interpellatione Job et David* by Ambrose.[19] As can be inferred from the title, this is not a proper commentary but a series of homilies in which the preacher presents the two famous characters as examples, in spite of their differences, of human frailty. Ambrose describes the work in detail, with ample references to the Scriptures, demonstrating that humanity can resist adversities only through the grace of divine protection. We have already introduced the commentary by the Arian *Anonymus in Job*, so that we pass now to the *Adnotationes in Job*, which Augustine dictated around 400.[20] This extremely concise commentary explains, through a literal interpretation, the book of Job in nearly its entirety, stopping only at Job 40:5 when Job humbly submits to the judgment of God. That comes at a point representing, for Augustine, the logical conclusion of the entire story of the vexed chief character. The commentary is not structured, as is usual in writings of this kind, in a succession of separate quotations from the text with their specific explanation, but in a continuous speech, in which quotations are embedded into the context of the explana-

---

[17]See U. and D. Hagedorn, *Olimpiodor Diakon von Alexandrien, Kommentar zu Hiob*, PTS 24 (Berlin and New York: De Gruyter, 1984).

[18]Cf. *Lives of Illustrious Men* 100. Jerome declares that the translation by Hilary was *ad sensum*, that is, very free, as was usual at the time.

[19]For this text, see the edition by C. Schenkl in CSEL 32.

[20]For this text, see PL 34:824-86.

tion. On the basis of his doctrine of the universality of sin, Augustine presents Job as aware, in spite of his righteousness, of this intrinsic sinfulness. The final statement of the chief character, who declares that he does not want to add anything else to what he had said formerly, indicates, in Augustine's opinion, the progress of the soul that cannot resist God any longer and takes refuge in the unfathomable nature of the mystery.

A few years after the publication of the Augustinian commentary, there appeared a work by the presbyter Philip. Philip was an almost unknown character. We only have proof that he was an *auditor*[21] of Jerome according to Gennadius.[22] This information was probably drawn from the mention of Jerome by Philip in the letter of dedication opening his commentary. However, the relationship to Jerome is evidenced especially by the fact that Philip used as the reference text for his commentary the new translation of the book of Job which Jerome had included in his *hebraica veritas*.[23] This work was Jerome's new Latin translation of the Bible, which he had based on the original Hebrew text and is now commonly indicated as Vulgate (Vg). This is a significant innovation in comparison with Ambrose and Augustine, who were still using the *Vetus Latina*,[24] and Philip often extols the translation by Jerome in his commentary. The transmission of Philip's work has been extremely complicated.[25] It was transmitted by several codices that attribute it to Philip, probably on the basis of a manuscript that transmitted it without the name of the author. The same text that had been printed under the name of Philip in its *editio princeps* of 1527 was reprinted in 1545 under the name of Bede. Later, it was also misattributed to Jerome, so that in the reprint of Migne (PL 26) it is included among the spurious works of Jerome. But the most important fact is that this reprint does not present the rather prolix original text of the commentary but a substantially abridged version. Consequently, the full text is not easily accessible now, while the abridged one that we have used in our commentary is easily available. The interpretation proposed by Philip is on two different levels. The first is the historical level which deals with the misfortunes of Job and explains them in a literal way. The second level is characterized by an extremely allegorical interpretation that considers Job as a figure of Christ and his three supposed friends as symbols of the heretics. These two kinds of interpretations run in parallel lines throughout the work. For instance, the seven sons of Job prefigure the sevenfold grace of the Holy Spirit, and his three daughters the law, the prophets and the gospel. Job, who curses the day of his birth, signifies Christ, who has taken upon himself the entire mortality of the human race and deprecates the transgression of Adam.[26]

Julian of Eclanum made use of the new translation of the Bible by Jerome but also referred often to the previous Latin translations. His commentary appears concise.[27] The only manuscript that has transmitted his work to us probably omits some sections of the original text. In addition, the story of this text is also

---

[21]Pupil, disciple.

[22]Cf. *Lives of Illustrious Men* 100.

[23]Hebrew truth.

[24]That is, the Latin Bible in use before the Vg and mostly based on the text of the LXX.

[25]See M. P. Ciccarese, "Una esegesi 'double face': Introduzione alla 'Expositio in Iob' del presbytero Filippo," *Annali di storia dell'esegesi* 9, no. 2 (1992): 483-92.

[26]See PL 26:658-61.

[27]Cf. the edition by de Conink in CCL 88, where there is also an ample introduction on the previous editions of this commentary.

quite complicated. The manuscript including this text, the *Codex Cassinensis* 371, indicates the presbyter Philip as its author. For this reason, Dom Amelli published the commentary under this name in 1897. Thanks to Father Vaccari, the genuine author was finally traced back. Now the attribution to Julian is considered certain, because the commentary has also used some material from those commentaries of Chrysostom and Polycronius. This feature points to Julian, the only Latin exegete who adhered to the Antiochian literalism and was in close relationship with Theodore of Mopsuestia, the brother of Polycronius. The substitution of the name of Julian with that of Philip was probably also due to reasons of opportunity, because Julian was a follower of Pelagius and a strong opponent of Augustine. For this reason, he was repeatedly condemned as a heretic. His interpretation is of a historical character and interprets the experience of Job, which is presented as exemplary, as a demonstration that virtue is accessible to those who want to reach it. The afflictions that Job endures are seen as temptations that God permits in order to try the soundness of the virtue which he has obtained and to corroborate it.

Gregory the Great is the author of the most extended and thorough commentary on the book of Job that has been transmitted to us from the patristic age. It consists of thirty-five books that were mostly composed after a long series of colloquial explanations given in Constantinople (c. 579), where he was the representative of the bishop of Rome. This ample and exacting work was completed, in any case, in Rome, when Gregory had already been appointed as pope. We know that he took extreme care with the final version and publication of his works. The unusual length of the Gregorian writing is due to the method of explanation used by Gregory more than to the size of the book of Job. Gregory places himself before the biblical text with the greatest liberty. He often drifts into the inspiration of the moment with little or no concern for precision or for wandering from the outline of the text that he is examining—a text that often seems to be only an occasion for ascetical and moral digressions. As he clearly explains in the prefatory letter addressed to his friend, Leander of Seville, if the exegete in the course of his explanation of the biblical text finds a good occasion to edify, he must not miss it. Later he can come back to the norm of the accurate explanation of the text, like a river when it meets along its bed a low valley, broadens to fill it and only later resumes its natural course.[28] We are here in the presence of the most authentic Alexandrian tradition that has the utmost certainty that the holy text nourishes every thought and every meditation of the committed Christian. It is not restricted to a given subject but is open, alive and new, so that it invites the interpreter to infer constantly from it new meanings, in accordance with the requirements of the moment and with the capacity of the interpreter. In the description of his hermeneutical method that Gregory makes in the prefatory letter, we read, "[The divine word] is, so to speak, like a river which is both deep and shallow, in which a lamb can walk and an elephant must swim." [29]

Gregory's interpretation of the book of Job is programmatically structured according to the hermeneutical method of Origen that had been spread in the West by Ambrose and Rufinus. In this method, Origen distinguished three different levels of interpretation. "First we lay the foundations of the literal sense (*historiae*); then, through the typological interpretation (*typicam*), we raise the building of our mind, so that it may be a fortress

---

[28]Gregory the Great *Ep. Leandro* 2.
[29]Gregory the Great *Ep. Leandro* 4.

of faith; finally, through the moral sense (*moralitas*), we cover, so to speak, the building with a layer of color" (*Ep. Leandro* 3). This means the first interpretation, since it is literal, has the explanation of the dramatic events in Job's life as its object. The other two interpretations, being of symbolic character, refer these events, on the one hand, to Christ and the church through an interpretation which we can define as collective [*collettivo*] (christological and ecclesiological) and, on the other, to the existential experience of each Christian through an individual, topical [*topico*] interpretation. In the transition from the theoretical proposal to practice, this exegetical method is employed without excessive rigor. In fact, in the first books, Gregory interprets each passage of the biblical text according to the three levels of interpretation; but later this procedure becomes freer, with an evident preference for the moral and typological interpretation. The fundamental allegory used by Gregory, according to his collective interpretation, sees Job as a figure of Christ as well as of the church, which is the body of Christ. Again, the three friends signify the heretics. By contrast, according to an individual interpretation, Job is a figure of the Christian, who is devoted to his spiritual progress that leads him to perfection through the afflictions and trials of life. For instance, according to the collective interpretation, the seven sons and the three daughters of Job are, respectively, figures of the apostles and the faithful of the simplest order (Job 1:19-20). According to the individual interpretation, they signify, respectively, the seven gifts of the Holy Spirit and the three virtues of faith, hope and charity (Job 1:38).

Among the writings of the Greek Fathers, we also possess a series of twenty-four homilies by Hesychius of Jerusalem (fourth-fifth century) which analyze the first twenty chapters of Job. This work, however, has not been transmitted in its original Greek language but only in an Armenian translation.[30] Even though it is extremely difficult to reconstruct the chronology of Hesychius's works, we can approximately date his commentary from the period between 412 and 439, when he was fully active as a priest and preacher in Jerusalem. As C. Renoux, the editor of the commentary, has pointed out,[31] Hesychius' works do not appear to be influenced by the other Greek writers such as Didymus or Julian the Arian who preceded him. In general, it presents only a vague similarity with that of Chrysostom. Scholars have tried to establish whether Hesychius' commentary originally extended beyond the twentieth chapter of the book of Job, but currently the most likely hypothesis is that it was conceived as a partial commentary on the first twenty chapters.[32] Hesychius appears to use allegory in his comments and explanations. He also makes typological references to Christ and the church. However, we cannot define his work as a product of the Alexandrian exegetical school, because the use of allegory is not systematic but is limited to certain passages. At the same time, we notice a constant attention to the moral and psychological aspects of Job in the course of his afflictions and arguments, and this undoubtedly reveals an openly pastoral purpose. Therefore we can conclude that Hesychius' commentary takes its starting point from the moral and literal exegesis of Chrysostom, to which it adds a reasonable amount of typological allegory.

In the context of eastern patrology, only two complete commentaries are extant, and both of them are written in Syriac. The first one has been transmitted among the works of Ephrem the Syrian, the greatest of the Syriac Fathers. He lived between 306 and 373 and is the author of numerous exegetical works on all

---

[30]See the edition by C. Renoux, PO 42.1:5-612.
[31]See Renoux, PO 42.1.1:12-13.
[32]See Renoux, PO 42.1.1:20-21.

the books of the Bible. The commentary on Job, which has been published only in the extensive collection edited by J. S. Assemani in the eighteenth century,[33] appears to be spurious and later than Ephrem's genuine exegetical writings.[34] However, the commentary appears to be quite interesting, even in its extreme conciseness, because, together with a typically Syriac historical and literal interpretation, it presents frequent typological and allegorical comments that reveal a phase in Syriac literature where the influence of Greek patrology, and especially of the allegorical school, was particularly strong. The second complete commentary on Job in Syriac[35] is that written by Isho'dad of Merv, who was ordained bishop of Hedatta, near Mossul in Mesopotamia around 850, and is therefore a much later author than Ephrem. Since Isho'dad was a Nestorian, his commentary, which is as concise as that by Ephrem, is extremely important for the history of Nestorian exegesis. Isho'dad also quotes numerous passages from Theodore of Mopsuestia and other sources, which would have been lost without his commentary, and this undoubtedly makes his work extremely precious. In general, Isho'dad favors a literal interpretation of the biblical text, according to the prevailing trend in Syriac exegesis, but also pays careful attention to any historical detail, so that he always tries to place Job and his personal experience in a precise and reliable historical context.

The Biblical Text Used by the Fathers

In his introduction to the ACCS volume on Genesis 1—11, Andrew Louth wrote, "Compiling a patristic commentary on any part of the Old Testament raises questions not raised by such a commentary on the New Testament. These questions are largely to do with the actual biblical text and to a lesser extent with the higher criticism of that text (that is, questions of composition and authorship). With the New Testament, the English text that we read nowadays is a translation of the New Testament more or less as the Greek Fathers themselves knew it. . . . However, with the Old Testament, there is a major difference. For the Christian Old Testament was the Greek Septuagint (usually abbreviated as LXX, the Latin numeral for seventy)."[36]

Without pursuing in detail the many questions concerning this ancient Greek translation[37] which, according to the majority of scholars, dates from the third century B.C., we can assert that it presents significant differences with the Hebrew text translated in the Revised Standard Version, which is used as a basis for our pericopes. These differences are due to two main reasons. In the first place, it has been ascertained that the Septuagint used a more ancient, lost Hebrew text that was ampler and different from the Masoretic one, that is, from the Hebrew text that we possess now, and that has been used as the reference text for all the modern translations of the Bible. In the second place, the different translators of the Septuagint were not all equally competent in Hebrew, so that they gave erroneous or controversial interpretations of Hebrew words in the course of their translations.[38] With all its evident idiosyncrasies and variants, the

---

[33]J. S. Assemani, ed., *Sancti Patris Nostri Ephraem Syri Opera omnia*, tomus II (Rome, 1740).

[34]Such as his commentaries on Genesis and Exodus (cf. CSCO 152-153 (Syri 71-72) (Louvain: Peeters, 1955).

[35]See C. Van Den Eynde, ed., *Commentaire d'Iso'dad de Merv sur l'Ancien Testament – III. Livres des Sessions*, CSCO 229 (Scriptores Syri 96) (Louvain: Peeters, 1962).

[36]See Andrew Louth (in collaboration with M. Conti), *Genesis 1-11*, ACCS Old Testament I, xl.

[37]For an updated, general introduction to the LXX, see Louth, *Genesis 1-11*, xl-xliv.

[38]Cf. L. L. Brenton, *The Septuagint Version of the Old Testament and Apocrypha* (Grand Rapids: Zondervan, 1980), iii.

Septuagint nonetheless was received into the first Christian communities and became the standard Christian Bible. This text was always the basis of the exegesis of the Greek Fathers.

In the West, the situation appears to be quite similar. The Latin Fathers, in fact, first used the *Vetus Latina*, that is, a Latin translation of the Bible that was based on the Septuagint, and then they later used the Vulgate, that is, the new Latin translation of the Bible made by Jerome (c. 347-419) at the end of the fourth century. The Vulgate was, in the intention of Jerome, a faithful translation from the Hebrew text, and we can assert with some accuracy that his basic Hebrew text did not differ significantly from the Masoretic text that we possess now. However, Jerome, in the course of his translations, constantly took into consideration the Septuagint and the later Greek translations of Aquila, Theodotion and Symmachus together with Hebrew hexaplar texts.[39] As a result, his translation frequently differs from the Masoretic text and consequently from modern translations of the Bible. Our annotation reveals many of these differences.

Finally, with regard to the Syriac Fathers, they used as their basic text the standard Syriac translation of the Bible that is generally defined as Peshitta (that is, the simple version). Scholars mostly agree on the fact that the Peshitta is generally a faithful, but not slavish, translation from the Masoretic Hebrew text.[40] One might expect here an agreement between the biblical text used by the Syriac Fathers and the modern translation of the RSV. However, this is not the case, because not only does the Peshitta reveal a dependence on the Targum[41] and even on the Septuagint, but it also presents significant variants derived from Hebrew versions different from the Masoretic one, that is, from lost Hebrew versions which were used by the translators of the Peshitta.

The differences between these three main translations (the LXX, Vulgate and Peshitta) and the Masoretic text are not quantitatively constant in all the books of the Bible but are more significant and frequent in some of them. In the case of the book of Job, we can say that the differences are extremely frequent and significant. For this reason, at the end of each pericope of our commentary we have added an ample apparatus that records all the significant variants between the text of RSV and those of the translations of the Septuagint, Vulgate and Peshitta. These were the biblical versions used by the Fathers in their commentaries. We invite the reader to always check these variants before reading each passage. Even though this might appear to be tedious at first, we are certain that the reader will soon be able to appreciate the richness of the biblical tradition transmitted by the ancient exegetes and to reflect on the different variants, which raise questions of great interest even in our modern context. In a sense, this commentary also wants to stimulate the creativity and personal meditation of the reader.

Editorial Note On the Present Commentary

After examining the whole of the available material on Job, we have sought to make a judicious selection of texts. In the first place, we have noticed that three of the extant patristic writings on Job, namely, the *Anonymus in Job*, the *De interpellatione Job et David* by Ambrose and the *Adnotationes in Job* by Augustine, are

---

[39]Hexaplar texts are defined as those texts that were used by Origen in his *Hexapla*, that is, a parallel presentation of the different biblical texts placed side by side on six different columns.

[40]See P. B. Dirksen, *La Peshitta dell'Antico Testamento*, edited by P. G. Borbone (Brescia: Paideia Edtirice, 1993), 103-4.

[41]That is, the explanatory translations in Aramaic of the Old Testament.

not suitable for a modern exegetical study of the book of Job. The first work is extremely verbose and incomplete, covering only the first two chapters of Job and part of the third, and its typological and allegorical interpretation appears to be more clearly and more maturely developed in the works of other authors. The work by Ambrose is heavily influenced by the rhetoric of his age and does not actually comment on the biblical text in a systematic way but turns out to be mostly a presentation and panegyric of the figure of Job. Finally, the *Adnotationes in Job* by Augustine, as the title suggests, are notes on the book of Job. Even though they present numerous interesting remarks, they are far from being a systematic commentary on the different sections of the biblical text. In fact, they appear to be extremely free treatments of passages from Job, where the biblical text is not isolated and analyzed but is embedded in each treatment. For all these reasons we have agreed that these three works could be eliminated from the present study. With a couple of exceptions, we have also decided not to include in our commentary all those occasional comments on Job that are scattered among the works of many patristic authors. Even though such comments can be interesting, nevertheless we thought it would be more consistent and organic to privilege the complete or proper commentaries on Job that give an ample and substantial image of the exegesis of each author.

Therefore we have used for our volume the following ancient commentaries on Job: the Greek Fathers—Origen, Didymus the Blind, Julian the Arian, John Chrysostom, Hesychius of Jerusalem, Olympiodorus; the Latin Fathers—Julian of Eclanum, Philip the Priest, Gregory the Great; and the Syriac Fathers—Ephrem the Syrian, Isho'dad of Merv.

Manlio Simonetti and Marco Conti

JOB

¹There was a man in the land of Uz, whose name was Job; and that man was blameless and upright, one who feared God, and turned away from evil.* ²There were born to him seven sons and three daughters. ³He had seven thousand sheep, three thousand camels, five hundred yoke of oxen, and five hundred she-asses, and very many servants; so that this man was the greatest of all the people of the east. ⁴His sons used to go and hold a feast in the house of each on his day; and they would send and invite their three sisters to eat and drink with them. ⁵And when the days of the feast had run their course, Job would send and sanctify them, and he would rise early in the morning and offer burnt offerings according to the number of them all; for Job said, "It may be that my sons have sinned, and cursed God in their hearts." Thus Job did continually.

*LXX from any evil

OVERVIEW: The Fathers emphasize the special position occupied by Job as a model of piety. It is evident that even though they do not assert it openly, Job represents in their views a figure and a foreshadowing of Christian piety, that is, a type of the perfect Christian who will be formed by the preaching of Christ and the gospel. Job is absolutely righteous and turns away from any kind of evil (CHRYSOSTOM). He is blessed by God, that is, he has the grace of God (EPHREM, CHRYSOSTOM). He possesses modesty and an interior wealth, like a true Christian (CHRYSOSTOM, HESYCHIUS). His family represents a model of harmony, that is, foreshadows the harmony of the Christian life (CHRYSOSTOM, DIDYMUS, ISHO'DAD).

1:1 There Was a Man

A BLAMELESS MAN. CHRYSOSTOM: Each of these epithets is sufficient to show the beauty of Job's soul. But, as a lover multiplies the details in order to describe the one he loves, so the same occurs here. "Blameless" the text says, that is, perfectly virtuous. "Upright," and also "true," and also "pious," and again, "he turned away from any evil." Notice the words "from any," and not simply from one evil and not from another. Where are those who assert that human nature is inclined

1

toward evil? What fear, what tribunals and what laws made Job as he is? COMMENTARY ON JOB 1.1.[1]

THE PIOUS JOB IS BLESSED BY GOD. EPHREM THE SYRIAN: Even though many others lived in Uz, no one was comparable to Job with regard to piety and innocence. He was of high reputation and was celebrated in everybody's words. And so that no one might think these things had been granted to Job thanks to his human ability, God never allowed a single possession of Job's to perish. [God] said, "My desire is that even a single hair, a loss that would be the very slightest, may be returned and increased for Job." COMMENTARY ON JOB 1.1.[2]

1:2 Seven Sons and Three Daughters

A PROSPEROUS PROGENY. CHRYSOSTOM: Notice how the author first of all speaks about Job's virtue and then of the goods Job has received from God. Observe the opportunity Job received to have children, and the proportion of children who are boys, desired as a source of greater benefit. Scripture says immediately why the man must receive our praise. It is because of the greatness of Job's virtue and the fruitfulness of his soul. And indeed we derive all such goods from virtue. That is why I speak about beautiful and plentiful progeny. "There shall not be," Scripture says, "male or female barren among you."[3] But Abraham was childless, so that you might learn that Abraham's goods were not the reward of virtue but of other goods. Therefore God has promised those goods in order to be generous to you. COMMENTARY ON JOB 1.2.[4]

1:3 A Great Man

MODESTY IN WEALTH. CHRYSOSTOM: The author calls Job a man of the East; he was superior to all in radiance and celebrity and could name distinguished and illustrious ancestors. How could Job not be incited to pride by the virtue that reigned in his soul, by the joy which his

children gave him and by the fact he was the only one who simultaneously possessed wealth and virtue and the privilege to descend from illustrious fathers? But when these goods fall into the hands of the impious, heed what the prophet says: "Since pride has completely grasped them, they have clothed themselves in their injustice and impiety."[5] But as for Job, he declares, "Why do the wicked live and grow old in their prosperity?"[6] Now it was not like that at all for Job. It is not the nature of wealth that causes bad conduct but the mind of those who do not use wealth properly. COMMENTARY ON JOB 1.3.[7]

JOB POSSESSES INTERNAL WEALTH. HESYCHIUS OF JERUSALEM: You see the greatness of Job's external wealth; but his internal wealth was even greater. The visible riches were splendid, but the invisible riches were even more splendid because they last; visible riches grow old, lose their value and continually collapse into the most pitiful corruption and destruction. HOMILIES ON JOB 1.1.2-3E.[8]

1:4-5 Sanctifying His Children

HARMONY IN JOB'S FAMILY. CHRYSOSTOM: Mutual understanding, the greatest good, was profound within Job's family. They were accustomed to have meals together, to hold a common banquet—a custom, to be sure, that significantly contributes to establishing a profitable mutual understanding. Do you perceive, dear brothers, the joy of the banquet mixed with security? Do you observe this brotherly table? Do you see that harmoniously united group? Profound affection is the source of all this. COMMENTARY ON JOB 1.4.[9]

PURITY OF JOB'S CHILDREN. DIDYMUS THE BLIND: Here the text stresses the great purity of Job's children. Since [Job] did not perceive any

---

[1]PTS 35:3. [2]ESOO 2:2. [3]Deut 7:14. [4]PTS 35:5. [5]Ps 73:6 (72:6 LXX). [6]Job 21:7. [7]PTS 35:6. [8]PO 42.1:70. [9]PTS 35:7.

sin in them, he sacrificed because of [the sons'] disposition. Job was aware that the human weakness and sluggishness that mark young persons often escalates. This is also why St. Paul said, "I am not aware of anything against myself."[10] And the psalmist, "Forgive my hidden faults."[11] Therefore we have to believe that the sons of Job did not die because of their own sins. COMMENTARY ON JOB 1.5.[12]

JOB'S RITES OF PURIFICATION. ISHO'DAD OF MERV: "Job would sanctify them," that is, Job purified them through the waters of cleansing

and through the sacrifices that he offered for them. And since the righteous man had full confidence in the fact that his children were free from manifest sins, thanks to the education and instruction which he had given them, he offered sacrifices for their secret sins and thoughts by saying, "It may be that my children have sinned and cursed God in their hearts." COMMENTARY ON JOB 1.5.[13]

---

[10]1 Cor 4:4. [11]Ps 19:12 (18:13 LXX). [12]PTA 1:56-58. [13]CSCO 229:236.

1:6-19 SATAN OBTAINS LEAVE TO TEMPT JOB

[6]*Now there was a day when the sons of God* came to present themselves before the LORD, and Satan[a] also came among them. [7]The LORD said to Satan, "Whence have you come?" Satan answered the LORD, "From going to and fro on the earth, and from walking up and down on it." [8]And the LORD said to Satan, "Have you considered my servant Job, that there is none like him on the earth, a blameless and upright man, who fears God and turns away from evil?" [9]Then Satan answered the LORD, "Does Job fear God for nought? [10]Hast thou not put a hedge about him and his house and all that he has, on every side? Thou hast blessed the work of his hands, and his possessions have increased in the land. [11]But put forth thy hand now, and touch all that he has, and he will curse thee to thy face." [12]And the LORD said to Satan, "Behold, all that he has is in your power; only upon himself do not put forth your hand." So Satan went forth from the presence of the LORD.*

[13]Now there was a day when his sons and daughters were eating and drinking wine in their eldest brother's house; [14]and there came a messenger to Job, and said, "The oxen were plowing and the asses feeding beside them; [15]and the Sabeans fell upon them and took them, and slew the servants with the edge of the sword; and I alone have escaped to tell you." [16]While he was yet speaking, there came another, and said, "The fire of God[†] fell from heaven and burned up the sheep and the servants, and consumed them; and I alone have escaped to tell you." [17]While he was yet speaking, there came another, and said, "The Chaldeans formed three companies, and made a raid upon the camels and took them, and slew the servants with the edge of the sword; and I alone have escaped to tell you." [18]While he was yet speaking, there came another, and said, "Your sons and

daughters were eating and drinking wine in their eldest brother's house; [19]*and behold, a great wind came across the wilderness, and struck the four corners of the house, and it fell upon the young people, and they are dead; and I alone have escaped to tell you."*

a Heb the *adversary* *LXX *the angels* †LXX *omits of God*

OVERVIEW: The Fathers in general view this section concerning the intervention of the devil as an allegorical narrative (ISHO'DAD, HESYCHIUS), where the trial of Job symbolizes the constant struggle of the righteous against the temptations and passions inspired by the malice of the devil (GREGORY). Job's wealth is the fruit of his righteousness, but he has to lose such wealth in the trial imposed by God (CHRYSOSTOM). The power of the devil can extend only to the limits set by God (JULIAN OF ECLANUM, HESYCHIUS, DIDYMUS, CHRYSOSTOM). The real instruction of the righteous, and the Christian, who is foreshadowed by Job, happens through the loss of material goods and the endurance of afflictions (GREGORY).

1:6 Satan Comes Before God

EVEN THE DEVIL'S THOUGHTS ARE KNOWN TO GOD. ISHO'DAD OF MERV: There was never a special meeting where Satan dared to speak, to formulate questions and receive answers—nothing of the sort—but these facts are reported in a narrative style for the edification of the listeners. . . . They never took place in reality, and here the devil did not address God or pose questions; Satan never had the faculty to speak to God or to see him who is the one that "the creatures of fire and spirit"[1] cannot see, but [the devil] meditated in his heart, and God, "who searches the hearts and examines the mind,"[2] knew the devil's malice. COMMENTARY ON JOB 1.6.[3]

AT THE SERVICE OF THE RIGHTEOUS. HESYCHIUS OF JERUSALEM: Was there ever a time when the angels did not stand before the Lord? Was it not written about them that "a thousand thousands served him, and ten thousand times ten thousand stood before him"?[4] But this coming, in our opinion, is that of the angels who had been sent to serve human beings. Paul actually says, "Are not all angels ministering spirits sent to serve those who will inherit salvation?"[5] HOMILIES ON JOB 2.1.6.[6]

1:7-8 Where Have You Come From?

CONSIDER MY SERVANT JOB. GREGORY THE GREAT: Satan's "going to and fro on the earth" represents his exploring the hearts of the carnal. In this way he is seeking diligently for grounds of accusation against them. He "goes round about the earth," for he surrounds human hearts in order to steal all that is good in them, that he may lodge evil in their minds, that he may occupy completely what he has taken over, that he may fully reign over what he has occupied, that he may possess the very lives of those he has perfected in sin. Note that he does not say he has been flying through the earth but that he has been "walking up and down it." For in fact he is never easily dislodged from whomever he tempts. But where he finds a soft heart, he plants the foot of his wretched persuasion, so that by dwelling there, he may stamp the footprints of evil practice, and by a wickedness similar to his own he may render reprobate all whom he is able to overcome. But in spite of this, blessed Job is commended with these words, "Have you considered my servant Job? There is no one like him on the earth, a blameless and upright man who fears God and turns away from evil." To him, whom divine inspiration strengthens to meet the enemy, God praises as it were even in the ears of Satan.

---

[1]Ps 104:4 (103:4 LXX). [2]Jer 17:10. [3]CSCO 229:237. [4]Dan 7:10. [5]Heb 1:14. [6]PO 42.1:84.

For God's praise of Job is the first evidence of Job's virtues, so that they may be preserved when they are manifested. But the old enemy is enraged against the righteous the more he perceives that they are hedged around by the favor of God's protection. MORALS ON THE BOOK OF JOB 2.65.66.[7]

1:9-10 Does Job Fear God for Nothing?

WEALTH RECEIVED FROM GOD. CHRYSOSTOM: Do you see that Job's wealth was a gift from God? Do you see that it was not the fruit of injustice? How Job had to suffer in order to demonstrate to people that his wealth was not the fruit of injustice! And behold, the devil himself bore witness to him from above and did not realize that he praised Job as well by saying that he had not acquired that wealth through illicit trading and through the oppression of others. Instead, Job owed his wealth to God's blessing, and his security came from heaven. You would have not rejoiced if Job had not been virtuous. But the devil praised and covered him with laurels without realizing what he was doing. COMMENTARY ON JOB 1.10.[8]

1:11-12 Stretch Out Your Hand

ALLEGORICAL MEANING OF GOD'S HAND. DIDYMUS THE BLIND: "[God's] hand" must be understood in a variety of ways. It is either the power that punishes or serves punishment, usually referred to in the Scripture as "tools of wrath,"[9] or the protecting and guarding power in the Scripture, "No one can snatch them out of the Father's hand."[10] Even the Son can be shielded by the hand which protects and supports those who are under it, in accordance with the word, "The right hand of the Lord [has] exalted [me]; the right hand of the Lord acts valiantly."[11] The quoted words prove that no one is tempted without God's permission. For God says, "See, I have given everything into your hand." But in order to show that this permission is given [only] with restrictions, it is added,

"Only do not stretch out your hand against him." Thus afflictions occur neither due to fate nor arbitrarily but due to God's permission, in order—as mentioned in the beginning—to proclaim Job's virtue, but sometimes for other reasons, concerning which we will speak later on. COMMENTARY ON JOB 1.11.[12]

GOD DOES NOT CONSIDER SATAN'S REQUESTS. CHRYSOSTOM: [Satan] himself willed and desired to receive power over Job, but he did not dare to say so. "But you," he says, "stretch out your hand." Then, so that he may not say, "you indulgently struck him as though he was a household servant," God does not do that which the devil asked. Certainly God could, in doing that, justify himself by saying, "I did what you wanted; it is you who told me to touch him." COMMENTARY ON JOB 1.11B.[13]

1:13-15 A Lone Servant Escapes

A DAY DELIBERATELY CHOSEN. JULIAN OF ECLANUM: The day of trial is chosen by the devil in order that he may now overwhelm the holy Job with the variety of damages and afflictions. For previously, after offering the sacrifices, by having his meals in the circle of his children, Job could be safe in God's protection. It was not without meaning that on the day of the theft of the oxen and donkeys mention was also made of what happened to the children as they were eating together. This was to show that all the misfortunes, by which the soul of the righteous man was to be crushed, happened simultaneously. EXPOSITION ON THE BOOK OF JOB 1.13-15.[14]

1:16 Sheep and Servants Destroyed

THE FIRE IS THE DEVIL. HESYCHIUS OF JERUSALEM: Who is "the fire"? The enemy himself, about whom David said, "You will throw burning

---

[7]LF 18:111-12. [8]PTS 35:19. [9]Rom 9:22. [10]Jn 10:29. [11]Ps 118:16 (117:16 LXX). [12]PTA 1:84-86. [13]PTS 35:20. [14]CCL 88:6.

coals at them."[15] In fact, he could not, as some people believe, cast thunderbolts, nor brandish lightning, nor set in motion any element. Therefore it is the devil in the semblance of fire who fell on the herds of sheep, with the intention of forcing Job to blaspheme God, as if it were he, who from heaven had destroyed the riches of the righteous. Homilies on Job 3.1.16.[16]

Proof of God's Action. Didymus the Blind: It is remarkable how the news from the second [messenger] increases Job's pain. "Fire fell from heaven," he says, "and burned up the sheep and the servants, and consumed them." Even if Job thoroughly knew the teachings of the truth and understood that afflictions did not occur without God's permission, the incident still brought him great suffering for the people's sake. They were confused by what occurred. It was as if God had turned against Job. That the intruders during the attack took the cattle and killed the servants could be interpreted by the less intelligent as if the intruders were simply acting in accordance with the hostile customs of battle. They had attacked and behaved in that way due to lack of discipline and hate. Therefore [one might conclude] that the event was not sent from God. But when the fire that had fallen from heaven was reported, one might have feared that the weak would believe that virtue was nothing admirable, if God even punishes the one who possesses it. Yet even during this incident the holy man did not fall down but focused his entire attention on God's work. Commentary on Job 1.16.[17]

1:17 A Chaldean Raid

The Power of the Devil. Chrysostom: Therefore we cannot consider these blows as coming directly from God. The devil amplifies the tragedy, as seen in the variety of the announced calamities. But, since Job was pious, he probably said, "It is God who strikes. Hence it is necessary to be patient." The devil then argues.

"Look!" the devil says. Consider what kind of men attack you. It is not only God who is fighting against you. Contemplate the great power of the devil and the way he has armed such numerous hordes. The devil has clothed himself in appearances. Even if you do not believe in the reality of divine judgment, you can see his ability to give demonic powers a visible form, even when he cannot create these powers. Commentary on Job 1.17.[18]

1:18-19 Job's Children Die

Loss Wisely Instructs the Human Heart. Gregory the Great: Sometimes, while the mind is sustained with the fullness and richness of a gift so large, if it enjoys uninterrupted security in these things, it forgets the source from which they have come. It imagines that it derives these things from itself in a way that never ceases. Hence it is that this same grace sometimes withdraws itself for our good and shows the presumptuous mind how weak it is in itself. For then we really learn the source from which our good qualities proceed. Only by seemingly losing them are we made aware that they can never be preserved by our own efforts. And so for the purpose of tutoring us in lessons of humility, it very often happens that when the crisis of temptation is upon us, such extreme folly comes down upon our wisdom. Then, the mind being dismayed, it does not grasp how to meet the evils that threaten or how to guard against temptation. But this very foolishness wisely instructs the heart. For whatever causes the mind to turn to foolishness for a moment is afterwards faced as reality. As the mind becomes more humble, it becomes wiser. In this way the very wisdom that seems to be lost temporarily is now held in more secure possession. Morals on the Book of Job 2.78.[19]

---

[15]Ps 140:10 (139:11 LXX). [16]PO 42.1:106. [17]PTA 1:96-98. [18]PTS 35:24. [19]LF 18:119-20*.

1:20-22 JOB BLESSES GOD IN HIS AFFLICTION

[20]*Then Job arose, and rent his robe, and shaved his head, and fell upon the ground, and worshiped.* [21]*And he said, "Naked I came from my mother's womb, and naked shall I return; the LORD gave, and the LORD has taken away; blessed be the name of the LORD."*

[22]*In all this Job did not sin or charge God with wrong.**

*LXX *insanity*

OVERVIEW: The Fathers agree in saying that Job preserves, in his affliction and inevitable despair, an undefeatable spirit of gratitude toward God (CHRYSOSTOM, EPHREM, HESYCHIUS). From this we learn that affliction must not become for us a cause of temptation (GREGORY). Nakedness is both gift and benevolence. Job's words concerning this may best be understood of evil and sin, and not simply of possessions. Our only true possession is godliness, which cannot be taken away even by death (CLEMENT). We should accept what God ordains for us, for he always ordains what is good (BASIL). Like a good servant, Job counted the will of the Lord his greatest possession (AUGUSTINE).

1:20-21 Job Worships God

A SIGN OF VICTORY. CHRYSOSTOM: Do not believe, dear brothers, that Job's gesture indicates a defeat. It is, above all, a sign of victory. Indeed, if he had done nothing, he would have appeared to be insensitive. Job actually demonstrates himself to be altogether wise, fatherly and pious. What damage did he suffer? He grieves not only for the loss of his children and his cattle but also for the way they died. Who would have not been shattered by such events? Which man of steel would have not been affected? Paul himself often expressed his tearful reaction to events, "What are you doing weeping and breaking my heart?"[1] We should admire Paul's response. In the same way, Job also deserves to be admired because, in

spite of the emotion that pushed him to make that moving gesture, he does not speak a single inappropriate word. COMMENTARY ON JOB 1.20.[2]

THE PURITY OF JOB. EPHREM THE SYRIAN: The text means that Job was not covered with crimes and evil deeds and would have returned "naked," that is, pure and innocent to "his mother's womb." He was so firm in his holy frankness that you may easily imagine he had never turned aside from righteousness nor would have ever passed from virtue to vice in the future. COMMENTARY ON JOB 1.21.[3]

GODLINESS IS OUR ONLY TRUE POSSESSION. CLEMENT OF ALEXANDRIA: Job's words may be more elegantly understood of evil and sin in this way: Naked was I formed from the earth at the beginning, as if from a mother's womb. Naked to the earth shall I also depart—naked[4] not of possessions, for that would be a trivial and common thing; rather, naked of evil and sin and of the unsightly shape which follows those who have led bad lives. Obviously all of us human beings are born naked and again are buried naked, swathed only in grave clothes. For God has provided for us another life, and made the present life the way for the course which leads to it. He appoints the supplies derived from what we possess merely as provisions for the way. And when we come to the end

---

[1]Acts 21:13. [2]PTS 35:25-26. [3]ESOO 2:2. [4]See also Clement's *Stromateis* 4.25.

of this way, the wealth, consisting of the things which we possessed, journeys no farther with us. For not a single thing that we possess is properly our own. We are properly owners of only one possession, that is, godliness. Death will not rob us of this when it overtakes us. It will, however, throw out everything else, although it will do so against our will. For it is for the support of life that we all have received what we possess; and after enjoying merely the use of it, each one departs, obtaining from life what amounts to a brief memento. For this is the end of all prosperity; this is the conclusion of the good things of this life. It is only right, then, that the infant upon opening its eyes after issuing from the womb, immediately begins with crying, not with laughter. For it weeps, as if bewailing life, at whose hands from the outset it tastes of deadly gifts. For immediately on being born its hands and feet are swaddled; and swathed in bonds, it begins nursing. O introduction to life, precursor to death! The child has but entered on life, and immediately there is put upon it the clothing of the dead; for nature reminds those that are born of their end. This is also why the child, on being born, wails, as if crying plaintively to its mother. Why, O mother, did you bring me out into this life in which prolongation of life is progress to death? Why have you brought me into this troubled world, in which, on being born, swaddled bands are my first experience? Why have you delivered me to such a life as this, in which both a pitiable youth wastes away before old age, and old age is shunned as under the doom of death? Dreadful, O mother, is the course of life, which has death as the goal of the runner. Bitter is the road of life we travel, with the grave as the wayfarer's inn. Perilous the sea of life we sail, for it has Hades as a pirate to attack us. Humankind alone is born in all aspects naked, without a weapon or clothing born with it. This does not mean you are inferior to the other animals, but the nakedness and the fact you bring nothing with you are designed to produce thought. That thought, in turn, may bring out dexterity, expel

sloth, introduce the arts for the supply of our needs, and beget a variety of ingenuity. For, naked, human beings are full of contrivances, being pricked on by their necessity, as by a goad, to figure out how to escape rains, how to elude cold, how to fence off blows, how to till the earth, how to terrify wild beasts; how to subdue the more powerful of them. Wetted with rain, they conceive of a roof; having suffered from cold, they invent clothing; being struck, they constructed a breastplate; their hands bleeding with the thorns in tilling the ground, they avail themselves of the help of tools; in their naked state liable to become a prey to wild beasts, they discovered from their fear an art which frightened the very thing that frightened them. Nakedness begat one accomplishment after another, so that even their nakedness was a gift and benevolence. Accordingly, Job also being made naked of wealth, possessions, of the blessing of children, of a numerous offspring, and having lost everything in a short time, uttered this grateful explanation: "Naked came I out of the womb, naked also I shall depart thither," to God and to that blessed lot and rest. CATENA, FRAGMENT 1.[5]

WHAT GOD ORDAINS IS ALWAYS GOOD. BASIL THE GREAT: Be perfectly assured of this, that though the reasons for what is ordained by God are beyond us, yet always what is arranged for us by him who is wise and who loves us is to be accepted, be it ever so grievous to endure. He himself knows how he is appointing what is best for each and why the terms of life that he fixes for us are unequal. There exists some reason incomprehensible to us why some are sooner carried far away from us, and some are left a longer while behind to bear the burdens of this painful life. So we should always adore his lovingkindness and not express discontent, remembering those great and famous words of the great athlete Job, when he had seen ten children at one table, in one short moment, crushed to death,

---

[5] ANF 2:577**.

"The Lord gave and the Lord has taken away."
As the Lord thought good so it came to pass. Let
us adopt those marvelous words. At the hands of
the righteous Judge, those who demonstrate similar good deeds shall receive a similar reward. We
have not lost the boy;[6] we have restored him to
the Lender. His life is not destroyed; it is
changed for the better. He whom we love is not
hidden in the ground; he is received into heaven.
Let us wait a little while, and we shall be once
more with him. The time of our separation is not
long, for in this life we are all like travelers on a
journey, hurrying on to the same shelter. While
one has reached his rest, another arrives, another
hurries on, but one and the same end awaits
them all. He has outstripped us on the way, but
we shall all travel the same road, and the same
hostel awaits us all. LETTER 5.2.[7]

WHAT HAVE YOU LOST? AUGUSTINE: Those
who lost all their worldly possessions in the sack
of Rome, if they owned their possessions as they
had been taught by the apostle who himself was
poor without, but rich within—that is to say, if
they used the world as though not using it—they
could say in the words of Job, heavily tried but
not overcome, "Naked I came out of my mother's
womb, and naked shall I return. The Lord gave,
and the Lord has taken away; as it pleased the
Lord, so it has happened: Blessed be the name of
the Lord." Like a good servant, Job counted the
will of his Lord his greatest possession and
through obedience to that will his soul was
enriched. It didn't grieve him while he was still
alive to lose those goods which he was shortly
going to have to leave at his death. But as to those
feebler spirits who, though they cannot be said to
prefer earthly possessions to Christ, still hang on
to them with a somewhat moderate attachment
to them, they have discovered by the pain of losing these things how much they were sinning in
loving them. For their grief is of their own making. In the words of the apostle quoted above,
"They have pierced themselves through with
many sorrows."[8] For it was well that they who

had so long despised these verbal admonitions
should receive the teaching of experience. For
when the apostle says "They that will be rich fall
into temptation,"[9] and so on, what he blames in
riches is not the possession of them but the desire
for them. For elsewhere he says, "Charge those
who are rich in this world not to be high-minded
or trust in uncertain riches but in the living God,
who gives us richly all things to enjoy; that they
do good, that they be rich in good works, ready to
distribute, willing to communicate; laying up in
store for themselves a good foundation against
the time to come, that they may lay hold on eternal life."[10] They who were making such a use of
their property have been consoled for light losses
by great gains, and have had more pleasure in
those possessions which they have securely laid
past, by freely giving them away, than grief in
which those they entirely lost by an anxious and
selfish hoarding of them. For nothing could perish on earth except what they would be ashamed
to carry away from the earth. Our Lord's injunction runs, "Do not lay up treasures for yourselves
on earth, where moth and rust corrupt, and
where thieves break through and steal; but lay up
for yourselves treasures in heaven, where neither
moth nor rust corrupt, and where thieves do not
break through or steal: for where your treasure is,
there will your heart be also."[11] And they who
have listened to this injunction have proved in
the time of tribulation how well they were
advised in not despising this most trustworthy
teacher and most faithful and mighty guardian of
their treasure. For if many were glad that their
treasure was stored in places which the enemy
chanced not to light upon, how much better
founded was the joy of those who, by the counsel
of their God, have fled with their treasure to a
citadel which no enemy can possibly reach! CITY
OF GOD 1.10.[12]

[6]Basil wrote this letter to comfort Nectarius who had lost his son.
[7]NPNF 2 8:114*. [8]1 Tim 6:10. [9]1 Tim 6:10. [10]1 Tim 6:17-19.
[11]Mt 6:19-21. [12]NPNF 1 2:7-8.

1:22 Job Did Not Sin

No Sin in Word or Thought. HESYCHIUS OF JERUSALEM: "Job did not sin" before God. That is, he was pure from sins committed with his tongue or in his thoughts, and he praised God by means of words in accordance with his thoughts. Actually "he did not charge God with insanity," that is, Job does not accuse the will of God or scorn the economy of the Creator, and he does not perceive insanity in the events that had occurred. He did not believe that the righteous are abandoned into the hands of sinners. HOMILIES ON JOB 3.1.22.[13]

GRIEF MUST NOT LEAD TO TEMPTATION. GREGORY THE GREAT: The mind that grieves over testing must be wary and diligent lest the temptation prompt it from within to utter words that are forbidden or to complain about being tested. It should be vigilant that the fire that tests it like gold not turn everything into mere chaff by the excesses of a lawless tongue. MORALS ON THE BOOK OF JOB 2.88.[14]

---

[13]PO 42.1.1:118.   [14]LF 18:126.

2:1-8 SATAN IS ALLOWED TO INFLICT SORES ON JOB

[1]*Again there was a day when the sons of God came to present themselves before the LORD, and Satan also came among them to present himself before the LORD.* [2]*And the LORD said to Satan, "Whence have you come?" Satan answered the LORD, "From going to and fro on the earth, and from walking up and down on it."* [3]*And the LORD said to Satan, "Have you considered my servant Job, that there is none like him on the earth, a blameless and upright man, who fears God and turns away from evil? He still holds fast his integrity, although you moved me against him, to destroy him without cause."* [4]*Then Satan answered the LORD, "Skin for skin! All that a man has he will give for his life.* [5]*But put forth thy hand now, and touch his bone and his flesh, and he will curse thee to thy face."* [6]*And the LORD said to Satan, "Behold, he is in your power; only spare his life*."*

[7]*So Satan went forth from the presence of the LORD, and afflicted Job with loathsome sores from the sole of his foot to the crown of his head.* [8]*And he took a potsherd with which to scrape himself, and sat among the ashes.†*

*Heb, LXX, Vg; Peshitta reads *his soul*   †LXX adds *outside the town*

OVERVIEW: All the events in Job's trial are ruled and controlled by divine providence (CHRYSOSTOM). In his affliction he foreshadows the suffering of Christ, after he assumed a human nature and human flesh (GREGORY). Job endures another test: he is attacked by disease, that is, the suffering moves to his own body (JULIAN OF ECLANUM, ISHO'DAD). But God commands that his natural state of mind and reason are not destroyed (EPHREM, DIDYMUS). Job is presented as a spectacle, that is, a model of behavior in affliction (ISHO'DAD).

2:1-2 God Questions Satan

THE DUTY OF THE ANGELS. CHRYSOSTOM: Why does the author describe the angels in the act of presenting themselves daily before the Lord? He does so that we might learn no actual event is overlooked by God's providence, and that the angels report what happens every day. Every day they are sent to settle some question, even though we ignore all this. That is the reason why they were created; that is their task, as the blessed Paul says, "They are sent to serve for the sake of those who are to inherit salvation."[1] "And the devil," the text says, "also came among them." You know why the angels are present. But why is the devil present? The latter is present to tempt Job; the former, in order to regulate our matters. Why is the devil questioned again before the angels themselves? Because he had said before them, "He will curse you to your face." What a shameless nature! He has dared come back! COMMENTARY ON JOB 2.1.[2]

2:3 Job Blameless and Upright

JOB'S LIKENESS WITH CHRIST. GREGORY THE GREAT: How could it be that the Lord says to Satan, "You incited me against him?" especially if we assume that blessed Job is an anticipation of the Redeemer in his passion? Truly the Mediator between God and man, the man Christ Jesus, came to bear the scourges of our mortal nature that he might put away the sins of our disobedience. But, seeing that he is of one and the self-same nature with the Father, how does the Father declare that he was moved by Satan against him, when it is acknowledged that no inequality of power, no diversity of will, interrupts the harmony between the Father and the Son? Yet he who is equal to the Father by the divine nature

came for our sakes to be flogged in his human nature. He would have never endured these stripes if he had not taken the form of accursed human beings in the work of their redemption. And unless the first man had transgressed, the second would never have come to the humiliation and disgrace of the passion. When Satan moved the first man from the Lord, then the Lord was moved against the second Man. And so, Satan then moved the Lord to the affliction of this second Man, when the sin of disobedience brought down the first man from the height of uprightness. For if the devil had not drawn the first Adam by willful sin into the death of the soul, the second Adam, being without sin, would have never come to the voluntary death of the flesh. MORALS ON THE BOOK OF JOB 3.26.[3]

2:4-5 Skin for Skin!

TESTING BY PERSONAL INJURY SHORT OF DEATH. JULIAN OF ECLANUM: Since the devil had seen that at the first attack of temptation the stability of the holy man had not tumbled down, the devil came again before God, and by claiming that the temptation was not serious enough, he asserted that Job had now to be tested. The test would focus on Job's own person, rather than his external circumstances. In fact, Satan supposed that Job had suffered the loss of his goods by hiding under a false appearance, according to the custom of all other people. Job did so to avoid the danger spiteful words against God would pose to his salvation. Humans typically drive away the greatest losses by suffering smaller damages. Often, by opposing the hand, we ward off a vital danger to the head. EXPOSITION ON THE BOOK OF JOB 2.4.[4]

2:6 Only Spare His Life

JOB MUST BE TESTED. EPHREM THE SYRIAN: "Only spare his soul." God does not say this as if

[1]Heb 1:14. [2]PTS 35:33. [3]LF 18:147-48*. [4]CCL 88:8-9.

he wanted to prevent the devil from snatching Job's life away, but he says "spare him." That is, be careful not to destroy the natural state of Job's mind and reason. So God arranged things in order that the devil, being convinced by the evidence of the facts, might acknowledge that Job, even though he was pressed by so many afflictions, could never be brought to blasphemy. Commentary on Job 2.6.[5]

The Meaning of "Spare His Life." Didymus the Blind: The Lord allows even this for our best, so that Job should be presented as an expression and image of perseverance—like a marked pillar—and that he may be for his contemporaries and his successors an example of such virtue. Indeed, this did happen. From the fighter and athlete himself one can hear the words, "I know that I shall be vindicated."[6] When the Lord surrendered him, he said, "Only spare his life." This phrase can be understood in the following way: often we see madness and confusion of mind in people. God alone, who knows the hidden, knows the reasons why these people have been surrendered [to testing] in such a way. What the Lord, therefore, wants to say is this: Do not numb or confuse Job's mind. You may have what you demanded. Touch his flesh and bones. Consider whether "Only spare his life" might mean, "Do not kill him!" Commentary on Job 2.6.[7]

2:7 Job Afflicted with Loathsome Sores

Nature of Job's Disease. Isho'dad of Merv: Job's disease is elephantiasis. When it strikes someone, his whole body putrefies, his flesh melts away, the features of his face decompose, his nostrils disappear, and a filthy, sour and corrosive pus constantly oozes from his body. [Job] inspires horror and disgust not only in his neighbors but in himself as well. Commentary on Job 2.7.[8]

2:8 Job Sat Among the Ashes

Job Is a Spectacle to the World. Isho'dad of Merv: God made Job sit "outside the town" in order to present him as "a spectacle to the world,"[9] so that afterwards no one might refuse to believe that it was him who had endured such tribulations. In the course of time, the visitors of that place might gain a profit from the experience of seeing Job. For the same reason our Lord left Lazarus in the grave for four days, so that his body might give a bad odor. After smelling his body, no one could refuse to believe in Lazarus's resurrection. Commentary on Job 2.8.[10]

---

[5]ESOO 2:2-3. [6]Job 13:18. [7]PTA 1:138. [8]CSCO 229:238-39. [9]1 Cor 4:9. [10]CSCO 229:239.

2:9-13 JOB'S FRIENDS COME TO CONSOLE HIM

[9]*Then his wife said to him, "Do you still hold fast your integrity? Curse God, and die."* [10]*But he said to her, "You speak as one of the foolish women would speak. Shall we receive good at the hand of God, and shall we not receive evil?" In all this Job did not sin with his lips.*

[11]*Now when Job's three friends heard of all this evil that had come upon him, they came each*

from his own place, Eliphaz the Temanite, Bildad the Shuhite, and Zophar the Naamathite. They made an appointment together to come to condole with him and comfort him. ¹²*And when they saw him from afar, they did not recognize him; and they raised their voices and wept; and they rent their robes and sprinkled dust upon their heads toward heaven.* ¹³*And they sat with him on the ground seven days and seven nights, and no one spoke a word to him, for they saw that his suffering was very great.*

OVERVIEW: After the physical trial of the loss of wealth and children, Job must now face the psychological opposition of his wife as a new test (HESYCHIUS). But Job is able to refute her argument by recognizing the absolute power of God (CHRYSOSTOM). Job's three friends symbolically represent the three classes of the high priests, priests and prophets (EPHREM). They come to Job in order to comfort him for his painful loss of children and wealth and for the present diseases which afflict him (DIDYMUS). Job's behavior in affliction is an eternal warning to transform evil actions into good and virtuous works (GREGORY).

2:9 Curse God, and Die

A NEW TEST CONFRONTS JOB. HESYCHIUS OF JERUSALEM: Now, since the betrayer had been defeated in every battle, had failed in all his attempts, had been hindered in all his hunts, had been deprived of all his schemes, and all his traps had been broken, after destroying Job's wealth, after the death of his numerous children, after ripping Job's body with his blows, as a last, and in the betrayer's opinion, most compelling resource, he leads his wife against Job. HOMILIES ON JOB 4.2.9.[1]

2:10 Job Did Not Sin with His Lips

GOD POSSESSES THE POWER TO DO WHATEVER HE DESIRES. CHRYSOSTOM: This text means that if we actually experienced only misfortunes, we would still need to bear them. God is Master and Lord. Does he not possess the power to send us anything? Why did God provide us with our goods? He did not do so because we

deserved them. God was absolutely free to send us only afflictions. If he has also granted us goods, why do we complain? Notice how [Job] does not speak anywhere about faults or good actions but only says that God has the power to do whatever he wants. Recall your former happiness, and you will have no problem in bearing the present difficulties. It is sufficient, as our consolation, to know that it is the Lord who sends them to us. Let us not speak about justice and injustice. COMMENTARY ON JOB 2.10C.[2]

2:11 Job's Friends Came to Console Him

SYMBOLIC MEANING OF JOB'S FRIENDS AND SONS. EPHREM THE SYRIAN: In the meantime, while the friends investigated Job's case and made preparations for their journey, there is no doubt that many days passed. They were all lords and men of princely rank. Job's three friends signified the class of the high priests, the priests and the prophets, who flourished among the Jews. And Job's seven sons represented the priests of the church, the apostles, the prophets, and those people endowed with the gift of miracles and healing, the assistants of the moderators, the presbyters and the deacons. COMMENTARY ON JOB 2.11.[3]

A COMFORT FOR PAST AND PRESENT AFFLICTIONS. DIDYMUS THE BLIND: Job's friends came to do both things, since he had suffered both. On the one hand, Job's possessions and his children were taken from him, and on the other hand his entire body was covered with leprosy. They arrived "together" at Job's place. Their simulta-

---

[1]PO 42.1:138. [2]PTS 35:47-48. [3]ESOO 2:3.

neous arrival was either due to their great zeal or because they who lived in different places had agreed to meet. They wanted to arrive together to comfort him. They realized that the evil had not yet ceased but was active at that time. COMMENTARY ON JOB 2.11.[4]

2:12-13 They Did Not Recognize Job

VICES TURNED INTO VIRTUES. GREGORY THE GREAT: If the heart feels true sorrow, the vices cannot speak against it. And when one genuinely seeks an upright life, it is fruitless to prompt that person to do evil. But frequently, if we vigorously brace ourselves against the incitements of evil habits, we transform even those very evil habits into virtue. For some people are possessed by anger. Yet if they bring their anger under reason's influence, it is transformed into service rendered to holy zeal. Some are lifted up by pride. But when they bow the mind before the fear of God, pride is transformed into a free and unfettered authority for the defense of justice. Physical strength is a snare to some. Yet when we control our physical strength through the practice of works of mercy, we purchase pity's gains and are freed from the prompting of wickedness. MORALS ON THE BOOK OF JOB 3.70.[5]

---

[4]PTA 1:162-64.   [5]LF 18:175-76.

3:1-12 JOB CURSES THE DAY OF HIS BIRTH

[1]After this Job opened his mouth and cursed the day of his birth. [2]And Job said:
   [3]"Let the day perish wherein I was born,
      and the night which said,
      'A man-child is conceived.'
   [4]Let that day be darkness!
      May God above not seek it,
      nor light shine upon it.
   [5]Let gloom and deep darkness claim it.
      Let clouds dwell upon it;
      let the blackness of the day terrify it.*
   [6]That night—let thick darkness seize it!
      let it not rejoice among the days of the year,
      let it not come into the number of
         the months.

   [7]Yea, let that night be barren;
      let no joyful cry be heard[b] in it.
   [8]Let those curse it who curse the day,
      who are skilled to rouse up Leviathan.†
   [9]Let the stars of its dawn be dark;
      let it hope for light, but have none,
      nor see the eyelids of the morning;
   [10]because it did not shut the doors of my
         mother's womb,
      nor hide trouble from my eyes.

   [11]"Why did I not die at birth,
      come forth from the womb and expire?
   [12]Why did the knees receive me?
      Or why the breasts, that I should suck?"

b Heb come *LXX (4-5) Let that night be darkness, and let not the Lord regard it from above, neither let light come upon it. But let darkness and the shadow of death seize it; let blackness come upon it. †Vg Let those curse it who curse the day, those who are ready to rouse up Leviathan.

OVERVIEW: In these words spoken by Job during his despair, the Fathers saw many allegorical meanings that could appear as a moral warning to Christians. First, they instruct us to avoid offending God, even when despair understandably overwhelms us (ISHO'DAD). However, Didymus suggests that Job is not cursing the day of his birth but the painful events that happened on that day (DIDYMUS). Job's words also remind us of our condition as fallen creatures before our redemption in Christ (HESYCHIUS, EPHREM). The darkness invoked by Job symbolizes the condemnation of sin (OLYMPIODORUS, JULIAN OF ECLANUM) and its judgment before God (GREGORY, PHILIP). Job's words also foreshadow the condemnation of Judas as it was pronounced by Jesus (CHRYSOSTOM).

3:1-2 Job Cursed the Day of His Birth

JOB CURSES THE DAY OF HIS BIRTH. ISHO'DAD OF MERV: Human beings are apt to curse and grumble against the misfortunes that befall them. God, in fact, does not expect insensitivity on our part. But when we are in tribulations and suffer those afflictions that strike us, God expects that we not abandon ourselves to blasphemous words but use those that demonstrate our grief and express the seriousness of our misery. COMMENTARY ON JOB 3.1.[1]

THE REAL MEANING OF JOB'S "DAY." DIDYMUS THE BLIND: The wise man is no babbler, nor does he utter through his mouth anything that cannot happen. Thus he does not curse the day as a period of time but those things that occurred on that day. For it is Scripture's custom to call occurrences a "day." This the psalmist teaches us, when he says, "The Lord delivers them in the day of trouble."[2] Thereby he does not refer to "day of trouble" as a period of time but to the trouble that happened on that day. Paul's statement, "because the days are evil,"[3] also has the same meaning. One can say that the day's events are good for some and bad for others. Thus, for the people of Israel who crossed the Red Sea against their expectations, the day was good. For the Egyptians, however, the day was bad, for "they sank like lead in the mighty waters."[4] COMMENTARY ON JOB 3.1.[5]

3:3 Let the Day Perish in Which I Was Born

A REFERENCE TO THE SIN OF EVE. HESYCHIUS OF JERUSALEM: "Let the day perish in which I was born," not the day in which I was formed but that "in which I was born." . . . God, in fact, forms me into goodness, but Eve, who transgressed, conceives me into sadness. And David himself did not ignore that, but after learning it from the Spirit, he introduces the concept into a prophetic psalm with these terms: "For, behold, I was conceived in iniquities, and in sins did my mother conceive me."[6] How? To be sure, Eve began to conceive and give birth after the fall in paradise and after the transgression due to the miserable nourishment of the tree. HOMILIES ON JOB 6.3.3.[7]

3:4-5 Let That Day Be Darkness!

THE REASON FOR CHRIST'S ADVENT. EPHREM THE SYRIAN: Learn here the reason which led the Emmanuel to a new birth in the flesh. Certainly the sin of the world was the reason for the advent of Christ. COMMENTARY ON JOB 3.4.[8]

CONDEMNATION OF SIN. OLYMPIODORUS: According to Job's words, he desires that the moon or the stars might not illuminate his night but that it may be obscured by thick darkness, which Job calls the shadow of death. If one carefully examines the text's meaning, Job demands through his prayers that sin may appear as it actually is in its great depravity, so that sin may not simulate virtue. Rather, after sin has been recognized as dark and deadly, it may be avoided and rejected. COMMENTARY ON JOB 3.4-5.[9]

---

[1] CSCO 229:240. [2] Ps 41:1 (40:2 LXX). [3] Eph 5:16. [4] Ex 15:10. [5] PTA 1:168. [6] Ps 51:5 (50:7 LXX). [7] PO 42.1:170. [8] ESOO 2:3. [9] PTS 24:39.

3:6-7 Let That Night Be Barren

**ADAM'S DECEITFUL JUSTIFYING OF SIN COM-
POUNDS HIS ERROR.** GREGORY THE GREAT:
The year of our illumination will be accomplished
at the appearing of the eternal Judge of the holy
church when the life of its pilgrimage is completed. [The church] then receives the recompense of its labors when, having finished this
season of warfare, [it] returns to its native country. Hence, the prophet says, "You shall bless the
crown of the year with your goodness."[10] For the
"crown of the year" is, as it were, "blessed" as the
reward of virtues is bestowed when the season of
toil comes to an end. But the days of this year are
the several virtues, and its months the many deeds
of those virtues. Moreover, note that when the
mind is erected in confidence, it has a good hope
that when the Judge comes it will receive the
reward of the mind's virtues. All the evil things
[the church] has done are also remembered. It
greatly fears lest the strict Judge, who comes to
reward virtues, should also examine and weigh
exactly those things that have been unlawfully
committed. Thus, when "the year" is completed,
the "night" is also reckoned. . . . There are some
people that not only have no remorse for what
they do but unceasingly uphold and applaud their
actions. Truly, a sin that is upheld is doubled. One
writer correctly condemns this attitude by saying,
"My son, have you sinned? Don't add on to what
you have done."[11] For a person "adds sin to sin"
who, over and above what he has done, justifies
his error. He does not "leave the night alone" who
also adds vindication's support to the darkness of
his fault. Thus, the first man Adam, when questioned concerning the night of his error, would
not allow his "night" to remain alone. God's questioning called Adam to repentance, but Adam
responded by justifying himself, saying, "The
woman whom you gave to be with me, she gave
me fruit from the tree, and I did eat."[12] Adam
covertly blames his Maker for the fault of Adam's
transgression. It was as if Adam said, "You provided me with an occasion for sin, because you

gave me the woman." Therefore, the branch of this
sin remains manifest in the human race up to the
present time. We continue to justify our misdeeds. MORALS ON THE BOOK OF JOB 4.37-39.[13]

3:8 Cursing the Day

SPIRITUAL INIQUITY COMES TO EARTH.
JULIAN OF ECLANUM: May this night or day of
detestation become what the horrible and cruel
dragon that is led from the sea to the earth
deserves. Indeed the Hebrew and Syrian tradition interpret Leviathan to be the one about
which David says, "There is that dragon that you
have made to delude him."[14] Even though the
dragon seems to represent, above all, a figure of
spiritual iniquity, it nonetheless, after getting out
and being cast onto earth, is said to possess the
ability to cause many massacres of people and
animals. Thus, with good reason, the curses of all
must be gathered against it. EXPOSITION ON THE
BOOK OF JOB 3.8.[15]

3:9 The Stars Darkened

A WARNING AGAINST SINNERS. PHILIP THE
PRIEST: "Let the stars of its dawn be dark," that
is, may the obscurity of blindness darken sinners
who pretend to shine in the night with the riches
and the honors of the world. May they not perceive, because of their fault, the gospel's light.
"Let it hope for light but have none." This is the
night of prevarication and death where the devil
has his kingdom. He cannot know the light of
Christ the Redeemer. Neither can those born on
that night if, after being regenerated through baptism, they do not destroy it. COMMENTARY ON
THE BOOK OF JOB 3.[16]

3:10-12 Why Did I Not Die at Birth?

A FORESHADOWING OF JESUS' WORDS. CHRY-

---

[10]Ps 65:11 (64:12 LXX).　[11]Sir 21:1.　[12]Gen 3:12.　[13]LF 18:207-9*.
[14]Ps 104:26 (103:26 LXX).　[15]CCL 88:11.　[16]PL 26:625.

sostom: Do not be amazed when I tell you that Job did not speak these words. I mistake him for another. These are words that I lend to Job and are contrary to his benevolence and profound goodness. In fact, Job had no desire to say anything of the sort. He suffered righteously what he was suffering, so that he reasonably and wisely said that "he was not born." This is exactly what Christ himself said about Judas: "It would have been better for that man if he had not been born."[17] And Job says much the same thing: "Why was I born? It would have been better if I had not been born." COMMENTARY ON JOB 3.11A-16B.[18]

---

[17]Mt 26:24.   [18]PTS 35:52.

3:13-26 JOB INVOKES THE REST OF DEATH

[13]For then I should have lain down and been quiet;
    I should have slept; then I should have been at rest,
[14]with kings and counselors of the earth
    who rebuilt ruins for themselves,*
[15]or with princes who had gold,
    who filled their houses with silver.
[16]Or why was I not as a hidden untimely birth,
    as infants that never see the light?
[17]There the wicked cease from troubling,
    and there the weary are at rest.
[18]There the prisoners are at ease together;
    they hear not the voice of the taskmaster.†
[19]The small and the great are there,

and the slave is free from his master.

[20]"Why is light given to him that is in misery,
    and life to the bitter in soul,
[21]who long for death, but it comes not,
    and dig for it more than for hid treasures;
[22]who rejoice exceedingly,
    and are glad, when they find the grave?‡
[23]Why is light given to a man whose way is hid,
    whom God has hedged in?§
[24]For my sighing comes as[c] my bread,
    and my groanings are poured out like water.
[25]For the thing that I fear# comes upon me,
    and what I dread** befalls me.
[26]I am not at ease, nor am I quiet;††
    I have no rest; but trouble comes.

---

c Heb before   *LXX who gloried in their swords   †Vg exactor   ‡Peshitta when they find the grave for the man, whose way is hidden and whom God covers?   §LXX Death is rest for man, but its way is hidden,[1] God has surrounded it with a wall.[2]   #Vg the fear that I feared   **Vg what I dreaded   ††Vg did not dissimulate and were I not quiet?

OVERVIEW: The Fathers see a source of moral instruction in the second half of Job's speech as well. Death is a departure from an impure world and a deliverance from pain (HESYCHIUS, GREGORY). Humility is an essential virtue of the righ- teous (CHRYSOSTOM). Death is as useful as life

---

[1]The reading "but its way is hidden" is attested only in a small part of the manuscript tradition of the LXX.   [2]The majority of the LXX mss read, "God has closed it upon him."

and must not be regarded as a calamity but as a gain (Chrysostom, Isho'dad). An affliction that goes beyond the limits of human nature authorizes anyone to express grief (Julian of Eclanum), but Job's words also reveal his willingness to fight in the struggle of the righteous against the opposing powers of evil (Didymus).

3:13 Then I Would Be at Rest

The Rest of the Righteous. Hesychius of Jerusalem: To enjoy the beauty of God's creation is desirable. It is a good thing to become a human being and to receive the image of God. It is not good to linger in an impure life. Many people are fascinated by an impure life, but not the righteous. Therefore, the departure from this world is no reason for sadness, for death is rest and deliverance from pain. Death is sleep. To depart from one's body is rest. Homilies on Job 6.3.13-16.[3]

3:14-16 Like a Stillborn Child

A Call to Humility. Chrysostom: It seems to me that Job attempts to humble these noble characters and to persuade them not to attach a great importance to human affairs, because he has not introduced the kings into this passage without purpose or at random. Job speaks of "those who gloried in their swords." Notice again how amid his afflictions Job possesses words full of wisdom. Their wealth, in fact, has granted the kings no protection; their power has been of no use; death has come at the end for everyone. "Or like a stillborn child that never sees the light," he says. Notice how, in order that he may not appear to be arrogant, he even compares himself with a stillborn child, so absolutely wretched and pitiful is he. Commentary on Job 3.20-23.[4]

3:17-19 The Weary Rest

Freedom from Sin Through the Love of God. Gregory the Great: Those who are endued with might in the love of their Maker are those who are strengthened in the love of God as the object of their desire. Yet they become in the same degree powerless in their own strength. The more strongly they long for the things of eternity, the more they are disenchanted with earthly objects. The failure of their self-assertive strength is wholesome. Hence the psalmist, wearied by the strength of his love, said, "My soul has fainted in your salvation."[5] For his soul did faint while making way in God's salvation, in that he panted with desire for the light of eternity, broken of all confidence in the flesh. Hence he says again, "My soul longs, yes, even faints for the courts of the Lord."[6] Now when he said "longs," he added correctly, "and faints," since that longing for the divine Being is small indeed if not similarly followed by a fainting in one's self. For it is fitting that one who is inflamed to seek the courts of eternity should be weakened in his love of his temporal state. He should become cold to the pursuits of this world in proportion as he rises with a soul more inflamed to the love of God. . . . Who else is to be understood by the title of the "taskmaster" other than that insatiate prompter who for once bestowed the coin of deceit upon humanity and from that time has not ceased daily to claim the debt of death? Who lent the man in paradise the money of sin, and by the multiplying of wickedness is daily exacting it with usury? Concerning this taskmaster, the truth is spoken in the Gospel, "And the Judge deliver you to the officer."[7] Therefore, when we hear the voice of this accuser, we are struck with this temptation. But the temptation does not have effect if we resist the one who accuses us. . . . And it is well added that "the slave is free from his master." For it is written, "Everyone that sins is the slave of sin."[8] For whoever yields himself up to evil desire bends the neck of his mind that previously was free to the dominion of wickedness. When we

---

[3]PO 42.1:186. [4]PTS 35:54. [5]Ps 119:81 (118:81 LXX). [6]Ps 84:2 (83:3 LXX). [7]Lk 12:58. [8]Jn 8:34.

struggle against the evil by which we had been taken captive, when we forcibly resist the bad habit, when we tread under all such desires, we withstand this taskmaster. When we strike our sin with penitence and cleanse the pollution with our tears, we uphold the right of our inborn liberty against this slavery. MORALS ON THE BOOK OF JOB 4.67-71.[9]

3:20-23 Life Given to Those Bitter in Soul

DEATH IS AS USEFUL AS LIFE. CHRYSOSTOM: "Why is light given," Job asks, "to those whose soul dwells in bitterness, and life to those souls who are in pain?" Again this is not the language—God forbid!—of someone who makes rebukes, but of someone who searches and suffers. In fact, when words are spoken with a different spirit, they must not be interpreted in the same manner. Therefore, when a philosopher asserts, "Why does a senseless person have riches at his disposal?"[10] he only shows that he is unworthy of riches. From this we learn that not only life but also death is useful, when it is more desired than evil. In this way Job speaks of "those who long for death," but, he says, "it does not come." That is why the Preacher in Ecclesiastes says, "For everything there is a season"[11] and, in another passage, "O death, how your memory is sweet."[12] When you hear Job's wife suggesting to him, "Curse God, and die,"[13] you should not suppose that he did not answer because of his love of life but because of his piety. Indeed he who considered death to be very desirable and saw it as a real goodness when he was allowed to obtain it did not dare speak against God. "Death is rest for man." This is what Job declares. Now if death brings rest, why don't the majority of people rush to it? Because God has made life desirable in order to prevent us from running to death. "Its way is hidden." In my opinion Job is speaking about death, but by pretending that his words are about the way of humankind. This indicates that Job's words concerning death are what has been said before,

especially in the expression, "they dig for it more than for hidden treasures," things that are evidently hidden. Our future is unknown, Job says. We do not uncover it. Please do not speak to me about those who hang themselves, because Job speaks about what conforms to nature and the commandments of God. "God has surrounded it," he says, "with a wall." As the gospel states, "The day of the Lord comes as a thief in the night."[14] To avoid the response, "Why do you not choose death?" Job answers, "The Lord has surrounded it with a wall." Its doors are closed. COMMENTARY ON JOB 3.20-23.[15]

THE PROTECTION OF DEATH. ISHO'DAD OF MERV: A person's actions are veiled and hidden by his death. God covers his way. The word *covers* means that God spares some afflictions through death, because the action of covering on God's part is an aid. COMMENTARY ON JOB 3.22.[16]

3:24-26 I Am Not at Ease

JOB IS FORCED TO REVEAL HIS SUFFERINGS. JULIAN OF ECLANUM: I did not ignorantly run into the things that I suffer. In fact, when I saw in others poverty's afflictions and the different diseases of the body, my communion with nature and my body warned me to fear lest anything of the same kind should happen to me. Therefore, I am also forced to fear an increase in the misfortunes I bear. This anticipation makes death look better than life. Job then adds, "Was I not quiet?" The Greek reads, "I was not quiet." That is to say, I did not continue in the fruition and prosperity of my goods. He says he feared he might encounter against his intention the evil necessity to reveal part of his vexations with wailing accents. Therefore Job says, "Was I not

---

[9]LF 18:232-38. [10]Prov 17:16 LXX. [11]Eccles 3:1. [12]Sir 41:1-2 (All LXX mss read "bitter" instead of "sweet," and this reading is attested only in Chrysostom). [13]Job 2:9. [14]1 Thess 5:2. [15]PTS 35:55-57. [16]CSCO 229:240.

quiet?" This means that while the harshness of my pain struck me, I wanted to hide in silence what I suffered, but such an abundance of raging misfortunes befell me that I am forced to reveal my tribulations with a feeble voice. EXPOSITION ON THE BOOK OF JOB 3.25-26.[17]

JOB IS READY TO FIGHT THE EVIL POWERS.
DIDYMUS THE BLIND: From this, Job's preparation against the adversary emerges. Even Paul, who possessed the hope and grace of the Spirit, was vigilant and fought the adversary, since he knew that for the holy the struggle "was not against enemies of blood and flesh but against the rulers, against the authorities, against the cosmic powers of this present darkness, against the spiritual forces of evil."[18] Our struggle is also against the archvillain himself, the devil, who prowls around "like a roaring lion . . . looking for someone to devour."[19] Even though Job was vigilant, the devil did not refrain from asking for permission to test him and to impose on him the burden he proceeds to place on him. Job's difficult experience seems like God's wrath, yet he knows that his sufferings are not the result of his sinfulness. For Job states, "I know that I shall be vindicated."[20] Even in other passages Scripture describes hardship as "wrath." It is said, "You sent out your fury; it consumed them like stubble."[21] When we hear about God's wrath, we do not consider it a condition of the soul similar to human emotions. Such an emotion cannot be sent, since it lives in the soul. The wrath of God, however, is sent, for "you sent out your fury," that is, hardship. Hardship is imposed. Job calls that which has affected him as "wrath." COMMENTARY ON JOB 3.26.[22]

---

[17]CCL 88:12. [18]Eph 6:12. [19]1 Pet 5:8. [20]Job 13:18. [21]Ex 15:7. [22]PTA 1:256-58.

4:1-11 ELIPHAZ EXHORTS JOB TO BE PATIENT

[1]Then Eliphaz the Temanite answered:
　[2]"If one ventures a word with you, will
　　you be offended?
　　Yet who can keep from speaking?*
　[3]Behold, you have instructed[†] many,
　　and you have strengthened the weak
　　hands.
　[4]Your words have upheld him who was
　　stumbling,
　　and you have made firm the feeble knees.
　[5]But now it has come to you, and you are
　　impatient;
　　it touches you, and you are dismayed.

　[6]Is not your fear of God your confidence,
　　and the integrity of your ways your hope?[‡]

　[7]"Think now, who that was innocent ever
　　perished?
　　Or where were the upright cut off?
　[8]As I have seen, those who plow iniquity
　　and sow trouble[§] reap the same.
　[9]By the breath of God they perish,
　　and by the blast of his anger they are
　　consumed.
　[10]The roar of the lion, the voice of the fierce
　　lion,

the teeth of the young lions, are broken.[#] *and the whelps of the lioness are*
[11]*The strong lion perishes for lack of prey,* *scattered."***

*LXX Have you often spoken in your suffering? And who will stand the violence of your words? Peshitta you have reproached †LXX Is not your fear founded in folly, your hope also, and the mischief of your way? §Vg grief #Peshitta The roar of the lion, the voice of the young lions, and the teeth of the lion are broken; the Peshitta version employed by Isho'dad reads the voice of the lioness and the young lions **LXX (10-11) The strength of the lion, and the voice of the lioness, and the exulting cry of serpents are quenched. The old lion has perished for want of food, and the lions' whelps have forsaken one another.*

OVERVIEW: In this initial speech of Eliphaz the Fathers recognize an ambiguous and reproachful attitude on the part of Job's friends and underline how their words have in themselves a part of truth that can be used as a starting point for moral issues and discussions. This kind of approach is constant in all Christian commentaries on Job, whether of the Greek, Latin or Syriac fathers. On the one hand, it is clearly asserted that Eliphaz blames and condemns Job as a sinner who is suffering because of his guilt (CHRYSOSTOM, DIDYMUS, JULIAN OF ECLANUM, GREGORY). On the other, it is emphasized how his words can be interpreted as a sincere invitation to patience (EPHREM), a warning against the arrogant (ISHO'DAD) and an acknowledgment of the natural power with which the righteous is endowed (CHRYSOSTOM).

4:1-2 Eliphaz Ventures to Speak

JOB'S WORDS ARE NOT SINFUL. CHRYSOSTOM: What does Eliphaz say? "Have you often spoken in your suffering?" By "suffering" the Scripture may signify "sin," as it states, "Under his tongue is mischief."[1] Eliphaz did not say, Have you committed any evil action? Eliphaz asks, "Have you spoken?" Indeed the fame of Job's life shone everywhere, and many still testified to Job's virtue. It is useless, Eliphaz says to Job, to say that your deeds are just and good, for the very reason that the fault is sometimes found in the words we speak. "And who can tolerate the violence of your words?" Consider now the expression "Have you often spoken?" The hesitation and uncertainty do not come from his moderation but from the fact that Eliphaz cannot convince Job about an evi-

dent fault on his part, "the violence of your words." What did Job say? He wished to die and to be delivered from his present life. Did Job actually say, "Is it in spite of my justice and virtues that I suffer such misfortunes"? No. He said, "I wanted to disappear with the impious, with my servants, with the stillborn. I wanted to have the same fate as the impious." He did not say, "I, who have such qualities and such importance." COMMENTARY ON JOB 4.2.[2]

4:3-5 Exhortation to Patience

AN INVITATION TO PATIENCE. EPHREM THE SYRIAN: "See, you have reproached many." Eliphaz shows Job that he has corrected many with his action and has brought them back to a fitting moderation with his advice and warnings. "And you have strengthened the weak hands," that is, since you exhorted others to endure with a strong soul the calamities that befell them, now it is fair that you exercise patience in your own afflictions. COMMENTARY ON JOB 4.3.[3]

WORDS OF CONSOLATION OR IRONIC REMARKS? JULIAN OF ECLANUM: "You have instructed many." The present facts battle with the former opinion. In fact, you supported others after they fell into despair and offered the aid of your hands to those lying down so that they might rise up. Why do you now not follow the stable footsteps of your constancy? Why are you unable to escape from your ruin? The things that you have often taught others should be sufficient

---

[1]Ps 10:7 (9:28 LXX). [2]PTS 35:59. [3]ESOO 2:3.

for your consolation. These words are spoken either as a consolation through the search for a more virtuous life or as an ironical remark, not because Job had actually helped others but because he had simply believed he was doing so. EXPOSITION ON THE BOOK OF JOB 4.3.[4]

4:6 Confidence Comes from Fear of God

ELIPHAZ BELIEVES JOB IS GUILTY. CHRYSOSTOM: "Is not your fear based on folly, as is your hope, and your mischievous ways?"[5] That is to say, was there not a foolish intention behind your actions? Eliphaz means, "Either you have not done these things, or your life is full of evil. Or you do not fear God with a righteous intention and all that you say is mere words. Your hope is based on folly." Eliphaz states that Job's hope was filled with foolishness. Why? Is it necessary to say that? Is it not possible that after often helping his neighbor, he has now fallen into misfortune? "No," says Eliphaz. COMMENTARY ON JOB 4.6.[6]

ELIPHAZ'S OPINION. DIDYMUS THE BLIND: While Scripture's spirit witnesses on behalf of Job that he has not committed any folly against God, Eliphaz incorrectly understands the reason behind what has been imposed upon Job. Eliphaz believes that Job suffers because of trespasses, and he thinks the words Job has spoken were motivated by his unacceptable behavior. "Is not your fear founded in folly," since you think you are righteous, "your hope also, and the mischief of your way?" Folly, Eliphaz says, is also the hope that you will be considered righteous. For such punishments are not imposed upon a righteous person. Eliphaz calls Job's way the "way of wickedness." He continuously thinks that the holy man suffers due to sins. This is also why Eliphaz ascribes folly to him. COMMENTARY ON JOB 4.6.[7]

4:7 Were the Upright Cut Off?

THE RIGHTEOUS MEET ALL THE ADVERSI-

TIES OF PRESENT LIFE. GREGORY THE GREAT: Whether it be heretics, of whom we have said that the friends of blessed Job bore an image, or whether any of the evil ones, they are as much to blame in their admonitions as they are immoderate in their condemnation. For Eliphaz says, "Who ever perished being innocent? Or where were the righteous cut off?" Since it often happens that in this life both "the innocent perish" and the "righteous are" utterly "cut off," yet in perishing they are kept for glory eternal. For if innocent people never perished, the prophet would not say, "The righteous perishes, and no man lays it to heart."[8] If God in his providential dealings did not carry off the righteous, Wisdom would never have said of the righteous person, "Yes, he was taken away quickly, to prevent wickedness from altering his understanding."[9] If no visitation ever struck the righteous, Peter would never foretell it, saying, "For the time has come that judgment must begin in the house of God."[10] They, then, are genuinely righteous who produce the love of the heavenly country to meet all the ills of the present life. For all who fear enduring ills in this life are clearly not righteous people. They have forgotten they suffer for the sake of eternal blessings. But Eliphaz does not take into account either that the righteous are cut off or that the innocent perish here. For people often serve God not in the hope of heavenly glory but for an earthly recompense. They make a fiction in their own head of that which they are seeking. Thinking themselves to be instructors in preaching earthly immunity, they show by all their pains what is the thing they love. MORALS ON THE BOOK OF JOB 5.34.[11]

4:8-9 Consumed by God's Anger

THE HARVEST OF GRIEF IS THE REWARD OF CONDEMNATION. GREGORY THE GREAT: To "sow grief" is to utter deceits, but to "reap grief" is to

---

[4]CCL 88:13. [5]LXX. [6]PTS 35:61. [7]PTA 1:274-76. [8]Is 57:1. [9]Wis 4:11. [10]1 Pet 4:17. [11]LF 18:267-68*.

prevail by speaking this way. Or, surely, they "sow grief" who do evil actions. They "reap grief" when they are punished for this wickedness. For the harvest of grief is the recompense of condemnation. The text immediately introduced the idea that they that "sow and reap grief," will "perish by the blast of God." They are "consumed by the breath of his nostrils." Yet in this passage the "reaping of grief" is not yet punishment but the still further perfecting of wickedness. For in the "breath of his nostrils," the punishment of that "reaping" is made to follow. Here, then, they "sow and reap grief," in that all that they do is wicked. They thrive in that very wickedness, as is said of the wicked person by the psalmist, "His ways are always grievous; your judgments are far above his vision. As for all his enemies, he puffs at them."[12] It is quickly added concerning him, "under his tongue is labor and grief."[13] Hence, he "sows grief" when he does wicked things. He "reaps grief" when from the same wickedness he grows to temporal greatness. How then is it that they who "perish by the blast of God" are for the most part permitted to abide long here below, and in greater prosperity than the righteous? Thus it is said of them again by the psalmist, "They are not in trouble as other men, neither are they plagued like other folk."[14] Therefore, Jeremiah asks, "Why does the way of the wicked prosper?"[15] Because it is written, "For the Lord is a longsuffering rewarder,"[16] he often puts up with for a long time those whom he condemns for all eternity. Yet sometimes God strikes quickly, in that he hastens to the aid of the fearful innocent. Thus, almighty God sometimes permits the wicked to have their way for a long time, so that the way of the righteous may be more purely cleansed. Yet some-

times he slays the unrighteous with speedy destruction, and by their ruin he strengthens the hearts of the innocent. MORALS ON THE BOOK OF JOB 5.35.[17]

4:10-11 The Lion Dies for Lack of Prey

THE ARROGANT HAVE PERISHED. ISHO'DAD OF MERV: The author signifies by "the lion" those powerful men who inspire people with fear, as lions do. By "lioness" he means their wives, who were evil and inspired fear simply by speaking. In the same manner, their children were arrogant and quite cruel. All these have perished. They were extinguished instantly. COMMENTARY ON JOB 4.10.[18]

THE NATURAL POWER OF THE RIGHTEOUS. CHRYSOSTOM: The writer mentions natural things, that is, nothing that is new or unusual. Certain laws regulate everything, and nothing has changed. Indeed, if what concerns wild beasts remains the same, even more so what concerns us remains unchanged. If it is not possible to restrain "the strength of the lion," then the righteous also cannot be prevented from talking frankly. In fact, as the wild beast naturally possesses strength, so also the righteous person possesses a natural power and force. Actually it is more likely for a lion to become weak than for a righteous person to allow others to manipulate him. COMMENTARY ON JOB 4.10.[19]

---

[12]Ps 10:5 (9:26 LXX). [13]Ps 10:7 (9:28 LXX). [14]Ps 73:5 (72:5 LXX). [15]Jer 12:1. [16]2 Thess 1:5. [17]LF 18:268-69*. [18]CSCO 229:241. [19]PTS 35:63.

4:12-21 ELIPHAZ RELATES HIS VISION AND THE WORDS THAT HE HEARD

¹²Now a word was brought to me stealthily,
*   my ear received the whisper of it.**
¹³Amid thoughts from visions of the night,
*   when deep sleep falls on men,*
¹⁴dread came upon me, and trembling,
*   which made all my bones shake.*
¹⁵A spirit glided past my face;
*   the hair of my flesh stood up.*
¹⁶It stood still,
*   but I could not discern its appearance.*
A form was before my eyes;
*   there was silence, then I heard a*
*   voice:†*
¹⁷"Can mortal man be righteous beforeᵈ
*   God?*

Can a man be pure beforeᵈ his Maker?‡
¹⁸Even in his servants he puts no trust,
*   and his angels he charges with error;*
¹⁹how much more those who dwell in houses
*   of clay,*
*   whose foundation is in the dust,*
*   who are crushed before the moth.*
²⁰Between morning and evening they are
*   destroyed;*
*   they perish for ever without any*
*   regarding it.*
²¹If their tent-cord is plucked up within
*   them,*
*   do they not die, and that without*
*   wisdom?"§*

ᵈ Or *more than* *LXX *If your sentences had contained a word of truth, none of these misfortunes would have befallen you* †Peshitta *a murmur and a voice* ‡LXX *What, shall a mortal be pure before the Lord? Or a man be blameless in regard to his works?* §LXX *And from the morning to evening they no longer exist, they have perished, because they cannot help themselves. For he blows upon them, and they are withered, they have perished for lack of wisdom.*

OVERVIEW: Job is blameless, and there is no ground for any accusation against him (CHRYSOSTOM). The words of Eliphaz, even though they reproach Job, can be interpreted allegorically and provide us with moral instruction (GREGORY). They also show us the limited and imperfect perception of God that human beings can attain (ISHO'DAD) and our weakness and powerlessness before God (HESYCHIUS, DIDYMUS), who can see every sin (OLYMPIODORUS).

4:12 A Word Came to Eliphaz

NO BASIS FOR BLAMING JOB. CHRYSOSTOM: In the present case Eliphaz wants to suggest, in my opinion, that Job has often spoken such words either, perhaps, to drive others to jealousy or with a different intention. You that ask such questions, see whom you resemble. Indeed, if Eliphaz has spoken so in these circumstances without obtaining forgiveness, it will be the same for us. Our situation will be even worse, because we have views similar to those of Eliphaz. And we have the advantage of the proofs the facts provide. We have been allowed to see the real reasons for the misfortunes that happened to Job. Yet we are just like those who believe they found a reason to blame him and to attack him without waiting for the evidence of the facts. COMMENTARY ON JOB 4.12.[1]

4:13-15 Dread Came upon Eliphaz

FIGURATIVE EXPRESSIONS OF SLEEP. GREGORY THE GREAT: Whoever is inclined to do worldly

[1]PTS 35:64.

things is, as it were, awake, but he who seeks inward rest eschews the riot of this world and is, as it were, asleep. Yet first we must know that when sleep is described figuratively in holy Scripture, it is understood in three senses. Sometimes we have used "sleep" to express the death of the body; sometimes "sleep" represents the grogginess of neglect; and sometimes "sleep" signifies tranquility of life. Earthly desires have been tramped underfoot. . . . What is denoted by the word *bones* but strong deeds? The prophet refers to the same thing when he writes, "He keeps all their bones."[2] In addition, it often happens that the things that people do are often reckoned to be of some account, largely because they do not realize how keen is God's inward discernment. However, when transported on the wings of contemplation, they behold things above. Somehow, they melt away from the security they felt in their presumption and quake all the more in the sight of God, a response proportionate to their awareness that whatever is excellent in them will not stand up to the searching eye of him whom they behold. . . . To "stand," then, is the attribute of the Creator alone, through whom all things pass away, though he himself never passes away, and in whom some things are held fast so that they might not pass away. Hence, our Redeemer, because the fixed state of his divine nature cannot be comprehended by the human mind, showed this to us as it were in passing, by coming to us, by being created, born, dead, buried, by rising again and returning to the heavenly realms. Christ foreshadowed this well in the gospel by enlightening the blind man, to whom Jesus promised hearing as he passed by, but he stood still as he healed his eyes.[3] For in the economy of his human nature he passed by, but in the power of his divine nature he stood still, demonstrating that he is present everywhere. MORALS ON THE BOOK OF JOB 5.54-63.[4]

4:16 *Hearing a Voice*

OUR PERCEPTION OF DIVINE NATURE. ISHO'DAD OF MERV: Eliphaz employs "murmur" and "voice" as words to express his ideas about God. As . . . the murmur and the voice strike our ears, they have no form or aspect. We only receive their sensation. Just as it is not possible to see a "murmur" or "voice," so we must realize the same is true of our thoughts about the divine nature. We receive our perception and knowledge of the divine nature as God gives us these thoughts, but this is not something that we can perceive through forms. COMMENTARY ON JOB 4.16.[5]

4:17 *Mortals Righteous Before God?*

NO SIN IS HIDDEN FROM GOD. OLYMPIODORUS: And do not think, Eliphaz says, that I am speaking these words to you reproachfully. No person, in fact, is totally blameless, and if he can hide his sins from people, he does not hide them from God's all-seeing eye that knows everything accurately. This indicates what is contrary to the Lord.[6] COMMENTARY ON JOB 4.17.[7]

4:18-19 *God Charges Angels and Humans with Error*

IF ANGELS FALL, DO NOT HUMANS MORESO? HESYCHIUS OF JERUSALEM: In truth, to be faultless is not easy for human beings. Faultlessness is beyond human possibilities. The order of the angels is itself subject to such weakness. This is what Eliphaz says, "Even in his servants God puts no trust." It is evident that God "puts no trust" in the righteous—like you, who have trusted yourself—because he knows the weakness of their nature and how easily their flesh falls. The fallen angels give God a reason not to trust in them, those whom "he charges with error." He has driven them away from the former honor of their rank and has reduced them to a lower position because they had evil thoughts against God. But if it is so for them, who even though they have a weak nature live nonetheless

---

[2]Ps 34:20 (33:21 LXX). [3]Jn 9. [4]LF 18:282-90*. [5]CSCO 229:24. [6]That is, to try to hide sins from him. [7]PTS 24:57.

in the heights among the virtuous powers, and if it is so for angels who in their own nature were above us, what will we say about our own human condition, one even more subject to sin? HOMI-LIES ON JOB 7.4.18-21.[8]

4:20-21 They Perish Forever

HUMAN POWERS ARE IMPOTENT. DIDYMUS THE BLIND: Eliphaz, still clinging to the same principle . . . that Job's critical circumstances were due to Job's own sins, adds these words, "Since they could not help themselves through virtue by repenting of their evils, these afflictions befell them." And Eliphaz suggests that he fully comprehends this situation. They perished since they could not drive away the most fearful accidents because of their weakness, demonstrating human power's worthlessness. COMMENTARY ON JOB 4.20-21.[9]

---

[8]PO 42.1:212. [9]PTA 1:306-8.

5:1-7 THE FOOL INCURS DISASTER

[1]Call now; is there any one who will
    answer you?
    To which of the holy ones will you turn?*
[2]Surely vexation kills the fool,
    and jealousy slays the simple.†
[3]I have seen the fool taking root,
    but suddenly I cursed his dwelling.
[4]His sons are far from safety,
    they are crushed in the gate,
and there is no one to deliver them.
[5]His harvest the hungry eat,
    and he takes it even out of thorns;[e]
    and the thirsty[f] pant after his[g] wealth.
[6]For affliction does not come from the dust,
    nor does trouble sprout from the
        ground;
[7]but man is born to trouble
    as the sparks fly upward.‡

e Heb obscure f Aquila Symmachus Syr Vg: Heb snare g Heb their *LXX Call for help, so that you may see whether you will be listened to, whether you will perceive one of the holy angels. †LXX For wrath destroys the foolish one, and ardour slays him that has gone astray. ‡LXX replaces the sentence just as sparks fly upwards with just as young vultures fly upwards; Peshitta and the young ones of the birds will lift their feathers over him.

OVERVIEW: The Fathers, in their writings on this section of the text, mostly emphasize the validity of Eliphaz's words. He shows the greatness of God and the lowliness of human beings. He declares that the wrath of God will inevitably punish the sinner, when the right time comes (CHRYSOSTOM). He foreshadows the infidelity and disbelief of the Jews (GREGORY) and demonstrates that human beings are always responsible for their sins and are punished because of them (EPHREM, ISHO'DAD). However, Didymus suggests that Eliphaz's principles reveal his narrowmindedness and human limitations (DIDYMUS).

5:1 Will Anyone Answer You?

THE EXCELLENCE OF GOD. CHRYSOSTOM: Through these words Eliphaz shows the excellence of God. Since it was natural for Job to examine his own situation on the ground of his personal reflections, observe what Eliphaz says: "Do not speak so." God is great. He does many things that we don't understand. Our lowliness is profound. . . . Whatever God might do, he does well. COMMENTARY ON JOB 5.1A.[1]

5:2 Vexation Kills the Fool

THE WRATH OF GOD. CHRYSOSTOM: But the wise person examines all with care, whereas the fool sees nothing. This certainly means that it is God who "causes the foolish to be destroyed by his wrath, while ardor makes him who has gone astray, perish." This refers to the ardor of God. "His wrath causes the foolish to disappear" means, in my opinion, that God's wrath causes the sinners to disappear. "Wrath destroys the foolish one," Eliphaz says, and therefore it does not destroy the sensible. Wrath, in fact, has no place among the sensible. COMMENTARY ON JOB 5.2.[2]

5:3 Fools Take Root

SINNERS ARE NOT DESTROYED IMMEDIATELY. CHRYSOSTOM: Notice how Eliphaz anticipates possible objections. "Do not say to me, 'Often they also had children.' Yes, but never for a long time." Since it made good sense to ask, "If Job was a sinner, how had he come to possess such great wealth?" Eliphaz responds, "I have seen fools taking root." You see that by fool he means the sinner. It is typical of the divine economy not to destroy sinners immediately. Rather, God grants them a delay so that they may repent, or so that others not be forced to act in a righteous manner. COMMENTARY ON JOB 5.3.[3]

5:4-5 The Hungry Eat Their Harvest

THE TRUE GATE. GREGORY THE GREAT: All who are given birth through the preaching of unbelief are "the children" of this foolish man.

These "are far from safety," for though they enjoy the temporal life without trouble, they are struck more severely with eternal vengeance. As the Lord says concerning these same sons of such a person, "Woe to you, scribes and Pharisees, hypocrites, for you travel over land and sea to make one proselyte, and when he becomes one, you make him twice as much a child of hell as you are."[4] The text continues, "And they are crushed, neither shall there be any to deliver them." Who else is to be understood by the name of "gate" but the Mediator between God and man, who says, "I am the gate; whoever enters through me will be saved."[5] The sons, then, of this foolish man do not advance through the gate. MORALS ON THE BOOK OF JOB 6.4.[6]

5:6-7 Human Beings Born to Trouble

SYMBOLISM OF THE EARTH AND THE BIRD. ISHO'DAD OF MERV: The author signifies all the silent and inanimate beings, and all those who are mute and without speech, through the two figures of the earth and the bird.[7] His point is that neither the earth nor a bird can commit any act of iniquity. Because they cannot sin they are beyond afflictions and punishment. But the human being, since he is endowed with reason and sins by using his freedom, is born and grows up among pains and tribulation to match his nature. COMMENTARY ON JOB 5.6-7.[8]

SIN CAUSES AFFLICTION. EPHREM THE SYRIAN: "And the young birds will raise their feathers over him."[9] This text indicates that sin is the cause of the calamities humans suffer. In a different sense we may understand the text to speak of angels as "sons of the winged ones," sent by God either for our correction and punishment when we transgress or for our protection and salvation after we have repented. COMMENTARY ON JOB 5.7.[10]

---

[1]PTS 35:68. [2]PTS 35:68-69. [3]PTS 35:69. [4]Mt 23:15. [5]Jn 10:9. [6]LF 18:314*. [7]See LXX. [8]CSCO 229:242. [9]Peshitta. [10]ESOO 2:4.

Human Beings Harvest the Fruits of Their Sins. Didymus the Blind: The text demonstrates that the curses with which Eliphaz cursed the evildoers . . . were said for a reason. "Afflictions are fitting for human beings but not for animals." The words may be meant as a comfort. As many people used to say, "What you have suffered is not beyond human nature. For our life consists of hardship. Even our birth occurs with hardship and suffering, since those who give birth must endure a thousand things. In addition, the life of a new born is cumbersome. One can aptly compare this text to the story in the Bible of the man born blind."[11] For it was regarding him that Jesus' disciples asked, "Who sinned, this man or his parents, that he was born blind?"[12] "Young vultures fly upwards" means "Punishment does not tame animals." The young vultures, he says, fly upward, meaning, "They are untroubled— they do not live in wickedness after all." His meaning is this: Lifeless things and animals—by the vulture's young he seems to refer to animals—do not experience vengeance themselves, whereas human beings harvest the fruits of their sins. Commentary on Job 5.6-7.[13]

---

[11]Jn 9. [12]Jn 9:2 [13]PTA 2:26-28.

5:8-16 IN DISTRESS WE MUST SEEK GOD

[8]As for me, I would seek God,
   and to God would I commit my cause;
[9]who does great things and unsearchable,
   marvelous things without number:
[10]he gives rain upon the earth
   and sends waters upon the fields;
[11]he sets on high those who are lowly,
   and those who mourn are lifted to safety.
[12]He frustrates the devices of the crafty,
   so that their hands achieve no success.

[13]He takes the wise in their own craftiness;
   and the schemes of the wily are brought
      to a quick end.
[14]They meet with darkness in the daytime,
   and grope at noonday as in the night.
[15]But he saves the fatherless from their
      mouth,[b]
   the needy from the hand of the mighty.
[16]So the poor have hope,
   and injustice shuts her mouth.

h Cn: Heb uncertain

Overview: Again the Fathers show in their commentary of these verses an oscillation between a positive interpretation of Eliphaz's words and an accusation against his hostile and reproachful attitude toward Job, which shows a certain narrow-mindedness. So on the one hand Eliphaz's words are seen as a reproach or veiled slander against Job (Hesychius) or as a proof of his limited human perspective (Didymus); on the other, as a demonstration of God's generosity and protecting benevolence toward humankind (Chrysostom, Gregory, Julian of Eclanum).

5:8 I Would Seek God

A Sharp Rebuke. Hesychius of Jerusalem: Eliphaz says, "You did not devote yourself to prayer. As for me, I would commit my cause to

God. You have reassured yourself and ceased from invoking 'the Lord of all things.' This is why the present afflictions befell you." After speaking, Eliphaz glorified God and aroused Job's anger. HOMILIES ON JOB 8.5.8.[1]

5:9-10 God Does Great Things

ELIPHAZ'S LIMITED HUMAN PERSPECTIVE. DIDYMUS THE BLIND: Eliphaz acknowledges that God is the ruler and creator of all things. It is likely that he has these convictions. He is a man who possesses wisdom in human things. Eliphaz also has an understanding of the invisible and visible, since he speaks of the inexplorable, the great, the honorable, and of water and rain. If he distinguishes that water from rain, he must have in mind water from wells, from creeks and from cracks in stone. One can find very wise thoughts of this kind in many places in Scripture, not least of all in Paul, who writes, "In him all things in heaven and on earth were created, things visible and invisible."[2] One has to imagine that Eliphaz became afraid in a human way because of the things that had happened to holy Job. He therefore admired the works of providence. Regarding the "things without number," one has to think that Eliphaz speaks from a human perspective. For God knows everything. That is no miracle. Doesn't Solomon say, "For it is he who gave me unerring knowledge of what exists, to know the structure of the world and the activity of the elements; the beginning and end and middle of times; the alternations of the solstices" and so on? For even what can't be counted due to its character is not uncountable for God, of whom it is said, "He determines the number of the stars,"[3] and "even the hairs of your head are all counted."[4] That knowledge is also given to those who are worthy of this benefit, as it is said about Solomon. COMMENTARY ON JOB 5.9-10.[5]

GOD'S GENEROSITY. JULIAN OF ECLANUM: "He does great and unsearchable things." Eliphaz enumerates the riches of divine providence that God properly bestows on each and every human being in common through each generation. "He gives rain on the earth." From the greatness of his power and the effusion of his liberality God gathers what is safe for humans. The defendant must place his hope of salvation not in his own merits but in the Lord's clemency. EXPOSITION ON THE BOOK OF JOB 5.9-10.[6]

5:11 God Lifts Up the Lowly

THOSE PERSECUTED ON EARTH WILL BE SAFE WITH GOD. GREGORY THE GREAT: "Those below are set on high," in that they, who are now despised for the love of God, shall return as judges along with God. The "Truth" pledges this which we have just named to the same humble ones, saying, "You who have followed me, in the regeneration, when the Son of man shall sit on the throne of his glory, you also shall sit upon twelve thrones, judging the twelve tribes of Israel."[7] Then "those that mourn the Lord safely exalt," because the desire for him is inflaming them; they flee prosperity, endure crosses, undergo tortures at the hands of persecutors, chasten their own selves with grieving. They are then promised a safety so much the more exalted that they now, from devout affection, consider themselves dead to all the joys of the world. Hence it is said by Solomon, "The heart knows his own soul's bitterness, and a stranger does not meddle impertinently with his joy."[8] For the human mind "knows its own soul's bitterness." When inflamed with aspirations after the eternal land, it learns by weeping its pilgrimage's sorrow. But "the stranger does not meddle impertinently with his joy" in that he, who is now a stranger to the grief of compunction, is not then a partaker in the joy of consolation. MORALS ON THE BOOK OF JOB 6.23.[9]

---

[1]PO 42.1:222. [2]Col 1:16. [3]Ps 147:4 (146:4 LXX). [4]Lk 12:7. [5]PTA 2:30-32. [6]CCL 88:17. [7]Mt 19:28. [8]Prov 14:10. [9]LF 18:328*.

5:12-13 Schemes Brought to an End

A VEILED SLANDER. HESYCHIUS OF JERUSALEM: What do these words mean? Eliphaz insults Job, who should be a crafty man. He has a desire for justice, without doing anything for which he boasts with real justice. However, God does not stand still without penetrating such schemes, and "the schemes of the wily are brought to a quick end." HOMILIES ON JOB 8.5.12-13.[10]

5:14-16 God Saves the Needy

GOD'S WONDERS. CHRYSOSTOM: Look! This is what God does, so the weak may hope for happiness and the powerful may not become proud. In fact, he said above, "Call for help in order to see whether you will be listened to," so that you may not think that there are things that escape providence.... Eliphaz dedicates the beginning of his speech to the defeat of Job. Indeed, God is accustomed to exalt the weak, to bring the powerful down and to confound the cunning. Now draw your own conclusions. COMMENTARY ON JOB 5.15B-16B.[11]

---

[10]PO 42.1:224. [11]PTS 35:72.

5:17-27 HAPPINESS AFTER GOD'S CORRECTION

[17]Behold, happy is the man whom God reproves;
therefore despise not the chastening of the Almighty.
[18]For he wounds, but he binds up;
he smites, but his hands heal.*
[19]He will deliver you from six troubles;
in seven there shall no evil touch you.
[20]In famine he will redeem you from death,
and in war from the power of the sword.
[21]You shall be hid from the scourge of the tongue,
and shall not fear destruction when it comes.†
[22]At destruction and famine you shall laugh,
and shall not fear the beasts of the earth.

[23]For you shall be in league with the stones of the field,
and the beasts of the field shall be at peace with you.
[24]You shall know that your tent is safe,‡
and you shall inspect your fold and miss nothing.
[25]You shall know also that your descendants shall be many,
and your offspring as the grass of the earth.
[26]You shall come to your grave in ripe old age,
as a shock of grain comes up to the threshing floor in its season.
[27]Lo, this we have searched out; it is true.
Hear, and know it for your good.[i]§

i Heb for yourself   *LXX For he causes a man to be in pain, and restores him again, he smites, and his hands heal.   †LXX He shall hide you from the scourge of the tongue, and you shall not be afraid of coming evils.   ‡Vg in peace   §LXX but reflect with yourself if you have done anything wrong

OVERVIEW: Eliphaz can show God to be benevolent, protecting and consistent in his providential plans and ways (JULIAN OF ECLANUM, CHRYSOSTOM, HESYCHIUS, ISHO'DAD, DIDYMUS, OLYMPIODORUS, GREGORY). At the same time, Eliphaz continues to consider Job guilty and to attribute the reason for his misfortune to his sins (CHRYSOSTOM).

5:17 The Discipline of the Almighty

NO REASON FOR DESPAIR. JULIAN OF ECLANUM: Since holy Job was dejected because of the misfortunes that befell him against his hope, Eliphaz now says that after his calamity Job must not despair about God being propitious again. Indeed, the restraint of sin's dissoluteness through scourging testifies to the divine love. "How happy is the one whom God reproves." Because he had enumerated different kinds of miseries that beset sinners, they did not want to appear to be guilty in anything or obtain forgiveness through the confession of their iniquity. He says that a person, when he is led through severity and the scourge to his correction and admission of guilt, must not consider himself as a man who is in misery. EXPOSITION ON THE BOOK OF JOB 5.17.[1]

5:18 God Wounds but Binds Up

GOD'S ACTIONS ARE CONSISTENT. CHRYSOSTOM: If God brings evils to an end and transforms them into their opposite, causing mortals to enjoy a profound peace, it is the same thought, not a different one, that guides God in his present attitude. COMMENTARY ON JOB 5.18.[2]

5:19 God Delivers from Troubles

NO LIMITATIONS TO DIVINE PROVIDENCE. ISHO'DAD OF MERV: We must not think that the author intends to limit divine providence by fixing a precise number of troubles. He means that God will completely save you from the afflictions that surround you. COMMENTARY ON JOB 5.19.[3]

5:20 Redeemed from Famine and War

JOB POSSESSES HAPPINESS. HESYCHIUS OF JERUSALEM: Without doubt Job possesses happiness. You see that, by necessity or willingly, while Job starves and keeps away from all the tables of this world, he cries, "Sighing is my nourishment."[4] Yet Job does not die and confirms with force this word of God, "Man shall not live by bread alone, but by every word that comes out from the mouth of God."[5] HOMILIES ON JOB 8.5.20-26.[6]

5:21 Not Fearing Destruction

VILIFICATION CANNOT HARM THE RIGHTEOUS. DIDYMUS THE BLIND: Again Eliphaz says this about the one who has been rebuked by the Lord, whereby he follows his own principle. Not even what Eliphaz says is stringent. Too often many righteous people have been vilified. Among them are Joseph, whom the Egyptian woman charged with excess in spite of his modesty, and Susanna, who suffered as a hostage the humiliations from the "lawless elders." Consequently, if he understands by "hidden from the scourge of the tongue" that one is neither humiliated nor vilified, this word is unfounded. It is more accurate to say that the one who lives after the will of God cannot be harmed by humiliation or vilification, called "scourge of the tongue." Virtue protects him from being found guilty of the false allegations. Nor does such a person fear expected destruction, since he says with Saint Paul, "Who will separate us from the love of Christ? Will hardship, or distress, or persecution, or famine, or nakedness, or peril or sword?"[7] Over all this he prevails through virtue's abundance. Likewise, he is protected from the intrigues of false wisdom, since God "takes the wise in their own craftiness."[8] . . . The same meaning as "you shall not fear destruction when

---

[1]CCL 88:17-18. [2]PTS 35:73. [3]CSCO 229:242-43. [4]Job 3:24. [5]Deut 8:3; Mt 4:4. [6]PO 42.1:228. [7]Rom 8:35. [8]Job 5:13.

it comes" has the following word from the prophet: "The calamity will come from far away."[9] This must be understood like this: The good comes from us. For it is said, "The kingdom of God is within you."[10] Thus we have an inclination toward virtue that Christ called "kingdom." But the punishment and damage and dishonor of sin come from the outside. For the human, who is created "after God's image,"[11] carries the seed of the good within. But if he deviates from the right path, he encounters evil, without having received such an inclination from God. COMMENTARY ON JOB 5.21.[12]

PROTECTION FROM SLANDER. OLYMPIODORUS: He will hide you from the evil tongue, which knows how to persecute unjustly. In fact, they call "scourge" the malice and slander of the tongue. Moreover, you will end up in complete safety. COMMENTARY ON JOB 5.19-21.[13]

5:22-24 Your Tent Is Safe

PERFECT PEACE. GREGORY THE GREAT: In holy Scripture complete peace is described in one way and initial peace in another. For "Truth" gave to his disciples peace from the beginning, when he said, "Peace I leave with you; my peace I give unto you."[14] And Simeon desired to have perfect peace. He sought it saying, "Now let your servant depart in peace, according to your word."[15] Our peace begins in longing for the Creator, but it is perfected by clarity of vision. Our peace will be perfect when our mind is neither blinded by ignorance nor moved by the assaults of the body. Forasmuch as we touch upon its first beginnings, when we either subject the soul to God or the flesh to the soul, the "tabernacle" of the righteous person is said to "have peace." The body he inhabits through his mind is restrained from the evil motions of its desires under the controlling hand of righteousness. But what advantage is it to restrain the flesh by continence if the mind has not been taught to expand itself through compassion in the love of our neighbor? For the body's chasteness is worth nothing if not recommended by sweetness of spirit. MORALS ON THE BOOK OF JOB 6.53.[16]

5:25-27 Ripe Old Age

HUMAN RESPONSIBILITY. CHRYSOSTOM: Notice how Eliphaz . . . has inflicted a severe blow. How and in what manner? By showing that Job is not among those who receive a warning or among those who keep faith. Indeed, Eliphaz has applied his words to the person of Job, but his speech has a general meaning. For he says: Here is what we have seen and understood; but if this did not occur in your case, and if you remain in your misfortunes, it is up to you to recognize your own perversity. COMMENTARY ON JOB 5.25-27.[17]

---

[9]Is 10:3. [10]Lk 17:21. [11]Gen 1:26. [12]PTA 2:80-84. [13]PTS 24:63. [14]Jn 14:27. [15]Lk 2:29. [16]LF 18:352*. [17]PTS 35:74.

6:1-7 JOB JUSTIFIES THE BITTERNESS
OF HIS COMPLAINTS

[1] *Then Job answered:*
[2] *"O that my vexation were weighed,*
and all my calamity laid in the
balances!
[3] *For then it would be heavier than the sand*
of the sea;
therefore my words have been rash.*
[4] *For the arrows of the Almighty are in me;*
my spirit drinks their poison;
the terrors of God are arrayed against me.

[5] *Does the wild ass bray when he has*
grass,
or the ox low over his fodder?
[6] *Can that which is tasteless be eaten*
without salt,
or is there any taste in the slime of
the purslane?[j]†
[7] *My appetite refuses to touch them;*
they are as food that is loathsome
to me."[k]‡

j The meaning of the Hebrew word is uncertain.   k Heb obscure   *Vg *my words are full of grief*   †Vg *Can anyone taste that which by being tasted brings death?*   ‡LXX *For my wrath cannot cease; for I perceive my food as the smell of a lion to be loathsome.*

OVERVIEW: Job expresses all his sorrow and vents his complaints about his present state. But around him he cannot find sympathy or understanding (CHRYSOSTOM, GREGORY, DIDYMUS, ISHO'DAD). Now even food has become a torture to him (CHRYSOSTOM), but through his love of future, heavenly aspirations, he can prepare to face his present sufferings (GREGORY).

6:1-2 Weighing Vexation

JOB'S PAIN CANNOT BE UNDERSTOOD. CHRYSOSTOM: This is what Job means, you show wisdom in the misfortunes of other people. Since you are far away from my misfortunes, you admonish me while you experience a peaceful life. This remark is an answer to the words that were said earlier, "You have instructed many."[1] "You have strengthened the feeble knees."[2] "But now misfortune has come to you, and you are impatient; it touches you, and you are dismayed."[3] Why does he say, "You are dismayed"? I wanted my affliction to become evident, so you would understand that nobody has ever suffered such tribulations. But I

perceive my bad luck. He who should have provided me with forgiveness makes me absolutely unforgivable. My misfortune's magnitude, he says, not only doesn't intercede for me, not only makes me seem unworthy of mercy, but condemns me. What should have obtained mercy for me instead makes me hateful and condemnable, and I cannot gain any mercy, in spite of what I say. And the proof is that Eliphaz imputed Job's misfortune to impiety. COMMENTARY ON JOB 6.2A-3A.[4]

6:3-4 The Arrows of God

FULL OF GRIEF. GREGORY THE GREAT: He who loves to sojourn abroad instead of in his own country does not know how to grieve, even in the midst of grief. But the words of the righteous person are full of grief. For as long as Job is subject to present ills, he sighs after something else in his speech. All that Job brought upon himself by sinning is set before his eyes. So that Job may return to the state of blessedness, he weighs carefully the

[1]Job 4:3. [2]Job 4:4. [3]Job 4:5. [4]PTS 35:75.

judgments that afflict him. MORALS ON THE BOOK OF JOB 7.3.[5]

ELIPHAZ'S LACK OF SENSITIVITY AND COMPASSION. DIDYMUS THE BLIND: Eliphaz believed that Job said all this out of desperation. Since Eliphaz's first words to Job were trustworthy—words that insisted that Job suffered because of sin—Job responds, "It seems my words are valueless and lack faith." Consequently, Job adds the reason why Eliphaz does not believe in him when he says, "For the arrows of the Almighty are in me," thus making the following clear, "This is why my words are valueless. The Lord's arrows are in my body." For most people usually disregard words uttered by people in distress, those aggrieved by poverty, even if their words are understandable. This is expressed in the words, "The poor person speaks and they say, 'Who is this fellow?'"[6] COMMENTARY ON JOB 6.3-4.[7]

6:5 Braying over Grass

WHEN BASIC NEEDS ARE PROVIDED. ISHO'DAD OF MERV: By mentioning the wild ass, the author speaks about all wild animals, and by referring to the ox, about all cattle. His point is that neither wild animals nor cattle complain when they have food to eat. Nor do humans complain when they can have at their disposal the necessary things they need and what is seasoned with salt. COMMENTARY ON JOB 6.5.[8]

6:6 Food Without Flavor

PREPARING THE SOUL TO FACE PRESENT AFFLICTIONS. GREGORY THE GREAT: "Can anyone taste poisonous food without dying?" For it is hard to seek that which torments or to follow that which destroys life. But very often the life of the righteous stretches itself to such a height of virtue that it rules within in the citadel of interior reason. It also rules without. By bearing with it, reason leads the folly of some to conversion. For we must bear with the weakness of those we are striving to draw on to strong things. No one can lift up another without bending down from the uprightness of his position. But when we empathize with the weakness of another, we are strongly encouraged to face courageously our own weaknesses. The result is that from the love of future things, the soul prepares itself to meet the ills of present times and watches for the hurts of the body that it used to fear. For the soul is increasingly straitened as its heavenly aspirations are enlarged. When it perceives how great is the sweetness of the eternal land, it fervently loves for the sake of the present life's bitter tastes. MORALS ON THE BOOK OF JOB 7.17.[9]

6:7 Food That Is Loathsome

A NEW AFFLICTION FOR JOB. CHRYSOSTOM: Sores and pus were not enough. A new affliction is added. Job's disease has destroyed his entire sensitivity to the extent that even his nourishment has become a torture for him. Indeed, Job says, the nauseating smell of gangrene has deprived him of the capability to distinguish sensations. Is there anything more painful than that torment? Neither sleep gave him rest nor food nourished him. "As the smell of a lion," Job says. That wild beast, in fact, gives a horrible stench. COMMENTARY ON JOB 6.7B.[10]

---

[5]LF 18:367*. [6]Sir 13:23. [7]PTA 2:132-34. [8]CSCO 229:243. [9]LF 18:375-76*. [10]PTS 35:77.

6:8-14 JOB WISHES FOR DEATH

⁸O that I might have my request,
　　and that God would grant my
　　　desire;
⁹that it would please God to crush me,
　　that he would let loose his hand and
　　　cut me off!*
¹⁰This would be my consolation;
　　I would even exult¹ in pain unsparing;†
　　for I have not denied the words of
　　　the Holy One.
¹¹What is my strength, that I

should wait?
　　And what is my end, that I should
　　　be patient?
¹²Is my strength the strength of stones, or
　　or is my flesh bronze?
¹³In truth I have no help in me,
　　and any resource is driven from me.

¹⁴He who withholds^m kindness from
　　a friend
　　　forsakes the fear of the Almighty.

l The meaning of the Hebrew word is uncertain.　m Syr Vg Compare Lg: Heb obscure　*Peshitta and finish me!　†Peshitta I would be finished again with violence and no
mercy; LXX Let the grave be my city, upon the walls of which I have leaped, I will have no cares.

OVERVIEW: Job does not boast about his good actions and does not claim to be unjustly punished. He appeals to God and wishes death because he cannot physically bear his sufferings (CHRYSOSTOM, ISHO'DAD). In his desperate endurance, he shows the strength of the righteous (DIDYMUS, GREGORY).

6:8-10 That God Would Crush Me

AN APPEAL TO GOD. CHRYSOSTOM: "I do not care to oppose your words," Job says. "It seems to me, in fact, that I have committed nothing resembling what you say. I don't state this openly. I simply say that I am suffering punishments that go beyond what human nature can endure. The vastness of my temptations extends far beyond what human bodies can actually bear." However, observe how, even in the midst of such grief, Job has not decided, in any case, to come and relate his good actions. He has hidden them so far. In addition, he who often with great honesty exposed his fault to public mockery before a brilliant audience is silent about his good actions, even while living

in such misery. In fact, Job does not say, "I experienced these sufferings, even though I am righteous." Rather, Job says he cannot bear them.... His language is not that of a man who asserts that he is unjustly punished but that of one who recognizes, on the contrary, the justness of his punishment. He simply cannot bear any more punishment and therefore demands that he obtain forgiveness. COMMENTARY ON JOB 6.10A.[1]

DESIRE FOR DEATH. ISHO'DAD OF MERV: "He would let loose his hand and finish me!" That is, may he put an end to my life by his intervention. Again Job speaks, "I would be finished again with violence and no mercy." In a word, "I desire that God inflict death on me violently and mercilessly. COMMENTARY ON JOB 6.9.[2]

JOB'S WILLINGNESS TO FULFILL HIS TASK.
DIDYMUS THE BLIND: He who asks to be wounded does not pray out of exhaustion that his prayer might be granted but in order to fulfill his

[1]PTS 35:78.　[2]CSCO 229:243.

task. This task was to fulfill the right deeds or to make visible to the friends for their benefit the reason for the hardships, [namely,] that they had been imposed as a test. Then they would not make mistakes against the righteous. Instead, with divine zeal they would be committed to emulate the endurance and steadfastness that the holy one exhibited and that led him to say, "O that I might have my request," rather than ... "that God would grant my desire." Job prays for two reasons. On the one hand, he prays that he himself may win the crown in the competition. On the other hand, Job prays that his friends may not consider his endurance in hardship as meaningless. His steadfastness even in such great hardships can be seen and admired in the fact that Job did not deny his friend an answer, even though preoccupation with his hardships could have served as an excuse. But even now Job speaks like a brave athlete who warlike meets his opponent, and with the consciousness that the imposed suffering did not occur without God's compliance. "That it would please God to crush me," yet "may he not extinguish me entirely," instead of, "May God mercifully allow me to endure the affliction until the end." Similar to this is the expression "and lead us not into temptation,"[3] which often has been interpreted in this way: "May it not come so far that we fall prey to the temptations." COMMENTARY ON JOB 6.8-9.[4]

6:11-14 What Is My Strength?

THE STRENGTH AND LOVE OF THE RIGHTEOUS. GREGORY THE GREAT: "What is my strength, that I should wait? And what is my end, that I should be patient?" It is necessary to bear in mind that the "strength" of the righteous is of one sort and the strength of the reprobate of another. For the strength of the righteous is to subdue the flesh, to thwart our own wills, to annihilate the gratification the present life offers, to be in love with the roughness of this world for the sake of eternal rewards, to consider as nothing the allurements of prosperity, to overcome in our hearts the dread of adversity. But the strength of the repro-

bate is to set their affection unceasingly on transitory things. To endure insensibly the strokes of our Creator (not even by adversity to be brought to cease loving temporal things); to attain vain glory even with a wasted life; to search out ever more wickedness; to attack the life of the good (not only with words and by behavior but even with weapons); to put their trust in themselves; to perpetrate iniquity daily without any diminution of desire.... "Is my strength the strength of stones, or is my flesh bronze?" ... Let the holy one, then, who amid the scourges eschewed the reprobate's hardness, exclaim, "Neither is my strength the strength of stones, nor is my flesh made of brass." It is as though Job openly confessed in plain words, "Under discipline's lash I keep clear of acting like the reprobate. For neither have I become like stones so hardened that under the lash's impulse I remained silent when I should have confessed, nor again have I like brass echoed the voice of confession, while not understanding the meaning of what I was saying. Yet under the scourge, the reprobate manifest a strength that is actually weakness and the elect a weakness that is actually strength. Blessed Job, while declaring that he is not strong due to the disease, makes it plain that he is strong in his state of saving health. So let him inform us as to the source from whom he received this same strength, lest Job ascribe to himself the powers that he possesses ... "Those who withhold kindness from a friend forsake the fear of the Almighty." Who else is here denoted by the name of a friend except every neighbor who is united to us in a faithful attachment proportionate to the good service received from us in this present time? Is this not he who effectually aids us in attaining hereafter the eternal country? For charity possesses two key principles: the love of God and the love of our neighbor. It is through the love of God that the love of our neighbor is born, and by the love of our neighbor the love of God is fostered. For one who does not care to love God truly knows nothing about how to love his neighbor. In turn,

---

[3]Mt 6:13. [4]PTA 2:144-46.

we advance more perfectly in the love of God if in the bosom of this love we first be suckled with the milk of charity toward our neighbor. For the love of God begets the love of our neighbor. The Lord, when proceeding to speak in the voice of the law the words "you shall love your neighbor"[5] prefaced it by saying, "You shall love the Lord your God."[6] The Lord desires to first plant the root of his love in our breast so that afterwards the love of our brothers should blossom in the branches. Again,

the love of God grows strong through the love of our neighbor. John testifies to this truth when he says, "For he that does not love his brother, whom he has seen, how can he love God, whom he has not seen?"[7] This love of God, though it is born in fear, is transformed by growing into affection. MORALS ON THE BOOK OF JOB 7.24-28.[8]

---

[5]Mt 22:39. [6]Deut 6:5; 10:12; Mt 22:37. [7]1 Jn 4:20. [8]LF 18:380-84

6:15-30 JOB'S DISAPPOINTMENT OVER HIS FRIENDS

[15]My brethren are treacherous as a
    torrent-bed,
  as freshets that pass away,
[16]which are dark with ice,
  and where the snow hides itself.
[17]In time of heat they disappear;
  when it is hot, they vanish from
    their place.
[18]The caravans turn aside from their course;
  they go up into the waste, and perish.*
[19]The caravans of Tema look,
  the travelers of Sheba hope.
[20]They are disappointed because they were
    confident;
  they come thither and are confounded.†
[21]Such you have now become to me;"
  you see my calamity, and are afraid.
[22]Have I said, "Make me a gift"?
  Or, "From your wealth offer a bribe
    for me"?

[23]Or, "Deliver me from the adversary's hand"?
  Or, "Ransom me from the hand of
    oppressors"?

[24]Teach me, and I will be silent;
  make me understand how I have erred.
[25]How forceful are honest words!
  But what does reproof from you reprove?
[26]Do you think that you can reprove words,
  when the speech of a despairing man
    is wind?‡
[27]You would even cast lots over the fatherless,
  and bargain over your friend.§

[28]But now, be pleased to look at me;
  for I will not lie to your face.
[29]Turn, I pray, let no wrong be done.
  Turn now, my vindication is at stake.#
[30]Is there any wrong on my tongue?
  Cannot my taste discern calamity?

n Cn Compare Gk Syr: Heb obscure *LXX (15-18) My nearest relations have not regarded me; they have passed me by like a failing brook, or like a wave. They who used to reverence me, now have come against me like snow or congealed ice. When it has melted at the approach of heat, it is not known what it was. Thus I also have been deserted of all; and I am ruined, and *become an outcast.*   †Vg (20) *They are confounded, because I have hoped. They came even unto me and were ashamed.*   ‡LXX (25-26) *But as it seems, the words of a true man are vain, because I do not ask strength of you. Neither will your reproof cause me to cease my words, for neither will I endure the sound of your speech.*   §LXX *You would even attack the orphan, and trample your friend underfoot.*   #Vg *Answer, I pray, without hostility, and judge by saying what is just.*

OVERVIEW: In their writings on this final section of Job 6, the Fathers emphasize the present, unbearable afflictions of Job, which do not cause any sympathy in his friends but merely raise their groundless accusations and unjustified reproaches (DIDYMUS, CHRYSOSTOM, GREGORY, OLYMPIODORUS, HESYCHIUS, JULIAN OF ECLANUM). Only Ephrem gives a positive interpretation of the images used by Job and sees in the waters of the streams a symbol of the prophecies given to the people of Israel (EPHREM).

6:15 Treacherous Companions

THE ABSENCE OF TRUE FRIENDS. DIDYMUS THE BLIND: Even this happened to test Job. For the absence of friends in the midst of suffering is no small pain. Even the holy David sang as he experienced similar suffering, "Look on my right hand and see—there is no one who takes notice of me."[1] Consider whether Job desired to show here that even the invisible holy powers "passed away" above him, so that his virtue may appear to be even greater. This interpretation fits for the one that has been given the words "the providence of the Lord has looked after me."[2] For the Lord of all did not neglect Job out of hate but in order to show the adversary that his wickedness is useless against human virtue. Likewise, perhaps the divine powers do not protect Job and allow him to struggle so that the righteous behavior of the saint would become even more visible, for one must assume that they know God's will. COMMENTARY ON JOB 6.15.[3]

THE SYMBOLISM OF THE STREAMS. EPHREM THE SYRIAN: The streams' waters fall from heaven and are symbols of the prophecies and oracles announced to the Jewish people through the prophets, just as through mystic clouds, as if the prophets' words were rains falling from heaven. COMMENTARY ON JOB 6.15.[4]

6:16-18 Disappearing in Adversity

NO TRACE OF JOB'S PROSPERITY. CHRYSOSTOM: Job means to say this: there is no memory or trace left of my former prosperity. And that is even worse than my misfortune itself. "Oh, that one would indeed weigh the wrath that is upon me and take up my sorrow in a balance together!"[5] And Job now tries to describe his sorrows. "I perceive my food to be loathsome [as the smell of a lion]."[6] I wish to die, but I do not die. I suffer so because I am a man and not a stone; I am an ephemeral human being, I do not enjoy the aid from above. Among my nearest relations, some pass me by without seeing me; others trample me underfoot. No trace of my former prosperity remains. COMMENTARY ON JOB 6.16-18B.[7]

6:19-21 Fearing Job's Calamity

RECKLESS INIQUITY WILL BE PUNISHED. GREGORY THE GREAT: "They are confounded, because I have hoped." When the wicked inflict evils upon the good, they are overjoyed at the success of their deceptions, if they see the good shaken from interior hope. For the wicked reckon the spread of their error to be the greatest gain, for they rejoice to have companions in perdition. But when the good person's hope is rooted within, never bent to the ground by outward evils, confusion seizes the soul of the wicked. Their inability to get at the innermost parts of the distressed results in shame for the wicked. Their cruelty has not produced the effect they

---

[1]Ps 142:4 (141:5 LXX).   [2]Job 6:14; RSV has a different rendering of this verse.   [3]PTA 2:160.   [4]ESOO 2:4.   [5]Job 6:2.   [6]Job 6:7.   [7]PTS 35:80.

expected. . . . "They came even to me and were ashamed." For lost sinners "come even to holy church" on the day of judgment, in that they are brought even then to behold its glory. For the punishment of their guilt is even greater when they see what they have lost as they are rejected. Then shame covers the wicked, when the conscience bears witness and convicts them in the sight of the Judge. At that time the Judge is beheld without and the accuser is convicted within. Every sin is called up before the eyes and the soul. The soul is tortured by its own fire, over and above the burnings of hell. MORALS ON THE BOOK OF JOB 7.46-47.[8]

6:22-24 A Plea for Understanding

MALICIOUSNESS IN JOB'S FRIENDS. CHRYSOSTOM: However, even in such a condition, Job does not refuse to learn. "You may say something useful. I will be silent, if you speak helpful words." But they could not, to be sure, present evidence, but simply proceeded through conjectures. And since Job's life was manifestly full of virtue, they supposed that it was not the ground of his punishments. COMMENTARY ON JOB 6.24A.[9]

6:25-26 Unjust Reproof

A DEFENSE AGAINST UNJUST ACCUSATIONS. OLYMPIODORUS: Job's words mean . . . "It is likely you have suffered the same in many things." Truth, however, is always hateful to many. Therefore, you despise my words of truth. "You do not come down to me," Job says, "nor do you speak about the gifts of grace like people who desire to encourage. On the contrary, you accuse me openly, whereas I have never accused you. I hope,

however, that after answering each of you, my words will defeat you." COMMENTARY ON JOB 6.24-27.[10]

6:27 Bargaining over a Friend

AN OFFENSE AGAINST GOD. HESYCHIUS OF JERUSALEM: "You would even attack the orphan," that is, me, for I am deprived of any human assistance. And since God is "the Father of the orphans,"[11] you make him angry by offending me. "And you would trample your friend underfoot" with your words. You trample him even more violently than with your feet, and you scorn the laws of friendship. But God takes these faults into account. He, who not only commands us to love our neighbor like ourselves, also wants to be called "love." HOMILIES ON JOB 9.6.27.[12]

6:28-30 I Will Not Lie to Your Face

UNSUBSTANTIATED ACCUSATIONS. JULIAN OF ECLANUM: While convincing his friends that they are not acting friendly but speaking against common sense, Job now tries to show that he cannot appropriately be accused of speaking harshly or of desiring death by just judges. "And judge by saying what is just." Be judges of the words that we said in common, so that your judgment may be in compliance with justice and not with a feeling of hostility. EXPOSITION ON THE BOOK OF JOB 6.29.[13]

---

[8]LF 18:401-2*. [9]PTS 35:81. [10]PTS 24:73. [11]Ps 68:5 (67:6 LXX). [12]PO 42.1:248-50. [13]CCL 88:21.

7:1-10 JOB'S REFLECTIONS UPON HUMAN LIFE

¹Has not man a hard service upon earth,
and are not his days like the days of
a hireling?
²Like a slave who longs for the shadow,*
and like a hireling who looks for
his wages,
³so I am allotted months of emptiness,
and nights of misery are apportioned
to me.
⁴When I lie down I say, "When shall
I arise?"
But the night is long,
and I am full of tossing till the dawn.
⁵My flesh is clothed with worms and
dirt;†

my skin hardens, then breaks out afresh.
⁶My days are swifter than a weaver's shuttle,
and come to their end without hope.‡

⁷Remember that my life is a breath;
my eye will never again see good.§
⁸The eye of him who sees me# will behold
me no more;
while thy eyes are upon me, I shall
be gone.
⁹As the cloud fades and vanishes,
so he who goes down to Sheol does
not come up;
¹⁰he returns no more to his house,
nor does his place know him any more.

*LXX Like a slave who fears his master and hid in shadows   †Vg with corruption and foulness of dust   ‡Vg My days are past more swiftly than a web is cut off by the weaver.   §Vg the eye of man   #Peshitta my eye will begin to see good again

OVERVIEW: The Fathers see in this second part of Job's speech both concrete meditations on human life and allegorical hints of the divine economy of salvation. Job describes the pain and fear of human life (HESYCHIUS) and its shortness and ephemeral nature (GREGORY), but also he foreshadows the new world in Christ (ISHO'DAD), the justice of our Savior, the corruption that will threaten the church of Christ and the eternal punishment of sin after the redemption of humankind (GREGORY).

7:1-4 Hard Service on Earth

A PAINFUL AND FRIGHTFUL LIFE. HESYCHIUS OF JERUSALEM: Not only is this life painful, but it is also frightful, because, after being wounded, I am now in the condition to fear the blows of the Lord. This is why I jump from one place to another in fright, like those slaves who are threat-

ened by their master. In addition, every day, like laborers who wait for their wages—and the wages are all their wealth and hope for nourishment—I also wait for the reward of my endurance, but I never meet it, because a long time and many months have passed. In those days I have exhausted myself in waiting for an empty hope. HOMILIES ON JOB 10.7.2-3.[1]

7:5 Clothed with Worms and Dirt

A FIGURE OF CORRUPTION. GREGORY THE GREAT: And yet if we take Job's words as the voice of the holy church universal, doubtless we find it at one time sunk to the earth by the "corruption" of the flesh, at another time by "the defilement of dust." For [the church] has many within it who, while devoted to the love of the

---

[1]PO 42.1:258.

flesh, become corrupt with the putrefaction of excess. In addition, there are some people who certainly keep from the gratification of the flesh, yet grovel with all their heart in earthly practices. So let holy church speak through the words of one of its members, let it express what it endures from either sort of person. "My flesh is clothed with corruption and the defilement of dust." It is as if [the church] said in plain words, "There are many who are members of me in faith, yet these are not sound or pure members in practice. For they either are mastered by foul desires and run to and fro in corruption's rottenness, or, being devoted to earthly practices, they are soiled with dust. For in those whom I have to endure, people filled with wantonness, I do plainly lament for the flesh turned corrupt. And in those from whom I suffer, those who are seeking the earth, what else is this but the defilement of dust that I bear?" MORALS ON THE BOOK OF JOB 8.23.[2]

7:6 Days That End Without Hope

TIME PASSES QUICKLY. GREGORY THE GREAT: "My days pass more swiftly than the weaving of cloth by the weaver." In a very suitable image, the time of the flesh is compared with a cloth web. As the web advances thread by thread, so this mortal life passes day by day; in proportion as the web increases, so it advances to its completion. Just as we said before, while the time in our hands passes, the time before us is shortened. Moreover, of the whole length of our lives, the days to come are proportionally fewer to those days that have gone by. MORALS ON THE BOOK OF JOB 8.26.[3]

7:7 My Life Is a Breath

HOPE IN THE NEW WORLD. ISHO'DAD OF MERV: "My eye will begin to see good again." Here the author refers to the hope that is reserved for people in the new world. COMMENTARY ON JOB 7.7.[4]

7:8 I Shall Be Gone

THE PITY AND JUSTICE OF OUR REDEEMER. GREGORY THE GREAT: For "the human eye" is the pity of the Redeemer that softens the hardness of our insensibility when it looks upon us. Hence, as the Gospel witnesses, it is said, "And the Lord turned, looked upon Peter, and Peter remembered the word of the Lord. And he went out, and wept bitterly."[5] However, when the soul is divested of the flesh, "the human eye" does not henceforth see anything. The Redeemer's pity never delivers anyone after death that it has not gracefully restored to pardon before death. MORALS ON THE BOOK OF JOB 8.30.[6]

7:9-10 Those Who Go Down to Sheol

PUNISHMENT FOR EARTHLY DESIRES. GREGORY THE GREAT: As the body's house is a bodily habitation, so it becomes to each separate mind "its own house to whatever the mind desires to have enter." And so "there is no more returning to his own house," because once a person is given over to eternal punishment, he is henceforth no more recalled from the place he had attached himself in love. MORALS ON THE BOOK OF JOB 8.34.[7]

---

[2]LF 18:432-33*. [3]LF 18:433-34*. [4]CSCO 229:244. [5]Lk 22:61-62. [6]LF 18:437*. [7]LF 18:440*.

7:11-21 JOB APPEALS TO GOD FOR DELIVERANCE

[11]*Therefore I will not restrain my mouth;*
I will speak in the anguish of my spirit;
I will complain in the bitterness of
my soul.
[12]*Am I the sea, or a sea monster,*
that thou settest a guard over me?
[13]*When I say, 'My bed will comfort me,*
my couch will ease my complaint,'
[14]*then thou dost scare me with dreams*
and terrify me with visions,
[15]*so that I would choose strangling*
and death rather than my bones.
[16]*I loathe my life; I would not live for ever.*
*Let me alone, for my days are a breath.**
[17]*What is man, that thou dost make*
so much of him,

and that thou dost set thy mind
upon him,
[18]*dost visit him every morning,*
and test him every moment?†
[19]*How long wilt thou not look away*
from me,
nor let me alone till I swallow my spittle?
[20]*If I sin, what do I do to thee, thou watcher*
of men?
Why hast thou made me thy mark?‡
Why have I become a burden to thee?
[21]*Why dost thou not pardon my*
transgression
and take away my iniquity?
For now I shall lie in the earth;
thou wilt seek me, but I shall not be.

*LXX (15-16) *You will separate life from my spirit; and yet keep my bones from death. For I shall not live forever, that I should patiently endure, depart from me, for my life is vain.* †LXX *judge them for the time of rest?* ‡LXX *If I have sinned, what shall I be able to do for you, O you that understand the mind of men? Why did you make me as your accuser?*

OVERVIEW: Job is overwhelmed by his pain and despair and cannot understand the reason for his afflictions (ISHO'DAD, CHRYSOSTOM). He opens the secret depths of his heart to express his absolute sorrow (GREGORY) and his wish for death (OLYMPIODORUS). At the same time he foreshadows the final day of judgment (HESYCHIUS).

7:11-12 In Anguish of Spirit

WHY AM I PUNISHED? ISHO'DAD OF MERV: "Am I the sea, or the dragon?" That is, you have imposed a limit that the sea must not trespass, so that it might not submerge the earth. You did the same with the dragon, that it might not go out and destroy all that it met. But why do you continue to punish me so harshly, for I am a feeble man with a short life? COMMENTARY ON JOB 7.12.[1]

7:13-14 Finding Comfort

A SYMBOL OF THE HEART'S DEPTHS. GREGORY THE GREAT: For in holy Scripture a "bed," a "couch" or "litter" usually represents the heart's secret depth. Hence, the spouse in the Song of Songs, urged by the piercing darts of holy love, speaks under the likeness of each separate soul: "By night on my bed I sought him whom my soul loves."[2] For "the beloved is sought by night and lying in bed," much as the appearance of the invisible Creator is found in the chamber of the heart, apart from every image of a bodily appearing. Thus "Truth" says to those same lovers of him, "The kingdom of God is within you."[3] And again, "If I do not go away, the Comforter will not come."[4] As if it were in plain words, "If I do not

[1]CSCO 229:244-45. [2]Song 3:1. [3]Lk 17:21. [4]Jn 16:7.

withdraw my body from your gaze, I will not lead you by the Comforter, the Spirit, to the perception of the unseen." The psalmist also states concerning the just, "The saints shall be joyful in glory, they shall rejoice upon their beds";[5] for when they flee the mischief of external things, they exult in safety within the recesses of their hearts. But the joy of the heart will then be complete when the fight of the flesh shall have ceased outwardly. It is as if when the wall of the house is shaken, the bed itself is disturbed. This is so as long as the flesh allures. MORALS ON THE BOOK OF JOB 8.41.[6]

7:15-16 I Loathe My Life

JOB LONGS FOR DEATH. OLYMPIODORUS: "I beg of you. Take away my life. Deliver me from my pains through death. In fact, you did not create me immortal. So . . . may [I] enjoy quiet and tranquility in the future. I do not demand, O Lord, anything contrary to your decree. You made me mortal, not immortal. Therefore bring me death." Moses prayed with these same words by saying, "If that is your purpose for me, then kill me."[7] COMMENTARY ON JOB 7.15.[8]

7:17-18 What Are Human Beings?

A REFERENCE TO JUDGMENT DAY. HESYCHIUS OF JERUSALEM: It is necessary, actually, to call that time "morning," because it is entirely light and drives the night away from this life. "You judge them for the time of rest," that is, not for the torments but for the delights and the reward. He, who is now constantly worthy of the "visit" of

God, will receive then his judgment "for the rest."[9] He is judged with the righteous, that is, is received [in heaven] together with the righteous, so that it may be known, in accordance with them what part is assigned to him and what is his destiny. Must he be placed with the patriarchs, or the prophets, or the apostles or the martyrs? HOMILIES ON JOB 10.7.18.[10]

7:19-21 Why Have You Made Me Your Target?

THE SCANDAL CAUSED BY JOB'S PUNISHMENT. CHRYSOSTOM: What does Job mean when he says, "What shall I be able to do for you?" What should I do in order to expiate my fault, in order to be reconciled with you? "O you who understand the human mind, why did you make me to be your accuser?" Job speaks this way not because he accuses God—God forbid!—but because what has happened to him raises a serious accusation against God. That is why he says, "You who understand the human mind." Even if they do not speak, you know their secret thoughts and all their intimate reflections, "such a righteous man has suffered such tremendous misfortunes!" But Job does not have the attitude of a man who tries to justify himself. In fact, he has not said, "I am righteous." Rather, they are deeply concerned about me, and that is why they have complained against you because of my trials. COMMENTARY ON JOB 7.20A-B.[11]

[5]Ps 149:5. [6]LF 18:447*. [7]Num 11:15. [8]PTS 24:78-79. [9]See LXX. [10]PO 42.1:270. [11]PTS 35:87.

8:1-7 BILDAD DEMONSTRATES
THAT GOD IS JUST

¹*Then Bildad the Shuhite answered:*
² *"How long will you say these things,*
    and the words of your mouth be a great
        wind?
³*Does God pervert justice?*
    Or does the Almighty pervert the
        right?
⁴*If your children have sinned against him,*
    he has delivered them into the power

of their transgression.
⁵*If you will seek God*
    and make supplication to the Almighty,
⁶*if you are pure and upright,*
    surely then he will rouse himself for you
    and reward you with a rightful
        habitation.
⁷*And though your beginning was small,*
    *your latter days will be very great."**

*LXX (5-7) But be early in prayer to the Lord Almighty. If you are pure and true, he will hearken to your supplication, and will restore to you the habitation of righteousness. Though then your beginning should be small, yet your end should be unspeakably great.

OVERVIEW: The Fathers' interpretation of Bildad's words is, in general, unfavorable. Even though they can discern a certain amount of correctness in his assertions (CHRYSOSTOM, JULIAN OF ECLANUM), they cannot help noticing his narrow views (EPHREM) and worldly mentality (DIDYMUS), which places human happiness only among material goods and riches (OLYMPIODORUS).

8:1-3 Does God Pervert Justice?

BILDAD CONSIDERS JOB'S WORDS TO BE ARROGANT. EPHREM THE SYRIAN: So Bildad the Shuhite reproached Job because he thought that the words that Job had said for the sake of truth and justice were, in fact, spoken out of arrogance and disdain. COMMENTARY ON JOB 8.2.[1]

JUSTICE ACCOMPANIES THE CREATOR. CHRYSOSTOM: Bildad says, "be unjust in his judgments, or will he who has created everything overturn what is just?" Observe what he means: justice accompanies the Creator. However, even though Bildad's words are not entirely applicable to Job, let us see what he means. Do you not per-

ceive the profound justice that reigns in the creation and its profound order? And how everything is well regulated and settled? Therefore, could he who maintains justice and order among the senseless creatures overturn the rules in your case? Further, why did God create everything? Is it not because of you, the human being? And so he who has created so many things, did he not give you what was right to share? He who has created you out of love and has created so many things for you, if he has shown his benevolence toward the universe, this is also a proof of his power. We often overturn justice because of our powerlessness, but "he has created everything," he says. Will he, who is so wise, so just, so powerful, be unjust? COMMENTARY ON JOB 8.2A-3B.[2]

8:4 Delivered into the Power of Transgression

PURIFICATION THROUGH CONFESSION. JULIAN OF ECLANUM: Even if your person is purified from guilt through your words, do not the sins of your house reflect the guilt of your principles?

---

[1]ESOO 2:4. [2]PTS 35:89.

Therefore, it is not proper that you make your pains into complaints. It is, however, useful that you are purified through confession and the offering of prayers. EXPOSITION ON THE BOOK OF JOB 8.4.[3]

JOB'S CHILDREN SINNED AS WELL. DIDYMUS THE BLIND: Even Bildad is confused in his speech and is pulled in different directions by various doctrines, when he says, "If you yourself have not sinned, your sons have." Thereby he does not believe one is punished for someone else. But he may be included (in his reasoning), for he delivered the transgression into their hand due to their own sin. In so doing, he alludes to the collapse [of the house], through which Job's children died. "Son" he says, referring to the superior part in his speech, because Job had also daughters. Thus he indicates, since the sons, who had great value for Job, have sinned, obviously the daughters have sinned as well. COMMENTARY ON JOB 8.4.[4]

8:5-7 Small Beginning, Great Ending

BILDAD'S WORLDLY MENTALITY. OLYMPIODORUS: Bildad says, "I suggest you pray to the Lord with all your devotion and diligence. Everything else should come after your prayers." This is what "be early" means. And if you are true and empty of any deceit and falseness, God will give you back a condition of life and a status worthy of a righteous person. You will enjoy an abundance of goods as great as you possessed earlier. Notice how Bildad demonstrates in this part of his discourse of praise his belief that the happiness of the righteous is found in the material goods of worldly life. COMMENTARY ON JOB 8.5-7.[5]

---

[3]CCL 88:24. [4]PTA 3:10. [5]PTS 24:83-84.

8:8-22 THE EXPERIENCE OF FORMER GENERATIONS PROVES THAT THE GODLESS SHALL PERISH

[8]For inquire, I pray you, of bygone ages,
   and consider what the fathers
     have found;
[9]for we are but of yesterday, and know
   nothing,
   for our days on earth are a shadow.
[10]Will they not teach you, and tell you,
   and utter words out of their
     understanding?

[11]Can papyrus grow where there is no marsh?
   Can reeds flourish where there is no water?

[12]While yet in flower and not cut down,
   they wither before any other plant.
[13]Such are the paths* of all who forget God;
   the hope of the godless man shall perish.
[14]His confidence breaks in sunder,[†]
   and his trust is a spider's web.°
[15]He leans against his house, but it does
    not stand;
   he lays hold of it, but it does not endure.
[16]He thrives before the sun,
   and his shoots spread over his garden.[‡]
[17]His roots twine about the stoneheap;

he lives among the rocks.ᵖ

¹⁸If he is destroyed from his place,
   then it will deny him, saying, "I have
      never seen you."

¹⁹Behold, this is the joy of his way;
   and out of the earth others will spring.

²⁰Behold, God will not reject a blameless

man,
   nor take the hand of evildoers.

²¹He will yet fill your mouth with laughter,
   and your lips with shouting.

²²Those who hate you will be clothed with
      shame,§
   and the tent of the wicked will be no
      more.

o Heb *house* p Gk Vg: Heb uncertain *LXX *So shall be the end* †Vg *He will not like their foolishness.* ‡LXX *For it is moist under the sun, and his branch shall come forth out of his dung heap.* §Vg *confusion*

OVERVIEW: In the second part of Bildad's speech the comments of the Fathers tend to give greater emphasis to the correct views and moral remarks contained therein, even when they appear to be fairly superficial (JULIAN OF ECLANUM, DIDYMUS, PHILIP, OLYMPIODORUS, GREGORY, ISHO'DAD). The unrighteous are portrayed as a dried-up herb (PHILIP) destined for death (OLYMPIODORUS), whose hypocrisy deceives, but only for a time (GREGORY), while the righteous do not forget God (HESYCHIUS), who brings them back to life (ISHO'DAD).

8:8-10 Ask Past Generations

"BYGONE GENERATIONS." JULIAN OF ECLANUM: In order to give authority to his words, Bildad calls the venerable past as a witness, so that he may appear to know through long experience what he has said or is about to say. In a different sense, Bildad wants Job to learn from ancient examples what he had said before, that is, that God is appeased by the prayers of the righteous. Through God's support not only are calamities dissolved but also prosperity and happiness are returned. Thus God, whom they had invoked, protected Abraham and his descendants in their distress. Observe a third sense in Bildad's words: "I want you to consider the ancient examples, so that you may not despise my advice because of my youth." EXPOSITION ON THE BOOK OF JOB 8.8.[1]

8:11-12 Nourishment Produces Fruit

GOD'S PROVIDENCE RULES OVER ALL THINGS. DIDYMUS THE BLIND: Previously Bildad said that the teaching is passed on from the ancestors and fathers to the following generations. Now he supports this with an example. He says, "As papyrus does not prosper without water and reeds do not grow if they are not watered . . . likewise someone cannot produce useful fruit whose spirit has not received nourishment from higher authorities." But one can also say that human affairs are watered by providence as with water; if water is not added, they easily decrease and vanish. If, therefore, someone is hit by hardships but recovers from them, this happens with thanks to Providence. Even if what humans do seems to have a human root, it still does not last if Providence does not preside over it. Similarly the psalmist says beautifully, "Unless the Lord builds the house, those who build it labor in vain."[2] [Bildad then comments], "They wither before any other plant." This means the same as Bildad's earlier comment but is said about every plant. He seems to mean that, big or small, everything in life is subjected to Providence and withers if it does not pay attention to it. COMMENTARY ON JOB 8.11-12.[3]

THE WICKED ARE LIKE PREMATURELY

[1]CCL 88:25. [2]Ps 127:1 (126:1 LXX). [3]PTA 3:24-26.

DRIED-UP HERBS. PHILIP THE PRIEST: Bildad means that as the papyrus and the reed cannot live without water, so you could not remain in your former happiness without the nourishment and liquid of justice. "While yet in flower and not cut down, they wither before any other plant." Bildad says that blessed Job flourished like a herb, but before reaching the maturity of stable glory, he was thrown into so many afflictions that he was not taken away by God's hand, on which all kingdoms are founded, in the fullness of his days or in a perfected and completed reign. "Therefore, since you did not act so that you might reach your grave in peace and after fulfilling your time, you are dried up by the ardor of the sun before all herbs, that is, before all sinners, who are often indicated with the word *herbs*. You ceased from the tribulations of your heart together with the impious." COMMENTARY ON THE BOOK OF JOB 8.[4]

8:13 Those Who Forget God

JOB HAS NOT FORGOTTEN GOD. HESYCHIUS OF JERUSALEM: Job has not really forgotten God. Being still subject to the test, Job has offered blessings and praise. That is why the final condition of the righteous is not comparable to the grass dried up by heat. But he "is like a tree planted by streams of water which yields its fruit in its season, and its leaves do not wither."[5] Indeed, by preserving the fruit of virtue, Job has caused the abundant foliage of this world's goods to bloom. HOMILIES ON JOB 11.8.13A.[6]

8:14-15 A House That Does Not Endure

A WARNING AGAINST HYPOCRISY AND PRIDE. PHILIP THE PRIEST: It is absolute foolishness and madness to act falsely and fraudulently before God, and this will never give them any advantage, because God sees into every heart and bosom.[7] These persons are so described in the Gospels. They are adorned outside with an appearance of holiness but inside are filled with the corruption of sin and are like the graves of the dead.[8] "If one leans against its house, it will not stand." He who confides in himself and relies on his own strength will not be able to stand, but his arrogance will fall more ruinously. COMMENTARY ON THE BOOK OF JOB 8.[9]

8:16 The Wicked Thrive for a Time

THE DOOM OF THE WICKED. OLYMPIODORUS: The papyrus and the reed are dried by the scorching heat of the sun and their shoots rot, even though they are moistened by water. In fact, this is what "his branch shall sprout from his dung heap" means. The impious will suffer the same destiny, when the wrath of God falls upon them. Bildad appears to allude to the death of Job's children through his use of "branch," which can indicate shoots, branches or flowers. COMMENTARY ON JOB 8.16.[10]

8:17-18 They Live Among the Rocks

A DESCRIPTION OF HYPOCRISY. GREGORY THE GREAT: Therefore, pay attention. Because they are called "rocks" but are not in any wise called "living stones," the lost and the elect may be mixed together by the bare appellation of "stones." Therefore this plant, "which lives among stones, wraps its roots around the heap of rocks," in that every hypocrite multiplies the thoughts of his heart in seeking out human admiration. For in all that hypocrites do, seeing that in their secret thoughts they look out for the applauses of their fellow-creatures, like rushes, as it were, they "send out roots into the heap of the rocks." For when they are about to act, they imagine the praises of others, and when applauded, they dwell upon these praises secretly within themselves in the thoughts of their heart. They rejoice that they have distinguished themselves first and foremost in the esteem of people; while they are puffed up and

---

[4]PL 26:636. [5]Ps 1:3. [6]PO 42.1:286. [7]Jer 17:10. [8]Mt 23:27. [9]PL 26:636. [10]PTS 24:85.

swollen in themselves by human applause, they often secretly wonder what they are. They long to appear day by day higher than they really are and grow to a height by practicing their extraordinary arts. As habits of virtue weaken everything bad, so presumption strengthens evil. . . . The hypocrite is "destroyed from his place" when death intervenes and he is separated from the applause of the present life. . . . When justly condemning the life of the pretender, "Truth" does not know him or recognize the good works he has done, for the pretender never acted with a right purpose in mind. Thus, when Christ comes to judge, he will say to the foolish virgins, "Truly, I say to you, I do not know you."[11] While he perceives a corrupt mind, he condemns even the corruption of the flesh. But would that hypocrites' own ruin alone were enough for them and that their wicked pains did not vehemently urge others to a life of duplicity. . . . Hence according to the hypocrites' perspective, every degree of simplicity of character is criminal. For they sit in judgment on people whose character is transparent. Purity of heart they term stupidity . . . and believe they have enlightened those persons whom they have forced to surrender the fortress of wisdom, purity of heart. MORALS ON THE BOOK OF JOB 8.81-85.[12]

8:19 Others Spring from the Earth

GOD'S JUSTICE AND POWER. ISHO'DAD OF MERV: "Out of the earth still others will spring." In other words, God inflicts these punishments on the impious as their just reward, but with regard to the righteous, regardless of the state of abasement in which he finds them, God will make them spring up again, rendering them glorious. COMMENTARY ON JOB 8.19.[13]

8:20-22 God Will Not Reject the Blameless

THE JOY OF THE RIGHTEOUS AND THE CONFUSION OF THE WICKED. GREGORY THE GREAT: Therefore, when all the elect are replenished with the delight of clear vision, they internally spring forth into the joy of laughter. We call it shouting when we conceive such joy in the heart as we cannot express through the force of words. Yet the heart's triumph expresses itself with a voice that external words cannot express. Now the mouth is correctly said to be filled with laughter, the lips with shouting, since in that eternal land, when the mind of the righteous is borne away in transport, the tongue is lifted up in the song of praise. And they, because they see so many inexpressible things, shout in laughter, for without understanding it, they resound with all the love that they feel. . . . "Confusion clothes" the enemies of the good in the final judgment, for when they see in the mind's eye their past misdeeds flooding their banks, their own guilt covers them on every side, weighing them down. For they then bear the memory of their actions in punishment, who now, as though strangers to the faculty of reason, sin with hearts full of joy. There they see how greatly they should have eschewed all that they loved. There they see how woeful that was which they now embrace in their sin. MORALS ON THE BOOK OF JOB 8.88-90.[14]

---

[11]Mt 25:12. [12]LF 18:482-87*. [13]CSCO 229:245. [14]LF 18:489-90*.

9:1-13 Job Is Helpless Before God's Power

[1]*Then Job answered:*
[2]*"Truly I know that it is so:*
*But how can a man be just before God?**
[3]*If one wished to contend with him,*
one could not answer him once in
a thousand times.
[4]*He is wise in heart, and mighty in strength*
—who has hardened himself against him,
and succeeded?†*—*
[5]*he who removes mountains, and they know*
it not,
when he overturns them in his anger;
[6]*who shakes the earth out of its place,*
and its pillars tremble;
[7]*who commands the sun, and it does not*
rise;
who seals up the stars;
[8]*who alone stretched out the heavens,*
and trampled the waves of the sea;[q]
[9]*who made the Bear and Orion,*
the Pleiades and the chambers of the
south;
[10]*who does great things beyond understanding,*
and marvelous things without number.
[11]*Lo, he passes by me, and I see him not;*
he moves on, but I do not perceive him.
[12]*Behold, he snatches away; who can hinder*
him?
Who will say to him, 'What doest
thou?'

[13]*"God will not turn back his anger;*
beneath him bowed the helpers of
Rahab."

q Or *trampled the back of the sea dragon* *Vg *and man formed by God will not be justified* †LXX (3-4) *For if he would enter into judgment with him, God would not hearken to him, so that he should answer to one of his charges of a thousand. For he is wise in mind, and mighty, and great, who has hardened himself against him and endured?*

Overview: Job discusses Bildad's words and expresses a mixed opinion. He approves his general and fairly superficial assertions on God's power and justice but opposes his conclusions, that is, the notion that his misfortunes derive from his sins (Julian of Eclanum, Didymus). Job is able to recognize the power of God and to foreshadow, in his prophetic words, the mystery of salvation (Chrysostom, Isho'dad). In his image of the heavens, Job describes the light of grace that spreads the unfailing justice of God. In his image of the sea he describes the bitterness and constantly changing nature of the material world (Gregory).

9:1-2 *Job Answers Bildad*

Agreement and Disagreement. Julian of Eclanum: "Then Job answered, 'Indeed I know that this is so, and that a mortal formed by God will not be justified.'" He asserts that he does not agree entirely with Bildad's judgment but only with a part of it. In fact, Bildad had maintained that God, who is equally endowed with justice and power, opposes the impious and supports the righteous. The holy Job agrees that this is true. But Job declares that the assumption that God wanted to show that he was a sinner on the basis of what had happened to him is false. In a different sense, Job does not agree with the judgment of Bildad's speech but states that the words that he had pronounced earlier are true. That is, "Inquire now of past generations, and consider what their ancestors have found." No one is found among mortals who, in Job's judgment, does not choose to oppress the inferior in an attempt to please the superior. EXPOSITION ON THE BOOK OF JOB 9.1.[1]

9:3-4 Who Can Resist God?

THE MYSTERY OF SALVATION. CHRYSOSTOM: "He is wise in mind, mighty and strong," with good reason. Indeed, since God is wise, his benefits are countless. But if you do not believe, O mortal, let us bring our reflection to its conclusion. If he pronounces one thousand words, we cannot answer a single one. These are wise words. In fact, that righteous man said, "Also the righteous will be happy." About what righteous man is he speaking? But where will we ever find a man who is righteous before God? "Not one of his thousand words." This is exactly what the prophet said as well: "No living person will be found righteous before you."[2] "If you observe our faults, O Lord, O Lord, who will survive?"[3] . . . God has created human nature. Why? Out of pure benevolence, as all the rest of creation. He has created the universe and all the rest for humans. He stated a commandment, but humanity did not consider it. Afterward he gave them the law, but they neglected it. Then he sent his Son, but they did not consider him either. Then he gave them repentance, but they did not ponder it. Then he threatened them with the punishment of hell, but they disregarded it. But why did he want to save them? Do you want us to ask Paul himself? Listen to what he says: "God dealt with me mercifully because I acted in the ignorance of disbelief."[4] And then, after being called, Paul testified to the profound and providential care, of which he was an object. COMMENTARY ON JOB 9.4A.[5]

9:5-6 The Power of God

JOB EXALTS THE POWER OF GOD. CHRYSOSTOM: "He removes mountains," Job says, "and they do not know it." The mountains, he says, and they do not notice it. And this is in perfect accordance with what David said: "He touches the moun-

tains, and they smoke."[6] In this passage he speaks about the power of God by stating that God can do anything through his avenging power. In fact, Job has testified to his justice and, at the same time, testifies to his power. COMMENTARY ON JOB 9.5.[7]

9:7 God Commands the Sun and Stars

EVIDENCE OF GOD'S MIGHT. ISHO'DAD OF MERV: Here the author is probably speaking about what happened in Egypt for three days,[8] or about what happens sometimes to the stars that become hidden. Perhaps he is alluding to what occurred at the beginning: God kept the light close to him, as though it was in a bag. The interpreter[9] says the author does not maintain that the things he mentions actually happened but that, if God desires it, they will certainly occur. COMMENTARY ON JOB 9.7.[10]

9:8-9 God Stretched Out the Heavens

THE HEAVENS AND THE SEA. GREGORY THE GREAT: For what does the name "the heavens" denote but this deeply heavenly life of those who preach, of whom the psalmist speaks, "The heavens declare the glory of God."[11] Thus the same persons are recorded to be the heavens, and the same to be the sun. Indeed they are the heavens, because they protect by praying for all; they are the sun, because they show the power of light by preaching. And so, as the "earth was shaken," "the heavens were spread out." For when Judea fed greedily on the violence of persecution, the Lord spread about the life of the apostles, so that all the Gentiles might acquaint themselves with them. . . . For what is denoted by the title of "the sea" but this world's bitter-

---

[1]CCL 88:26. [2]Ps 143:2 (142:2 LXX). [3]Ps 130:3 (129:3 LXX). [4]1 Tim 1:13. [5]PTS 35:92-93. [6]Ps 104:32 (103:32 LXX). [7]PTS 35:93. [8]Allusion to the plague of the darkness: see Ex 10:21. [9]That is, Theodore of Mopsuestia. Isho'dad is referring to a lost work by Theodore. [10]CSCO 229:245. [11]Ps 19:1 (18:1 LXX).

ness raging in the destruction of the righteous? The psalmist also speaks concerning this: "He gathers the waters of the sea together as in a skin."[12] For the Lord "gathers the water of the sea together as in a skin" as he disposes all things with wonderful governance. He restrains the carnal threats pent up in their hearts. Thus "the Lord treads upon the waves of the sea." When the storms of persecution lift up themselves, they are dashed to pieces in astonishment at his miracles. Since he that brings down the swellings of humanity's madness, as it were, treads the waters as they stand in a heap. MORALS ON THE BOOK OF JOB 9.10-11.[13]

9:10 Things Beyond Understanding

THE GLORIOUS AND UNFATHOMABLE RESOLUTIONS OF GOD. DIDYMUS THE BLIND: Whoever is great necessarily does great things. But the one who does great things is not necessarily great. The disciples who did great things received their ability from God. Taking an example from the human realm, I want to say that the grammarian writes correctly; but not everyone who writes correctly does so because of studies in grammar. Rather, he does so by chance and habit. Job demonstrates regarding greatness that only the one who is great makes great the things he does. Analogously and in accordance with our ability, we perceive God in the greatness of creatures and so receive an idea of God.[14] He says this, however, so that his friends—who think there is only one reason for hardship—may consider that he who does great and dreadful things also has deep and unfathomable resolutions that are glorious. These things are filled with glory, so to speak. Paul writes something similar when he says, "O the depth of the riches and wisdom and knowledge of God! How unsearchable are his judgments and how inscrutable his ways! For who has known the mind of the Lord?"[15] COMMENTARY ON JOB 9.10.[16]

9:11-13 Who Will Question God?

THE ACTS OF GOD. GREGORY THE GREAT: For the human race, being shut out from interior joy as the result of sin, lost the eyes of the mind. Where the mind is now going in the steps of its deserved punishments, it cannot tell. Often the mind identifies the gift of grace as wrath. In turn, it is the wrath of God's severity that it supposes to be grace. For very commonly it reckons gifts of virtue as grace, and yet being uplifted [pridefully] by those gifts is brought to the ground. Very often it dreads the opposition of temptations as wrath, and yet being bowed down by those temptations, arises with even greater concern for the safe keeping of his virtuous attainments. For who would not reckon himself to be near to God when he sees that he is magnified with gifts from on high? When either the gift of prophecy or the mastery of teaching has been granted to him, or when he is empowered to exercise the grace of healing? Yet it often happens that while the mind may become careless in its self-satisfaction over its virtues as the adversary plots against it, it is pierced with the weapon of unexpected sin. The mind is forever put far away from God by the very means by which for a time it was brought near to him without the caution of attentiveness. . . . The acts of our Maker ought always to be reverenced without scrutiny, for they can never be unjust. For to seek a reason for God's secret counsel is nothing else than to erect one's own pride against his counsel. So when the motive of God's acts cannot be discovered, in humility we should remain silent under those acts, for the senses of the flesh are not equal to the task of penetrating the secrets of God's majesty. He, then, who sees no reason for the acts of God, on considering his own weakness, does see although he does not see. MORALS ON THE BOOK OF JOB 9.20-22.[17]

---

[12]Ps 33:7 Vg (32:7 LXX). [13]LF 18:500-502*. [14]See Wis 13:5. [15]Rom 11:33-34. [16]PTA 3:52-54. [17]LF 18:509-11*.

9:14-35 DOES JOB DOUBT GOD'S JUSTICE?

¹⁴How then can I answer him,
　choosing my words with him?
¹⁵Though I am innocent, I cannot answer
　　him;
　I must appeal for mercy to my accuser.^r
¹⁶If I summoned him and he answered me,
　I would not believe that he was
　　listening to my voice.
¹⁷For he crushes me with a tempest,
　and multiplies my wounds without cause;
¹⁸he will not let me get my breath,
　but fills me with bitterness.
¹⁹If it is a contest of strength, behold him!
　If it is a matter of justice, who can
　　summon him?^s*
²⁰Though I am innocent, my own
　　mouth would condemn me;
　though I am blameless, he would prove
　　me perverse.
²¹I am blameless; I regard not myself;
　I loathe my life.
²²It is all one; therefore I say,
　he destroys both the blameless and the
　　wicked.
²³When disaster brings sudden death,
　he mocks at the calamity^t of the
　　innocent.
²⁴The earth is given into the hand of
　　the wicked;

he covers the faces of its judges—
　if it is not he, who then is it?

²⁵My days are swifter than a runner;
　they flee away, they see no good.
²⁶They go by like skiffs of reed,
　like an eagle swooping on the prey.[†]
²⁷If I say, "I will forget my complaint,
　I will put off my sad countenance, and
　　be of good cheer,"
²⁸I become afraid of all my suffering,[‡]
　for I know thou wilt not hold me
　　innocent.[§]
²⁹I shall be condemned;
　why then do I labor in vain?
³⁰If I wash myself with snow,
　and cleanse my hands with lye,
³¹yet thou wilt plunge me into a pit,
　and my own clothes will abhor me.[#]
³²For he is not a man, as I am, that I
　　might answer him,
　that we should come to trial together.
³³There is no^u umpire between us,
　who might lay his hand upon us both.
³⁴Let him take his rod away from me,
　and let not dread of him terrify me.
³⁵Then I would speak without fear of
　　him,
　for I am not so in myself.

r Or *for my right*　s Compare Gk: Heb *me*. The text of the verse is uncertain.　t The meaning of the Hebrew word is uncertain.　u Another reading is *Would that there were*　*LXX *For indeed he is superior in power, who then shall resist his judgment?*　†LXX (25-26) *But my life is swifter than a post, my days have fled away, and they knew it not. Or again, is there a trace of their path left by ships? Or is there one of the flying eagle as it seeks its prey?*　‡Vg *works*　§Vg *I know that you would not spare one that offends.*　#LXX (29-31) *If I am ungodly, why have I not died? For if I should wash myself with snow, and purge myself with pure hands, you had thoroughly plunged me in filth, and my garment had abhorred me.*

Overview: This section of Job's speech appears to be quite controversial in different respects, especially because it may suggest the idea that Job seriously doubts God's justice. The Fathers tried to solve these evident difficulties mainly through a moral interpretation of Job's words. As a consequence, Job's assertions become an instrument of moral instruction to the Christian (Gregory, Chrysostom, Hesychius, Didymus). At the same time Job's words appear to contain a prophetic message that hints at the sacrifice of Christ (Ephrem, Julian of Eclanum). Finally, Job's despair demonstrates the frailty of human nature, so that his doubts are psychologically interpreted as a consequence of his excessive and unbearable sufferings (Gregory, Chrysostom, Philip).

9:14-16 Appeal for Mercy to My Accuser

Righteousness Must Be Seasoned by Prayer and Humility. Gregory the Great: It is as though Job said in plain words, "If a created being unburdened by a physical body cannot think clearly about God, how can I dispute God's judgments, as I am hampered by the burden of corruption?" God's words to us are frequently his judgments, declaring God's sentence upon our actions. Our words to God are the deeds that we set forth. A human being, however, cannot use words to reason with God. For in the eye of God's exact judgment, he cannot rely on his own actions. Hence, Job appropriately adds, "Even if I possessed anything righteous, I would not answer. Rather, I would make supplication to my Judge." For, as we have often said, all human righteousness is proved to be unrighteousness, if it is judged by strict rules. And so there is need for prayer to follow righteous actions.... The human mind with difficulty puts into practice the truths that it apprehends, and the things that it apprehends are nothing more than the outskirts. Therefore, let Job say, "Though I possessed nothing righteous, yet I would not answer, but I would make supplication to my Judge." It is as if Job acknowledged in plainer words, "And if I should grow to the practicing of virtue, I am strengthened to life not by merit but by pardoning grace." Therefore, we must be strenuous in prayer when we act rightly, so that all the righteous ways in which we live may be seasoned by humility. Morals on the Book of Job 9.27-28.[1]

9:17 Wounds Multiplied

Two Different Meanings. Ephrem the Syrian: These words mean two different things, either that Job had not sinned, even though he was, nevertheless, undergoing a punishment; or that Christ, as if he were guilty of sin, would have suffered resolutely the temptation of blameless passions. Commentary on Job 9.17.[2]

9:18-19 A Contest of Strength

God's Power Is Unlimited. Chrysostom: "He will not let me catch my breath." That is, I am filled with a multitude of afflictions. "He has filled me with bitterness, for indeed he is superior in power. Who, then, shall resist his judgment?" Job does not want to say simply that God is superior to him in power but also that God is able to do whatever he wants. Commentary on Job 9.18-19.[3]

9:20-21 Blameless but Reproached

The Sin of Pride. Hesychius of Jerusalem: "If I think I have attained purity in my actions, I will be proved perverse in my words. If I am found blameless in my words, I will be reproached for my actions." In the same manner, if one is righteous in his actions and proclaims that loudly with ostentatious words, his mouth commits impiety, because he has fallen into pride, a pride appropriate to the betrayer, the real impious one.[4] If one is blameless but ignores the source of his purity, and as a consequence places his trust in himself and becomes proud and arrogant, he will

---

[1]LF 18:516*. [2]ESOO 2:4. [3]PTS 35:96. [4]In Armenian, "the informer."

become perverse. Evidently, the hand of God has abandoned him. HOMILIES ON JOB 12.9.20.[5]

9:22-24 It Is All One

EARTHLY SUFFERINGS FORESHADOW THE PASSION. JULIAN OF ECLANUM: "The earth is given into the hand of the wicked." With regard to the context of the passage, Job seems to state that his earthly part, that is, his body, is given to torments and vexations. The permission to afflict it is granted to the impious. Therefore, it certainly happens that those who see cannot express a fair judgment on the merits of the one who is afflicted. Passing to the prophetic aspect, that which vindicates the merits of the person, Job appears to wander from the context of the debate and to speak of future mysteries. The passion of the Lord is predicted. Job's friends could not recognize this because the earthly vileness of Job's external appearance is his internal dignity. EXPOSITION ON THE BOOK OF JOB 9.24.[6]

9:25-26 Days That Flee Without Seeing Good

THE SPEED AND PERSEVERANCE OF THE RUNNER. DIDYMUS THE BLIND: The swift runner does not appear to touch the ground; he appears as though he has wings. [Job says], "'My life is swifter than a runner.' I look at what is above. 'I do not run aimlessly.'[7] I do not touch the ground." Because they want to reach the finish line, the righteous keep on running, even when they run into obstacles. For example, when they encounter a distressful situation they continue to run. Even David ran, for he said, "I have run without unrighteousness, always running straight ahead."[8] And, "I ran the way of your commandments, for you enlarge my understanding."[9] Job also hints at this twofold interpretation: First, "judges," whose faces are completely covered, is a reference to the people's leaders who run away in fear of the righteous because they saw no successful outcome of the [righteous person's] race. [Their faces are covered]

because they are unworthy [to be judges or leaders.] Secondly, however, consider whether Job may not also be speaking about the righteous as well. They fled from the [corrupt] judges according to the passage "but run away, do not stay in one place."[10] And they [the judges] did not perceive the poignancy of virtue [anymore]. And so they stopped running. Maybe it is also appropriate to compare this with the passage, "I have not known an evil person, seeing that he turns away from me."[11] COMMENTARY ON JOB 9.25-26.[12]

JOB'S LOSS OF AWARENESS. CHRYSOSTOM: He means, "My memories themselves are dead, and I don't even know what I am talking about, as my pain is so great! In the moment itself, in which I speak, I forget, as the storm around me is so strong!" COMMENTARY ON JOB 9.25-27.[13]

9:27-28 Fear in Suffering

RECOGNITION OF HUMAN LIMITATION. GREGORY THE GREAT: For we say that "we never ought to speak this way" when we transgress the limits of our frail nature by excessive questioning. We reproach ourselves in dread and are restrained by reminding ourselves of heavenly awe, in which our mind's face is altered. The mind, in the first instance, failing to comprehend its limits, is boldly investigating things above. Afterwards, discovering its own infirmity, it begins to entertain awe for what it is ignorant of. However, in this very change there is pain, for the mind is very greatly afflicted that, in payment for the first sin, it is blinded to the understanding of things touching it. . . . Therefore, because our very good actions themselves cannot escape the sword of ambushed sin unless they are guarded every day by anxious fear, it is rightly said by the holy man in this place, "I was afraid of all my works." It is as if he said with humble confession, "What I have done publicly, I

---

[5]PO 42.2:318. [6]CCL 88:28-29. [7]1 Cor 9:26. [8]See Ps 59:4 (58:5 LXX). [9]Ps 119:32 (118:32 LXX). [10]Prov 9:18; RSV has a different rendering of this verse. [11]Ps 101:4 (100:4 LXX). [12]PTA 3:86-90. [13]PTS 35:97.

know, but what I may have been secretly subject to through this I cannot tell." For often our good points are spoiled by deceit robbing us, in that the earthly desires unite themselves to our righteous actions. Oftentimes they come to nothing from sloth intervening, in that, when love grows cold, they are starved of the fervor in which they began. Therefore, because the stealth of sin has scarcely got the better of those even in the very act of virtue, what safeguard remains for our security? Even in our virtue, we always tread with fear and caution. What he adds after this presents itself as a very great difficulty to the mind: "I know that you would not spare one that offends." For if there be no "sparing of one that offends," who can be rescued from eternal death, seeing that there is no one to be found clear of sin? Or does this mean, alternatively, that God does spare one who repents but not one that offends (on the premise that when we bewail our offenses, we are no longer offending)? MORALS ON THE BOOK OF JOB 9.51-54.[14]

9:29-31 Cursed and Impure

JOB IS SEEN AS CURSED AND IMPURE. CHRYSOSTOM: "If I am ungodly, why have I not died?" You see how he does not deny being a sinner. "Why have I not died?" he says. This is not the expression of a man who accuses but who searches. I do not know at all, he says, God's plans. "For if I should wash myself with snow and purge myself with pure hands [that would be useless]. You have thoroughly plunged me in filth, and my garment has abhorred me." He means, before everybody's eyes I am an example of impiety. It would be necessary that the wicked disap-

peared, so that I might not play the role of master for the others anymore. If I become purer than the sun, I still retain filthiness, and not an ordinary filthiness. "My garment has abhorred me." What can I say about people, if even my garment despises me? This is what he more or less means. Even my closest relations have begun to hate me. They have turned away from me not because I am condemned but because they think I am cursed and impure. COMMENTARY ON JOB 9.29-31.[15]

9:32-33 Impossible to Come to Trial Together

GOD'S JUDGMENT IS OVERWHELMING. CHRYSOSTOM: This is what he means, if he who punishes were a man, his punishment would not have entirely condemned the one in affliction. I could have been judged before him and proved that he too is unjust. But since you are God, that is impossible. It is sufficient to be punished and to suffer the greatest condemnation. COMMENTARY ON JOB 9.32A.[16]

9:34-35 Speaking Without Fear

ABSOLUTE POWER AND ABSOLUTE SUFFERING OVERWHELM. PHILIP THE PRIEST: "I will be able to speak safely and constantly, when he removes these two things from me: the greatness of his power and the affliction of these torments." COMMENTARY ON THE BOOK OF JOB 9.[17]

---

[14]LF 18:532-35. [15]PTS 35:98. [16]PTS 35:98. [17]PL 26:641.

10:1-17 JOB WONDERS WHAT IS GOD'S PURPOSE IN AFFLICTING HIM

¹I loathe my life;
I will give free utterance to my complaint;
  I will speak in the bitterness of my
    soul.*
²I will say to God, Do not condemn me;
  let me know why thou dost contend
    against me.†
³Does it seem good to thee to oppress,
  to despise the work of thy hands
  and favor the designs of the wicked?
⁴Hast thou eyes of flesh?
  Dost thou see as man sees?
⁵Are thy days as the days of man,
  or thy years as man's years,
⁶that thou dost seek out my iniquity
  and search for my sin,
⁷although thou knowest that I am not
    guilty,
  and there is none to deliver out of thy
    hand?‡
⁸Thy hands fashioned and made me;
  and now thou dost turn about and
    destroy me.ᵛ
⁹Remember that thou hast made me of
    clay;ʷ

and wilt thou turn me to dust again?
¹⁰Didst thou not pour me out like milk
  and curdle me like cheese?
¹¹Thou didst clothe me with skin and flesh,
  and knit me together with bones and
    sinews.
¹²Thou hast granted me life and steadfast
    love;
  and thy care has preserved my spirit.
¹³Yet these things thou didst hide in thy
    heart;
  I know that this was thy purpose.§
¹⁴If I sin, thou dost mark me,
  and dost not acquit me of my iniquity.#
¹⁵If I am wicked, woe to me!
  If I am righteous, I cannot lift up
    my head,
  for I am filled with disgrace
  and look upon my affliction.
¹⁶And if I lift myself up,ˣ thou dost hunt
    me like a lion,**
  and again work wonders against me;
¹⁷thou dost renew thy witnesses against me,
  and increase thy vexation toward me;
  thou dost bring fresh hosts against me.ʸ

v Cn Compare Gk Syr: Heb *made me together round about and thou dost destroy me*   w Gk: Heb *like clay*   x Syr: Heb *he lifts himself up*   y Cn Compare Gk: Heb *changes and a host are with me*   *LXX *Weary in my soul, I will pour my words with groans upon him, I will speak being straitened in the bitterness of my soul.*   †Vg *Show me why you judge me so.*
‡LXX (4-7) *Or do you see as a mortal sees? Or will you look as a man sees? Or is your life human, or your years the years of a man, that you have enquired into my iniquity, and searched out my sins? For you know that I have not committed iniquity, but who is he that can deliver out of your hands?*   §LXX *Having these things in yourself, I know that you can do all things; for nothing is impossible to you.*   #Vg *If I have sinned, and you spared me at the hour, why do you not let me be clean from my iniquity?*   **LXX *I am caught in the hunt like a lion for slaughter.*

OVERVIEW: In Job 10, where Job's speech continues, we find the same elements of Job 9, and therefore the same lines of interpretation used by the Fathers. Job's complaints and doubts are an instrument of moral instruction (OLYMPIODORUS, GREGORY, CHRYSOSTOM, HESYCHIUS). They demonstrate the frailty and weakness of human nature (Chrysostom, Gregory); they also contain a prophetic hint of Christ's sacrifice (Ephrem). Even in the embryo the soul is being clothed with skin and flesh and knit together with bones and sinews. Didymus sees in this passage an attestation of the priority of the soul to the body (Didymus).[1] The pains of temporary affliction purify each of the elect (Gregory). The righteous, by preserving the honor of God, are dreadful to their enemies, like lions (Hesychius).

10:1 I Loathe My Life

Job Expresses His Fears. Chrysostom: But he also said above, "God would not hearken to him, so that he should answer to one of his charges or of a thousand."[2] How can Job speak so here? "In the bitterness of my soul," he says. Therefore it is not him who speaks but his bitterness, insofar as the reflections of Job allow us to express what he means. "Would that one were present who should hear the cause between both"[3] not in order to examine his life in detail and to show that he is unjustly suffering. He does not say that actually, as in the previous passages. He has often said that it is "because of his iniquity."[4] He wants to demonstrate that the persisting oppression overwhelms him. And this is what Isaiah says, "You became angry, and we, we are distraught,"[5] and in another passage, "Why did you lead us astray from your path?"[6] "I fear, [Job] says, lest I fall or capsize; I am afraid to be forced, one day, to blaspheme or to commit suicide." Commentary on Job 9.32b-10.1.[7]

10:2-3 Why Do You Contend Against Me?

Doubts Generated by Fear and Distress. Gregory the Great: Therefore it often happens that the mind of the righteous man, in order to be made more secure, is the more penetrated with fear, and when he is beset with scourges, he is troubled with misgivings about the judgment of the Most High. He fears lest all that he suffers

should be the forerunner of an ensuing doom. In his heart, he questions the Judge with the result that under his visitation he is full of doubts about the merit of his life. However, when the goodness of his life is brought before the eyes of the mind, it is as if the Judge gave comfort in the answer whereby he never strikes to destroy but strikes to sustain the innocency of life and conduct. Therefore, it is justly said here, "Show me why you judge me so." As if it were expressed in plain words, "Whereas you exercise judgment upon me by scourging me, show me that by these scourges you are making me secure against judgment." . . . This same thing is also said by way of a negating interrogation, as though it were said in plain terms: "You who are supremely good, I know do not hold it good to oppress the poor man by calumny. Therefore, I know that it is not unjust that I am suffering, and I am the more grieved that I cannot tell the causes of its justness." Morals on the Book of Job 9.69-70.[8]

10:4-7 Do You See As Humans See?

We Can Only Take Refuge in God. Olympiodorus: "Do you judge things according to human views? May anything hide from your careful examination, as it is hidden from human beings? Are your years few, and do you ignore what was previous to your age? Do you need to make an enquiry and an investigation about what happened to me, in order to understand that I am not impious?" He says these words by bringing forward God as the witness of his righteousness and by demanding the benefit of his infinite benevolence. People, in fact, ask for similar things, and God, in his benevolence, reveals few of them to the many. "But if I have not committed iniquity," he says, "I know, in my heart, that it is not possible to escape

[1]Didymus, who was a faithful follower of Origen, agreed with some of his heretical ideas. See the discussion on the preexistence of soul in R. A. Layton, *Didymus the Blind and His Circle in Late-Antique Alexandria* (Urbana, Ill.: University of Illinois Press, 2004), 72-74, 108-10, 151-52. [2]Job 9:3. [3]Job 9:33 LXX. [4]Cf. Job 7:21. [5]Is 64:5 (64:4 LXX). [6]Is 63:17. [7]PTS 35:99. [8]LF 18:545-46*.

from your will; and if I did not know this by myself, your will which knows human things better than us, would have mastered me." The blessed Job pronounces all these words by teaching us that in temptation we can only take refuge in God and supplicate that his mercy may spare his creature. COMMENTARY ON JOB 10.4-7.[9]

10:8-9 You Made Me

THE DIGNITY OF HUMANITY SET BEFORE GOD. GREGORY THE GREAT: For he, who declares himself both "made and fashioned altogether round about" by God, leaves to the people of darkness no part either in his spirit or in his flesh. For he described himself as "molded" in virtue of the interior image, but he spoke of being "fashioned altogether round about" insofar as he consists of a covering of flesh. Yet, it is to be observed that he declares himself made by the hands of God. He is setting before the divine mercy the dignity of his creation. For though all things were created by the Word which is coeternal with the Father, yet in the very account of the creation it is shown how greatly humankind is preferred above all animals; how much greater than celestial things that are without sense. MORALS ON THE BOOK OF JOB 9.74-75.[10]

10:10-12 Clothed with Skin and Flesh

A FIGURE OF INCARNATION. EPHREM THE SYRIAN: Here [Job] foreshadows the incarnation of the divine Word through the assumption of human nature. These words, in fact, appear to be addressed to the Father, as if they were said by the person [the Son] of the Lord. COMMENTARY ON JOB 10.11-12.[11]

THE HUMAN SOUL. DIDYMUS THE BLIND: The seed from which life emerges he calls "milked milk," for as milk curdles and becomes cheese, so the seed becomes "nature" when it curdles. This is a condition before the embryo. For the seed that sinks into the channels of the vagina becomes "nature" when it curdles like cheese. This formation is further developed or, as Scripture says, "formed out of an image" and takes on shapes . . . when the limbs are formed and every part emerges and finally moves. Just as the hand or foot of a living being, the delivery of the embryo brings the creature to the light of day. It is clear that "skin and flesh" here signify the body, for he adds in what follows with what holds it together and says, "knit me together with bones and sinews." The whole procedure and the harmony of the formation of the body he proclaims in the previous [section] and in what is quoted here. It is remarkable that these seem to be words from his soul; for it is [the soul] that is "clothed with skin and flesh" and "knit together with bones and sinews." That makes it clear that [the soul] is before the clothing and dressing, for it is clothed (already) as that which is the basis. Since skin and flesh, bones and sinews do not live by themselves but move due to the presence of the soul—if it leaves, they do not have life anymore—he says, "You have not only formed me, made flesh, skin, bones and sinews for me and clothed me with them, but you have also given me life and love." COMMENTARY ON JOB 10.10-12.[12]

10:13 Things Hidden in Your Heart

THE POSSIBILITY TO KNOW GOD. CHRYSOSTOM: Do you see that "the possibility to know God is manifest in creatures,"[13] that our creation was already sufficient to show me the nature of God and his power, without any help from heaven? Indeed the fact that we are so created from a germ, are supported, are not left in perils, is sufficient to show the strength of God and his power, as well as the fact that a sinner is preserved and not punished, whereas a righteous person is punished and chastised. COMMENTARY ON JOB 10.13.[14]

---

[9]PTS 24:105. [10]LF 18:549*. [11]ESOO 2:4. [12]PTA 3:142-46. [13]Rom 1:19. [14]PTS 35:101.

10:14-15 *If I Am Wicked, Woe to Me!*

SUFFERING LIBERATES THE RIGHTEOUS FROM SIN. GREGORY THE GREAT: Therefore let the holy person take note of the wretchedness of the human mind, how often it defiles itself with unhallowed thoughts. After the Judge's remission of the guilt of our actions, even while Job bewails his own case, let him show to us our sin, for us to bewail, "If I have sinned, and you spare me at the hour, why do you not allow me to be clean from my iniquity?" It is as if Job said in plain words, "If your forgiveness has taken away my sin, why does it not sweep it from my memory also?" Often the mind is so shaken from its center at the recollection of sin that it is prompted to the commission of far worse things than it had been before being subjected to the memory of prior sins. And when entangled the mind is filled with fears, and being driven with different impulses, throws itself into disorder. It dreads lest it should be overcome by temptations, and in resisting, it shudders at this very fact that it is harassed with the long toils of conflict. Hence it is fitly added, "If I am wicked, woe to me! If I am righteous, I cannot lift up my head, for I am filled with disgrace and look upon my affliction." Certainly the wicked person has "woe" and the righteous person "affliction," in that everlasting damnation follows the lost sinner and the pains of temporary affliction purify each of the elect. The wicked person lifts up his head, yet when so lifted up he cannot escape the woe that pursues him. The righteous person, faring ill with the toils of his conflict, is not allowed to lift up his head, but while hard pressed, he is freed from everlasting affliction. The one who sets himself up in pleasure is plunging himself to the earth in sorrow and hides himself from the weight of eternal visitation. MORALS ON THE BOOK OF JOB 9.55.84-85.[15]

10:16-17 *You Hunt Me Like a Lion*

A ROYAL ANIMAL. HESYCHIUS OF JERUSALEM: A human being is called "lion" with good reason, because he is a royal animal, and even more so the righteous, because, by preserving the honor of God's form, he is dreadful to his enemies. That is why he has been properly called so in Proverbs, "the righteous is as bold as a lion."[16] Yet if he stoops down to the lustful temptations presented by his enemies, he is "caught in the hunt like a lion for slaughter" and becomes an object of mockery for his hunters, like a lion, who, after being deluded by them, "has been caught in the hunt." HOMILIES ON JOB 13.10.16-17A.[17]

---

[15]LF 18:556-57*. [16]Prov 28:1. [17]PO 42.2:344.

10:18-22 PRAYER FOR A BRIEF RESPITE BEFORE DEATH

[18]*Why didst thou bring me forth from the womb?*
Would that I had died before any eye had seen me,

[19]*and were as though I had not been, carried from the womb to the grave.*
[20]*Are not the days of my life few?[z]*

*Let me alone, that I may find a little
comfort[a]*
[21]before I go whence I shall not return,

*to the land of gloom and deep darkness,
[22]the land of gloom[b] and chaos,
where light is as darkness.*

z Cn Compare Gk Syr: Heb *Are not my days few? Let him cease*   a Heb *brighten up*   b Heb *gloom as darkness, deep darkness*

Overview: The events in Job's life and his personal experience become a poignant instrument of moral instruction for all those who are around him (Hesychius, Didymus). It is not inconsistent for the righteous amid affliction to pray for an end to their affliction (Hesychius). Nonetheless, Job endured the pain with the help of God's power by praying in gratefulness (Didymus).

10:18-22 A Plea to Be Let Alone

Job Is an Example for Everyone. Hesychius of Jerusalem: In order to avoid scandalizing many who see his life end in affliction and sadness, it is not without reason that the righteous man asks for the termination of his ordeals. That is why [Job] said, "Before I go, never to return," evidently, to his human life, as if to say "In fact, if I return down here and receive here the reward of my toils, I will not be worn out and will not renounce the fight to the death in my ordeals. Those who are here, knowing my justice, will see that I receive my reward by coming back here. But if they see me die now in my ordeals, they will either think that Job is wicked or will believe that nothing useful comes from justice." Homilies on Job 13.10.20b-22.[1]

A Model of Humanity and Virility. Didymus the Blind: Someone could think that Job's statement comes from desperation, but that is proven wrong by what God has said: "Do you believe I treated you like this for any other reason than to reveal your righteousness?"[2] Job, who previously had said, "If I am wicked, woe to me,"[3] does not contradict this assumption but reveals the bitterness of life. An evil person would not do that, for he rejoices in this [life]. Above all, Job wants to reveal to his friends the reason why he

did not die at the moment of his birth, namely, because he was to be an example of energy and strength. According to a different interpretation, even the life in the flesh is indicated, about which Paul writes, "If for this life only we have hoped in Christ, we are of all people most to be pitied."[4] Job experiences the pleasant as well as the bitter sides of life; no one who has rid himself of the flesh rejoices in wealth or excess, nor is he plagued by hardship. Job has tasted this life and its pleasures, for he was blessed with many good children and was rich and healthy. But since his situation turned into its opposite, he also experienced the reverse of his previous life and acknowledged in real life the vanity of these things. This is why Job teaches us not to long for them by saying, "Why did you bring me forth from the womb? Would that I had died before any eye had seen me, and were as though I had not been."

Job expresses this in the form of a prayer, for his burdens were not light and he endured the pains not without feeling them. For it would not have been manful had he not felt his sufferings. But he teaches that he endured the pain with the help of God's power, by praying in gratefulness. Paul also expresses this: "It was not I, but the grace of God that is with me."[5]

Job wants to find relief before he has to go from where he cannot return. Therefore, he does not pray for himself, but to teach the friends who think that those who suffer hardship are evil but those who are free from hardship are righteous. He desired that they should gain certainty regarding the divine resolutions about him. One should not assume that Job denies the resurrection of the dead. Rather, Job says, "From where I

[1]PO 42.2:348. [2]Job 40:8; RSV has a different version of this verse.
[3]Job 10:15. [4]1 Cor 15:19. [5]1 Cor 15:10.

will not return to lead a mortal life." Job knows that he will rise as immortal.

Although the brave one was in pain, he talked about the coming age. So he says—not to deny the resurrection—"Before I go from where I will not return." Job calls the land "a land of gloom and deep darkness, where light is like darkness," since the holy one ascribes only little to himself.

For it would not have been suitable to say, "Before I am in the kingdom of the heavens and in the land of our promises, my God." Job wants his listener to be instructed about the divine judgment. There has not yet been restitution for deeds done. COMMENTARY ON JOB 10.18-22.[6]

[6]PTA 3:166-76.

11:1-12 ONLY GOD CAN CLEARLY SEE HUMAN SINS

[1]Then Zophar the Naamathite answered:
  [2]"Should a multitude of words go
      unanswered,
    and a man full of talk be vindicated?*
  [3]Should your babble silence men,
    and when you mock, shall no one shame
      you?[†]
  [4]For you say, 'My doctrine is pure,
    and I am clean in God's eyes.'
  [5]But oh, that God would speak,
    and open his lips to you,
  [6]and that he would tell you the secrets of
      wisdom!
    For he is manifold in understanding.[c‡]
  Know then that God exacts of you less than
      your guilt deserves.

[7]"Can you find out the deep things of God?
    Can you find out the limit of the
      Almighty?[§]
  [8]It is higher than heaven[d]—what can you do?
    Deeper than Sheol—what can you
      know?
  [9]Its measure is longer than the earth,
    and broader than the sea.[#]
  [10]If he passes through, and imprisons,
    and calls to judgment, who can hinder
      him?
  [11]For he knows worthless men;**
    when he sees iniquity, will he not
      consider it?
  [12]But a stupid man will get understanding,
    when a wild ass's colt is born a man."[††]

c Heb obscure d Heb The heights of heaven *Vg Will he, who speaks many words, not listen, or will a loquacious man be justified? †LXX Be not a speaker of many words; for is there none to answer you? ‡Vg For her law is manifold §The Peshitta version employed by Ephrem reads Can you know the manifestation of God? Can you rise over the limit of the Almighty? #LXX (8-9) Heaven is high; and what will you do? And there are deeper things than those in hell; what do you know? Or longer than the measure of the earth, or the breadth of the sea. **Vg If he overturns all things, or shuts them up together, who will contradict him? ††LXX But man is vainly supported by his words; and a mortal born of a woman is like an ass of the desert.

OVERVIEW: In their interpretation of Zophar's speech the Fathers notice again an unjustified and reproachful attitude toward Job. At the same time, they are able to take the words of Job's friend as a starting point for moral reflections about the power, justice and benevolence of God and about the limits of the human mind to grasp divine truths. Therefore, Zophar appears to be a false accuser and a man full of resentment (JULIAN OF ECLANUM, CHRYSOSTOM, DIDYMUS, HESYCHIUS), but, at the same time, his words contain some truth that can be used for the moral instruction of the faithful (CHRYSOSTOM, GREGORY, EPHREM). The secret works of supreme wisdom are when God forsakes those whom he has created, enlightening them yet by permitting temptation of the flesh. When one is at the same time being enlightened by contemplation's uplifting and obscured by the pressure of temptation, the soul then strains forward all the more to see what it should desire (GREGORY).

11:1-2 Should Words Go Unanswered?

ZOPHAR'S AUDACIOUS WORDS. DIDYMUS THE BLIND: Since Zophar does not recognize Job's virtue and the goal of his consistent remarks, he says to Job, "Do not talk much." The word of holy Scripture teaches us to control our words. It says, "When words are many, transgression is not lacking."[1] Here Scripture calls the utterance of inappropriate things "many words." But it is not the number of uttered words that make a babbler. The apostle shows this when he "continued speaking until midnight."[2] One can, however, be astonished about Zophar's audacity toward Job. Although he answered Job, Zophar claimed that there was no one to answer him. Thereby Zophar shows one should not speak too audaciously, yet he does so himself in maintaining that Job is suffering due to his personal wickedness. COMMENTARY ON JOB 11.3.[3]

ACCUSATIONS OF VERBOSITY. JULIAN OF ECLANUM: Do you think that by speaking many words you will improve your position and reduce us to silence and amazement with a long speech? Since the holy Job was not only proven innocent of any crime by using just arguments but also called God to his trial as a witness of his upright life, Zophar tries to accuse him first of verbosity

and then of unrighteousness. By demonstrating Job's biased opinion about God's power and wisdom, Zophar tries to show what had inconsiderately erupted in the freedom of Job's words. It would have been fitting [for Job] to remember the weakness of his nature. EXPOSITION ON THE BOOK OF JOB 11.1-2.[4]

11:3 Babbling and Being Shamed

ZOPHAR'S RESENTMENT. CHRYSOSTOM: Zophar means, "Is there none to answer you?" meaning other than we ourselves. Or it could mean: "There is nobody who knows your misfortunes, apart from God, and if he had wanted to disgrace you, then you would have been already dead." Notice that, since Job does not say anywhere that he is unjustly suffering and that he has no faults, this is exactly what they resentfully bring up to him. COMMENTARY ON JOB 11.3B.[5]

11:4 Clean in God's Sight

ZOPHAR REFUSES GOD'S TESTIMONY. HESYCHIUS OF JERUSALEM: Previously Job had already said, "If I am ungodly, why have I not died?"[6] Did he not define himself as "blameless"?[7] These words do not belong to Job but to God. It is God, in fact, who designated Job as blameless in his actions and as a man "who turns away from evil."[8] Therefore you (i.e., Zophar) refuse the testimony of God himself. HOMILIES ON JOB 14.11.4-6.[9]

11:5-6 Telling the Secrets of Wisdom

THE SECRET WORKS OF SUPREME WISDOM. GREGORY THE GREAT: The public works of the supreme wisdom are when almighty God rules those whom he creates, brings to an end the good things which he begins and aids by his inspiration those whom he illuminates with the light of his

---

[1]Prov 10:19. [2]Acts 20:7. [3]PTA 3:184-86. [4]CCL 88:32. [5]PTS 35:103. [6]Job 9:29 LXX. [7]Job 1:1, 8; 2:3. [8]Job 1:1, 8; 2:3. [9]PO 42.2:358.

visitation. For it is plain to the eyes of all people that those whom God created of his free bounty, he provides for with lovingkindness. And when he grants spiritual gifts, he himself brings to perfection what he has himself begun in the bounty of his lovingkindness. But the secret works of supreme wisdom are when God forsakes those whom he has created . . . when he enlightens us with the brightness of his illumination and yet by permitting temptation of the flesh, strikes us with the mists of blindness. Or when he does not care to preserve the good gifts he has bestowed to us, when he at the same time prompts the desires of our soul toward himself and yet by a secret judgment presses us with the powerlessness of our weak nature. . . . "For her law is manifold." What should the "law" of God be understood to mean here except for "charity," whereby we ever read in the inward parts in what way the precepts of life should be maintained in outward action? For concerning this law the voice of "Truth" says, "This is my commandment, that you love one another."[10] Concerning it, Paul says, "Love is the fulfilling of the law."[11] In relation to it Paul says again, "Bear one another's burdens, and so fulfill the law of Christ."[12] For how can the law of Christ be more aptly understood than to mean the charity that we then truly fulfill when we bear the burdens of our brothers from the principle of love? MORALS ON THE BOOK OF JOB 10.6-7.[13]

11:7 The Deep Things of God

THE LIMITS OF HUMAN KNOWLEDGE. EPHREM THE SYRIAN: These words mean, "Do you know what the Almighty will do at the end of his works?" I certainly grant that we have experience of things that are otherwise evident and manifest, but they only disclose to us the loftiness of heaven and all divine things. COMMENTARY ON JOB 11.7.[14]

11:8-9 Higher Than Heaven

HOW SMALL HUMANS ARE! CHRYSOSTOM: He

means either, "Can you do anything similar?" or "You are a humble creature in the universe, and consequently you can do nothing; and you are as far from God as 'heaven is removed from earth.'"[15] COMMENTARY ON JOB 11.8A.[16]

11:10-11 God Sees Iniquity

VANITY AND INIQUITY. GREGORY THE GREAT: It very often happens that the spirit already lifts the mind on high, while nonetheless the flesh assails it with pressing temptations. When the soul is led forward to the contemplation of heavenly things, it is repelled by the images of unlawful practice presented to it. The sting of the flesh wounds him suddenly, whom holy contemplation was bearing away beyond the flesh. Therefore, heaven and hell are shut up together, when one and the same mind is simultaneously enlightened by contemplation's uplifting and obscured by the pressure of temptation. The result is the soul strains forward to see what it should desire and yet, because it is bowed down in its thought, is subject to things that should make it blush. For light springs from heaven, but hell is held in darkness. Heaven and hell then are brought into one when the soul that already sees the light of the land above also sustains the darkness of secret temptation coming from the warfare of the flesh. . . . As if we were appending the explanation of the things premised, saying, "Because he sees that by suffering them evil habits gain growth, by judging he brings to nothing his gifts." Now the right order is observed with the account that vanity is to be known, and afterwards iniquity to be considered. For all iniquity is vanity, but not all vanity, iniquity. For we do vain things as often as we give heed to what is transitory. Something is said to vanish that is suddenly withdrawn from the eyes of the beholder. Hence the psalmist says, "Every living human being is altogether vanity."[17] For in this, by living he only tends to destruction and is rightly

[10]Jn 15:12. [11]Rom 13:10. [12]Gal 6:2. [13]LF 18:579-81. [14]ESOO 2:5. [15]Is 55:9. [16]PTS 35:104. [17]Ps 39:5 (38:6 LXX).

called "vanity" indeed. But by no means is his living also rightly called "iniquity." For though it is in punishment of sin that he comes to nothing, yet this particular circumstance is not itself sin that passes swiftly from life. Thus all things are vain that pass by. Solomon speaks the words, "All is vanity."[18] But "iniquity" is fitly introduced immediately after "vanity." For while we are led onwards through some things transitory, we are, to our injury, tied fast to some of them. When the soul does not hold its seat of immutability, running out from itself it goes headlong into evil ways. From vanity, then, the mind sinks into iniquity. Iniquity, being familiar with things mutable, while it is ever being hurried from one sort to another, is defiled by sins springing up. It is also possible that "vanity" may be understood as sin, and that by the title of "iniquity" weightier guilt may be designated. MORALS ON THE BOOK OF JOB 10.17-21.[19]

11:12 Gaining Understanding

THE VANITY OF WORDS. CHRYSOSTOM: Zophar is right in saying, "Like an ass of the desert." The ass does not stop braying. There is no difference, he says, between our words and those incomprehensible sounds that an ass produces at random and foolishly. We criticize everything, with regard to everything, and we put the blame on everything. Again they exhort Job to take care of his life. But that is useless. That is why Job had said, "If I am righteous, I cannot lift up my head."[20] What is the use of that? Job says, I am righteous, but in his judgment, I am impure. COMMENTARY ON JOB 11.8B-12.[21]

---

[18]Eccles 1:2.   [19]LF 18:592-94.   [20]Job 10:15.   [21]PTS 35:104.

11:13-20 THE BLESSING OF REPENTANCE

[13]If you set your heart aright,
     you will stretch out your hands toward
          him.
[14]If iniquity is in your hand, put it far away,
     and let not wickedness dwell in
          your tents.*
[15]Surely then you will lift up your face
          without blemish;†
     you will be secure, and will not fear.
[16]You will forget your misery;
     you will remember it as waters that
          have passed away.‡
[17]And your life will be brighter than the

          noonday;
     its darkness will be like the morning.
[18]And you will have confidence, because
          there is hope;
     you will be protected[e] and take your
          rest in safety.
[19]You will lie down, and none will make you
          afraid;
     many will entreat your favor.
[20]But the eyes of the wicked will fail;
     all way of escape will be lost to them,
     and their hope is to breathe their
          last.

e Or you will look around   *LXX (13-14) For if you have made your heart pure, and lifted up your hands towards him; if there is any iniquity in your hands, put it far from you, and let not unrighteousness lodge in your habitation.   †LXX your face will shine again like pure water   ‡Peshitta you will be led like passing waters

OVERVIEW: The Fathers view the second part of Zophar's speech in an extremely unfavorable light. They perceive his insincerity (OLYMPIODORUS), ignorance (DIDYMUS, CHRYSOSTOM) and hypocrisy (GREGORY). Only Isho'dad reads in Zophar's words an announcement of Job's forthcoming liberation from his afflictions (ISHO'DAD). Zophar wrongly and incessantly repeats that Job's faults have caused his misfortunes (CHRYSOSTOM). Moral virtue must correspond to purity of soul (DIDYMUS). Whoever is rooted in the desire of eternity alone is neither uplifted by good fortune nor shaken by adverse fortune (GREGORY).

11:13-14 Put Wickedness Far Away

INSINCERE ADVICE. OLYMPIODORUS: Here times are changed, and the meaning is, "If you want to obey me, open your arms in prayer to God with a pure heart, and you will never commit iniquity or transgression, and those things which Zophar mentions later will happen to you." And here it seems that Zophar is giving advice to Job, save that he himself strikes him by saying that Job is punished for his sins. COMMENTARY ON JOB 11.13-14.[1]

ZOPHAR IS WRONG. DIDYMUS THE BLIND: Zophar introduces himself as teacher and exhorts Job with the words, "Even if you are very clean, so clean that you stretch your hands continuously in prayer and ask for God's gifts, be still prepared to reject the evil that remains within you. Iniquity shall not reside in you." That means, "Even if you somehow start to do unrighteousness, iniquity shall not stay to nest in your life." Here Zophar means the following: Moral virtue must correspond to the purity of soul [and reason]. Similar to this is, "Lifting up holy hands without anger or argument."[2] But Zophar is wrong if he deems it possible to have a pure heart and unjust deeds [at the same time]. The opposite, one could say, would be possible, namely, to have righteous deeds and an impure heart. One

would thereby indicate that if someone acts mercifully with an impure heart only to be seen by the people, the deed looks the same. COMMENTARY ON JOB 11.13-14.[3]

11:15 Then You Will Not Fear

THE IGNORANCE OF ZOPHAR. CHRYSOSTOM: For Job said, in fact, that a change was impossible: "If I wash myself with snow [that will be of no use], you have deeply plunged me into the mire."[4] That is why Zophar says, "Your face will shine again like pure water." The whole of Zophar's reflections is certainly excellent. The fact, however, that he incessantly repeats that Job's faults have caused his misfortunes is undoubtedly wrong. It is as though Zophar wanted to exhort Job to be converted to virtue, while he was not in sin at all. To say such things demonstrates Zophar's ignorance and the fact that he understood nothing. COMMENTARY ON JOB 11.15-16.[5]

11:16 Your Affliction Will Pass Away

JOB'S AFFLICTIONS WILL END. ISHO'DAD OF MERV: The words "You will be led like passing waters" mean that your tribulations will leave you at once, like the waters of rain which, when it stops raining, disappear as well. COMMENTARY ON JOB 11.16.[6]

11:19-20 You Will Not Fear

ZOPHAR'S HYPOCRITICAL WORDS. GREGORY THE GREAT: Whoever seeks present glory doubtless dreads contempt. He who is ever hungering for gain is ever surely in fear of loss. For that very object, which seems medicine to him, wounds him with its loss. As he is riveted under fetters to things mutable and destined to perish, so he lies groveling beneath them far away from the strong-

[1]PTS 24:113. [2]1 Tim 2:8. [3]PTA 3:206-8. [4]Job 9:30-31. [5]PTS 35:105. [6]CSCO 229:246.

hold of security. But, on the other hand, whoever is rooted in the desire of eternity alone is neither uplifted by good fortune nor shaken by adverse fortune. For while he has nothing in the world that he desires, there is nothing that he dreads from the world. . . . But herein, it is to be known, that when bad people deliver right sentiments, it is very hard for them not to let themselves be revealed by those things that they are secretly pursuing within. Hence Zophar adds, "Many will entreat your favor." For the righteous do not keep themselves on the narrow paths of innocence with the aim in view that others may implore them. Whether heretics or any others that are perverse, all of them live with an appearance of innocence among each other; they have the desire to show themselves as intercessors on behalf of others when in their speech they convey the holy truths they are longing for. They also promise them to others as something great. And while they tell of heavenly things, they soon show by their pledges what their hearts are bent on. But lest by long continuance of promising earthly things, they may be made to appear as they are, they quickly return to words of uprightness. Then it is immediately added, "But the eyes of

the wicked shall fail, and refuge shall perish from them." By designation of "eyes," the energy of the intention is presented to us. "Truth" testifies in the Gospel, saying, "If your eye shall be single, your whole body shall be full of light."[7] For in view of the fact that a pure intention has preceded our action, it may seem otherwise to men. Yet, to the eyes of our interior Judge, the body of the deed that follows is presented pure. Therefore "the eyes" of the wicked are the intentions of carnal desires in them; these fail for the reason that they are careless of their eternal interests and are ever looking for transitory interests. . . . What does the sinner hope for here in all his thoughts except to surpass others in power, to go beyond all people in the abundance of his possessions, to bow down his rivals in lording it over them, to display himself as an object of admiration to his followers, to gratify anger at will, to make himself known as kind and gracious when he is commended, whatever his appetite may long for, to acquiesce in all that pleasure dictates by the fulfilling of the thing? MORALS ON THE BOOK OF JOB 10.39-42.[8]

---

[7]Mt 6:22. [8]LF 18:607-10*.

12:1-6 JOB'S IRONIC REMARKS ON HIS FRIENDS' WISDOM

[1] Then Job answered:
[2]"No doubt you are the people,
    and wisdom will die with you.*
[3]But I have understanding† as well as
    you;
  I am not inferior to you.
  Who does not know such things as these?

[4]I am a laughingstock to my friends;
  I, who called upon God and he
    answered me,
  a just and blameless man, am a
    laughingstock.
[5]In the thought of one who is at ease there
    is contempt for misfortune;

it is ready for those whose feet slip.[‡]
    [6]*The tents of robbers are at peace,*

and those who provoke God are secure,
    who bring their god in their hand."[f§]

[f] Hebrew uncertain   *LXX *So are you really men, and shall wisdom die with you?*   [†]Vg *a heart*   [‡]LXX *For it had been ordained that I should fall under others at the appointed time and that my houses should be spoiled by transgressors.*   [§]Vg *The tents of robbers are abundant, and they provoke God, since he gave everything into their hands.*

OVERVIEW: All the Fathers agree in considering Job's reproachful and critical words against his friends to be amply justified and correct. In their speeches Job's friends show only false wisdom and conceit (HESYCHIUS, PHILIP, DIDYMUS). Though Job is blameless and in the power of God (CHRYSOSTOM), his friends want to show that he is punished because of his sins, while they are secure from afflictions (JULIAN OF ECLANUM). God tests the righteous and shows tolerance with sinners (HESYCHIUS).

12:1-2 No Doubt You Are the People

NO DEMONSTRATION OF WISDOM. HESYCHIUS OF JERUSALEM: Job speaks in an admirable way. Instead of briefly saying, "You would not be able to be men," he questions them, and what does he ask? "So are you really men, and shall wisdom die with you?" This means, "Is the honor of rational beings really intact within you? Do you know the decisions that God forms with regard to sinners and righteous people?" It is convenient, in fact, that people are aware of this. Know that God tests the righteous and shows tolerance with sinners. That is why the latter are wealthy and the former in the ordeal, because for sinners God's long tolerance will be the reason for a return to repentance, while to the righteous the long battle will offer the occasion to be crowned. If you knew that, you would not condemn the righteous person who is in the ordeal, and you would not consider the sinner who is wealthy, as the righteous. HOMILIES ON JOB 15.12.2.[1]

12:3 Job Also Has Understanding

ABSOLUTE CONCEIT. PHILIP THE PRIEST: Job is saying, "Do you consider yourselves the only one who is wise? And do you think that after you there will be no wise person?" COMMENTARY ON THE BOOK OF JOB 12.[2]

WRONG PERCEPTIONS. DIDYMUS THE BLIND: Job wants to reveal their wrong perceptions with the words, "But I have understanding as well as you," and still I do not think the same thoughts as you. Or do you think that your thinking is unsurpassed? I am reasonable too, and reason is not different from reason, but the difference is in the application. So it is said for example about the evil ones, "Listen to me, you stubborn of heart,"[3] for not the creature but its evil activity he calls "stubbornness of heart." COMMENTARY ON JOB 12.3.[4]

12:4-5 I Am a Laughingstock

A BLAMELESS MAN IN THE POWER OF GOD. CHRYSOSTOM: "Did I lose my common sense, by any chance," Job says, "because I fell into misery?" Here he presents himself as a righteous man, not by testifying to his perfect virtue but to the fact that he did not do anything wrong to anyone and that nobody can blame him. "And that my houses should be spoiled by transgressors,"[5] it was necessary that this happened, he says. It had been ordained from above. "However," he says, "do not believe that these misfortunes will stop for me. Indeed, if I, who have committed no act of injustice, suffer so, the wicked will suffer even more so." COMMENTARY ON JOB 12.2-5.[6]

---

[1]PO 42.2:374.   [2]PL 26:645.   [3]Is 46:12.   [4]PTA 33.1:40-42.   [5]See LXX.   [6]PTS 35:106.

12:6 The Wicked Are Secure

A CHARGE AGAINST GOD'S JUSTICE. JULIAN OF ECLANUM: Certainly the subtlety of your entire conjecture leans toward this, that is, to a reflection on the merits for prosperity and misfortune, so that you want to show that I am guilty, and you righteous, because not even a contrary breath blows against you. This is a plain accusation against the justice of God or a way to lay blame on his patience. "The tents are abundant," those, whom above he had called "rich," he now accuses of corruption by the name of "robbers." EXPOSITION ON THE BOOK OF JOB 12.6.[7]

---

[7]CCL 88:35.

12:7-25 JOB RECOGNIZES GOD'S OMNIPOTENCE AND REFLECTS ON HIS JUSTICE

[7]But ask the beasts, and they will teach
    you;
  the birds of the air, and they will tell
    you;
[8]or the plants of the earth,[g] and they will
    teach you;
  and the fish of the sea will declare to you.
[9]Who among all these does not know
  that the hand of the LORD has done this?
[10]In his hand is the life of every living thing
  and the breath of all mankind.
[11]Does not the ear try words
  as the palate tastes food?*
[12]Wisdom is with the aged,
  and understanding in length of days.

[13]With God[h] are wisdom and might;
  he has counsel and understanding.[†]
[14]If he tears down, none can rebuild;
  if he shuts a man in, none can open.
[15]If he withholds the waters, they dry up;
  if he sends them out, they overwhelm
    the land.

[16]With him are strength and wisdom;
  the deceived and the deceiver are his.
[17]He leads counselors away stripped,
  and judges he makes fools.[‡]
[18]He looses the bonds of kings,
  and binds a waistcloth on their loins.
[19]He leads priests away stripped,[§]
  and overthrows the mighty.
[20]He deprives of speech those who are
    trusted,
  and takes away the discernment of the
    elders.[#]
[21]He pours contempt on princes,
  and looses the belt of the strong.**
[22]He uncovers the deeps out of darkness,
  and brings deep darkness to light.[††]
[23]He makes nations great, and he destroys
    them:
  he enlarges nations, and leads them away.
[24]He takes away understanding from the
    chiefs of the people of the earth,
  and makes them wander in a pathless
    waste.

^{25}*They grope in the dark without light;*
and he makes them stagger like a drunken man.‡‡

g *Or speak to the earth* h *Heb him* *LXX *It is reason which discerns words, and the palate which recognizes the taste of foods.* †LXX (12-13) *In length of time is wisdom, and in long life knowledge. With him are wisdom and power, with him counsel and understanding.* ‡Vg (16-17) *He knows both the deceiver and deceived, he brings counselors to a foolish end and judges to dullness.* §Peshitta *He leads priests away in amazement.* #Vg *By changing the lips of those, who speak truly, and by taking away the doctrine of the elders.* **Vg *and lifts up those who were oppressed* ††LXX *Revealing deep things out of darkness, and he has brought into light the shadow of death.* ‡‡LXX (24-25) *Perplexing the minds of the princes of the earth, and he causes them to wander in a way, they have not known, saying, Let them grope in darkness, and let there be no light, and let them wander as a drunken man.*

OVERVIEW: In the second part of Job's speech, the Fathers distinguished and underlined two main aspects: the moral and edifying content of his words and an openly prophetic and allegorical meaning that is constantly placed side by side. So they describe, through Job's words, the power of God, and they discuss the possibility granted to the faithful to grasp it (CHRYSOSTOM, DIDYMUS, GREGORY, JULIAN OF ECLANUM). At the same time, they recognize in Job's words constant hints and figures of the advent and passion of Christ and of his universal and eternal power (CHRYSOSTOM, PHILIP, OLYMPIODORUS). Ephrem reads in Job's words a foreshadowing of the figure of the high priest who symbolically represents both Christ and the new priest in the church of Christ. God's true priests are led away sacrificially in order that they may be astonished at the prodigies that are brought out against the impious (EPHREM). Christ destroyed death when he took it by humbling himself to die in it (PHILIP).

This passage gave the Fathers occasion to distinguish sense and reason. As God has granted us a palate to recognize the taste of foods, he has also given us reason to make our decisions; in the former we are like the animals, and the latter, unlike (CHRYSOSTOM, DIDYMUS). Even if we possess reason to discern, we need a long time to find things out (CHRYSOSTOM). To us he first gives the lesson of mildness, and afterwards at the judgment he will show his strength (GREGORY). God finally manifests the things which are hidden to all (OLYMPIODORUS). Viewed in the light of his providence, everything is shown according to his will and authority (JULIAN THE ARIAN).

12:7-10 *Life and Breath Are in God's Hand*

THE PASSION OF CHRIST FORESHADOWED. CHRYSOSTOM: Why do you behave as if you had made a great and wonderful discovery? It was necessary, in fact, that such a man died, and nobody ignores it. At the same time, we all know that "in his hand is the life of every human being." Do you see how not only creation but Providence also testifies to God? They both give witness that he controls everything and supports both the life and soul of human beings, so well that he can, when he wants, punish and correct them. COMMENTARY ON JOB 12.7A-10B.[1]

12:11 *The Ear Tests Words*

THE GIFT OF HUMAN REASON. CHRYSOSTOM: "It is reason that discerns words, and the palate that recognizes the taste of foods." Job means, if animals know those things, we, who are endowed with reason, and not only with a palate to eat, know them even better. Or it means, since I am not devoid of reason, I know that. In fact, if God has granted us a palate to recognize the taste of foods, he has also given us reason to make our decisions and the time to acquire knowledge. COMMENTARY ON JOB 12.11A.[2]

WHO CAN UNDERSTAND THE RESOLUTIONS OF PROVIDENCE? DIDYMUS THE BLIND: Consider if this does not refer to the following words, "But ask the animals, and they will teach you."[3]

---

[1]PTS 35:107. [2]PTS 35:107. [3]Job 12:7.

The sequence of these two thoughts makes it clear that it is not given to unreasonable animals or soulless things to understand the resolutions of Providence, but it is given to reason. There is an example, as the palate judges food, so reason judges what is said and what is in the nature of the cosmos. "Consider also this yourselves," he says to his friends, "and you will find out the nature of what happened to me." COMMENTARY ON JOB 12.11.[4]

12:12-13 Wisdom and Understanding

TIME IS NEEDED TO UNDERSTAND. CHRYSOSTOM: "In the length of time is wisdom, and in long life knowledge." In this passage it can be gathered that reason is natural to humanity as well as eating; or, at the beginning he said, "Are you really the only men?"[5] Since I am a man, he means, I can understand what you also understand. "In length of time," he says, "is wisdom." It seems to me that he is criticizing them. "Do you believe," he says, "that you have found out all things?" Even if we possess reason to discern, we need a long time to find out things. "With him are wisdom and power, with him counsel and understanding." "All wisdom indeed," he says, "is in God, in his fullness, and it is in him without any need of time." . . . Therefore, is it possible that since we know that, we also know all things? I know that the wicked are punished; but I am punished despite my justice, so time is needed to understand this. COMMENTARY ON JOB 12.12-13.[6]

12:14-15 Waters Withheld or Sent Out

AN ALLUSION TO CHRIST'S POWER. PHILIP THE PRIEST: It is clear that after [God] has decreed to dissolve or destroy something, according to the judgment of his wisdom, nobody will ever be able to oppose his will. As he destroyed the tower and the kingdoms of many nations, so he announced beforehand that also Jerusalem, where the precepts of his law had been engraved as in stone, had to be torn down under the presence of his grace. And so, according to the prophecy of Job, Christ, who made a new peace in himself by establishing two men in a single new man, destroyed the wall of enmity, that is, the law of the commandments.[7] The God, Christ, destroyed and opened the gates of hell and deposed from his reign the devil, who had the power of death. The God, Christ, destroyed death, when he took it by deigning to die in it. And while he destroyed the body of sin on the cross, he annihilated the old man in us by killing it, so that he might give eternal life back to us. COMMENTARY ON THE BOOK OF JOB 12.[8]

12:16-17 Strength and Wisdom with God

STRENGTH, KNOWLEDGE AND JUSTICE OF GOD. GREGORY THE GREAT: When almighty God in the mystery of his mercy was made man, he first gave the lesson of mildness, and afterwards at the judgment he will show his strength. It is correct to say that in the place above, wisdom is mentioned before strength, as the thing is spoken of the only begotten Son of the Father, "With him is wisdom and strength."[9] In view of the fact that as he comes to judge, he will appear in the terribleness of his power, and the damned being cast off, he will manifest to his elect in his everlasting kingdom. How he is "the wisdom of the Father" is rightly said in the subsequent sentence, that with him is first "strength" and then "wisdom." . . . Whereas everyone who strives to deceive his neighbor is wicked, "Truth" says to the wicked, "I never knew you; depart from me, you evildoers." In what sense is it said here that "the Lord knows the deceiver"? But God's "knowing" sometimes means his taking notice or acknowledging, sometimes his approving; God at once knows a wicked person, in that in taking notice of him he judges him (for he would never judge any wicked person, if he did not take notice

---

[4]PTA 33.1:52. [5]Job 12:2. [6]PTS 35:107-8. [7]Eph 2:14-15. [8]PL 26:645-46. [9]Mt 7:23.

of him), and yet he does not know a wicked person in that he does not approve of his actions. So, God both knows him, in that he finds him out, and doesn't know him, in that he does not acknowledge him in a likeness of his own wisdom. . . . The only begotten Son of the most high Father, because he was made man and preached eternal truths, is therefore called the "Angel of great counsel." We rightly interpret "the counselors" as those preachers who furnish the counsel of life to their hearers. However, when any preacher preaches the truths of eternity that he may acquire temporal gains, he is assuredly brought to a foolish end; he is aiming to reach that point by laborious effort. Hence, he ought to have fled in uprightness of mind. And it is rightly added, "And the judges to dullness." For all that are set over the examination of other people's conduct are rightly called "judges." But when he who has this oversight does not diligently examine the lives of those under his authority or acquaint himself with whom he should correct, "the judge is brought to dullness," in that he, who should have judged things that were ill, never finds out those things that are to be judged. MORALS ON THE BOOK OF JOB 11.17-20.[10]

12:18-19 Overthrowing the Mighty

A REFERENCE TO JOB AND MELCHIZEDEK. EPHREM THE SYRIAN: These words must not refer to the sons of Aaron, who did not live anymore at that time, but to priests such as Job himself and Melchizedek. If the narrative is about real and holy priests, how is it said that they are led away in amazement? Evidently, [they are led away] in order that they may be astonished and admire the prodigies that are brought agains the impious through the decision of God and through the godhead. And so Job proceeds to relate here the admirable things that through the power and will of God happen in the sea, among the nations, among the kings and the leaders, and among all those, who prevail with force, deal with weapons and are called to war. Therefore, he sub-

mits. COMMENTARY ON JOB 12.19.[11]

12:20-21 Contempt Poured on Princes

THE ABSOLUTE POWER OF GOD ON MORTALS. JULIAN OF ECLANUM: "By changing the speech of those who speak truly." He is not referring here to those who speak truly, so much as to those who believe they speak truly. He convinces them of their falsehood when he makes what they had predicted happen in a different way.

"By taking away the doctrine of the elders," Job shows them that the frustration of their projects occurs without any consideration for their authority. "He pours contempt on princes," both those who are entrusted with teaching and the leaders who take care of the administration of common goods. When God opposes them, they lose completely the high position they previously had where they stood. "He lifts up those who were oppressed." After showing what God can do to these people, who are considered to be illustrious, he includes the wealth and protection he can grant to the humble, so that the divine power may be known by both these classes of people. EXPOSITION ON THE BOOK OF JOB 12.20-21.[12]

12:22 Bringing Darkness to Light

A PROPHECY OF CHRIST'S ADVENT. OLYMPIODORUS: "Revealing deep things out of darkness, and he has brought into light the shadow of death." The literal meaning is, "He manifests the things which are hidden to all, and preserves those who are in danger and close to death." He calls danger "the shadow of death," because, as shadow is very close to the body that produces it, so danger is very close to the death that causes it. However, the profound meaning of this sentence appears to announce prophetically the advent of the Lord, who said to the prisoners, "Come out, and to those who are in the shadow, show yourselves,"[13] "and appeared to those, who sit in dark-

---

[10]LF 21:12-14. [11]ESOO 2:5. [12]CCL 88:36. [13]Is 49:9.

ness and in the shadow of death."[14] COMMEN-
TARY ON JOB 12.22.[15]

12:23-25 Making and Destroying Nations

JOB UNDERSTANDS GOD'S PROVIDENCE. JULIAN
THE ARIAN: And after that Job said, "He brought
the shadow of death into light"[16] (that is, the fear
of death. In fact, when such a thing is feared,
understanding it redeems us from such fear) by
mentioning the details of the many facts and by
showing the providence deriving from them. Job
did this so that no one may believe that simply
from the details of the facts one is able to understand the providence of God, or that God exercises his control on people one by one [and not in
a general way]. And, in the same way, Job finally
produces the general truth on the nations. That
is, that the nations that sinned were destroyed
because of their thoughtlessness, like the Sodomites, the Canaanites and the Egyptians, who,
for this reason, were wiped out in their catastro-
phe by the wrath of God. Also, the Israelites who,
after being guided by God, settled down in the
land of Palestine. Even though one may announce
that these nations are now pacified in harmony
with one another, nothing can be gained by them.
In fact, their thoughtlessness misled them, and
for this reason they were wiped out without
understanding their ruin. The night took them
instead of daylight, and they staggered like a
drunkard, falling into shadow in their belching.
"Therefore, I can observe the whole of his providence, in detail and in general, and nothing
remains hidden from me, as you think; indeed I
do not ignore his power and his justice. Everything is shown according to his will and authority." COMMENTARY ON JOB 12.23-25.[17]

---

[14]Lk 1:79. [15]PTS 24:123. [16]Job 12:22 LXX. [17]PTS 14:92.

13:1-12 JOB CRITICIZES
THE WORDS OF HIS FRIENDS

¹Lo, my eye has seen all this,
  my ear has heard and understood it.
²What you know, I also know;
  I am not inferior to you.
³But I would speak to the Almighty,
  and I desire to argue my case with
    God.*
⁴As for you, you whitewash with lies;
  worthless physicians are you all.
⁵Oh that you would keep silent,
  and it would be your wisdom!†
⁶Hear now my reasoning,
and listen to the pleadings of my
  lips.
⁷Will you speak falsely for God,
  and speak deceitfully for him?‡
⁸Will you show partiality toward him,
  will you plead the case for God?
⁹Will it be well with you when he searches
    you out?
  Or can you deceive him, as one deceives
    a man?
¹⁰He will surely rebuke you§
  if in secret you show partiality.

¹¹Will not his majesty terrify you,
and the dread of him fall upon you?

¹²Your maxims are proverbs of ashes,
your defenses are defenses of clay.

LXX Nevertheless I will speak to the Lord, and I will reason before him, if he wants to.   †LXX (4-5) But you are all bad physicians, and healers of diseases. But would that you were silent, and it would be wisdom to you in the end.   ‡LXX But hear the reasoning of my mouth, and attend to the judgment of my lips. Do you not speak before the Lord, and utter deceit before him?   §LXX (8b-10a) Or will you draw back? Nay, do you yourselves be judges. For if God follows your traces, even though you do all things in your power to place yourselves in his way, he will nonetheless condemn you.

OVERVIEW: Job's reproaches and critical remarks against his friends' positions and opinions continue in Job 13. The attitude of the Fathers does not change and is consistent with what they had expressed in the previous chapter. They emphasize again how Job's words are a source of moral instruction for the faithful (HESYCHIUS, DIDYMUS, CHRYSOSTOM, OLYMPIODORUS) and how his teaching contains prophetic references to the near and distant future (GREGORY, CHRYSOSTOM, ISHO'DAD). Job heard and saw with understanding things past and future things as if they were all in the present (GREGORY). With deep humility he seeks to argue his case with God (HESYCHIUS). Silence is better than senseless words (DIDYMUS, CHRYSOSTOM). God hears false speech (OLYMPIODORUS).

13:1-2 I Have Seen and Understood

SEEING, HEARING AND UNDERSTANDING.
GREGORY THE GREAT: For Job saw what was to follow as present in him; it was not as if future things came to Job or things from the past; but all things are present at once and together before his eyes. And because he saw the very things that were to come were in part works and in part words, it is rightly said, "My eye has seen and my ear has heard all this." However, words are without use if those who use them do not understand them. Hence it is fitly added, "And I have understood it." For if something is shown or heard but the understanding of it is not bestowed, it is insignificant as prophecy. Thus Pharaoh saw in a dream things that were to come upon Egypt, but because he could not understand what he saw, he was no prophet. King Belshazzar "saw the fingers of the hand that wrote"[1] on the wall, but he was no prophet, because he did not attain to the understanding of that which he saw. Therefore, in order that blessed Job might testify that he had the spirit of prophecy, he declares not only that he had "seen and heard" but also that he had "understood all this." Yet Job is not elated on the grounds of such understanding; his appended words bear witness when he says, "What you know, I also know; I am not inferior to you." By these same words, he made known what exceeding humility he had, who says that he was "not inferior" to them. Job by far surpassed them in holiness of life. For he proves that "what they knew he knew," who by knowing all things of heaven transcended their earthly thoughts through the spirit of prophecy. MORALS ON THE BOOK OF JOB 11.31-32.[2]

13:3 I Desire to Argue My Case with God

JOB ACKNOWLEDGES GOD'S POWER AND JUSTICE. HESYCHIUS OF JERUSALEM: This means, "I know the tremendous greatness of God, the endless wisdom of the Creator and his prodigious power; but even though I know that, 'I will speak to the Lord,' because if I know his power, I also know his justice. For he is just, he supports those who in the meantime, without rendering themselves accusers, speak to him. This teaches people that even though they are very righteous, they have to accept the judgments given to them. That is why 'I will reason before him, if he wants to.' For if he does not want, I will remain silent, because I know what is honorable to the servant.

---

[1]Dan 5:5.   [2]LF 21:22*.

It is according to the command of the Lord that I will speak and will have the boldness to 'reason before him.'" HOMILIES ON JOB 15.13.3.[3]

13:4-5 If You Would Only Keep Silent!

A TIME TO SPEAK AND A TIME TO REMAIN SILENT. DIDYMUS THE BLIND: A worthless physician is literally one who applies curing strategies that are not useful for the suffering. This happens in two ways: either it is due to lack of experience in the physician or to his wickedness. The friends who are contradicted here speak out of a lack of knowledge rather than wickedness in saying, "You suffer due to your sins." They think they are bringing words of comfort. They were worthless physicians since they did not discover the true reason. "Whitewash with lies," Job says against them, who think highly of themselves as if they could cure the affliction that occurs in others. He wishes that they had knowledge of the right times, to speak when it is appropriate and to be silent when it is appropriate, since they have realized their mistake. For that would be the beginning and commencement of wisdom for them. For once they learn that one can also be suffering for a different reason, namely, for inherent virtue to become visible, then Job's friends will possess wisdom. Even for those who long for insight, it is beneficial to restrain their speech. In Proverbs it is said, "Even fools who keep silent are considered wise."[4] For if someone realizes that he needs the illuminating teaching of a teacher, this will make him wise. As someone who can talk and teach about wisdom is wise and a teacher, likewise is the one partially wise, who is able to ask what needs to be asked. He did not call him "fool" because he lacked insight altogether but because he had deficiency of insight. The word "If you would only keep silent" is similar to "There is a time, when one has to be silent." However, since one has to talk, when one has become wise, he adds, "But there is a time to speak."[5] COMMENTARY ON JOB 13.4-5.[6]

SILENCE IS BETTER THAN SENSELESS WORDS. CHRYSOSTOM: Indeed, when senseless words are spoken, it is better to remain in silence, and in being silent, one will show greater wisdom than in speaking. COMMENTARY ON JOB 13.4-5.[7]

13:6-7 Will You Speak Falsely for God?

GOD HEARS FALSE SPEECH. OLYMPIODORUS: "Consider now the words which I am about to say in order to correct you, and then judge whether I pronounce them thoughtfully." "Do you not speak before the Lord and utter deceit before him?" "Do you not realize that God hears your speeches? How do you dare, while he hears you, say false words?" Consider also these words from that blameless and truthful man, how falsehood is able to blame everything, even when one appears to speak according to God. Therefore Job ponders with truth and frankness all the words that are spoken, so that God himself may approve him, as God is the truth. Falsehood, in fact, comes from the evil one,[8] as the Savior says. COMMENTARY ON JOB 13.6-7.[9]

13:8-10 God Will Rebuke

GOD WILL PUNISH PARTIALITY. CHRYSOSTOM: "If he follows your traces," Job says. Therefore you, who speak so now would have not spoken so, if you were directly involved in the case that is judged. That is, if you were in my place and God were judging your matters with severity, you would have not judged my words as you do now. Or, to say things in a different manner, you, who speak so, would have not been judges of my words. In fact, Job says, even if you speak more, and you do everything to speak in God's favor, he will not confound you any less and will ask you for explanations. COMMENTARY ON JOB 13.8-10A.[10]

---

[3]PO 42.2:396. [4]Prov 17:28. [5]Eccles 3:7. [6]PTA 33.1:84-86. [7]PTS 35:109. [8]See Mt 5:37. [9]PTS 24:125. [10]PTS 35:110.

13:11-12 God's Majesty Will Terrify Them

TERRIFIED BY GOD. ISHOʻDAD OF MERV: The author seems to say that Job's friends will abstain from pronouncing reproaches, because of the fear of God and the terror that he inspires. COMMENTARY ON JOB 13.11.[11]

---

[11]CSCO 229:247.

13:13-28 JOB PLEADS WITH GOD TO KNOW HIS SINS

[13]Let me have silence, and I will speak,
  and let come on me what may.
[14]I will take[i] my flesh in my teeth,
  and put my life in my hand.[*]
[15]Behold, he will slay me; I have no hope;
  yet I will defend my ways to his face.[†]
[16]This will be my salvation,
  that a godless man shall not come before him.[‡]
[17]Listen carefully to my words,
  and let my declaration be in your ears.
[18]Behold, I have prepared my case;
  I know that I shall be vindicated.
[19]Who is there that will contend with me?
  For then I would be silent and die.[§]
[20]Only grant two things to me,
  then I will not hide myself from thy face:
[21]withdraw thy hand far from me,
  and let not dread of thee terrify me.
[22]Then call, and I will answer;
  or let me speak, and do thou reply to me.
[23]How many are my iniquities and my sins?
  Make me know my transgression and my sin.
[24]Why dost thou hide thy face,
  and count me as thy enemy?
[25]Wilt thou frighten a driven leaf
  and pursue dry chaff?
[26]For thou writest bitter things against me,
  and makest me inherit the iniquities of my youth.
[27]Thou puttest my feet in the stocks,
  and watchest all my paths;
  thou settest a bound to the soles of my feet.[#]
[28]Man[j] wastes away like a rotten thing,
  like a garment that is moth-eaten.

i Gk: Heb Why should I take?   j Heb He   *Peshitta Even if he kills me, I will be ready.   †LXX (13-14) Be silent, that I may speak, and cease from my anger, while I may take my flesh in my teeth, and put my life in my hand.   ‡LXX (15-16) Though the mighty One should lay hand upon me, forasmuch as he has begun, verily I will speak to him, and plead before him. And this shall turn to me for salvation; for fraud shall have no entrance before him.   §LXX (17-19) Hear, hear my words, for I will declare in your hearing. Behold, I am near my judgment, I know that I shall appear evidently just. For who is he that shall plead with me, that I should now be silent, and expire?   #Peshitta you observe the strength of my feet

OVERVIEW: In the second part of Job's speech the Fathers notice three main aspects: an expression of despair and grief that is proper to the weakness of human nature (CHRYSOSTOM, GREGORY, ISHO'DAD); a prophetic foreshadowing and invocation of the redemption in Christ (GREGORY); and an absolute faith in God that is not destroyed by Job's afflictions and sufferings (EPHREM, OLYMPIODORUS, DIDYMUS, CHRYSOSTOM). Job prays both for his hearing and his being heard (GREGORY). There are two ways of hiding before God: hiding from God and being hidden in God. To be hidden in God is salvation, but to hide oneself from God is ruinous. The righteous are consoled to know the reason for their punishment. The human mind is agitated by as many gusts as it undergoes temptations (CHRYSOSTOM).

13:13-14 Job's Life in His Own Hand

JOB'S CONSOLATION. CHRYSOSTOM: As those, Job says, who devour themselves have a consolation, as those who bite their flesh feel a certain relief in their sufferings, so it is the same with me, when I express myself in these terms, "And I may put my life in my hands." Consider, above all, this sentence, "I may put my life in my hand." This means, I will destroy myself! Like those who destroy themselves, I also find a consolation; and that is my consolation, if God does not cause me to perish, my consolation is to give expression to my thoughts. COMMENTARY ON JOB 13.13-14B.[1]

13:15 Job Will Defend His Ways

ABSOLUTE FAITH. EPHREM THE SYRIAN: These words mean, "Even if he kills me, I will support myself with my hope and faith in him." O admirable man, who, being destined to be killed, praises his killer and looks at him. Indeed Job knew that if he had taken away his life, the same one who is the Lord of Abraham, would have given it back to him. He believed that God was able to make alive those who had died. COMMENTARY ON JOB 13.15.[2]

13:16 Job's Salvation

JOB'S HONEST WORDS. CHRYSOSTOM: "And he shall turn to me for salvation; for fraud shall gain no entrance before him." This means, my consolation is that "fraud shall gain no entrance before him." "You see, I do not speak like you, with hidden thoughts. I know that there is no dissimulation in him." COMMENTARY ON JOB 13.15B-16.[3]

13:17-19 I Shall Be Vindicated

JOB'S TRUST IN GOD. OLYMPIODORUS: The Lord is near those, it is said, who invoke him, and therefore God is kindly disposed toward them. So listen, Job says, to what I am about to say: I will maintain my kindly disposed judgment upon God, who is just and speaks truthfully; and by trusting his truthfulness, I believe that I will appear to say words more righteous than yours. Or, in a different sense, "I am near my judgment," that is, I am ready to suffer what God has decreed. Confiding in his truthfulness, I hope I will be seen to be righteous. COMMENTARY ON JOB 13.17-18.[4]

13:20-21 Two Requests

AN INVOCATION FOR THE SEASON OF GRACE AND REDEMPTION. GREGORY THE GREAT: What are we to understand here by the "face of God," except his visitation? While God beholds, he also punishes our sins from which no just person is even hidden if the two things that he entreats are not removed. About this, Job adds, "Withdraw your hand far from me, and do not let dread of you terrify me." Concerning the two, what else does Job ask for in a voice of prophecy, but the season of grace and redemption? For the law held the people abhorrent to the stroke of vengeance, that whoever committed sin under its yoke should be immediately punished with death. Nor did the Jewish people serve God from a principle

---

[1]PTS 35:111. [2]ESOO 2:5. [3]PTS 35:111. [4]PTS 24:127.

of love but of fear. But righteousness can never be perfected by fear, seeing that according to the voice of John, "perfect love casts out fear."[5] And Paul comforts the children of adoption by saying, "For you have not received the spirit of bondage again to fear, but you have received the Spirit of adoption, whereby we cry, Abba, Father."[6] Therefore in the voice of humankind, longing for the hardness of the law's stroke to pass away and eagerly desiring to advance from fear to love, Job names in prayer the "two things God should put far from him," saying, "Withdraw your hand far from me, and do not let dread of you terrify me"; that is, remove from me the hardness of the stroke, take away the weight of dread, and while the grace of love illuminates me, pour upon me the spirit of assurance. If I am not removed far from the rod and from dread, I know that I shall not be withdrawn from the strictness of your searching since he cannot be justified before you, who serves you on a principle of love but of fear. Hence he seeks the very presence of his Creator, as if it were a familiar and bodily way, that he may thereby both hear what he is ignorant of and be heard in the things that he knows. MORALS ON THE BOOK OF JOB 11.54-55.[7]

TO BE HIDDEN BY GOD BRINGS SALVATION. DIDYMUS THE BLIND: The lack of clarity in the text could be explained in the following way. Job says, "If you want to treat me as the friends say, as if you wanted to show my wickedness, I will hide from your face." But if I am right, then "withdraw your hand far from me, and do not let your dread terrify me!" Every sinner hides from God's face, since he does unworthy things. Thus Adam was hiding from God's face.[8] The opposite of this is to be hidden by God according to the word, "In the shelter of your presence you hide them from human plots."[9] This brings salvation since God protects the righteous so that he is not stumbling due to human confusion. The "hiddenness of God's face" in contrast to the revealed might be the mystical thoughts. To gain insight from the works of Providence and God's creation does not happen in hiddenness but in the open. It is written, "For what can be known about God is plain to them, because God has shown it to them. Ever since the creation of the world his eternal power and divine nature, invisible though they are, have been understood and seen through the things he has made."[10] To be hidden by God, as mentioned, is bringing salvation. But to hide oneself as Adam did is ruinous. Since this is not true for Job, because he had no sin, he says, "Withdraw your hand from me" so that the friends may experience that I am not suffering because of sin. For the friends did not believe anything else but that Job suffered for his sins. COMMENTARY ON JOB 13.20-21.[11]

13:22-24 Make Known My Sins

THE PRISON OF JOB'S ANGUISH. CHRYSOSTOM: Why, Job says, do you not act clearly? Why do you not say, See, this is the reason why I punish you? It is no small consolation for those who are chastised to know the reason for their punishment. That is why Job says, "Make me know my transgressions," but God will not let him know. COMMENTARY ON JOB 13.24-25B.[12]

13:25-26 Bitter Things

HUMAN WEAKNESS AND DIVINE SEVERITY. GREGORY THE GREAT: For what is a human being but a leaf who fell in paradise from the tree? What but a leaf is he who is caught by the wind of temptation and lifted up by the gusts of his passions? For the human mind is agitated as it were by as many gusts as it undergoes temptations. Thus very often anger agitates it; when anger is gone, empty mirth follows. It is driven by the goading of lust. The fever of avarice causes the mind to stretch itself far and wide to compass the things that belong to the earth. Sometimes pride lifts it up, and sometimes excessive

---

[5]1 Jn 4:18. [6]Rom 8:15. [7]LF 21:34-35*. [8]Gen 3:8. [9]Ps 31:20 (30:21 LXX). [10]Rom 1:19-20. [11]PTA 33.1:112-14. [12]PTS 35:112.

fear sinks it lower than the dust. Therefore, perceiving that he is lifted and carried by so many gusts of temptation, a human is compared well with a "leaf." . . . For seeing that everything we speak passes away but what we write remains, God is said not to "speak" but to "write bitter things," in that his scourges upon us last for long. For it was once said to man when he sinned, "Dust you are, and into dust you shall return." And angels many times appearing gave commandments to people. Moses, the lawgiver, restrained sins by severe means. The only begotten Son of the most high Father himself came to redeem us. He swallowed up death by dying. He announced that everlasting life to us that he exhibited in himself. Yet that sentence that was given in paradise concerning the death of our flesh remains unaltered from the very beginning

of the human race up to the end of the world. Morals on the Book of Job 11.60-61.[13]

13:27-28 Bounds Set

AFFLICTIONS IMPOSED WITH FORCE AND CARE.
ISHO'DAD OF MERV: "You observe the strength of my feet." The words "you observe" signify God's consideration, because we keep our eye on what we care for. And the words "my feet" refer to the firmness, because feet are supports. But these words are also analogous to the roots of the plants. That is, you have sent me tribulations and imposed them on me with force and care. COMMENTARY ON JOB 13.27.[14]

---

[13]LF 21:37-38*. [14]CSCO 229:247.

14:1-6 HUMAN LIFE IS FRAIL AND SHORT

[1]Man that is born of a woman
  is of few days, and full of trouble.
[2]He comes forth like a flower, and withers;
  he flees like a shadow, and continues
    not.*
[3]And dost thou open thy eyes upon such
  a one
  and bring him[k] into judgment with thee?[†]
[4]Who can bring a clean thing out of
  an unclean?

There is not one.
[5]Since his days are determined,
  and the number of his months is
    with thee,
  and thou hast appointed his bounds
    that he cannot pass,
[6]look away from him, and desist,[l]
  that he may enjoy, like a hireling,
    his day.[‡]

k Gk Syr Vg: Heb *me* l Cn: Heb *that he may desist* *The version of the LXX employed by Hesychius reads *A mortal born of a woman has a short life full of wrath. He, like a flower that has come to bloom, fell after being shaken; and he fled like a shadow, and will not last.* †Vg *Do you deign to open your eyes on such a one, and to bring him into judgment with you?* ‡LXX *stay away from me, so that I may be peaceful, and satisfied about my life like a laborer*

OVERVIEW: The final part of Job's speech is constituted by a detailed reflection on the frailty and

weakness of human life. The Fathers take Job's words as a starting point for further commentary on the human condition in this world and on the reasons that have caused humanity to live in frailty and misery (HESYCHIUS, GREGORY, CHRYSOSTOM). However, God concedes a space for remorse to every human being, who can save themselves from their misery through repentance (DIDYMUS). Analogies between Adam and Job are explored (HESYCHIUS).

14:1-2 Humans Frail and Fleeting

HUMANITY'S CONDITION AFTER THE FALL. HESYCHIUS OF JERUSALEM: Man, who is born of a woman, "has a short life," because he has been ordered to return to the earth.[1] With regard to the expression "full of wrath," Job thinks about that moment in which man received the order to observe the commandment[2] but transgressed it.[3] And therefore "like a flower that has finished blooming, he fell after being shaken"; he bloomed in paradise, so that he imposed a name on every animal. But "he fell after being shaken," when Adam was enticed into the deception of the dragon. At that stage "he fled like a shadow," because, being naked, he concealed himself away from God and hid under a tree of the paradise. When God called him, "Adam, where are you?"[4] he did not show up. . . . Therefore our hope was destroyed. Since he had fallen from paradise, man was deprived of his goods and perished completely, because with a single blow he was condemned as someone who had fallen, without any possibility for us to hope of judgment. In fact, if there is hope for judgment, there is also hope for crowns. HOMILIES ON JOB 16.14.1-2.[5]

14:3 Bringing to Judgment

A SURVEY OF GOD'S POWER AND HUMAN FRAILTY. GREGORY THE GREAT: Job has surveyed both the power of Almighty God and his own frailty. Before he brought himself and God together, he considered who would come into judgment and who would judge. He saw on the one side man, and on the other side his Creator,

that is, dust and God. And Job rightly exclaims, "Do you deign to open your eyes on such a one?" With almighty God, to open the eyes is to execute his judgments, to look upon whom to smite. For as it were, with eyes closed, God does not wish to look at him whom he does not wish to smite. Hence it is immediately added also about the judgment itself, "To bring him into judgment with you?" But whereas Job had viewed God coming to judgment, he again takes a view of his own frailty. He sees that no one who comes forth from uncleanness can be clean by his own will. MORALS ON THE BOOK OF JOB 11.69.[6]

14:4-5 Clean from Unclean?

IMPURITY AND MISERY. CHRYSOSTOM: You see Job taking refuge again in his nature, because it is impossible, he says, to be pure. [He implores God] not only because of our weakness or our ephemeral nature or the disheartening that fills our life, but because it is also impossible to be pure. "Stay away from me, so that I may be peaceful and satisfied about my life like a laborer." Job expresses again the ephemeral, miserable and unhappy character of life. "And since I am overwhelmed and unhappy, I ask only to be left in peace." Then Job demonstrates that human beings are the unhappiest of all, more than trees, rivers and the sea. COMMENTARY ON JOB 14.4-6.[7]

14:6 Look Away from Them

GOD GRANTS A BREAK FOR REMORSE. DIDYMUS THE BLIND: Since God is with Job through the hardships he lays upon him, Job says, "Look away!" in the sense of "Bring your anger to an end!" God approaches in different ways by allowing participation and through anger. The friends had come to the conclusion that Job suffers for his sin. He therefore harshly responds that "The human being has a short life and is like a withered

---

[1]See Gen 3:19. [2]See Gen 2:17. [3]See Gen 3:6. [4]Gen 3:9. [5]PO 42.2:420-22. [6]LF 21:43-44**. [7]PTS 35:114.

flower and a shadow" and "God sees him." In this Job was demonstrating for them that he was not suffering because of sin. He says, "Look away!" If God delivers someone into such a flood of afflictions, the human being has no calm for remorse. Job therefore teaches his friends that their opinion is unreasonable. For he says, "Look away from him and desist, that he may enjoy, like a hireling, his day." In such affliction he would not be able to have calm or to enjoy his life. . . .

But Job spoke this to his friends so that it might be clear that God grants a break in order for remorse to occur. This is why Paul says, "Or do you despise the riches of his kindness and forbearance and patience? Do you not realize that God's kindness is meant to lead you to repentance?"[8] That "desist" is said instead of "end your wickedness and be virtuous" becomes plain in the words "If you have sinned, desist!"[9] And "the earth feared and was still when God rose up to establish judgment."[10] When people realize that God is judge, they desist from sinning. COMMENTARY ON JOB 14.6.[11]

---

[8]Rom 2:4 [9]Gen 4:7. [10]Ps 76:8-9 (75:9-10 LXX). [11]PTA 33.1:132, 134.

14:7-22 IS THERE LIFE AFTER DEATH?

[7]For there is hope for a tree,
    if it be cut down, that it will sprout
        again,
    and that its shoots will not cease.
[8]Though its root grow old in the earth,
    and its stump die in the ground,
[9]yet at the scent of water it will bud
    and put forth branches like a young
        plant.
[10]But man dies, and is laid low;
    man breathes his last, and where is he?
[11]As waters fail from a lake,
    and a river wastes away and dries up,
[12]so man lies down and rises not again;
    till the heavens are no more he will not
        awake,
    or be roused out of his sleep.
[13]Oh that thou wouldest hide me in Sheol,
    that thou wouldest conceal me until thy
        wrath be past,

    that thou wouldest appoint me a set
        time, and remember me!
[14]If a man die, shall he live again?
    All the days of my service I would wait,
    till my release should come.*
[15]Thou wouldest call, and I would answer
        thee;
    thou wouldest long for the work of thy
        hands.
[16]For then thou wouldest number my steps,
    thou wouldest not keep watch over my
        sin;
[17]my transgression would be sealed up in a
        bag,
    and thou wouldest cover over my
        iniquity.

[18]But the mountain falls and crumbles
        away,
    and the rock is removed from its place;

^{19}the waters wear away the stones;
> the torrents wash away the soil of the
> earth;
> so thou destroyest the hope of man.†
^{20}Thou prevailest for ever against him, and
> he passes;
> thou changest his countenance, and

> sendest him away.
^{21}His sons come to honor, and he does not
> know it;
> they are brought low, and he perceives
> it not.
^{22}He feels only the pain of his own body,
> and he mourns only for himself.‡

*LXX (13-14) For oh that you had kept me in the grave, and had hidden me until your wrath should cease, and you should set me a time in which you would remember me! For if a man should die, shall he live again, having accomplished the days of his life? I will wait till I exist again?   †Vg you destroy mortals   ‡LXX (20-22) You drove man to an end, and he is gone, you set your face against him, and sent him away; and even though his children are multiplied, he does not know it; and if they are few, he is not aware. But his flesh is in pain, and his soul mourns.

OVERVIEW: Job's reflections on life and death and on life after death are mostly interpreted by the Fathers as prophetic hints of the rebirth of humankind in Christ. They see in this part of Job's speech a section of the Old Testament that is extremely suitable to a typological interpretation (EPHREM, GREGORY, HESYCHIUS, OLYMPIODORUS, DIDYMUS). At the same time Job's words are edifying and suggest a moral reflection on human pride and ignorance (PHILIP, CHRYSOSTOM). Job pleads to be in God's custody in the netherworld awaiting resurrection rather than to remain alive with these troubles (OLYMPIODORUS).

14:7-10 Cut Down but Sprouting Again

A PROPHECY OF THE REBIRTH IN BAPTISM.
EPHREM THE SYRIAN: Here the blessed Job assumes the role of teacher and prophet, and through the symbol of the tree coming to life again, he predicts his return to his former state. At the same time, Job prophesies that human nature in its entirety will be renewed. Giving vigorous thanks to the perfume of the baptismal waters, the human race will sprout again. Endowed with a new growing foliage, human nature will regain the dignity of its former beauty. After, it will be planted again through the death of the Lord. COMMENTARY ON JOB 14.7.[1]

THE SYMBOL OF THE TREE. GREGORY THE

GREAT: Now because Job's words are clear according to the letter, we must refer the sense to the inward things and search how they are to be understood spiritually. Thus, in holy Scripture by the name of "tree" we have represented sometimes the cross, sometimes the righteous person or even the unrighteous person, and sometimes the Wisdom of God incarnate. Therefore, the cross is denoted by the "tree" when it is said, "Let us put the tree into his bread,"[2] for to "put the tree into the bread" is to apply the cross to the body of our Lord. Again by the title of the "tree" we also have the just person, or even the unjust person, set forth, as the Lord says by the prophet, "I the Lord have brought down the high tree and exalted the low tree."[3] According to the word of the self-same Truth, "Whoever exalts himself shall be humbled; and he who humbles himself shall be exalted."[4] Solomon also says, "If the tree falls towards the south or toward the north, in the place where the tree fell, there it shall be."[5] For in the day of their death the just person does "fall to the south," and the unjust "to the north," as both the just person favored by the Spirit is brought to joy, and the sinner, together with the apostate angel, who said, "I will sit also upon the mount of the testimony, in the sides of the north,"[6] is cast away in his frozen heart. Again, the "tree" represents the Wisdom of God incar-

---

[1]ESOO 2:6. [2]Jer 11:19. [3]Ezek 17:24. [4]Lk 14:11. [5]Eccles 11:3. [6]Is 14:13.

nate. As it is written, "She is a tree of life to them that lay hold on her."[7] And as she herself says, "If they do these things when the tree is green, what shall be done when it is dry?"[8] And so in this text, whereas a tree is preferred above a man, what is man understood as but every carnal person? And what is denoted by the title of the tree but the life of the righteous? "There is the hope that a tree, if it is cut down, will be green again." For when in a death of painful endurance the just person is hard pressed for the truth, in the greenness of everlasting life he is recovered again; and he who here proved green by faith, there becomes green in actual sight. "And his branches shoot," in that it is most often the case that by the sufferings of the just person, all faithful persons are redoubled in the love of the heavenly country. They receive the greenness of the spiritual life, while they are glad for what he courageously did here in God's behalf. MORALS ON THE BOOK OF JOB 12.4.5.[9]

14:11-12 They Will Not Awake

RESURRECTION ON THE DAY OF JUDGMENT. HESYCHIUS OF JERUSALEM: By calling death "sleep," Job has clearly given us the hope for resurrection. However, he says, we will not awake "until heavens are no more." That is obvious, because, as Isaiah said, it is necessary that "they shall be rolled together like a scroll."[10] It is necessary that all their powers are shaken, that the sun and the moon are obscured and that the stars, after being unsettled, fall like leaves. Then, at the sound of the trumpet,[11] the angels will raise us from the dead, as from "sleep," obviously under the order and the sign of God. HOMILIES ON JOB 17.14.12.[12]

14:13-14 Waiting for Release

HOPE FOR RESURRECTION. OLYMPIODORUS: The meaning is, "Oh that in the time when you were inflamed with rage against me, you would have kept me in custody in the netherworld—there, in fact, custody is not due to faults—and that you would not have forgotten me completely but

would have set a time for my custody there!" Job has given us a reason for his desiring death. Without trials, he says, while being kept there, I will wait for resurrection. In fact, Job says, if a person dies after completing the days of this life, he does not withdraw into nonexistence but lives in his soul and waits for resurrection. COMMENTARY ON JOB 14.13-14.[13]

14:15-17 Call and Answer

A FORESHADOWING OF THE RESURRECTION. GREGORY THE GREAT: We are said to answer anyone, when we work in a way answerable to what another requires. Thus, in that change the Lord "calls," and a person "answers." Thus, before the brightness of the Incorrupt, humankind is shown forth as incorrupt even after being corrupted. For now so long as we are subject to corruption, we do not in any way "answer" our Creator, seeing that whereas corruption is far from incorruption, there is no similarity suitable to our answering. But of that change it is written, "When he shall appear, we shall be like him, for we shall see him as he is."[14] Then, therefore, we shall truly "answer God," who "calls," when at the bidding of the supreme Incorruption we shall arise incorruptible. MORALS ON THE BOOK OF JOB 12.18.[15]

RESURRECTION OF BODY AND SOUL. DIDYMUS THE BLIND: Since Job wants to show that not only the body is resurrected but also the soul whose thoughts are fixed on God, he says, "You would call, and I would answer you." For listening when God calls is a quality of a creature endowed with reason, that is, the soul. COMMENTARY ON JOB 14.15B.[16]

14:18-19 Mountains Fall

PRIDE SWELLS UP LIKE A MOUNTAIN, ONLY TO

---

[7]Prov 3:18. [8]Lk 23:31. [9]LF 21:47-48*. [10]Is 34:4. [11]See Mt 24:31; 1 Cor 15:52. [12]PO 42.2:434. [13]PTS 24:132. [14]1 Jn 3:2. [15]LF 21:57. [16]PTA 33.1:152.

FALL. PHILIP THE PRIEST: I believe that we must interpret "the mountain" as the devil, or as the human pride that swells up like a mountain before God through arrogance of mind, so that, after rising up, this mountain tumbles down and is destroyed, and after being reduced to dust, it is totally annihilated. I think that by "rock" are signified those who had to remain in the goodness of nature like rocks with a strength similar to that of the ground but who are brought, by their will, to a certain obtuseness and hardness of heart, so that, after turning down their dwelling place, which they presumed to possess thanks to their merits, they must be rejected toward suitable places for them. These "waters" that always flow towards lower things, and through which sometimes ruin comes, represent the hostile powers and the storms and whirlwind of the world. These waters, I say, waste with an incessant dripping those people who assume to be very strong and stable and have confidence in their virtue, and therefore they are compared with rocks. I think that the "soil of earth" is those who by withdrawing from dangers and temptation give themselves to destruction. COMMENTARY ON THE BOOK OF JOB 14.[17]

14:20-22 Pain and Mourning Only for Self

IGNORANCE AS A FURTHER CAUSE OF MISERY. CHRYSOSTOM: "A person is punished," Job says, "and, even if he has many descendents, he does not know them. In fact, after his death, he is often deprived of the pleasures that he was accustomed to enjoy while alive. What is the pleasure of leaving children after one who has departed?" You see, everywhere Job emphasizes the ephemeral character of life. It is impossible to come back and to return down here. Even if he leaves children after him, he does not know how they will prosper. He does not know at all whether his descendants will be numerous or scarce. What is more painful than to ignore one's successes and to go away alone by only knowing one's afflictions? Even if something good happens to him after his death, he does not know, nor will he ever know it [in this life]; but what he surely knows now is that "his flesh is in pain and his soul mourns." COMMENTARY ON JOB 14.20-22.[18]

---

[17]PL 26:650. [18]PTS 35:116.

15:1-16 ELIPHAZ ACCUSES JOB OF IMPIETY

[1] Then Eliphaz the Temanite answered:
  [2]"Should a wise man answer with windy
      knowledge,
    and fill himself with the east wind?
  [3]Should he argue in unprofitable talk,
    or in words with which he can do no good?*
  [4]But you are doing away with the fear of
      God,
    and hindering meditation before God.

[5]For your iniquity teaches your mouth,
    and you choose the tongue of the crafty.†
  [6]Your own mouth condemns you, and not I;
    your own lips testify against you.

  [7]"Are you the first man that was born?
    Or were you brought forth before
      the hills?
  [8]Have you listened in the council of God?

And do you limit wisdom to yourself?
⁹What do you know that we do not know?
    What do you understand that is not clear
      to us?
¹⁰Both the gray-haired and the aged are
      among us,
    older than your father.
¹¹Are the consolations of God too small
      for you,
    or the word that deals gently with
      you?
¹²Why does your heart carry you away,

    and why do your eyes flash,
¹³that you turn your spirit against God,
    and let such words go out of your mouth?†
¹⁴What is man, that he can be clean?
    Or he that is born of a woman, that he
      can be righteous?
¹⁵Behold, God puts no trust in his holy ones,
    and the heavens are not clean in his
      sight;§
¹⁶how much less one who is abominable and
      corrupt,
    a man who drinks iniquity like water!"#

*Vg (2-3) *Will the wise answer as if he speaks in the wind, or will he fill his stomach with ardor? You accuse with your words him who is not equal to you, and say what is not profitable to you.* †LXX *You are guilty by the words of your mouth, and you have not examined the words of the powerful.* ‡Vg (11-13) *Is it a great thing that God should console you? But your evil words prevent this. Why does your heart lift you up, and have your eyes astonished you as if you were thinking of great things? Why does your spirit swell against God, that you let such words go out of your mouth?* §LXX (14-15) *For who, being a mortal, is such that he shall be blameless? Or, who that is born of a woman, that he should be just? Forasmuch as he trusts not his saints; and the heaven is not pure before him. Alas then, abominable and unclean is man, drinking unrighteousness as a draught.* #Peshitta *as he will drink iniquity like water*

OVERVIEW: The Fathers interpret Eliphaz's second speech as falsely accusatory and groundlessly reproachful, that is, as the speech of a resentful and irritated man who is trying to distort the words of his opponent (JULIAN OF ECLANUM, HESYCHIUS, CHRYSOSTOM, GREGORY). At the same time, according to the interpretive line followed by the Fathers throughout their commentaries on the book of Job, they recognize in Eliphaz's words a certain amount of truth that they underline for moral and edifying purposes (OLYMPIODORUS, ISHO'DAD). The unrighteous attribute arrogance to the righteous (GREGORY) and distort their words (JULIAN OF ECLANUM), while the wicked enjoy uttering blasphemies (ISHO'DAD). Job pleaded his case with a humble heart, not arrogance (GREGORY).

15:1-3 How Should the Wise Answer?

AN ATTEMPT TO DISTORT JOB'S WORDS. JULIAN OF ECLANUM: Holy Job had not only shown that Zophar's words were ridiculous but also had reproved all his friends in common. They all thought that wisdom had to be judged according to the limits of their age. Since he had also discussed many issues concerning both human and divine nature, Eliphaz gets offended. He tries to accuse [Job] openly of different iniquities; since he has no decisive evidence, Eliphaz takes refuge by drawing a comparison with the people of previous generations, without showing any humility but by considering himself to be wiser than anybody else. "Will the wise answer as if he speaks in the wind, or will he fill his stomach with ardor?" [Eliphaz] wants to demonstrate that Job's longwinded speech is a proof of foolishness and that the words Job said were dictated by anger and not suggested by reason. "Will the wise answer as if he speaks in the wind?" Since holy Job, after the beginning of his speech, had left his antagonists behind and had turned his words to God, Eliphaz says that it is not worthy of a wise man, after neglecting the opponent in a debate, to speak as if in the wind and to pronounce whatever he wants without the fear of an adversary. "You accuse with your words him who is not equal to you and say what is not profitable to you." Your purification is an accusation against God. In fact, if you are afflicted undeservedly, he who is afflicting you is undoubtedly accused of iniquity. EXPOSITION ON THE BOOK OF JOB 15.1-3.[1]

15:4-6 You Condemn Yourself

ELIPHAZ'S IRRITATION. HESYCHIUS OF JERUSALEM: Because Job reproached his friends with confidence, they were irritated and hurt. This did not demonstrate any arrogance before God. In fact, since Job trusted in his own innocence, he did not take seriously at all the vain power of his accusers. Feeling ashamed in rebuking Job for his former words, [Eliphaz] says, in a vain attempt at useless chatter, that Job spoke of him with arrogance before God. And then, without waiting any longer, he hastens to reveal the reason why he denigrated Job, because Job had no consideration for "the words of the powerful." HOMILIES ON JOB 18.15.5B.[2]

15:7-10 Are You Ancient and Filled with Wisdom?

JOB EXPOSES HIS FRIENDS' PRIDE. CHRYSOSTOM: Eliphaz is just about to say, did you by any chance exist before the entire world, so that you learned about the most ancient times? Or did you learn anything from the mouth of God? You are not superior to us in knowledge at all. Since you had said that "wisdom is found in a long time,"[3] are you not caught in a trap now? In fact, you are not aged at all, nor were you born before the universe. But Job said that so that his friends might show their pride. COMMENTARY ON JOB 15.7A-10B.[4]

15:11-13 You Dare to Speak So?

HOW THE UNRIGHTEOUS READ THEIR OWN FEELINGS INTO THE MOTIVES OF THE RIGHTEOUS. GREGORY THE GREAT: It is as if Eliphaz said to Job in plain words, "If you would amend your profession of faith, you might long ago have possessed consolation in your scourges."

"Why does your heart puff you up? Have your eyes astonished you as though you were thinking of great things?" Often the mind of the righteous is so suspended in contemplating things on high that outwardly their face seems to have been struck with astonishment. Because heretics are not taught to enforce the power of contemplation in secret, they think that when the just and those that are imbued with right understanding do so, it is more out of hypocrisy than truth. They believe that whatever they themselves cannot obtain possession of must not exist in others in any genuine way either. "Why does your spirit swell against God, that you let such words go out of your mouth?" Very often when the righteous are afflicted with any woes, they are forced to confess their works, as blessed Job had done, who after living righteously was beaten down by the stokes of the rod; but when the unrighteous hear the sayings of the righteous, they think that they are uttered in self-exaltation rather than in truth. For they weigh the words of the righteous by their own feelings and do not think that good words can be said in a humble spirit. For as it is a great sin for a person to ascribe to himself what is not there, so it is commonly no sin at all if he speaks the good that there is with humility. Hence it often happens that the just and unjust speak words that are similar, but always a heart that is widely dissimilar. By the same sayings for which the Lord is offended by the unrighteous, he is even propitiated by the righteous. Thus the Pharisee, when he entered the temple, said, "I fast twice in the week; I give tithes of all that I possess."[5] But the publican went out justified more than he. Hezekiah too, the king, when he was afflicted with sickness of the body and brought to the last point of life, said with his heart pierced in prayer, "Remember now, O Lord, I beseech you, how I have walked before you in truth, and with a perfect heart."[6] Nor yet did the

---

[1]CCL 88:41-42. [2]PO 42.2:454. [3]Job 12:12 LXX. [4]PTS 35:117. [5]Lk 18:12. [6]Is 38:3.

Lord disregard this confession of his perfection, or refuse him, whom he immediately heard effectually in his prayers. See, the Pharisee justified himself in act, and Hezekiah maintained himself to be just in thought as well, and by the same act the one offended and the other propitiated God. Does not almighty God estimate the words of each by the thoughts within, and in his ear are not those high that are uttered with a lowly heart? Hence blessed Job, when he put forward his deeds, did not in the least degree act proudly against God, in that those things that he had really done, he spoke with a humble spirit. MORALS ON THE BOOK OF JOB 12.34-36.[7]

15:14-16 God's Purity

ONLY GOD IS ABSOLUTELY PURE. OLYMPIODORUS: "Who is the person," Eliphaz asks, "who can be blameless or can proclaim, I am righteous?" If, in fact, those who are very holy, both men and angels, and the purity itself of heaven before the judgment of the most pure God appear to be unclean, what should we say about the damnable and impure human being who drinks iniquity like a draught? He has said this because humans commit sin deliberately. The words "as he does not trust his saints" may also be interpreted in this manner, since the angels themselves can become different in their nature, and actually some of them slipped away from their own former position. Heaven is not pure because of this, and it is also often obscured by clouds. COMMENTARY ON JOB 15.14-16.[8]

THE PLEASURE OF SIN. ISHO'DAD OF MERV: "He will drink iniquity like water." The author says these words in order to show that [human beings] enjoy uttering blasphemies. COMMENTARY ON JOB 15.16.[9]

---

[7]LF 21:66-67. [8]PTS 24:139-40. [9]CSCO 229:247.

15:17-35 THE ANGUISH OF THE WICKED

[17]I will show you, hear me;
    and what I have seen I will declare
[18](what wise men have told,
    and their fathers have not hidden,
[19]to whom alone the land was given,
    and no stranger passed among them*).
[20]The wicked man writhes in pain all his
    days,
    through all the years that are laid up for
    the ruthless.
[21]Terrifying sounds are in his ears;
    in prosperity the destroyer will come
    upon him.
[22]He does not believe that he will return out
    of darkness,
    and he is destined for the sword.
[23]He wanders abroad for bread, saying,
    "Where is it?"
    He knows that a day of darkness is ready
    at his hand;
[24]distress and anguish terrify him;
    they prevail against him, like a king
    prepared for battle.†
[25]Because he has stretched forth his hand

against God,
and bids defiance to the Almighty,
[26]running stubbornly against him
with a thick-bossed shield;
[27]because he has covered his face with
his fat,
and gathered fat upon his loins,[‡]
[28]and has lived in desolate cities,
in houses which no man should inhabit,
which were destined to become heaps
of ruins;
[29]he will not be rich, and his wealth will not
endure,
nor will he strike root in the earth;[m]
[30]he will not escape from darkness;
the flame will dry up his shoots,

and his blossom[n] will be swept away[o] by
the wind.[§]
[31]Let him not trust in emptiness, deceiving
himself;
for emptiness will be his recompense.
[32]It will be paid in full before his time,
and his branch will not be green.[#]
[33]He will shake off his unripe grape, like the
vine,
and cast off his blossom, like the olive
tree.
[34]For the company of the godless is barren,
and fire consumes the tents of bribery.
[35]They conceive mischief and bring forth
evil
and their heart prepares deceit.

m Vg: Heb obscure   n Gk: Heb mouth   o Cn: Heb will depart   *LXX marched against them   †LXX (20-24) All the life of the ungodly is spent in anguish, and the years granted to the oppressor are numbered. And his terror is in his ears, just when he seems to be at peace, his overthrow will come. Let him not trust that he shall return from darkness, for he has been already made over to the power of the sword. And he has been appointed to be food for vultures; and he knows within himself that he is doomed to be a carcass, and a dark day shall carry him away as with a whirlwind. Distress also and anguish shall come upon him, he shall fall as a captain in the first rank.   ‡Vg (25-27) For he has lifted his hands against the Lord, and he has become strong against the almighty Lord. And he has run against him with an upright neck, and has armed himself with a fat neck. For he has covered his face with fat, and from his loins fat hangs.   §LXX (28-30) And let him lodge in desolate cities and enter into houses without inhabitant, and what they have prepared, others shall carry away. Neither shall he at all grow rich, nor shall his substance remain, he shall not cast a shadow upon the earth. Neither shall he in any wise escape the darkness, let the wind blast his blossom, and let his flower fall off.   #Vg Before his days are fulfilled he shall perish, and his hands shall wither.

Overview: In their comments on the second part of Eliphaz's speech, the Fathers are consistent with the interpretive line that they had begun in the first part of the speech. On the one hand, they emphasize Eliphaz's pride and groundless accusations (Gregory, Philip); on the other, they isolate Eliphaz's most truthful and acceptable remarks to develop them in a moral and edifying sense (Chrysostom, Ephrem, Philip, Olympiodorus, Gregory). The proud always look for ways to lift themselves up (Gregory), but at their apex, they fall (Chrysostom), in their stubborn opposition to God (Philip). The proud inhabit a desolation they have created for themselves (Olympiodorus). The alms of the proud have no efficacy to redeem (Gregory). God's view of Job's innocence is to be trusted rather than that of his detractors (Philip).

15:17-19 What the Wise Have Said

A Further Proof of Eliphaz's Pride. Gregory the Great: All arrogant persons have this characteristic that when they have a right notion, though the thing is little, they wrest it to serve their pride. By the same act from understanding they attempt to raise themselves higher. From swollen pride they fall into the pit of self-exalting and account themselves better instructed than the learned. They exact respect for themselves from their superiors and stand upon it to teach as with authority those who are holier people. Hence it is now said, "I will demonstrate; listen to me." MORALS ON THE BOOK OF JOB 12.40.[1]

15:20-24 The Wicked in Pain

A COMPARISON OF THE WISE AND THE WICKED. CHRYSOSTOM: Eliphaz adds, "No stranger marched against them," that is, the wise are those who enjoy peace and transmit it to their descendants. "No stranger marched against them." This means they made no war nor saw any fight nor knew any revolt, but they stood with nobility and bravery. They did not only survive but also possessed great force and power and enjoyed a profound peace. "All the life of the ungodly," he says, "is spent in anguish," and when they experience peace, their conscience will know this anguish. "The years granted to the oppressors," who are unjust, "are numbered," he says, because the tyrants are ephemeral. "Just when he seems to be at peace, his overthrow will come." Here Job learns that war comes from above, and there will be no change in his misfortunes. "He has been appointed to be food for vultures." "He has already been given over to the power of the sword." Notice this again. His death is pitiful. It is not conformed to the common law of nature but is the result of violence, war and battle. After his death, he will not have a burial or a funeral and will not only be deprived of a tomb but will also be "food for vultures." "He knows within himself that he is doomed to be a carcass." The foreboding of these events makes them even more painful for Job when they are predicted to him and announced beforehand. COMMENTARY ON JOB 15.17-23B.[2]

THE WICKED IS DEFEATED BY DISTRESS. EPHREM THE SYRIAN: This means that pain and anguish catches [the wicked] in the middle, just like in a field where on one side a king threatens with inimical banners and on the other side pillaging robbers impend, so that his mind and soul cannot be at rest. COMMENTARY ON JOB 15.24.[3]

15:25-27 The Wicked Opposed God

A DESCRIPTION OF INSANE PRIDE. PHILIP THE PRIEST: "He has lifted his hands against the Lord, and he has become strong against the almighty Lord." Through the lifting or stretching of the hand Eliphaz indicates the one who opposes God, and he calls him strong for the arrogance of his swollen mind. "And he has run against him with an upright neck." Here Eliphaz indicates the precipitous and abrupt mind of the proud. Being indeed possessed by his insanity, he does not proceed with slow steps in his bold opposition. "And he has armed himself with a fat neck." By mentioning the fatness of the neck, Eliphaz has indicated an overabundant and almost excessively flowing arrogance. COMMENTARY ON THE BOOK OF JOB 15.[4]

15:28-30 Living in Desolation

THE DOOM OF THE IMPIOUS. OLYMPIODORUS: He describes the absolute solitude of the impious and says that because of their misery, they inhabit desolation instead of prosperous cities and houses. "In fact," Eliphaz says, "their wealth will not last." COMMENTARY ON JOB 15.28-29.[5]

15:31-33 Emptiness for the Wicked

GOODNESS MUST COME FROM THE HOLY SPIRIT. GREGORY THE GREAT: As often as we do alms after sin, we, as it were, pay a price for bad actions. Wherefore, the prophet says concerning him who does not do these things, "He will not give God his propitiation or the price of the redemption of the soul."[6] But sometimes the rich, being elated, oppress those below them and seize the things of another. Yet, in a certain way they give some things to others. And while they oppress multitudes, they sometimes render defensive support to particular persons; for the

---

[1]LF 21:69-70*. [2]PTS 35:119. [3]ESOO 2:7. [4]PL 26:654. [5]PTS 24:142. [6]Ps 49:7-8 (48:8-9 LXX).

iniquities that they never abandon they seem to offer a price. But the price of alms then frees us from sins, when we lament and renounce things of which we are guilty. For he who is both always sinning, and, as it were, always bestowing alms, pays a price in vain, in that he does not redeem his soul, which he does not keep from evil habits. Hence it is now said, "Let him not believe, being vainly deceived, that he is to be redeemed with any price." For the alms of the rich and proud person has no efficacy to redeem him, seeing that his robbery of the poor person committed simultaneously will not allow his alms to rise up before the eyes of God. . . . Very commonly we see persons that both lead wicked lives and attain to the very extreme of old age. How then is it said, "Before his days are fulfilled, he shall perish," when, in the case of particular persons we often see that their limbs already fail from age, and yet their passions do not cease to carry out their wickedness? For there are some, who after losing their way in life, come to their senses, and with their conscience accusing them, they forsake their evil ways, alter their actions, resist their old wickedness, flee earthly courses and pursue heavenly aims. However, before they become firmly rooted in those holy aims, from deadness of mind they return to the things from which they began to pass sentence, and they fall back to the evil habits that they had determined to shun. For it often happens that for the profit of many, even holy people bow their necks to external actions and are busied with the governance of a people. The weak observing this, and from their former pride still within them, seeking to follow their example, they set themselves in outward ways of action. But in proportion, for they do not come to their actions well imbued with the things of the Spirit, and they execute them in a carnal manner. For until the heart is first confirmed in heavenly desires by long application and a habitual manner of living, when the heart is poured back again for the executing of things exterior, it is rooted out from all its standing in good practice. MORALS ON THE BOOK OF JOB 12.57-59.[7]

15:34-35 The Wicked Plot Deceit

WE MUST BELIEVE GOD. PHILIP THE PRIEST: With these words [Eliphaz] identifies holy Job as a robber and a pretender who hides his violent actions. He had also spoken so against Job in his first speech, when Eliphaz had compared him with a lion, a lioness and a cub of lions and tigers. But we must believe in God, who by praising Job did not call him a deceiver but declared him to be innocent and simple. COMMENTARY ON THE BOOK OF JOB 15.[8]

---

[7]LF 21:80-81*. [8]PL 26:656-57.

16:1-6 JOB REPROVES HIS FRIENDS FOR THEIR UNMERCIFUL ATTITUDES

[1] Then Job answered:
[2]"I have heard many such things;
    miserable comforters are you all.

[3]Shall windy words have an end?
    Or what provokes you that you
    answer?

⁴I also could speak as you do,
*   if you were in my place;*
I could join words together against
*   you,*
*   and shake my head at you.*
⁵I could strengthen you with my mouth,

and the solace of my lips would assuage
*   your pain.*

⁶"If I speak, my pain is not assuaged,
*   and if I forbear, how much of it leaves*
*   me?"*

OVERVIEW: In his reply, Job demonstrates his wisdom (HESYCHIUS, CHRYSOSTOM), his willingness to sacrifice himself (HESYCHIUS) and his benevolence and mercy (GREGORY).

16:1-2 Miserable Comforters

WICKED COUNSELORS. HESYCHIUS OF JERUSALEM: You are "comforters" but very wicked ones. No word of yours is for the good, but they are all for the bad. You teach, you give advice, and you propose not how ordeals must be avoided, but how [new] ordeals will be obtained from affliction! [You do not teach] how a storm must be abated but how harmful agitations can be raised from peace. HOMILIES ON JOB 19.16.2B.[1]

SUPERFICIAL JUDGMENTS. CHRYSOSTOM: Since Eliphaz speaks so, as if the matter were of extraordinary importance, and talks as if his speech derived from the wisdom of the ancestors, Job also resumes the argument he had used at the beginning. Is what you say not evident, he says? Therefore, since you speak superficially and utter what comes to your mind without checking your words, do not be annoyed with me if I express the thoughts of my mind. COMMENTARY ON JOB 16.1-2.[2]

16:3-4 I Could Talk As You Do

THE AFFLICTIONS OF OTHERS. HESYCHIUS OF JERUSALEM: Job has phrased this in the form of a question and not in order to look for an argu-

ment. This means "Will I really join words together against you? Or will I really shake my head at you? Not at all! It is convenient for the righteous to take upon himself the afflictions of others and not to trample underfoot or to exaggeratedly insist wickedly, as you do concerning my torments." HOMILIES ON JOB 19.16.4C-D.[3]

16:5-6 I Could Encourage You

A PRAYER RATHER THAN A CURSE. GREGORY THE GREAT: It is sometimes necessary that wicked minds, which are incapable of being corrected by human preaching, should have the comfort of God desired for them in a spirit of kindness; and while this is done with great earnestness in love, plainly not the punishment but the correction of the guilty person is the thing aimed at, and it is shown to be a prayer rather than a curse. In these words blessed Job is shown to aim at this, that the friends, who didn't know how to sympathize with his grief through charity, might learn by experience how they ought to have pitied the affliction of another. Those subdued by grief may learn to draw from their own suffering a better way to minister consolation to others. They would then live ever more healthfully within as they are made more sensitive to frailty without. MORALS ON THE BOOK OF JOB 13.5.[4]

---

[1]PO 42.2:474. [2]PTS 35:121. [3]PO 42.2:476. [4]LF 23:89*.

16:7-22 IN HIS DISTRESS JOB ASSERTS HIS INNOCENCE

⁷Surely now God has worn me out;
he has *made desolate all my company.*
⁸And he has *shriveled me up,*
which is a witness against me;
and my leanness has risen up against
me,
it testifies to my face.
⁹He has torn me in his wrath, and hated
me;
he has gnashed his teeth at me;
my adversary sharpens his eyes
against me.
¹⁰Men have gaped at me with their
mouth,
they have struck me insolently upon the
cheek,
they mass themselves together against
me.
¹¹God gives me up to the ungodly, *
and casts me into the hands of
the wicked.
¹²I was at ease, and he broke me asunder;
he seized me by the neck and dashed me
to pieces;
he set me up as his target,
¹³his archers surround me.

He slashes open my kidneys, and does
not spare;
he pours out my gall on the ground.
¹⁴He breaks me with breach upon breach;
he runs upon me like a warrior.
¹⁵I have sewed sackcloth upon my skin,
and have laid my strength in the
dust.†
¹⁶My face is red with weeping,
and on my eyelids is deep darkness;
¹⁷although there is no violence in my hands,
and my prayer is pure.‡

¹⁸O earth, cover not my blood,
and let my cry find no resting place.
¹⁹Even now, behold, my witness is in
heaven,
and he that vouches for me is on high.
²⁰My friends scorn me; §
my eye pours out tears to God,
²¹that he would maintain the right of a
man with God,
*like*q *that of a man with his neighbor.*
²²For when a few years have come
I shall go the way whence I shall not
return.

---

p Heb *thou hast* q Syr Vg Tg: Heb *and* *Peshitta *God has given me up to an iniquitous angel.* †Vg (12-15) *God locked me beside the iniquitous and delivered me into the hands of the impious. I, who was once rich, was suddenly trampled underfoot. He held my neck, broke me and set me as a sign. He abandoned me to his spears, wounded my loins and did not spare them, and he scattered my entrails on the ground. He struck me with wound after wound, ran over me as a giant.* ‡Vg *I have suffered this without committing iniquity (verses 17-18 are numbered 18-19 in the Vg)* §Vg *are full of words*

OVERVIEW: In his sincere description of his afflictions and sufferings, Job demonstrates again his profound wisdom (JULIAN OF ECLANUM) as well as his sensitivity (EPHREM), his accurateness in language (ISHO'DAD) and his willingness to please God (GREGORY). At the same time, his words contain a prophetic message announcing the passion of Christ and his apostles (PHILIP). It is especially reserved for the righteous that their sufferings and their deaths not be hidden (JULIAN). Although never attained in this life, people hope that in all they say they will be accurately heard, even as they wish that they could hear rightly all that is said about them (GREGORY). Ephrem provided a poetic paraphrase of this passage.

16:7-10 Worn and Desolate

JOB'S AFFLICTIONS. EPHREM THE SYRIAN: Your words cruelly pierce me, because you endeavor to present me as a false witness before God, whose wrath "has torn me." Even in the middle of my mourning, where the loss of the children and cattle had dragged me, bodily pains invaded me. And I certainly remained silent, but he struck me with ominous reports and harsh news. COMMENTARY ON JOB 16.9.[1]

16:11 Given to the Ungodly

JOB'S INIQUITOUS ANGEL. ISHO'DAD OF MERV: "God has given me up to an iniquitous angel." These words are said because it is believed that an angel accompanies each human being. Job calls his angel iniquitous because of the effects of Job's misfortunes that he observes, just as David calls the angel evil who kills the firstborn of the Egyptians.[2] COMMENTARY ON JOB 16.11.[3]

16:12-15 God Like a Warrior

A PROPHECY ABOUT CHRIST AND HIS APOSTLES. PHILIP THE PRIEST: "God locked me beside the iniquitous and delivered me into the hands of the impious," that is, beside the devil and his angels. But [this sentence] must also be interpreted as a reference to Christ when he was delivered into the hands of the Jews. "I, who was once rich, was suddenly trampled underfoot. He held my neck, broke me and set me as a sign," that is, from rich he became poor, or as Christ, who, from being God, was born a man. "He abandoned me to his spears, wounded my loins and did not

spare them, and he scattered my entrails on the ground." The spears mentioned in this passage can be seen as the seizures of pain that Job suffered, but they must also be interpreted as the blasphemies that Christ suffered from the Jews. . . . The words "he wounded my loins" must also be read as a reference to Christ. In fact, the Jews persecuted the apostles to such a degree that they wounded with the injury of infidelity and the denial of Christ those [holy men] who were born, in a sense, from the loins of Christ's doctrine. Peter, in fact, said, "I do not know the man."[4] COMMENTARY ON THE BOOK OF JOB 16.[5]

16:16-19 Do Not Cover My Blood

THE SUFFERING OF THE RIGHTEOUS MUST NOT BE HIDDEN. JULIAN OF ECLANUM: "I have suffered this without committing iniquity." You have a good reason to be upset, because there was no cause for such a torment. "I have suffered this." Job is knowingly in pain against his merits. Therefore, he does not want the fact that he has been given to torments to remain hidden, but he desires what he suffers to be under the light. Job has no desire for the memory of his passion to be buried in oblivion but wants what he suffers to reach everybody's ears, because he is certain of the innocence of his life. . . . Therefore it is especially reserved for the righteous that their passions and their deaths not be hidden in the course of their struggles. EXPOSITION ON THE BOOK OF JOB 16.18-19.[6]

16:20-22 I Weep to God

THE INTENT OF JOB'S HEART IS TO PLEASE GOD. GREGORY THE GREAT: Yet this voice may together with blessed Job suitably apply to each one of us as well; for every person who aims at human praises in what he does, seeks a "witness" on earth. But he that is eager to please almighty

---

[1]ESOO 2:7. [2]See Ps 78:48-51 (77:48-51 LXX). [3]CSCO 229:248. [4]Mk 14:71. [5]PL 26:658-59. [6]CCL 88:46.

God by his deeds takes into account that he has a "witness in heaven." It often happens that inconsiderate people find fault with even the very best things in us; but one who "has a witness in heaven" has no need to fear human reproofs. Hence it is further added, "My friends are full of words; my eye pours out tears to God." For what is denoted by the eye but the intent of the heart? As it is written, "If your eye is good, your whole body shall be full of light."[7] For when anything is done with a good intention, the enacting of that intention gains no favor in the sight of God. And so when friends are full of words, that is, when the very same persons deny they are joined with us in faith, "the eye" must "pour out tears to God," so that the whole bent of our heart may run out into the piercing of interior love and lift itself up to the things of the interior. Being forced back by external reproaches, it is driven to turn back within, lest it should vanish. . . . As if it were expressed in plain words, "As in all that I say, I am heard, so would that I heard all that is said concerning me." But this can never be brought about in this life, because there is a great obstruction before the eyes of our heart,

blocking from our sight the subtle nature of God, even our mere frailty by itself. But we shall then see him with clarity by whom we are now searchingly beheld. When this frailty is laid aside, we will receive that grace of inward contemplation of which Paul says, "For then shall I know, as also I am known."[8] Hence blessed Job, seeing that that knowledge can never be in the fullest way perfected here, groans indeed over the blindness of the present life, yet consoles himself by life's brevity, saying, "For when a few years have come, I shall go the way from which I shall not return." Everything that passes is short, even though it should seem slow in being finished, but in the way of death we "go and do not return by it," not because we are not brought back by rising again to the life of the flesh but because we do not come again to the labors of this mortal life or to earn rewards by our labors. MORALS ON THE BOOK OF JOB 13.28-31.[9]

---

[7]Mt 6:22. [8]1 Cor 13:12. [9]LF 21:103-5*.

17:1-16 JOB SEES HIS HUMILIATION

[1] *My spirit is broken, my days are extinct,*
the grave is ready for me.
[2]Surely there are mockers about me,
and my eye dwells on their provocation.

[3]Lay down a pledge for me with thyself;
who is there that will give surety for me?
[4]Since thou hast closed their minds to
understanding,
therefore thou wilt not let them triumph.

[5]He who informs against his friends to get a
share of their property,
the eyes of his children will fail. *

[6]He has made me a byword of the peoples,
and I am one before whom men spit. †
[7]My eye has grown dim from grief,
and all my members are like a shadow.
[8]Upright men are appalled at this,
and the innocent stirs himself up against

the godless.

⁹Yet the righteous holds to his way,
    and he that has clean hands grows
    stronger and stronger.‡

¹⁰But you, come on again,§ all of you,
    and I shall not find a wise man among
    you.

¹¹My days are past, my plans are broken off,
    the desires of my heart.#

¹²They make night into day;
    "The light," they say, "is near to the

darkness."ʳ

¹³If I look for Sheol** as my house,
    if I spread my couch in darkness,

¹⁴if I say to the pit,†† "You are my father,"
    and to the worm, "My mother," or "My
    sister,"

¹⁵where then is my hope?
    Who will see my hope?

¹⁶Will it go down‡‡ to the bars of Sheol?
    Shall we descend together into the
    dust?

r Heb obscure   *Vg (3-5) Set me free and put me beside you, and let the hand of anyone fight against me. You have removed their heart far from discipline. Therefore they shall not be exalted. He promised prey to his friends; and the eyes of his children shall fail.   †Peshitta I will rise in authority among the peoples and will be a veil on their faces.   ‡LXX But let the faithful hold on his own way, and let him who is pure of heart take courage.   §Vg turn and come now   #Vg my thoughts are scattered, racking my heart   **Vg hell   ††Vg putrefaction   ‡‡LXX Will they go down

OVERVIEW: The Fathers comment on the final part of Job's speech according to three main lines of interpretation: in the first place, Job shows through his words the weakness and frailty of his human body and mind (EPHREM, PHILIP); in the second, his personal experience of suffering is a model for the faithful and an eternal moral warning (ISHO'DAD, HESYCHIUS); in the third, his words include prophetic truths announcing the advent of Christ, the new judgment and the universal church (GREGORY, CHRYSOSTOM). It is quite natural for us upon hearing a horrible thing to veil our eyes (ISHO'DAD). Job thought he was already experiencing hell (PHILIP). Even while we remain free to foolishly pursue the lowest enjoyments, we are always ever longing for the higher good. The elect are exhorted to turn by faith and repentance away from evil and come to do good (GREGORY).

17:1-2 Broken in Spirit

BODILY AND SPIRITUAL PAIN. EPHREM THE SYRIAN: "My spirit is broken" in bitterness and pain, because my ulcers torture me, or, on the other hand, because of my friends, who are ready to burst out against their friend. COMMENTARY ON JOB 17.1-2.[1]

17:3-5 Who Will Make a Pledge for Me?

A FORESHADOWING AND A WARNING. GREGORY THE GREAT: "Set me free and put me beside you, and let the hand of anyone fight against me," for Christ did not sin, either in thought or deed. He was made to "abide in bitterness" by his passion. He was "set free" by resurrection. He was "put beside" the Father by his ascension, in that having gone up into heaven he sits on the right hand of God. And because, after the glory of his ascension, Judea was stirred up in persecuting his disciples, it is rightly said here, "Let the hand of anyone fight against me." For the madness of the persecutors did then rage on Christ's members, and the flame of cruelty blazed out against the life of the faithful. But where should the wicked go, or what should they do, while he whom they persecuted on earth is now seated in heaven? Concerning whom it is yet further added, "You have removed their heart far from discipline. Therefore they shall not be exalted." If they had been acquainted with the keeping of discipline, and had not ever despised the precepts of our Redeemer, the mere mortal condition of their

[1]ESOO 2:7.

flesh by itself would have excited them to the love of immortal life. For this reason even the fact that we are subject to corruption in this life is due to our need for learning discipline. . . . Therefore, insofar as the heart is under discipline, it seeks after the things above; it is not enthralled with transitory good things. But of those whose heart is not under discipline, it is rightly said, "Therefore they shall not be exalted," for even while they are freed to pursue the lowest enjoyments, they are ever longing for the good things of the earth. MORALS ON THE BOOK OF JOB 13.35-37.[2]

17:6-7 An Object of Scorn

HEARING OF HORROR PROMPTS VEILING THE EYES. ISHO'DAD OF MERV: "I will rise in authority among peoples," because of the stupefaction for all that has happened to me. And the words, "I will be a veil on their faces,"[3] that is, whoever hears about my horrible misfortunes will veil his face. This is said as an analogy of the fact that when one hears a horrible thing, he brings his hand to his forehead and veils his eyes. COMMENTARY ON JOB 17.6.[4]

17:8-9 The Righteous Appalled

A CALL TO A NEW JUDGMENT. CHRYSOSTOM: I cannot say, in fact, that I receive mercy, which is the only privilege common to those who suffer. On the contrary, I am a laughingstock for the senseless; the righteous are frightened because of me. How can the faithful continue on his way? . . . "Let the faithful remain on his own way," Job says, "and let him who is pure of heart take courage." But how will a pure person keep his courage after these events happened in this manner against all hopes? Let us disregard what concerns me. How will others stand in the way of righteousness? Therefore I call you to a new judgment. COMMENTARY ON JOB 17.8A-9B.[5]

17:10-12 No Sensible Person Found

AN EXHORTATION AND A FIGURE. GREGORY THE GREAT: It is to the elect that Job frames these words, whom he calls to the eternal world. They are exhorted in two ways, namely, that they should "turn" and that they should "come" (meaning "turn" by faith and "come" by practice), that is, "turn" by abandoning evil deeds and "come" by doing good. As it is written, "Depart from evil, and do good."[6] But Job amazingly adds, "I shall not find a sensible person among you." What does it mean that Job bids them to wisdom and yet wishes that he may not find them wise? Concerning them it is written, "Woe to you that are wise in your own eyes and prudent in your own sight;"[7] and to whom it is said again, "Be not wise with your own selves."[8] Hence that same great preacher desired that those whom he found carnally wise, in order that they might attain true wisdom, should first become foolish, saying, "If anyone among you seems to be wise in this world, let him become a fool, that he may be wise."[9] And the living Truth said elsewhere, "I thank you, O Father, Lord of heaven and earth, because you have hidden these things from the wise and prudent and have revealed them to babes."[10] And so because they that are wise in themselves cannot come to true wisdom, blessed Job, being anxious for the conversion of his hearers, rightly desires that he may not "find any wise man among them." It is as if Job said to them in plain speech, "Learn to be foolish in your own selves, that you may be truly wise in God." . . . The holy church of the elect perceives that the spaces of its life pass in periods of day and night. This suggests that the church in adversity is experiencing a night to be followed by a day of prosperity. For there rises, as it were, light on it from the tranquility of peace and night from the grief of persecution. Now after each pause of rest [the church] returns to the labor of persecution, growing to a head against it. [The church] testifies that "its days have past." In these days, however, it is accustomed to be weighed down proportionally

[2]LF 21:106-7**. [3]See Peshitta. [4]CSCO 229:249. [5]PTS 35:123. [6]Ps 37:27 (36:27 LXX). [7]Is 5:21. [8]Rom 12:16. [9]1 Cor 3:18. [10]Mt 11:25.

with so many heavier cares. As [the church] things of the true tranquility of rest, a more exact reckoning is required of it by the Judge.... Hence blessed Job, whether in his own voice or the voice of the universal church, after testifying that "his days were past," thereupon added, "My thoughts are scattered, racking my heart." MORALS ON THE BOOK OF JOB 13.44-46.[11]

17:13-15 Who Will See My Hope?

MORTALITY AND BODILY CORRUPTION.
PHILIP THE PRIEST: "If I look for hell as my house, if I spread my couch in darkness." Bodily pains and the torment of his thoughts incessantly vexed [Job]. Therefore, he declared he was suffering already the punishment of hell. Or perhaps, in this passage, the separation from human society that he had undergone, so that he sat outside the town in a dung pit called darkness, because it did not have the light of human comfort. "If I say to putrefaction, 'You are my father,' and to the worms, 'My mother,' or 'My sister.'" I am putrefying, Job says, for such a long time that I can certainly call putrefaction itself and the worms generated in its pus "parents." ... And appropriately he called "father" Adam, the firstborn of the human race, who was made corruptible by corruption. And he called "mother" human nature, which is infected by corruption. And finally he called "sister" Adam's entire posterity, which was born from the corruption of mortality as from the pus of corruption. COMMENTARY ON THE BOOK OF JOB 17.[12]

17:16 Descending into Dust

MATERIAL GOODS ARE USELESS. HESYCHIUS OF JERUSALEM: Why do we build palaces? Why do we care for the drapery of beds and for the different garments? Why do we add estate to estate, strangle the poor and strike the needy? Why do we want to increase those riches that will not come together with us? And why do we not bend our ears to the truthful oracles? Why do we not believe in the commandment of the Judge and do not obey what he said, "Do not lay up for yourselves treasures on earth, where moth and rust corrupt, and where thieves break through and steal. But lay up for yourselves treasures in heaven, where neither moth nor rust corrupt and where thieves do not break through nor steal"?[13] For our angels protect our treasures, and, above all, the Lord of the angels. HOMILIES ON JOB 20.17.16.[14]

---

[11]LF 21:111-12. [12]PL 26:661-62. [13]Mt 6:19-20. [14]PO 42.2:510.

18:1-4 BILDAD REPROACHES JOB FOR HIS CONCEIT

[1] Then Bildad the Shuhite answered:
 [2]"How long will you hunt for words?
  Consider, and then we will speak.*
 [3]Why are we counted as cattle?

 Why are we stupid in your sight?†
 [4]You who tear yourself in your anger,
  shall the earth be forsaken for you,
  or the rock be removed out of its place?"‡

*LXX How long will you continue? Forbear so that we also may speak   †LXX For where have we been silent before you like cattle?   ‡LXX Anger has possessed you, for what if you should die; would the stretches under heaven be desolate? Or shall the earth be deprived of its foundations?

OVERVIEW: The beginning of Bildad's second speech is severely criticized by the Fathers. They perceive in it ignorance and callousness toward Job's points and opinions (HESYCHIUS) and malice and bad faith in the accusations against him (JULIAN OF ECLANUM, CHRYSOSTOM).

18:1-2 Consider Your Words

JOB'S WISDOM IGNORED BY BILDAD. HESYCHIUS OF JERUSALEM: It seems that Bildad ignores Job when he draws his resolutions, or when the logic of his words comes to him or when the power of his words comes to him, and where his will leads him, because the fighter "continues" to fight. The more Job sees his enemies increase, the more he grows strong against them. The more he sees the number of the slanderers grow, the more he renews himself to fight back in favor of truth. It is not only by exhorting but also by becoming firmer that Job makes the truth appear. But Bildad ignores that, and that is why he has said, "How long will you continue?" It is necessary that Job respond, and since he has not said that, we will say it instead of him, "He will continue until his spirit animates you, until he makes sources spring, until he blows wisdom into sincere vases, until you are tortured by his words as by the strikes of a whip. For you do not understand the wisdom of God and do not know his economy with regard to the righteous and the sinners." HOMILIES ON JOB 21.18.2-3.[1]

18:3 Considered Cattle

BILDAD'S ACCUSATION. JULIAN OF ECLANUM: "Why are we considered to be as cattle?" After taking away from us the right to speak, you now claim that it is only reserved to you, if you are wise. EXPOSITION ON THE BOOK OF JOB 18.3.[2]

18:4 You Tear Yourself in Anger

FOOLISH ACCUSATIONS AGAINST JOB. CHRYSOSTOM: Bildad speaks these words because Job did not refrain from complaining by saying that he wanted to die. What sort of consolation is this? How could he have disheartened him in another way? He said, in fact, that the "stretches under heaven would be desolate," or did he mention his death as if it brought a great contribution to this life that is common to us? Actually Bildad says the opposite: a man is nothing and deserves no mention. Why do you[3] say that? Then he also foolishly and haphazardly accuses the impious, in order to support his present argument. They cannot put the blame on [Job] for any evil action. But notice their perversity; by saying that great misfortunes will befall the impious, they mention those afflictions suffered by Job, naming his miseries in their words, as if they wanted to show that they alluded to him. Notice and observe that their remarks about others are addressed to him. COMMENTARY ON JOB 18.4B-C.[4]

---

[1]PO 42.2.516. [2]CCL 88:49. [3]That is, Bildad. [4]PTS 35:125.

18:5-21 AFFLICTIONS OVERTAKE THE WICKED

⁵Yea, the light of the wicked is put out,
    and the flame of his fire does not shine.
⁶The light is dark in his tent,
    and his lamp above him is put out.
⁷His strong steps are shortened
    and his own schemes throw him down.

⁸*For he is cast into a net by his own feet,*
    and he walks on a pitfall.
⁹*A trap seizes him by the heel,*
    *a snare lays hold of him.**
¹⁰*A rope is hid for him in the ground,*
    a trap for him in the path.
¹¹*Terrors frighten him on every side,*
    and chase him at his heels.†‡
¹²*His strength is hunger-bitten,*
    and calamity is ready for his stumbling.
¹³*By disease his skin is consumed,ˢ*
    the first-born of death consumes his
    limbs.
¹⁴*He is torn from the tent in which he*
    trusted,
    and is brought to the king of terrors.§
¹⁵*In his tent dwells that which is none of his;*

brimstone is scattered upon his
    habitation.
¹⁶*His roots dry up beneath,*
    and his branches wither# above.
¹⁷*His memory perishes from the earth,*
    and he has no name in the street.
¹⁸*He is thrust from light into darkness,*
    and driven out of the world.
¹⁹*He has no offspring or descendant*
    among his people,
    and no survivor where he used to live.
²⁰*They of the west are appalled at his day,*
    *and horror seizes them of the east.***
²¹*Surely such are the dwellings of*
    the ungodly,
    such is the place of him who knows
    not God.

s Cn: Heb *it consumes the limbs of his skin* *LXX (7-9) Let the meanest of men spoil his goods, and let his counsel deceive him. His foot also has been caught in a snare, and let it be entangled in a net. And let snares come upon him; he shall strengthen those that thirst for his destruction. †LXX Let pains destroy him completely, let many enemies come about him. ‡Vg *entrap their feet* §LXX (13-14) Let the soles of his feet be devoured, and death shall consume his beauty. And let health be utterly banished from his tabernacle, and let distress seize upon him with a charge from the king #Vg *their crops are ruined* **Vg In his days the last shall be astonished, and horror shall seize on the first.

OVERVIEW: In the second part of Bildad's speech, the Fathers recognize again how his reproaches and accusations against Job are wrong and groundless (HESYCHIUS, JULIAN OF ECLANUM). At the same time, they are able to find in his words partial truth that provides them with the matter for moral meditations on the ephemeral nature of human glory (GREGORY), on the desperate life and the inevitable punishment of the impious and the proud (OLYMPIODORUS, PHILIP, EPHREM).

18:5-6 The Wicked Are Extinguished

A FLAME OF EXTERNAL AND EPHEMERAL GLORY. GREGORY THE GREAT: For every ungodly person has "a flame of his own fire" that he kindles in his heart from the heat of temporal desires, while he burns now with these, now with those lusts and fans his thoughts into a bigger flame by the diverse flatteries of the world. But if a fire has no flame, it does not shine by shedding any light. And so the flame of the fire is his outward beauty or power that comes from his burning within. What he anxiously desires to get, he very often wins, to the heaping up of his own ruin; and whether in the power of the loftiest pitch or in the wealth of multiplied increase, he, as it were, shines in external glory. But "the flame of his fire shall not shine," in that in the day of his departure, all the fair outward show is removed, and he is consumed by his own burning within. And "so the flame" is removed from "the fire" when his exterior glory is separated from his interior burning. . . . Now it is well that it is not said of this lamp, "which is by him" but "which is above him," in that earthly enjoyments possess the mind of the bad and so swallow it up in delight, that they are "above" it and not "by it." But the righteous, even when they have the good fortune of the present life, are taught to force it to bow beneath them. That is, when they are made glad in themselves with good things, they may get above it by the counsel of a steadied mind and surmount it by the control of virtue. And so "the lamp" of the wicked person, "which is above him, is put out," in that his joy is quickly brought to an end, a joy that possessed him wholly in this life; and the person who now wickedly lets himself out at large in pleasures is punished hereafter being closely encompassed round about in woe. MORALS ON THE BOOK OF JOB 14.9-10.[1]

18:7-9 Walking into a Trap

THE DOOM OF THE IMPIOUS. OLYMPIODORUS: Bildad says these things using the metaphor of the birds or the animals that are captured in the hunt. In fact, as they can no longer escape after falling into snares and nets, so the impious are caught by inevitable calamities that overwhelm them. And what is worse, after all their schemes have been overturned and reversed, their riches are taken away from them not by the powerful but by people of the lowest class. COMMENTARY ON JOB 18.7-9.[2]

18:10-11 A Rope Hidden for Them

THE DANGER AND ANGUISH HIDDEN IN PRIDE. PHILIP THE PRIEST: "A rope is hid for them in the ground, a trap for them in the path." They do not realize in what dangers they are lost, and what rope, that is, the binding of sin, in which they entangle their feet, is hidden in them. In the violence of their life, through which they believe they are proceeding righteously, the trap of this error is hidden. "Terrors" or pains "frighten them on every side and entrap their feet." The proud will be always frightened by the terror of impending calamities. Here terrors can also be interpreted not as feelings but as the ministers of the devil. In fact, they tried to terrify holy Job in many ways, so that he might surrender to them. COM-

MENTARY ON THE BOOK OF JOB 18.[3]

18:12 Hunger and Calamity for the Wicked

JOB IS A RIGHTEOUS MAN. HESYCHIUS OF JERUSALEM: These words are appropriate to the impious but not at all to Job, because "pains have not destroyed him" but have made him appear to be a powerful fighter, have made him appear doubly just. Many have come, and "the soles of their feet have been devoured";[4] therefore, those who have come must complain about themselves and not about the righteous, because Job, thanks to his patience, deserves crowns and happiness. HOMILIES ON JOB 21.18.12.[5]

18:13-14 Consumed by Disease

THE IMPIOUS ARE CONDEMNED TO FAILURE. OLYMPIODORUS: He calls the "soles of their feet" the products of their journeys, in order to say that the impious are not prosperous in their travels when they fall into "a violent ruin."[6] But also their fruits of season, that is, their children, are insatiately consumed by death; and from this entire condition, in which they find themselves, all healing withdraws. That is, their results will always be incorrigible and incurable. It is also possible to interpret the "soles of their feet" as their offspring or descendants. COMMENTARY ON JOB 18.12-14.[7]

18:15-16 The Wicked Dry Up

AN ABSOLUTE PUNISHMENT. EPHREM THE SYRIAN: These words mean that the punishment of the impious will be similar to the massacre of the Sodomites. "Their roots dry beneath, and their branches wither above" so that nothing useful to the impious may remain anywhere, beneath or above the ground. COMMENTARY ON JOB 18.15-16.[8]

---

[1]LF 21:122-23*. [2]PTS 24:159. [3]PL 26:663. [4]Cf. Job 18:13. [5]PO 42.2:522. [6]Job 18:12 LXX. [7]PTS 24:160. [8]ESOO 2:8.

18:17-19 The Wicked Perish

OBLIQUE ALLUSIONS TO JOB. JULIAN OF ECLANUM: "Their memory perishes from the earth." In order that Bildad may not appear to speak inconsistently after saying, "Their roots dry up beneath," he had added, "Their crops are ruined above." He then concludes with what he wanted to convey through such a sequel of expressions, that is, "Their memory perishes from the earth." In fact, it could happen that the ripening of the fruits occurred before the drying up of the roots, which takes place over a long period of time. "Their memory perishes from the earth." All the things that happen to the impious are described in general but also obliquely referred to Job, because he suffers these same things under the scourge of God. EXPOSITION ON THE BOOK OF JOB 18.17.[9]

18:20-21 The Place of the Wicked

A REFERENCE TO THE ANTICHRIST AND HUMAN HYPOCRISY. GREGORY THE GREAT: That these words are to be understood as speaking of the antichrist is shown when it is added, "In his days the last shall be astonished, and horror shall seize on the first." He will then let himself loose against the righteous with such a measure of iniquity that even the hearts of the very elect shall be struck with no small consternation. Hence it is written, "Insomuch that if it were possible, they shall deceive the very elect,"[10] which clearly isn't said because the elect shall fall but because they shall tremble with terrible alarms. Now, at that time, both the latest elect and the first elect are described as maintaining the conflict for righteousness against him. They that shall be found among the elect at the end of the world are destined to be laid low in the death of the flesh. And they too who proceeded from the former times of the world, that is, Enoch and Elijah, shall be brought back among humankind and shall be exposed to the savageness of his cruelty while still in their mortal flesh. This one's forces will be let loose with such terrible power that "the latest are astonished at, and the first do dread." . . . Then he adds, "Surely such are the dwellings of the ungodly, such is the place of those who do not know God," in that he who is now lifted up from ignorance of God is then brought to his own "dwellings" where his own wickedness plunges him into woes. One day he finds "darkness his place," who while he made himself glad here in the counterfeit light of righteousness, was occupying the place of another. For bad people act deceitfully, striving to possess for themselves the righteous person's good name, as of another place. But they are then brought to their own place, when they are tormented with everlasting fire, as the deserved punishment of their iniquity. MORALS ON THE BOOK OF JOB 14.26-28.[11]

---

[9]CCL 88:51. [10]Mt 24:24. [11]LF 21:133-34*.

19:1-22 JOB'S AFFLICTION BEFORE GOD AND HUMANKIND

[1] Then Job answered:
[2]"How long will you torment me,
and break me in pieces with words?
[3]These ten times you have cast reproach

upon me;
are you not ashamed to wrong me?*
⁴And even if it be true that I have erred,
my error remains with myself.
⁵If indeed you magnify yourselves against
me,
and make my humiliation an argument
against me,
⁶know then that God has put me in the
wrong,
and closed his net about me.
⁷Behold, I cry out, 'Violence!' but I am not
answered;
I call aloud, but there is no justice.¹
⁸He has walled up my way, so that I cannot
pass,
and he has set darkness upon my paths.
⁹He has stripped from me my glory,
and taken the crown from my head.
¹⁰He breaks me down on every side, and
I am gone,
and my hope has he pulled up like a
tree.
¹¹He has kindled his wrath against me,
and counts me as his adversary.‡
¹²His troops come on together;
they have cast up siegeworksᵗ against
me,§
and encamp round about my tent.

¹³"He has put my brethren far from me,
and my acquaintances are wholly
estranged from me.#
¹⁴My kinsfolk and my close friends have
failed me;
¹⁵the guests in my house have forgotten
me;
my maidservants count me as a stranger;
I have become an alien in their eyes.
¹⁶I call to my servant, but he gives me no
answer;
I must beseech him with my mouth.
¹⁷I am repulsive to my wife,
loathsome to the sons of my own mother.
¹⁸Even young children despise me;
when I rise they talk against me.
¹⁹All my intimate friends abhor me,
and those whom I loved have turned
against me.
²⁰My bones cleave to my skin and to my
flesh,
and I have escaped by the skin of
my teeth.
²¹Have pity on me, have pity on me, O you
my friends,
for the hand of God has touched me!
²²Why do you, like God, pursue me?
Why are you not satisfied with my
flesh?"**

---

t Heb *their way*   *LXX *Only know that the Lord has dealt with me thus. You speak against me; you do not feel for me, but bear hard upon me.*   †LXX *(4-7) I have erred in truth, but the error abides with me, in having spoken words which it was not right to speak; and my words err and are inopportune. But alas! Since you magnify yourselves against me and insult me with reproach, know then that it is the Lord that has troubled me and has raised his bulwark against me. Behold, I laugh at reproach; I will not speak, or I will cry out, but there is nowhere judgment; I still contend.*   ‡LXX *(8-11) I am fenced round about and can by no means escape; he has set darkness before my face. And he has stripped me of my glory and has taken the crown from my head. He has torn me around about, and I am gone, and he has cut off my hope like a tree. And he has dreadfully handled me in anger and has counted me for an enemy.*   §Vg *His robbers came on together, and through me they made their own way and surrounded my tent with siegeworks.*   #LXX *My brothers have withdrawn from me; they have recognized strangers rather than me*   **LXX *(20-22) My flesh is corrupt under my skin, and my bones are held in my teeth. Pity me, pity me, O friends; for it is the hand of the Lord that has touched me. Wherefore do you persecute me as also the Lord does, and are not satisfied with my flesh?*

OVERVIEW: The Fathers emphasize how in his reply Job demonstrates the heartlessness of his friends (CHRYSOSTOM), who are not able to express respect for him, who fight against Job in his trials and wait for God's judgment (Chrysostom, Origen, Olympiodorus, Julian of Eclanum, Isho'dad). They are so malicious and disloyal that they represent a foreshadowing of the heretics (Gregory). The visitors are reprimanded for lack of empathy (Origen). Job wonders why they add their wrath to divine wrath without doing this according to God's will (Olympiodorus). One whom God strikes does not always suffer because of his faults, but in order to be tested (Chrysostom). At the same time, Job's sufferings prefigure Christ's passion (Hesychius) and announce the Christian message that will be received by the Gentiles and refused by the Jews (Gregory).

19:1-2 How Long Will You Torment Me?

A Type of the Heretics to Come. Gregory the Great: The sayings of the holy man, as we have already often said, are to be understood as spoken sometimes in his own person, as sometimes in the voice of the Head and sometimes as a prefigurement of the universal church. Now the soul of the righteous is deeply distressed when people launch severe sentences against the good; they have not learned to lead good lives. By their words they claim righteousness for themselves, while in their actions they prove to be its enemies. To the friends of blessed Job, who bear the type of heretics, he rightly answers, "How long will you torment me and break me in pieces with words?" For good people are "broken into pieces" by the words of the wicked. They come out against them with words of the lips while they lie low either in a corrupt faith or in bad habits. Morals on the Book of Job 14.29.[1]

19:3 Reproach and Wrong

Heartlessness and Impiety of Job's Friends. Chrysostom: "Only know that the Lord has dealt with me thus. . . . You speak against me; you do not feel for me but bear hard upon me. . . . May the dignity of him who pun-

ishes me make you change your mind," he says. We do not have to trample underfoot the people who are punished by God, but we must shed tears and grieve over their fate. Above all, we must not rejoice over the death of anybody, because such an action will not be left unpunished. Who would have not respected Job's misfortune, at least because of the dignity of him who chastised him? Commentary on Job 19.3a.[2]

19:4-7 God Has Put a Net Around Me

The Test of Suffering. Chrysostom: Job says this as a concession. He always acts in this manner, by multiplying his concessions. He does not allow the discussion to languish on the same point but begins his fight again. Let us admit, he says, that you reprove my words for being foolish, vain and inopportune. You, nonetheless, had no reason to insult me, even if things were so, but it was necessary to respect my distress, to fear him who had struck me, to forgive because of the greatness of my misfortunes.

"But alas! Since you magnify yourselves against me and insult me with reproach," he says, "know then that it is the Lord that has troubled me." What do these words mean? That it is necessary to have respect and fear? In my opinion, Job wants to suggest in this passage that if he was suffering so much, it was not because of his faults—in fact, if God strikes one, does one always suffer because of his faults? Not Job, and not many others—but in order to be tested and to achieve more victories. Commentary on Job 19.3b-6a.[3]

The Visitors Reprimanded for Lack of Sympathy. Origen: "And if I—let us suppose—had done things that should not have been done, even if I had been in such a condition, was it not necessary just the same that you felt ashamed while seeing my afflictions, disease, worms and loss of goods? But you approach me without commiserating with me and without

---

[1]LF 21:135**. [2]PTS 35:127. [3]PTS 35:127-28.

feeling any sympathy for my adversities." . . . "I will cry out, and there is nowhere judgment; I still contend." This is as if Job had said, "I cried out like an athlete in the stadium, but my judgment is nowhere there. Indeed, I still fight. But if I do not bring my fight to a close, I will not get my crown." We actually say these things lest we accuse God of the fact that Job suffered such misfortunes and there was judgment for him nowhere. Fragments on Job 13.15, 29.[4]

19:8-11 Darkness and Obstacles

Job's Patience Is Tested. Olympiodorus: "No speech," Job says, "can describe my misfortunes. As those who are surrounded on every side by a wall or are oppressed by darkness, I cannot proceed any further. So, it is impossible for me to escape these calamities." He says that his crown was taken away from him, that is, he also was a king before, or . . . [5] "He tore me off," he says, "and like a tree he cut away all my hopes from the roots. Like an enemy who is inflamed with anger, he destroyed all my prosperity." Job correctly says "like an enemy," because God does not inflict torments with an angry or hostile mind. He says these things in order to persuade his friends and himself that his punishment exceeds the limits of human crimes. Indeed, that righteous man was suffering not because of his crimes but in order that his patience might be tested. Commentary on Job 19.8-11.[6]

19:12 Besieged

Job Metaphorically Describes His Misfortunes. Julian of Eclanum: "His robbers came together, and through me they made their own way." Either Job employs use of the simile that he had chosen in order to say that he is exposed to the attack of the enemies and that they go back and forth without any obstacle on their open way, or he refers to the messenger who announced to him those misfortunes that had befallen him. Indeed, the text says, "While he was still speaking, another messenger came."[7] "His robbers came together." He has developed the metaphor that he had suggested with the name *enemy*. In fact, since Job said that God came as a king to fight him as an enemy, he now adds, "His robbers came together." It is as if he said, his soldiers, because Scripture usually calls the spies of the enemies "robbers." Exposition on the Book of Job 19.12.[8]

19:13-15 Estranged from Family and Friends

Figures of Events in the Life of Christ. Hesychius of Jerusalem: The grace of the Gospel testifies that these words have been said about the Lord in truth. John, in fact, says, "His brothers did not believe in him,"[9] when they said to him, "Leave from here, and go into Judea, so that your disciples may also see the works that you do. For there is no man that does anything in secret, and he himself seeks to be known openly. If you do these things, show yourself to the world."[10] They said that because they did not know his ability and "recognized strangers rather than" him. This certainly referred to the Jews, that is, they looked after their own interests, and when he had to be admired, they despised him. Homilies on Job 22.19.13a-b.[11]

Christ's Own People Did Not Recognize Him. Gregory the Great: We shall show this more effectively if we introduce the testimony of John, who says, "He came to his own, and his own did not receive him."[12] For his "brothers were put far from him," and his "acquaintances were estranged" from him, concerning whom the Hebrews that held the law were taught to prophesy and never realized they should acknowledge when present. Thus it is rightly said, "My relatives and my close friends have failed me." The Jews,

---

[4]PTS 48:283, 287. [5]There is a lacuna in Olympiodorus' text. [6]PTS 24:165-66. [7]Job 1:17. [8]CCL 88:52-53. [9]Jn 7:5. [10]Jn 7:3-4. [11]PO 42.2:546. [12]Jn 1:11.

"relatives" in the flesh, an "acquaintance" by the teaching of the law, forgot him whom they had foretold. They sang of him in the words of the law as destined to become incarnate. When he was made incarnate, they denied him with words of unbelief. The text continues, "The guests in my house have forgotten me; my serving girls count me as a stranger." The inhabitants of God's house were the priests, whose race was once set apart in the service of God and continued henceforth by office in that state. But the "serving girls" are not improperly taken as the souls of the Levites, servants to the hidden parts of the tabernacle, as it were, by a more familiar service to the interior of the bedchamber. Therefore, let Job say of the priests, serving with diligent care, let him say of the Levites attending in the interior of the house of God, "The guests in my house have forgotten me; my serving girls count me as a stranger." For they refused to acknowledge and reverence the incarnate Lord, whom they had for long foretold in the words of the law. And yet, Job more plainly shows that he was not understood by their wicked will when he adds, "I have become an alien in their eyes." This prefigures our Redeemer who, because he was not recognized by the synagogue, was rendered, "as it were, an alien" in his own house. The prophet plainly witnesses to this, saying, "Wherefore shall you be as a settler in the land and as a wayfaring man that turns aside to tarry?"[13] When Christ was not heard as the Lord, he was not accepted as the owner but as "a settler of the land." He only "turned aside to tarry as a wayfaring man," in that he bore away only a few people out of Judea, and proceeding to the calling of the Gentiles finished the journey that he had begun. MORALS ON THE BOOK OF JOB 14.47-49.[14]

19:16-19 They Speak Against Me

A TARGET OF SCORN. ISHO'DAD OF MERV: "When I rise, they speak against me." Like a target, Job says, I rise before them, and they will spit upon me all the words of abuse that they want to say. COMMENTARY ON JOB 19.18.[15]

19:20-22 Have Pity!

A WARNING AGAINST ABUSE. OLYMPIODORUS: "My flesh is corrupt under my skin, and my teeth grip my bones." "While I am alive," Job says, "my flesh putrefies, and my bones are chewed by the teeth of some wild animal." "Pity me, pity me, O friends, for it is the hand of the Lord that has touched me." "You are not ashamed before the one who says righteous words. As benevolent persons, you have compassion upon me and take pity by considering also the respect due to what has been inflicted on me by God. You will not be tested by God through the same calamities." "Why do you persecute me as also the Lord does, and are not satisfied with my flesh? Why do you add your wrath to divine wrath without doing this according to God's will? Even though God punishes, he, nonetheless, wants to be good to us— and therefore, why do you insatiably use the harshness of your words against me?" In fact, abusive words are sufficient to devour flesh. So let us fear invectives and insults, because we are aware of the fact that they wound our brothers. COMMENTARY ON JOB 19.20-22.[16]

---

[13]Jer 14:8. [14]LF 21:148-49*. [15]CSCO 229:249. [16]PTS 24:168-69.

19:23-29 JOB'S HOPE IN GOD THE REDEEMER

²³Oh that my words were written!
    Oh that they were inscribed in a book!
²⁴Oh that with an iron pen and lead
    they were graven in the rock for ever!
²⁵For I know that my Redeemer" lives,
    and at last he will stand upon the
    earth;ᵛ
²⁶and after my skin has been thus destroyed,
    then fromʷ my flesh I shall see God,ˣ
²⁷whom I shall see on my side,ʸ

and my eyes shall behold, and not
    another.
    My heart faints within me!*
²⁸If you say, "How we will pursue him!"
    and, "The root of the matter is found in
    him";†
²⁹be afraid of the sword,†
    for wrath brings the punishment of the
    sword,
    that you may know there is a judgment.

u Or Vindicator v Or dust w Or without x The meaning of this verse is uncertain. y Or for myself *LXX (25-27) For I know that he who is about to deliver me on earth is immortal, and he will raise up my body that endures these sufferings, for it is the Lord, who caused them; which I am conscious of in myself which my eye has seen, and not another, but all have been fulfilled to me in my bosom. †Vg Why do you say now, Let us persecute him and find out the root of the word against him? ‡Vg fly from the face of the sword

OVERVIEW: In the second part of Job's speech, the prophetic aspect of his words prevails, according to the interpretation of the Fathers. Job declares the Truth (JULIAN OF ECLANUM) and announces the advent of Christ, his judgment and the resurrection of the body (EPHREM, CHRYSOSTOM, GREGORY). Job here anticipates the later teaching of the resurrection (CHRYSOSTOM). Those who are behaving badly do not grasp the coming judgment (GREGORY).

19:23-24 O That My Words Were Written Down!

JOB SPEAKS TRULY AND DELIBERATELY.
JULIAN OF ECLANUM: We desire what we have said with a troubled mind not be confusedly relegated to oblivion as a cause of shame. On the contrary we want what we have said seriously and carefully to be fixed in the memory and remain in the mouth of many people. Therefore also holy Job, intending to show that he had not poured out what he had said with a troubled mind but that his words were truthful and reasonable, wishes that his words are not only written on

paper but also engraved on lead and stone, so that they may be preserved for a long time. EXPOSITION ON THE BOOK OF JOB 19.23-24.[1]

19:25-27 My Redeemer Lives

A PROPHECY. EPHREM THE SYRIAN: "For I know that my Redeemer lives and that at last he will be revealed upon the earth." Here the blessed Job predicts the future manifestation of Emmanuel in the flesh at the end of time. COMMENTARY ON JOB 19.25.[2]

JOB'S REDEEMER LIVES. CHRYSOSTOM: "For I know that he, who is about to deliver me on earth, is immortal." That is, he who has to deliver me on earth is God. What does this mean? If God is immortal, why do you want your words to be written and their memory to remain eternally, in an imperishable manner? Notice the state of the soul of those who are in distress. They want not only those who are seeing these events now, but also those, who will come later, to be witnesses of

¹CCL 88:53. ²ESOO 2:8.

their own misfortunes, in order to obtain, in a sense, a certain sympathy from everyone. This is evidently what the rich man[3] tried to do when he wanted to inform everybody about his own misfortunes and about the situation in which he who previously lived in luxury finally finds himself.

"He will raise up my body that endures these sufferings, for it is the Lord who caused them." Did Job know the doctrine of resurrection? I believe so, and the doctrine concerning the resurrection of the body, unless he says here that the resurrection that he speaks about is the deliverance from the afflictions that pressed him. That is why, Job says, even after my deliverance, I want my afflictions to be immortal. This is an extremely wise way to keep always before one's eyes the punishments of God even after they have gone. . . . "For it is the Lord," he says, "who caused these sufferings." Job is correct in saying that the Lord will be the actual cause of his change. "He strikes," Job says, "and he heals."[4] COMMENTARY ON JOB 19.25-26.[5]

19:28-29 Know There Is a Judgment

WE MUST FEAR CHRIST THE JUDGE. GREGORY THE GREAT: Everyone who does wicked things, even he who is too indifferent to fear this, does not know of the judgment of God. If he did know that this was a thing to be feared, he would never do things that are destined to be punished. For there are very many who know that there is a final judgment as far as the words go, but by acting wickedly they bear witness that they do not know it. Since one does not dread this as he ought, he does not yet know with what a tempest of terror judgment will come. For if he had been taught to estimate the weight of the dreadful scrutiny, surely in fearing he would guard against the day of wrath. Moreover, "to fly from the face of the sword" is to propitiate the sentence of the strict visitation before it appears. For the dread and terror of the Judge cannot be avoided, except before the judgment. Now he is not discerned but is appeased by prayers. But when he shall sit on that dreadful inquest, he is both able to be seen and no longer able to be propitiated in that the deeds of the wicked, which he bore long in silence, he shall pay back all of them together in wrath. Hence it is necessary to fear the Judge now, while he does not yet execute judgment, while he bears patiently for long, while he still tolerates the wickedness that he sees, lest when he has once stretched out his hand in the awarding of vengeance, he strikes the more severely in judgment in proportion as he waited longer before judgment. MORALS ON THE BOOK OF JOB 14.79.[6]

---

[3]See Lk 16:19-31. [4]Job 5:18. [5]PTS 35:130-31. [6]LF 21:170-71*.

20:1-29 ZOPHAR EXPLAINS THAT GOD'S JUSTICE NEVER FAILS

[1] Then Zophar the Naamathite answered:
[2]"Therefore my thoughts answer me,
  because of my haste within me.

[3]I hear censure which insults me,
  and out of my understanding a spirit
  answers me.

⁴Do you not know this from of old,
    since man was placed upon earth,
⁵that the exulting of the wicked is short,
    and the joy of the godless but for
        a moment?*
⁶Though his height mount up to the
        heavens,
    and his head reach to the clouds,
⁷he will perish for ever like his own dung;
    those who have seen him will say,
        'Where is he?'
⁸He will fly away like a dream, and not be
        found;
    he will be chased away like a vision
        of the night.
⁹The eye which saw him will see him no
        more,
    nor will his place any more behold
        him.
¹⁰His children will seek the favor of the
        poor,
    and his hands will give back his wealth.†
¹¹His bones are full of youthful vigor,
    but it will lie down with him in the dust.‡

¹²"Though wickedness is sweet in his mouth,
    though he hides it under his tongue,
¹³though he is loath to let it go,
    and holds it in his mouth,
¹⁴yet his food is turned in his stomach;
    it is the gall of asps within him.
¹⁵He swallows down riches and vomits them
        up again;
    God casts them out of his belly.§
¹⁶He will suck the poison of asps;
    the tongue of a viper will kill him.
¹⁷He will not look upon the rivers,#
    the streams flowing with honey and
        curds.

¹⁸He will give back the fruit of his toil,
    and will not swallow it down;
 from the profit of his trading
    he will get no enjoyment.
¹⁹For he has crushed and abandoned the
        poor,
    he has seized a house which he did not
        build.

²⁰"Because his greed knew no rest,
    he will not save anything in which he
        delights.
²¹There was nothing left after he had eaten;
    therefore his prosperity will not endure.**
²²In the fulness of his sufficiency he will be
        in straits;
    all the force of misery will come upon
        him.
²³To fill his belly to the full
    Godᶻ will send his fierce anger into him,
    and rain it upon him as his food.ᵃ††
²⁴He will flee from an iron weapon;
    a bronze arrow will strike him through.
²⁵It is drawn forth and comes out of his
        body,
    the glittering point comes out of his gall;
    terrors come upon him.‡‡
²⁶Utter darkness is laid up for his treasures;
    a fire not blown upon will devour
        him;
    what is left in his tent will be consumed.
²⁷The heavens will reveal his iniquity,
    and the earth will rise up against him.
²⁸The possessions of his house will be
        carried away,
    dragged off in the day of God'sᵇ wrath.
²⁹This is the wicked man's portion from
        God,
    the heritage decreed for him by God."§§

z Heb *he*   a Cn: Heb *in his flesh*   b Heb *his*   *LXX *that the mirth of the impious is a ruinous downfall and the joy of the iniquitous is destruction*   †LXX (9-10) *The eye has looked upon him but shall not see him again; and his place shall no longer perceive him. Let his inferiors destroy his children, and let his hands kindle the fire of sorrow.*   ‡Peshitta *Their bones are full of marrow and will lie down in the dust with them.*   §Vg *of his belly;* LXX *a messenger of wrath shall drag him out of his house*   #Peshitta *They will not see the division of the rivers.*   **LXX (19-21) *For he has broken down the houses of many poor men, and he has plundered an habitation, though he built it not. There is no security to his possessions; he shall not be saved by his desire. There is nothing remaining of his provisions; therefore his goods shall not flourish.*   ††LXX (22-23) *But when he shall seem to be just satisfied, he shall be straitened; and all distress shall come upon him. If by any means he would fill his belly, let God send upon him the fury of wrath; let him bring a torrent of pains upon him.*   ‡‡Vg *Terrible ones come and go upon him*   §§LXX (28-29) *Let destruction bring his house to an end; let a day of wrath come upon him. This is the portion of an ungodly man from the Lord, and the possession of his goods appointed him by the all-seeing God.*

OVERVIEW: The Fathers give an almost unanimous interpretation of Zophar's second speech. They recognize how his words are morally correct and worthy of attention when they refer to a general context (GREGORY, CHRYSOSTOM, ISHO'DAD, ORIGEN, OLYMPIODORUS), but also how they appear to be groundlessly reproachful and falsely accusatory when they are referred to Job's specific case (PHILIP, HESYCHIUS). Zophar's words also have a prophetic value, as they announce the gifts of the spirit and final judgment (EPHREM, GREGORY).

20:1-3 Hear My Words!

ZOPHAR ASSERTS JOB'S GUILT. PHILIP THE PRIEST: Therefore, Zophar says, I burn inside and am confused in my mind, because you assert that you are enduring these calamities from God, the judge, for no reason, when no evil can be expected from God. "I hear censure that insults me, and a spirit beyond my understanding answers me." I will listen to you while you reproach and correct me. For I do not have to scold one who has been placed in calamities by chance. I can really say what is more appropriate about God. In fact, you could not be punished so by him if you were not aware of your evils and guilty of many crimes. COMMENTARY ON THE BOOK OF JOB 20.[1]

20:4-5 Shortlived Joy and Exultation

ZOPHAR'S IMPUDENT WORDS. HESYCHIUS OF JERUSALEM: In this passage Zophar speaks impudently and seriously insults Job. By scorning him, as the other two friends had already done, Zophar also defamed him for the following reason. After the beginning, after human beings came into existence, they felt "joy" and happiness in the fall "of the impious" and the "destruction of the iniquitous." Zophar wants to include Job among them as well, according to what he says afterwards. Actually, forgetting that great number of people, Zophar addresses his words to a single person. HOMILIES ON JOB 24.20.5.[2]

20:6-8 Hypocrites Will Perish Forever

THE IRRELEVANT AND DAMNABLE LIFE OF THE HYPOCRITE. GREGORY THE GREAT: The pride of the hypocrite is said to "mount up as high as the heavens," when his highmindedness has the appearance of leading a heavenly life. And his "head, as it were, reaches to the clouds," when the leading part, that is, his intellect, is thought to equal the merits of the saints that have gone before. Yet "he perishes at last like his own dung," because at his death, when he is led to torments, being full of the dung of evil habits, he is trampled underfoot by evil spirits. . . . It generally happens that the life of the hypocrite is discovered by all people at the end to be damnable, for it to be made apparent by plainer marks of what sort it was. Those who formerly saw him happy shall then say of him when dead, "Where is he?" For neither is he seen here, where he was elated, nor in the rest of eternity, which he was supposed to receive. Concerning the brevity of the hypocrite's life, it is yet further added fittingly, "He will fly away like a dream and not be found; he will be chased away like a vision of the night." What else is the life of

---

[1]PL 26:668.   [2]PO 42.2:574.

the hypocrite but the vision of a phantom that exhibits the facade that it does not possess in truth? MORALS ON THE BOOK OF JOB 15.5-7.[3]

20:9-10 They Will No Longer Be Seen

SUDDEN RUIN COMES FROM GOD. CHRYSOSTOM: This means that their ruin comes suddenly, so that you may not believe that their calamity comes from a natural condition but that it is in accordance with a divine and extraordinary power. Moreover, this concerns not only their crimes but also their sacrifices. If they offer any, they turn out to be useless. "Let his inferiors," Zophar says, "destroy his children." This sentence also demonstrates clearly that the blow comes from God, because inferior people prevail on those who are stronger, and those who are outcast prevail on those who have power. COMMENTARY ON JOB 8-10.[4]

20:11-14 Bodies Lying Down in Dust

A MISERY GREATER THAN DEATH. ISHO'DAD OF MERV: "Their bones are full of marrow and will lie down in the dust with them." By the "marrow" that is inside the bones, the author signifies prosperity. That is, from his former prosperity he will pass to a profound abasement, so that he will not be inferior to the dead. COMMENTARY ON JOB 20.11.[5]

AN ALLUSION TO THE BITTERNESS OF HERESY. ORIGEN: They have theories that are not sweet but as the gall of asps, that is, evil; and those theories come from the wine of their doctrine. "For their wine comes from the vine of Sodom."[6] The gall of asps is in the belly of the heretics and those who declare impious dogmas contrary to truth. FRAGMENTS ON JOB 14.41.[7]

20:15 The Wicked Are Condemned

THE HYPOCRITE SPEAKS SAGELY BUT DOES NOT LIVE SO. GREGORY THE GREAT: The hypocrite desires to know the revelations of God, yet [he does] not to practice them. He would speak sagely but not live so. For this reason, then, he does not do what he knows, and even that which he knows he loses. For since he does not unite wholesome practice with his knowledge, despising purity of right practice, he loses the knowledge also. Therefore, the "riches" of the sacred law that he "swallowed" in reading, he vomits in forgetting. And God "casts them out of his belly," in that what he fails to do is by a righteous judgment rooted altogether out of his memory. God will not allow him to keep the precepts of God with his words only, but which he did not practice in his life. Hence it is said by the prophet, "But to the wicked God said, 'Why should you declare my statutes? For what reason should you take my covenant in your mouth?'"[8] If at any time the hypocrite should seem to retain these words of instruction in his mouth until the end, he will be condemned the more on those very grounds; whereas not even a bad person is ever deprived of the good gift of God. For it is written, "To those who remember his commandments."[9] . . . He then that keeps his commandments in mind but never does them, holds in the words of instruction the very sentences by which he is condemned. MORALS ON THE BOOK OF JOB 15.17.[10]

THE RICHES OF THE WICKED AND THE HERETIC ARE DOOMED. ORIGEN: What other riches are unjustly gathered but those which are in their speeches? Indeed, they are unjustly gathered. But God, in his benevolence, does not allow those mad people to keep forever their unjustly gathered riches. He will cause them to vomit them up again. . . . The angel, in fact, through the action and benevolence of God, drags him out of his wickedly built house, that is, the church of those who behave wickedly; it is their house. But the

---

[3]LF 21:175-76*. [4]PTS 35:133. [5]CSCO 229:249. [6]Deut 32:32. [7]PTS 48:324. [8]Ps 50:16 (49:16 LXX). [9]Ps 103:18 (102:18 LXX). [10]LF 21:181-82**.

angel drags him out of his house. FRAGMENTS ON JOB 14.43, 47.[11]

20:16-18 The Wicked Will Not Look on the Rivers

A PREDICTION OF THE GIFTS OF THE SPIRIT. EPHREM THE SYRIAN: "They will not rejoice on the division of the rivers,[12] the streams flowing with honey and curds." These words mean that those rivers were divided on Mount Calvary, and the streams derived from the rivers signify the gifts of the Spirit communicated by the revelation of the Gospel. COMMENTARY ON JOB 20.17.[13]

20:19-21 Gaining No Enjoyment

WEALTH GAINED WITH VIOLENCE WILL NOT LAST. OLYMPIODORUS: "For he has broken down the houses of many poor men, and he has plundered a dwelling, though he did not build it. His possessions provide no security." He has broken down, that is, has shattered mercilessly [their houses], has carried off all their properties and has not given them back. In fact, he has not mended this situation, that is, has not returned what he has stolen. But, as he has carried off the properties of the poor and has not restored them, so his own possessions will not be saved either. "He shall not be saved by his desire. There is nothing remaining of his provisions; therefore his goods shall not flourish." The impious, Zophar says, will not save himself through his desire, and then he will not have any provision left, because he does not possess anything that has been left to him by his absolute misery. COMMENTARY ON JOB 20.19-21.[14]

20:22-23 Misery Will Come on Them

A SEVERE PUNISHMENT WILL FOLLOW. OLYMPIODORUS: Perhaps not even his goods will flourish, but they will become corrupted while still in bloom. In fact, if he appears to be full and abundant in all goods, then every need and affliction

will assault him, so that he fills his belly, that is, fills his soul with every pain. "Let God send upon him the fury of wrath; let him bring a torrent of pains upon him." God, by striking him with the most severe punishment, will bury him in pains as under a snowstorm. COMMENTARY ON JOB 20.21-23.[15]

20:24-25 Terrors

OVERRUN BY EVIL SPIRITS. GREGORY THE GREAT: For you may often see the bad person, who is set in earthly power, agitated with furious passion and executing all that his rage suggests. When his fury is gone, then lust directly ravages his soul. When lust is stopped for a time, his continence produces self-exaltation that immediately occupies his heart. So that others may fear him, he aims to present himself as an object of terror. But when the occasion requires that he should say anything deceitfully, he seems to lay aside the horror of his pride and flatters with an easy address. When he ceases to show himself proud, he does not dread to act deceitfully again. And so it is rightly said of him, in whose mind one vice takes the place of another, "Terrible ones come and go upon him." Since all the evil habits weigh him down with their coming and going in taking each other's place, his soul is, as it were, overrun by as many evil spirits departing and returning. MORALS ON THE BOOK OF JOB 15.33.[16]

20:26-27 Devoured by Fire

A REFERENCE TO THE FINAL JUDGMENT. GREGORY THE GREAT: What do we understand by "the heavens," but the righteous, and what by "the earth," but sinners? Hence, in the Lord's Prayer we pray, "Your will be done on earth as it is in heaven." This means that the will of our Cre-

---

[11]PTS 48:325-26. [12]The version of the Syriac Bible employed by Ephrem differs from the Peshitta in this passage and reads: "they will not rejoice on the division" instead of "they will not see the division." [13]ESOO 2:8-9. [14]PTS 24:177-78. [15]PTS 24:178. [16]LF 21:193-94*.

ator, in the same way as it is accomplished in all the righteous, may be fulfilled in all sinners as well. Moreover, of the righteous it is said, "The heavens declare the glory of God."[17] To man, when he sinned, the sentence is pronounced, "You are earth, and to earth you shall return." And so of this ungodly man, when dragged to that awful judgment, "the heavens reveal his iniquity, and the earth rises up against him," that that man, who never spared either the good or the bad, should in that tremendous inquest have the life of the righteous and of sinners alike accusing him. MORALS ON THE BOOK OF JOB 15.37.[18]

20:28-29 The Day of God's Anger

A WARNING TO THE MINISTERS OF THE CHURCH. OLYMPIODORUS: "Let a day of wrath come upon him. This is the portion for the ungodly man from the Lord, and the possession of his goods appointed him by the all-seeing[19] God." Since he did not recognize the benevolence of God while he possessed his goods, the fullness of wrath is given him as his property and reward. Therefore the bishops, when they hear in holy Scripture that God is invoked with this name, must protect the dignity of his name by taking care of the safety of their herd with watchful guard and faith, being irreprehensible in life and adorned with doctrine. COMMENTARY ON JOB 20.28-29.[20]

BISHOPS MUST EMULATE THE MODEL OF JESUS. ORIGEN: [The wrath of God strikes] both the circumcised, who act impiously against Christ, and the heretic and indeed any who are ungodly. The retribution of each is according to what has been shown above. Do you understand who is the overseer[21] mentioned here? God is called "overseer," and his bishops must endeavor in every way to put into practice his model, if they are good. And as one who emulates a royal model is honored, because he has emulated it in a proper way, so the blessed bishop who meditates upon the true bishop and imitates him also becomes like a god among humans. He really has in himself that bishop and has made himself a bishop in Jesus Christ. FRAGMENTS ON JOB 14.106, 110.[22]

---

[17]Ps 19:1 (18:2 LXX). [18]LF 21:196*. [19]*Episkopos* (i.e.,"bishop") in the Greek text. [20]PTS 24:180. [21]The word *episkopos* ("bishop") literally means "overseer" in Greek. [22]PTS 48:341-43.

21:1-16 JOB CONSIDERS THE PROSPERITY OF THE WICKED

[1] Then Job answered:
[2]"Listen carefully to my words,
    and let this be your consolation.
[3]Bear with me, and I will speak,
    and after I have spoken, mock on.*
[4]As for me, is my complaint against
        man?
Why should I not be impatient?[†]
[5]Look at me, and be appalled,
    and lay your hand upon your mouth.
[6]When I think of it I am dismayed,
    and shuddering seizes[‡] my flesh.
[7]Why do the wicked live,
    reach old age, and grow mighty in power?

⁸*Their children are established in their presence,*
and their offspring before their eyes.
⁹*Their houses are safe from fear,*
and no rod of God is upon them.
¹⁰*Their bull breeds without fail;*
their cow calves, and does not cast her calf.
¹¹*They send forth their little ones like a flock,*
and their children dance.
¹²*They sing to the tambourine and the lyre,*
and rejoice to the sound of the pipe.

¹³*They spend their days in prosperity,*
and in peace they go down to Sheol.
¹⁴*They say to God, 'Depart from us!*
We do not desire the knowledge of thy ways.[§]
¹⁵*What is the Almighty, that we should serve him?*
And what profit do we get if we pray to him?'
¹⁶*Behold, is not their prosperity in their hand?*
The counsel of the wicked is far from me."[#]

Vg (2-3) Hear I pray you my speech, and practice penitence. Suffer me that I may speak; and after my words, if it shall seem so, laugh. †LXX (3-4) Raise me, and I will speak; then you shall not laugh me to scorn. What! Is it a mortal who blames me? And why should I not be angry? ‡LXX pains seize §LXX (7-14) For what reason do the ungodly live, and grow old even in wealth? Their seed is according to their desire, and their children are in their sight. Their houses are prosperous, neither have they anywhere cause for fear, neither is there a scourge from the Lord upon them. Their cow does not cast her calf, and their beast with young is safe and does not miscarry. And they remain as eternal sheep, and their children play before them, taking up the psaltery and harp; and they rejoice at the voice of a song. And they spend their days in wealth and fall asleep in the rest of the grave. Yet such a man says to the Lord, Depart from me; I desire not to know thy ways.   #Vg But because their good things are not in their hand, may their counsel be far from me.

OVERVIEW: Job's extended and detailed reflection on the prosperity of the wicked on earth is not interpreted by the Fathers as criticism against God's way of ruling and administering our material world but as a constant source of moral instruction and meditation for the righteous and the faithful (GREGORY, CHRYSOSTOM, EPHREM, OLYMPIODORUS, ORIGEN). Even if he is unable to avail his hearers, Job must speak in order to avoid the sin of silence (GREGORY). As his soul is dismayed, he speaks not for himself alone (CHRYSOSTOM). The faithful understandably ask the burning question of why the ungodly prosper while the godly suffer (OLYMPIODORUS); meanwhile God patiently offers his love to the unrighteous (EPHREM), who continue to mock the oracles of God (ORIGEN). Whoever loves temporal things excessively subjects himself all the more to them than them to himself. The eyes of their body indeed are open, but they cannot perceive anything because the sense of sight is gone. One "holds his good things in his hand" who in despising temporal things overcomes them under the dominion of the mind (GREGORY).

21:1-3 Listen with Care

THE WORDS OF THE RIGHTEOUS. GREGORY THE GREAT: For when good people speak, there are two points that they regard in their discourse (viz. , that they should be of use to themselves and their hearers, or to themselves alone), if they are unable to be of use to their hearers. For when the good things they deliver are heard with good purpose, they benefit both themselves and their hearers. But even when they are turned to ridicule by the hearer, doubtless they were of use to themselves, by no longer consenting to the sin of silence. And so let blessed Job, that he might serve both himself and his hearers, speak the words, "Hear, I pray you, my speech, and practice repentance." In order that he may discharge himself of the obligation that he owes, even if he is unable to avail his hearers, he adds, "Suffer me that I speak; and after my words, if it shall seem so, laugh." I observe that whereas he added, "and practice repentance," he first premised, "Hear," but when he added the words "and after my words, if it shall seem so, laugh," he premised, "Permit me to speak"; for "hearing" is of one who acts of free will, but "bearing" of one who acts against his own inclination. And so if his friends desire to be taught, let them "hear," but if they are ready to mock, let them "suffer" the things that are said seeing that to a proud mind instruction in humility is a grievous and onerous weight. MORALS ON THE BOOK OF JOB 15.41.[1]

21:4-6 Dismayed in Soul

NO MORTAL CAN BLAME ME. CHRYSOSTOM: Let us admit, he says, that I am iniquitous and impious; but I gain no profit from these remarks and know that you will mock me; therefore, I do not yield. "And what!" he says, "is it a mortal who blames me?" that is, no mortal can blame me. I am not fighting against a man. "When I think of it, I am dismayed and pains seize my flesh." Notice how he always stands up, how he puts forward his sufferings, how he indicates the reason for the terrible words he is going to speak, because he does not talk in this manner by himself or from a fixed position but because his soul is dismayed and his thoughts are darkened. COMMENTARY ON JOB 21.3-6.[2]

21:7-14 Why Do the Wicked Continue?

GOD'S MERCY. EPHREM THE SYRIAN: Certainly God does not cease from benefiting the wicked, in order to show that he has no hate against them, so that they may not say, "Since God hates us, he will never open the door of repentance to us." And while he severely and sternly acts with the righteous, he nevertheless offers his love to the unrighteous. The rewards to be granted in time for [righteous] virtues are the future signs of the good works they do. COMMENTARY ON JOB 21.3-7.[3]

HOW CAN WE EXPLAIN THE PROSPERITY OF THE WICKED? OLYMPIODORUS: Since you believe to be wise and to know the reason why I suffer these afflictions, now answer my question. Why does it happen that very often many impious persons reach an old age in their wealth? . . . Their fields produce large crops, and they are delighted by their children and enjoy a constant abundance. They fear no one and receive no blow sent them by God. Their plowing cow does not give birth to an immature fetus, that is, it does not generate an imperfect or dead fetus, and their wives have no miscarriages. And they remain in prosperity like a flock, that is, free from care. COMMENTARY ON JOB 21.6-14.[4]

THE HERETICS' EMPTY IMITATION OF THE CHRISTIAN CHURCH. ORIGEN: "And they remain as eternal sheep."[5] What is the meaning of these words? They are those words that Christ spoke, "My sheep hear my voice, and I give them eternal life."[6] The faithful are the eternal sheep; the heretics are imitators. They want to imitate the flock of Christ. They ordain their own bishops, presbyters, deacons, doctors, congregation and catechumens, and by imitating the eternal sheep they fulfill the prediction, "And they appear as eternal sheep." They clearly are not eternal sheep but "appear as eternal sheep." FRAGMENTS ON JOB 15.23.[7]

THE HERETICS DO NOT PRAISE OR GLORIFY GOD. ORIGEN: "And their children play before them, taking up the psaltery and harp."[8] Our children take up the psaltery and the harp, praising and glorifying God. But "their [the heretics'] children," who are foolish in themselves, also "play taking up the psaltery and the harp." Every time they usurp the words of the Old Testament, they play and mock the oracles of the Law and

---

[1]LF 21:199-200*. [2]PTS 35:135. [3]ESOO 2:9. [4]PTS 24:184. [5]Job 21:9 LXX; see also the apparatus at the foot of the text of the pericope. [6]See Jn 10:27-28. [7]PTS 48:354. [8]Job 21:11 LXX; see also the apparatus at the foot of the text of the pericope.

the Prophets. By taking up the harmonies that were once the psaltery of the law and the prophetic harp, they play with them. FRAGMENTS ON JOB 15.25.[9]

21:15-16 Why Serve the Almighty?

OUR EYES FIXED ON HEAVENLY THINGS ONLY. GREGORY THE GREAT: For it very often happens that people make it more their aim to serve their fellow creatures, whom they see with bodily sight, than to serve God, whom they do not see. For in all that they do, their eyes reach out only for what they can see. But they cannot stretch the eyes of the body to God. They become scornful of paying god homage. They grow weary. For, as has been said, they do not serve him whom they do not behold with bodily sight. If they would but seek God, the author of all things, in a spirit of humility, they would in themselves experience that something not seen is preferred to an object that is seen. For they themselves exist by virtue of an invisible soul and a visible body. But if that which is not seen is withdrawn from them, what is seen at once perishes. The eyes of the body indeed are open, but they cannot see or perceive anything, for the sense of sight is gone, because the indweller has quit, and the house of the flesh remains empty, since that invisible spirit has departed which was wont to look through its windows. . . .

Rather, to us, the eternal world ought to be viewed in both thought and intent, yet in the way the world of time views it, one is "given" and the other "added" over and above in superabundance. And yet it very often happens that when people pray for temporal good things but do not look for eternal rewards, they seek the thing that is added and do not want that to which it should be added. They do not count it to be worthy of their prayer, if here they are poor in temporal things, and there live for everlasting wealth in blessedness. Having their eyes fixed on visible things alone, as has been said, they refuse to purchase for themselves

the invisible by the labor of asking God for it. If they only sought first that which is above, they would fill their labor already with fruit. When the mind employed in prayers pants after the form and fashion of its Maker, burning with divine longings, it is united to that which is above and liberated from that below. It opens itself in the affection of its fervent passion that it may take in [that which is above], and, while taking in, kindles itself. Merely to love things above is already to mount on high, and while with longing desire, the soul is already participating in heavenly things. In a marvelous way it tastes the very thing it longs to get. It goes on, "But because their good things are not in their hand, may their counsel be far from me." He "holds his good things in his hand" who in despising temporal things overcomes them under the dominion of the mind. For whoever loves them overly much subjects himself all the more to them than them to himself. For many of the righteous were rich in this world. Sustained by their substance and by their honor, they seemed to possess many things. Yet, because their mind was not possessed by the excessive enjoyment of these things that were theirs, "their good things were [seemingly possessed] in their own hands," because they were held subordinate to the authority of the soul. But on the other hand the wicked so discharge themselves with all their hearts in aiming toward outward things that they do not themselves hold the things possessed but are held with minds in bondage by the things they possess.

Therefore, because "their good things are not in their hand," it is rightly added, "let their counsel be far from me." For what is "the counsel of the wicked" except to seek earthly things and neglect eternal glory, to aim at temporal wellbeing at the cost of interior detriment and to exchange transitory sorrows for eternal woes? MORALS ON THE BOOK OF JOB 15.52-54.[10]

---

[9]PTS 48:354-55. [10]LF 21:205-8*.

21:17-34 THE WICKED OFTEN REMAIN UNPUNISHED IN THIS WORLD

^{17}How often is it that the lamp of the
    wicked is put out?
That their calamity* comes upon
    them?
That God^c distributes pains in his anger?
^{18}That they are like straw before the wind,
    and like chaff that the storm carries
    away?†
^{19}You say, "God stores up their iniquity for
    their sons."
Let him recompense it to themselves, that
    they may know it.
^{20}Let their own eyes see their destruction,
    and let them drink of the wrath of the
    Almighty.
^{21}For what do they care for their houses
    after them,
when the number of their months is cut
    off?
^{22}Will any teach God knowledge,
    seeing that he judges those that are on
    high?‡
^{23}One dies in full prosperity,
    being wholly at ease and secure,
^{24}his body^d full of fat
    and the marrow of his bones moist.
^{25}Another dies in bitterness of soul,
    never having tasted of good.

^{26}They lie down alike in the dust,
    and the worms cover them.

^{27}Behold, I know your thoughts,
    and your schemes to wrong me.
^{28}For you say, "Where is the house of the
    prince?
Where is the tent in which the wicked
    dwelt?"
^{29}Have you not asked those who travel the
    roads,
and do you not accept their testimony
^{30}that the wicked man is spared in the day
    of calamity,
that he is rescued in the day of wrath?§
^{31}Who declares his way to his face,
    and who requites him for what he has
    done?
^{32}When he is borne to the grave,
    watch is kept over his tomb.
^{33}The clods of the valley are sweet to him;
    all men follow after him,
    and those who go before him are
    innumerable.
^{34}How then will you comfort me with empty
    nothings?
There is nothing left of your answers but
    falsehood.$^#$

c Heb *he* d The meaning of the Hebrew word is uncertain *Vg *flooding* †In the Vg the sentences at Job 21:17-18 are not presented as questions but as positive statements. ‡LXX (19-22) Let his substance fail to supply his children, God shall punish him, and he shall know it. Let his eyes see his own destruction, and let him not be saved by the Lord. For his desire is in his house with him, and the number of his months has been suddenly cut off. Is it not the Lord who teaches understanding and knowledge? And does not he judge murders? #Peshitta *Emptiness* §Vg (29-30) *Ask every one of them that go by the way; and you will know that he understands this same. Because the wicked is reserved to the day of destruction, and he is brought to the day of wrath.*

OVERVIEW: In the second part of Job's speech, the Fathers demonstrate that if there is any criti- cism in Job's words, it is addressed to Zophar and his ignorance of divine justice (CHRYSOSTOM,

Julian of Eclanum). The form of justice that the visitors think they understand is lame (Julian of Eclanum). They bring Job even more suffering instead of consolation (Isho'dad). At the same time the fathers also emphasize the moral content of Job's speech (Philip, Gregory, Isho'dad) and its eternal context (Philip). No one can discern the secret plans of God (Chrysostom). Only one who has already removed his heart from the love of the present world can find equanimity in the fact that here the wicked thrive (Gregory).

21:17-18 The Lamp of the Wicked Extinguished

The Eternal Light of Faith. Philip the Priest: Truly the light of the righteous is forever, because in this night of the world the lamp of faith is not extinguished by any wind of temptation and is prepared for the glory of the eternal light above. On the other hand, the light of the sinner is extinguished within the short time of human life, because he is temporary like a shadow. His light will not last, and a flooding will overwhelm the impious, as Job says, that is, in an abundance of torments. And [God] distributes the pains of his anger for each of them. Undoubtedly, he has said, God distributes pains, because he rewards each one with the punishment that he deserves. Commentary on the Book of Job 12.[1]

21:19-22 God Judges Those on High

Zophar Shows His Ignorance. Chrysostom: Since he spoke before him [Zophar] and said "from the time man was set upon the earth,"[2] things go on in this manner. Job addresses his reproaches to him, because he ignores what is clear and evident. He says to him, you asserted that things are not as I said, but quite the opposite. Therefore, no one must know the secret plans of God, who rules the entire creation. Now tell me, why are those who are not impious punished? One is in need, the other in wealth, but

their wickedness is the same. Commentary on Job 21.19-22a.[3]

21:23-26 Divine Justice

A Wrong Concept of Divine Justice. Julian of Eclanum: In order to refute the argument of [his friends], who wanted to refer everything to [their concept] of divine equity, he shows how they are inferior to him in merits and successes, so that it may clearly appear that in the present state of things the form of justice that they think they understand is lame. Exposition on the Book of Job 21.23-25.[4]

21:27-30 Are the Wicked Spared?

The Righteous Longs to Reach the Eternal World. Gregory the Great: The weak desire to thrive in this world's fortune. They dread scourges as evils of great magnitude. In the case of those they see smitten, they measure the offence by the punishment. For those they see struck with the rod, they suppose them to have displeased God. Hence blessed Job's friends were persuaded that he, whom they beheld under the rod, had been ungodly, that is, as reckoning that if he had not been ungodly, his "dwelling places would have remained." But no one thinks so except he who still travails with the weariness of infirmity, who firmly sets the footstep of his thoughts in the gratification of the present life, who is not taught to pass on with perfect desires to the eternal land. Hence, it is well added, "Ask every one of them that go by the way. You will know that he understands this same, because the wicked is reserved to the day of destruction, and he is brought to the day of wrath." Often the patience of God long suffers with those whom it already condemns to a foreknown punishment. It suffers those to go on thriving whom it sees still committing worse things. One who sees the pit of condemnation to which they are going is viewed

---

[1]PL 26:673. [2]Job 20:4. [3]PTS 35:137. [4]CCL 88:60.

as nothing to them. The wicked multiply here things that must be abandoned. But one who is wedded to the glory of the present life counts it great happiness to thrive here according to his wishes, though hereafter he is driven to undergo eternal punishment. Therefore, that person only sees it as nothing for the wicked to thrive, who has already removed his heart from the love of the present world. Hence, in speaking of the future condemnation of the wicked, it is rightly premised, "Ask every one of them that go by the way, and you will know that he understands this." For he is called a "wayfarer," who minds that the present life is to him only a way and not a native land, who thinks it beneath him to fix his heart on the love of this passing state of being, who longs not to continue in a transitory scene of things but to reach the eternal world. MORALS ON THE BOOK OF JOB 15.67-68.[5]

21:31-33 Who Repays the Wicked for Their Deeds?

A REFERENCE TO THE DEVIL CONQUERED BY

CHRIST. PHILIP THE PRIEST: It seems to me that here Job is appropriately speaking about the devil, even though his words can also be interpreted as a general reference to all sinners. Who among men could ever declare to his face his most polluted way, into which he led the entire universe? Or which creature was ever able to give him back what he deserved, except the only Lamb of God, who did not commit sin and in whose mouth no deceit was ever found?[6] COMMENTARY ON THE BOOK OF JOB 21.[7]

21:34 Nothing Left but Falsehood

JOB'S IMPOTENCE. ISHO'DAD OF MERV: "There is nothing left of your answers but emptiness," that is, you, he says, have brought me suffering and torments instead of consolation; and what I gain from speaking a great deal is only emptiness. Your answers, he says, are vanity to me. COMMENTARY ON JOB 21.34.[8]

---

[5]LF 21:217-18^A. [6]1 Pet 2:22. [7]PL 26:674. [8]CSCO 229:250.

22:1-20 GOD PUNISHES ONLY IN THE NAME OF JUSTICE

[1] Then Eliphaz the Temanite answered:
[2]"Can a man be profitable to God?
   Surely he who is wise is profitable
     to himself.*
[3]Is it any pleasure to the Almighty if you are
   righteous,
   or is it gain to him if you make your ways
     blameless?
[4]Is it for your fear of him that he

   reproves you,
   and enters into judgment with you?†
[5]Is not your wickedness great?
   There is no end to your iniquities.
[6]For you have exacted pledges of your
   brothers for nothing,
   and stripped the naked of their clothing.
[7]You have given no water to the weary
   to drink,

and you have withheld bread from the
    hungry.
[8]The man with power possessed the
    land,
    and the favored man dwelt in it.[‡]
[9]You have sent widows away empty,
    and the arms of the fatherless were
    crushed.
[10]Therefore snares are round about you,
    and sudden terror overwhelms you;
[11]your light is darkened, so that[e] you
    cannot see,[§]
    and a flood of water covers you.

[12]"Is not God high in the heavens?
    See the highest stars, how lofty they
    are!
[13]Therefore you say, 'What does God
    know?
    Can he judge through the deep darkness?

[14]Thick clouds enwrap him, so that he does
    not see,
    and he walks on the vault of heaven.'[#]
[15]Will you keep to the old way[**]
    which wicked men have trod?
[16]They were snatched away before their
    time;
    their foundation was washed away.
[17]They said to God, 'Depart from us,'
    and 'What can the Almighty do to
    us?'[f]
[18]Yet he filled their houses with good
    things—
    but the counsel of the wicked is far
    from me.
[19]The righteous see it and are glad;
    the innocent laugh them to scorn,[††]
[20]saying, 'Surely our adversaries are cut
    off,
    and what they left the fire has consumed.'"

---

e Cn Compare Gk: Heb or darkness   f Gk Syr: Heb them   *LXX Is it not the Lord that teaches understanding and knowledge?   †LXX (3-4) For does it matter to the Lord if you were blameless in your works? Or does he gain any profit from the righteousness of your conduct? Or, in order to make a case against you, will he accuse you and enter into judgment with you?   ‡Vg In the strength of your arm you possessed the land and obtained it in your great power.   §Vg and you thought you would have not seen the darkness   #LXX (12-14) Does not he that dwells in the high places observe? And has he not brought down the proud? And you have said, What does the mighty One know? Does he judge in the dark? A cloud is his hiding-place, and he shall not be seen; and he passes through the circle of heaven.   **Peshitta the way of the world   ††Vg The righteous will see it and will be glad; the innocent will laugh them to scorn.

OVERVIEW: In their comments on Eliphaz's third speech, the Fathers show, in general, an extremely critical attitude. Eliphaz's accusations against Job appear to them to be groundless and only become a starting point to show how an impious mind can deny the role of providence, distort facts and give a false and negative picture of a righteous man (CHRYSOSTOM, ORIGEN, GREGORY, PHILIP, OLYMPIODORUS, JULIAN OF ECLANUM, ISHO'DAD). When unrestrained, the tongue is always descending to what is worse (GREGORY). The charges against Job multiply without restraint—madness, criminality, unfairness to the poor (PHILIP, OLYMPIODORUS).

22:1-2 Can the Wise Be of Service to God?

THE ROLE OF PROVIDENCE. CHRYSOSTOM: "Then Eliphaz the Temanite answered and said, 'Is it not the Lord who teaches understanding and knowledge?'" After being defeated, Eliphaz eventually agrees with this. Then, since what had been said allowed everyone to come to the conclusion that Job was not impious and that the conduct of a person could not be judged on the basis of his punishments, notice the perfidy at which he almost arrives to suppress the role of Providence. COMMENTARY ON JOB 22.2.[1]

---

[1]PTS 35:138.

ONLY GOD CAN TEACH US VIRTUE. ORIGEN: The things that are administered by the Holy Spirit are worthy of description. Therefore, they are described, so that the reader may take advantage of the things being read. If the speeches of those three who came to Job were not useful, so that the reader might gain nothing from what was said to Job through them, to be sure the divine Providence would have not reported the speeches of those three in the book of Job. It is possible, therefore, to obtain a certain advantage from their speeches by observing carefully their doctrine.

Notice that the fault in their speeches is singular: every time they accuse Job, they believe that he is suffering his misfortunes because he had sinned. They do not see that there are many reasons why adversities happen to people. It was established that these are the things that happen, both good and bad, or whatever you want to call them.

"Is it not the Lord that teaches understanding and knowledge?" This statement is wise. Indeed, the true doctor of virtue cannot be a person. "He that teaches man knowledge"[2] is also mentioned in the psalms and is no one else but God. And the prophet says, "Teach me your ordinances,"[3] because he knows that God is the true and perfect doctor. In truth God teaches, by lighting the soul of the pupil from him and by illuminating his mind with his light, his truthful word. For this reason, the righteous men, who received the grace of teaching, teach us. FRAGMENTS ON JOB 16.4.[4]

22:3-4 Does Your Righteousness Please the Almighty?

JOB'S AFFLICTIONS DO NOT COME FROM GOD. CHRYSOSTOM: "What does it matter to the Lord, if you were blameless in your works?" That is, it has no importance for God. "Or does he gain any profit from the righteousness of your conduct?" It cannot be said that, in fact, it contributes to him any advantage, he says. Since Job in every possible manner had said that God did this and because of him I am suffering, Eliphaz wants to show that [his afflictions] do not come from God. "Or, in order to make a case against you, will he accuse you and enter into judgment with you?" Yes, you can be as righteous as you want, it does not matter for him, and he has no consideration for you, that is, what you do deserves little interest on the part of God. In fact, if he really wanted to judge you, he would have found your faults. COMMENTARY ON JOB 22.3-4.[5]

22:5-6 Exacting Pledges

THE MEANING OF "PLEDGE." GREGORY THE GREAT: Note that from a deadened heart one may throw out words or promises, and from idle words he may in the heinousness of lying blaze out into insults. For these are the corrosions of increasing sin, that the tongue when not restrained should never lie still where it has fallen but is always descending to what is worse. . . .

In holy Scripture the term *pledge* [promise] may denote either the gifts of the Holy Spirit or the confession of sin. Thus pledge is taken as the gift of the Holy Spirit, such as where it is said by Paul, "And given the earnest of the Spirit in our hearts."[6] For we receive a pledge for this, that we may have an assurance of the promise that is made to us. And so the gift of the Holy Spirit is called a pledge, because through this [Spirit] our soul is strengthened to the assuredness of the inward hope. Again by the name of "a pledge," confession of sin is also intended, as it is written in the law, "If your brother owes you something, and you take away a pledge from him, restore the pledge before the setting of the sun." When any fellow creature is proven to have done anything wrong against us, our brother is made a debtor to us. Sins we call "debts." Thus it is said to the servant when he sinned, "I forgave you all that debt." And in the Lord's Prayer we pray daily, "Forgive us our debts, as we forgive our debtors."

---

[2]Ps 94:10 (93:10 LXX). [3]Ps 119:12 (118:12 LXX). [4]PTS 48:370-71. [5]PTS 35:138. [6]2 Cor 1:22.

Now we "take a pledge" from our debtor, when from the lips of him who is found to have sinned against us, we receive a confession of his sin, whereby we are asked to remit the sin that was committed against us. For anyone who confesses the sin that he has done and begs pardon has already, as it were, given a "pledge" for his debt. This pledge we are bidden to "restore before the sunset," because before that, in ourselves through pain of the heart, the Sun of righteousness shall set. We are bound to render back the acknowledgment of pardon to him from whom we receive the acknowledgment of transgression, that he who remembers that he has done amiss toward us may be made aware that what he has done wrong is forgiven by us at once. MORALS ON THE BOOK OF JOB 16.4-6.[7]

22:7 Withholding Bread from the Hungry

JOB IS UNJUSTLY ACCUSED. ORIGEN: All these things are accusations, and certainly very reproachful ones. But they are not true with regard to Job and are unjustly pronounced against him. These things happen in times of hardship. Sometimes, when one has only a piece of bread, even though he does not have an entire loaf, we take it away from him by saying, "You are in debt." FRAGMENTS ON JOB 16.22-23.[8]

THE CRIME OF MERCILESSNESS. OLYMPIODORUS: A criminal act not only causes harm but also denies any benefit. Therefore, notice to what point our benevolence must be extended. As there is a certain crime, when those thirsty do not drink, so we have a reward for a glass of cool water, according to the truthful voice of the Savior.[9] COMMENTARY ON JOB 22.7.[10]

22:8-9 Crushing Orphans and Widows

JOB IS COMPARED WITH A CRUEL TYRANT. PHILIP THE PRIEST: "In the strength of your arm you possessed the land and obtained it in your great power." He suggests that [Job] was like a proud tyrant who did not rule the people of his kingdom according to justice and equity but submitted them to an oppressive bondage according to his cruel ways as under the power of his arm. . . . "You have sent widows away empty-handed." You did not give them succor when they, being wretched and vexed by afflictions and humiliated, came. You dismissed each of them empty-handed, when they could not obtain what they expected from you. "And the hands of the orphans you have crushed." If they still had some strength, through which they could support themselves, you took it away and broke their souls into despair or did not defend them from evil people. You destroyed their virtue of hope, through which they looked to you, while you allowed them to be oppressed. COMMENTARY ON THE BOOK OF JOB 22.[11]

22:10-11 Terror and Darkness Overwhelm You

ELIPHAZ INVOKES REVENGE. JULIAN OF ECLANUM: Since [Eliphaz] had said that [Job] had sinned not mildly or, so to speak, with feeble strength but greatly and with much force, he now fervently invokes revenge against him, so that it may appear that the crime and the revenge are weighed for him at the same time. "And a sudden terror overwhelms you." Another version of the text reads, "a sudden force."

"And you thought that you would have not seen the darkness." You also added this crime to your iniquities—the fact that you believed that revenge would have not followed. If you had thought about it, it would have turned you from the dangerous ways of your actions or frightened you less by being already foreseen. EXPOSITION ON THE BOOK OF JOB 22.10-11.[12]

---

[7]LF 21:226-27*. [8]PTS 48:378. [9]See Mt 10:42. [10]PTS 24:193. [11]PL 26:675-76. [12]CCL 88:62.

22:12-14 *What Does God Know?*

A SERIOUS ACCUSATION OF IMPIETY. OLYMPI-ODORUS: Eliphaz pronounces a serious accusation of impiety and madness against Job. "In fact," he says, "you committed iniquities, as if [God] did not realize they were [committed] in the land of the Lord, but as if he judged in darkness. That is, as if, in judging, he did not see what happened in his land. You said, in fact, that since he is invisible and separates himself with clouds from what happens among us, and only goes around the circle of heaven, he does not deem it worthy to take care of earthly things." This is what the pagan philosophers thought, when they said that God does not take care of what is under the moon. COMMENTARY ON JOB 22.13-14.[13]

22:15-20 *The Wicked and the Righteous*

REPEATING THE SINS OF THE WORST. ISHO'DAD OF MERV: These words mean, "You imitate the actions of the ancestors." [The author] is alluding to the Cainites, those who lived at the time of the deluge, to the Sodomites, etc.; these are those whom he calls "the way of the world." COMMENTARY ON JOB 22.15.[14]

THE JOY OF THE RIGHTEOUS AND THE PUNISHMENT OF THE WICKED. PHILIP THE PRIEST: "But the plans of the wicked are repugnant to me." He places among the blasphemers holy [Job] as well, who is now detested like them. "The righteous will see it and will be glad." Or, as others said, he will laugh. Here he speaks about the abasement of faithless people. "The innocent will laugh them to scorn." How can this not be said about the saints too? When the faithful see that the sinners are condemned by the just judgment of God, they will see and will be glad. They like God's justice, as well as God likes them. But Eliphaz, even though he perhaps spoke correctly here, has the wrong idea of comparing holy Job with the impious and the sinners....

"And what they left, the fire has consumed." What they left, that is, their most serious sins, must be punished on the day of judgment, because in this world no punishment condemns the wickedest of sinners as much as they deserve. COMMENTARY ON THE BOOK OF JOB 22.[15]

---

[13]PTS 24:195. [14]CSCO 229:250-51. [15]PL 26.676-77.

22:21-30 ELIPHAZ EXHORTS JOB TO AGREE WITH GOD

[21]*Agree with God, and be at peace;*
thereby good will come to you.
[22]*Receive instruction from his mouth,*
and lay up his words in your heart.
[23]*If you return to the Almighty and humble yourself,[g]*
if you remove unrighteousness far from your tents,
[24]*if you lay gold in the dust,*
and gold of Ophir among the stones of the torrent bed,
[25]*and if the Almighty is your gold,*
and your precious silver;
[26]*then you will delight yourself in the Almighty,[*]*

and lift up your face to God.
[27]You will make your prayer to him, and
he will hear you;
and you will pay your vows.
[28]You will decide on a matter, and it will
be established for you,

and light will shine on your ways.
[29]For God abases the proud,[h]
but he saves the lowly.
[30]He delivers the innocent man;[i]
you will be delivered through the
cleanness of your hands.[†]

g Gk: Heb *you will be built up*   h Cn: Heb *when they abased you said, Proud*   i Gk Syr Vg: Heb *him that is not innocent*   *Vg *you will abound with delicacies over the Almighty*
†Vg (29-30) *For he that has been abased shall be in glory, and he that has bent down his eyes, the same shall be saved. The innocent will be saved, but he will be saved by the cleanness of his hands.*

OVERVIEW: The second part of Eliphaz's speech is commented on by the fathers under a more favorable light. They are able to recognize a certain correctness in some of his opinions (ORIGEN, EPHREM) and show how an allegorical interpretation of his words can suggest useful moral reflections. God's grace first works in us without our help so that our own free will follows in order that the good may be accomplished (GREGORY).

22:21-25 Good Will Come to You

THE ENDURANCE OF ADVERSITIES PURIFIES US. ORIGEN: This is what he means, in my opinion: "Confess your sins; receive from God's mouth his support after your confession; and take his words into your heart." Certainly Eliphaz said these things, as he believed, by making himself equal to Job. . . . However, he pronounces a correct dogma here. He, in fact, thinks that Job suffers his adversities because of his sins but also so that he will be purified through the endurance of his afflictions. Once he is purified, he will be delivered from any extraneous element and freed from any involvement with iniquity. And like gold refined in a melting pot, he will appear to be tested. If you, he says, endure what has happened to you, God will make you pure, like silver purified with fire. FRAGMENTS ON JOB 16.61, 69.[1]

THE POWER OF REPENTANCE. EPHREM THE SYRIAN: This means that you will be restored to your former state. And God will be your helper

while before it seemed that he had completely neglected the care of your salvation, as if he had been absent. COMMENTARY ON JOB 22.23.[2]

22:26-30 Delighting in the Almighty

HISTORICAL, MORAL AND ALLEGORICAL INTERPRETATION OF ELIPHAZ'S WORDS. GREGORY THE GREAT: "You will abound with delicacies over the Almighty" is to be entirely filled with the banquet of holy Scripture in the love of God. In those words surely we find as many delicacies for our profiting as we obtain diversities of meaning. The bare history should now be our food veiled under the text of the letter, the moral allegory should refresh us from our inmost soul, and, to the deeper things, contemplation should hold us suspended, already, in the darkness of the present life, shining in upon us from the light of eternity. . . . To "lift up the face" to God means to raise up the heart for searching into what is loftiest. For as by the bodily face we are known and distinguishable to people, so by the interior figure we are known to God. Yet because of the guilt of sin, we are weighed to the earth, and we are afraid to lift the face of our heart to God. When it is not buoyed up by any of the confidence of good works, the mind is too full of fear to gaze upon the highest things, because conscience of itself, it accuses itself. But when by the tears of penance sins are now washed out and lament is completed, a great

---

[1]PTS 48:389, 392. [2]ESOO 2:10.

confidence springs up in the mind for contemplating the joys of the recompense from above; "the face of our heart is lifted up." . . .

"You will pray to him, and he will hear you," for they make their prayer to God but never obtain to be listened to, who set at nothing the precepts of the Lord, when he enjoins them. Hence it is written, "He that turns away his ear from hearing the law, even his prayer shall be an abomination." So long then as Eliphaz believed the blessed Job was not heard, he determined that that person had surely done wrong in his practice. And hence he adds further, "And you will pay your vows." He that has vowed but is unable from weakness to pay the same, has it dealt to him in punishment of sin, that while willing good, having the power should be taken away from him. But when, in the sight of the interior Judge, the sin that hinders is done away, it is immediately brought to pass that one is able to attend the vow.

It goes on, "You will decide on a matter, and it will be established for you." This used to be the special conclusion of those going weakly, that in such proportion they esteem a person righteous as they see him obtain all that he desires; whereas, in truth, we know that earthly goods are sometimes withheld from the righteous while they are bestowed with liberal bounty on the unrighteous. When sick people are despaired of, physicians order whatever they need to be supplied. But those whom they foresee may be brought back to health when the things which they long for they refuse to have given them. Now if Eliphaz introduced these declarations with reference to spiritual gifts, it must be known that "a thing is decreed and is established" in a person when the virtue that is longed for in the desire, is, by God's granting it, happily forwarded by the carrying out of it as well.

And hence it is yet further added, "And the light will shine on your ways." The light that shines on the ways of the righteous shines by extraordinary deeds of virtue to scatter the tokens of their brightness. Wherever they go in the bent of the mind, from the hearts of those beholding them, they may dispel the might of sin and by the example of their own practice pour into them the light of righteousness. But, whatever justness of practice there may be, in the eye of the interior Judge it is nothing, if pride of the heart uplifts it. Hence it is added, "For he that has been abased shall be in glory, and he that has bent down his eyes shall be saved." This sentence is not at variance with the mouth of "Truth," when it says, "For whosoever exalts himself shall be abased, and he that humbles himself shall be exalted."[3] Therefore, it is said by Solomon, "Before destruction the heart of man is haughty, and before honor is humility."[4] However, it is properly said, "For he that has bent down his eyes, the same shall be saved." Insofar as it is to be discovered through the ministering of the members, the first manifestation of pride is with the eyes. . . .

"The innocent will be saved, but he will be saved by the cleanness of his hands." This sentence [from Eliphaz], if it is delivered in relation to the recompense of the kingdom of heaven, is supported by truth, in that it is written concerning God, "He renders to every man according to his deeds." The justice of the eternal Judge saves that person in the last inquest. His mercy sets him free from impure deeds.

But if the person here purported is supposed to be saved by the cleanness of his own hands, that by his own powers he should be made innocent, then assuredly it is an error. For if grace above does not prevent him when faulty, assuredly it will never find any one faultless to recompense without fault. It is said by the truthful voice of Moses, "And no man of himself is innocent in your sight." So, heavenly pity first works something in us without our help, that, our own free will follows as well, so the good which we now desire may be accomplished. Yet the good that is bestowed by grace, in the last judgment, God rewards to us as if it had come only from ourselves. MORALS ON THE BOOK OF JOB 16.24-30.[5]

---

[3]Lk 14:11. [4]Prov 18:12. [5]LF 21:239-43*.

23:1-7 JOB SEEKS GOD'S JUSTICE

¹*Then Job answered:*
²*"Today also my complaint* is bitter,ʲ*
* hisᵏ hand is heavy in spite of my*
*   groaning.†*
³*Oh, that I knew where I might find him,*
* that I might come even to his seat!*
⁴*I would lay my case before him*
* and fill my mouth with arguments.*
⁵*I would learn what he would answer me,*

and understand what he would say to
* me.*
⁶*Would he contend with me in the greatness*
* of his power?*
* No; he would give heed to me.*
⁷*There an upright man could reason*
* with him,*
* and I should be acquitted for ever by my*
*   judge."‡*

j Syr Vg Tg: Heb *rebellious* k Gk Syr: Heb *my* *Peshitta *my speech* or *my report* †LXX (1-2) *Then Job answered and said, "Yes, I know that my accusation comes from my hands. His hand has been made heavy upon me, and I groan over me."* ‡Vg (5-7) *That I may know the words that he will answer me, and understand what he will say to me. I would not that he should contend with me with great power or oppress me with the weight of his mightiness. Let him put forth equity against me, and my judgment will come to victory.*

OVERVIEW: In Job's reply the Fathers see the bitterness of a man who has been unjustly accused. He has been driven to harsh words (EPHREM), yet with no intention on his part to blame God (CHRYSOSTOM). In his words they also read a prophecy about the advent of Christ the Redeemer (GREGORY). Anticipating the end of the book, we will find that Job obtains exactly what he here desires: pleading his case in justice and learning what God answers (CHRYSOSTOM). Finally Job in his plea is prefiguratively praying that his ways will be corrected by the sending of God's incarnate Son (GREGORY).

23:1-2 My Complaint Is Bitter

JOB'S BITTERNESS. EPHREM THE SYRIAN: "Today also my speech is bitter," that is, my words happen to be harsh and irksome to both our ears. In a different sense [we may interpret the passage as] you, indeed, to use harsher speech against you, drive me with your words. COMMENTARY ON JOB 23.2.[1]

NO INTENTION TO ACCUSE GOD OF INJUSTICE. CHRYSOSTOM: "Then Job answered and said, 'Yes, I know that my accusation comes from my hands.'" This means, I carry along with me the evidence that accuses me. I draw from myself the demonstration of my afflictions. "His hand has been made heavy upon me, and I groan over me." If it were possible, he says, to discuss my punishments with him, it would also be possible to find them out. If only I could plead my case in justice, he says, and meet him and learn what he would have answered me! See how he obtained exactly what he desired. That is, in fact, what occurs at the end of the book. I wanted to know what he would have said to me and whether he would have punished me just the same; and, by saying so, I had no intention of condemning any injustice on his part. COMMENTARY ON JOB 23.2B.[2]

23:3-7 Oh, That I Knew Where I Might Find Him

FORESHADOWING REPENTANCE AND REDEMPTION. GREGORY THE GREAT: We bewail our sins when we begin to weigh them. We weigh them

---

[1]ESOO 2:10. [2]PTS 35:140.

the more exactly when more anxiously we bewail them. By our lamentations it rises up more perfectly in our hearts that the severity of God threatens those who commit sin. What will be those reproofs on the children of perdition, what terror, what the abhorrence of the unappeasable majesty? Great things shall the Lord then, being angry, declare to the lost, as great as he permits them of justice to undergo. . . .

Who else except the Mediator between God and humankind, the man Christ Jesus, is denoted by the title of "equity"? Concerning whom it is written, "Who of God is made to us wisdom and righteousness."[3] And whereas this same righteousness came into this world against the ways of sinners, we get the better of our old enemy, by whom we were held captive. So let him say, "I do not want him to contend with me with great power or oppress me with the weight of his mightiness. Let him judge me justly, and my judgment will come to victory." In other words, for the correction of my ways let him send his incarnate Son. Then by the sentence of my absolution, I will turn out as a victor over the plotting foe.

If the only begotten Son of God had so remained invisible in the strength of divine nature as not to have admitted anything derived from our weakness, when could weak people ever have found the access of grace to him? For the weight of his greatness, being considered, would rather have oppressed than aided things. Yet he agreed with us by assuming our weakness, that he might elevate us to his own abiding strength. MORALS ON THE BOOK OF JOB 16.36-37.[4]

---

[3]1 Cor 1:30. [4]LF 21:247-48*.

23:8-17 JOB FOLLOWS GOD'S PATH IN HIS AFFLICTIONS

[8]Behold, I go forward, but he is not there;
   and backward, but I cannot perceive him;
[9]on the left hand I seek him,[l] but I cannot behold him;
   I[m] turn to the right hand, but I cannot see him.*
[10]But he knows the way that I take;
   when he has tried me, I shall come forth as gold.[†]
[11]My foot has held fast to his steps;
   I have kept his way and have not turned aside.
[12]I have not departed from the commandment of his lips;

I have treasured in[n] my bosom the words of his mouth.
[13]But he is unchangeable and who can turn him?
   What he desires, that he does.
[14]For he will complete what he appoints for me;
   and many such things are in his mind.
[15]Therefore I am terrified at his presence;
   when I consider, I am in dread of him.
[16]God has made my heart faint;
   the Almighty has terrified me;
[17]for I am[o] hemmed in by darkness,
   and thick darkness covers my face.[p‡]

l Compare Syr: Heb *on the left hand when he works* **m** Syr Vg: Heb *he* **n** Gk Vg: Heb *from* **o** With one Ms: Heb *am not* **p** Vg: Heb *from my face* *LXX (8-9) *For if I shall go first and am no longer, still what do I know concerning the latter end? If he acts on the left, I cannot grasp him; he hides his right, and I will not see.* †Vg *he will try me like gold that passes through fire* ‡LXX (16-17) *The Lord has made my heart melt; the Almighty set himself against me; I did not know that darkness would have come upon me and that obscurity would have covered me before my face.*

OVERVIEW: Job is in the darkness of his affliction (CHRYSOSTOM) and unable to grasp God's invisible and incomprehensible nature (OLYMPIODORUS). However, he proceeds in the path leading to God (GREGORY) and declares his devotion to him (JULIAN OF ECLANUM), trusting fully in God's hidden wisdom.

23:8-9 I Cannot Perceive God

GOD'S INVISIBLE AND INCOMPREHENSIBLE NATURE. OLYMPIODORUS: The real meaning is this, "Suppose I willingly submit the judgment of my actions to the eyes of the Lord." What happens to me? God is invisible in his nature. Will I look for him in those material things that are before me? He cannot be seen. He is before me, but I do not perceive him. When he moves to the left, I cannot grasp him, and when he is on the right, I cannot see him at all. These words do not mean that God passes from one place to another bodily or by moving, but they intend to show that he is present everywhere and, nonetheless, escapes our perception and cannot be comprehended by us. "If I am no longer," that is, "If I further extend my research, I will be out of myself and dizzy in reflection while I try to comprehend what is incomprehensible." COMMENTARY ON JOB 23.8-9.[1]

23:10-12 God Knows My Way

THE PATH LEADING TO THE FULFILLMENT OF GOD'S WILL. GREGORY THE GREAT: "But he knows the way that I take." This is as if he said in plain terms, "I for my own part search myself strictly and am not able to know myself thoroughly; yet he, whom I have no power to see, sees most minutely all the things that I do."

It goes on, "And he will try me like gold that passes through fire." Gold in the furnace is advanced to the brightness of its nature while it loses the dross. And so like "gold that passes through fire" the souls of the righteous are tried. Their defects are removed through and through, and their good points are increased by the fire of tribulation.

The holy man [Job] compared himself with one who is being tested through fire as gold. This was not said out of pride. He who by the voice of God was pronounced righteous before his suffering was not out of pride being permitted to be tried in order that bad qualities might be cleared off and that excellences might be heightened. Gold is purified by fire. As he was being delivered over to suffer tribulation, he believed that he was being purified, although he had nothing in him to be purified. . . .

"My foot has held fast to his steps." It is by examining the footsteps of God, so to speak, that we see how both the good and bad are governed and the righteous and unrighteous distinguished. By this means everyone [by divine Providence] may be led on day by day to better things, or one who is in rebellion against the good plunges headlong into worse.

It is of these same footsteps that the prophet said, "Your goings have been seen, O God."[2] And so we, when we behold the efficacy of his long-suffering and mercy and strive to imitate them, may follow the "footsteps of his goings" and thus imitate in some fashion his method of proceeding. . . .

"I have kept his way and have not turned aside." For he who keeps the way and does not turn aside practices the thing on which his mind is bent. To continue to follow the temperament of one's own mind is to fail in practice. Every day

---

[1]PTS 24:203. [2]Ps 68:24 (67:25 LXX).

the righteous are concerned that they test their actions by the ways of truth. So they propose these as a rule to themselves, that they should not turn aside from the track of their right course.

Thus, day by day, they strive to move ahead, a step above their present position in proportion as they are being lifted up toward the summit of virtues, while they judge with heedful censure whatever there is of themselves that remain below themselves. And they are quick to press themselves wholly toward that point to which they find that they have been brought in part.

The text goes on, "I have not departed from the commandment of his lips." The servant who serves well is ever intent upon the master's facial expression in order that the things they may be asked to do, they may hear readily and strive to fulfill. In this way the minds of the righteous become bent toward almighty God. So, according to Scripture, the faithful fix their eyes on his face that reveals all that he wills, in order that they may not be at variance with his will in proportion to what they learn of that will in his revelation. When this happens, his words do not pass superfluously through their ears, but they fix these words in their hearts.

So it is added here, "I have treasured in my bosom the words of his mouth." For we "treasure the words of his mouth in the bosom of our heart" when we hear his commandments not in a passing way but to fulfill them in practice. Thus, of the Virgin Mother herself it is written, "But Mary kept all these things and pondered them in her heart." Even when these same words come forth to be practiced, they are said to lie hidden in the recesses of the heart if by what is done outwardly the mind of the doer is not lifted up within. When the word conceived is carried on to the deed, human praise is aimed within, for the word of God assuredly is not "hidden in the bosom of the mind." Why then, blessed man, do you examine yourself with so much earnestness, and why do you take yourself to task with so much anxiety? MORALS ON THE BOOK OF JOB 16.39-44.[3]

23:13-15 I Dread God

JOB DECLARES HIS DEVOTION TO GOD. JULIAN OF ECLANUM: He declares the reason by which he walks in the narrow path of God without his feet ever turning aside. This compels him to be the dedicated guardian of his precepts, "I conceived with my mind, he says, this esteem for God, because he is the only one for whom this name [of God] is truly fitting." As for those who are called gods, he does not accept any of those who are called gods, who do not participate in his power. For him everything is easy to do and nobody can oppose his force and will. EXPOSITION ON THE BOOK OF JOB 23.13.[4]

23:16-17 Vanishing in Darkness

THE DARKNESS OF DEJECTION. CHRYSOSTOM: This unexpected disaster, he says, did not happen according to human logic. I discern that this blow comes from the hand of God. And he is right in speaking of the darkness that "covers my face," because this darkness is not ordinary darkness but is of his own dejection. COMMENTARY ON JOB 23.16-17.[5]

---

[3]LF 21:250-53**. [4]CCL 88:65. [5]PTS 35:142.

24:1-25 VIOLENCE AND INIQUITY
PREVAIL ON EARTH

[1]Why are not times of judgment kept by the
    Almighty,
    and why do those who know him never
      see his days?
[2]Men remove landmarks;
    they seize flocks and pasture them.*
[3]They drive away the ass of the fatherless;
    they take the widow's ox for a pledge.
[4]They thrust the poor off the road;
    the poor of the earth all hide themselves.
[5]Behold, like wild asses in the desert
    they go forth to their toil,
  seeking prey in the wilderness
  as food[q] for their children.[†]
[6]They gather their[r] fodder in the field
    and they glean the vineyard of the wicked
      man.
[7]They lie all night naked, without clothing,
    and have no covering in the cold.
[8]They are wet with the rain of the
      mountains,
    and cling to the rock for want of shelter.
[9] (There are those who snatch the fatherless
      child from the breast,
    and take in pledge the infant of the poor.)
[10]They go about naked, without clothing;
    hungry, they carry the sheaves;
[11]among the olive rows of the wicked[s] they
      make oil;
    they tread the wine presses, but
      suffer thirst.
[12]From out of the city the dying groan,
    and the soul of the wounded cries for help;
    yet God pays no attention to their prayer.[‡]

[13]"There are those who rebel against the
      light,
    who are not acquainted with its ways,
    and do not stay in its paths.
[14]The murderer rises in the dark[t]
    that he may kill the poor and needy;
    and in the night he is as a thief.[§]
[15]The eye of the adulterer also waits for the
      twilight,
    saying, "No eye will see me";
    and he disguises his face.
[16]In the dark they dig through houses;
    by day they shut themselves up;
    they do not know the light.
[17]For deep darkness is morning to all of them;
    for they are friends with the terrors
      of deep darkness.[#]

[18]You say, "They are swiftly carried away**
      upon the face of the waters;
    their portion is cursed in the land;
    no treader turns toward their vineyards.
[19]Drought and heat snatch away the snow
      waters;
    so does Sheol those who have sinned.[††]
[20]The squares of the town[u] forget them;
    their name[v] is no longer remembered;
    so wickedness is broken like a tree."

[21]They feed on the barren childless woman,
    and do no good to the widow.
[22]Yet God[w] prolongs the life of the mighty by
      his power;
    they rise up when they despair of life.[‡‡]

*²³He gives them security, and they are
supported;
and his eyes are upon their ways.
²⁴They are exalted a little while, and
then are gone;*

*they wither and fade like the mallow;^y
they are cut off like the heads of grain.^{§§}
²⁵If it is not so, who will prove me a liar,
and show that there is nothing in what
I say?^{##}*

q Heb food to him   r Heb his   s Heb their olive rows   t Cn: Heb at the light   u Cn: Heb obscure   v Cn: Heb a worm   w Heb he   y Gk: Heb all   *Vg (1-2) Times are not hidden from the Almighty, and those who know him ignore his days. Others removed the landmarks.   †LXX And they have departed like asses in the field, having gone forth on my account according to their own order, his bread is sweet to his little ones.   ‡LXX (9-12) They have snatched the fatherless from the breast and have deprived the outcast. And they have wrongfully caused others to sleep without clothing and taken away the morsel of the hungry. They have unjustly laid ambush in narrow places and have not known the righteous way; they have been cast forth from the city and their own houses, and the soul of the children has groaned aloud.   §LXX (13-14) Why then has he not visited these? Forasmuch as they were upon the earth and took no notice, and they knew not the way of righteousness, neither have they walked in their appointed paths? But having known their works, he delivered them into darkness, and in the night one will be as a thief.   #Vg If the morning suddenly appears, it is to them even as the shadow of death. And they walk so in darkness as in the light.   **Vg He is light.   ††Vg (18b-19) May his portion of the land be cursed, and may he not walk in the way of the vineyard. May he pass from the snow waters to the highest heat, and his sin to hell.   ‡‡LXX For he has not treated the barren woman well and has had no pity on a feeble woman. And in wrath he has overthrown the helpless; therefore when he has arisen, a man will not feel secure of his own life.   §§LXX (23-24) When he has fallen sick, let him not hope to recover, but let him perish by disease. For his exaltation has hurt many; but he has withered as mallows in the heat or as an ear of corn falling off of itself from the stalk.   ##Peshitta If it is not so, may his wrath make me lie, and may my speech be judged before God.

Overview: The second half of Job's speech, in which he describes the prevalence of wickedness on earth, is not, according to the Fathers, an acknowledgment of the fact that God allows evil to prevail; on the contrary, it demonstrates that God observes every human action and will strike the wicked with severe punishment (Julian of Eclanum, Gregory, Olympiodorus, Ephrem). Job thoroughly understands human wickedness and condemns it with all his scorn (Chrysostom, Isho'dad, Olympiodorus, Philip). The fact that the wicked are prosperous on earth, while the righteous Job is in affliction, only demonstrates that God has no solicitude for the evildoers, whereas he visits his beloved children and corrects them through suffering (Olympiodorus).

24:1-4 Times Kept by God

A Reflection on Divine Justice and Human Evilness. Julian of Eclanum: "Times are not hidden from the Almighty." [Job] raises the same question he had discussed above, but now with a profession of faith. He says that he certainly knows that parts of his censorship in blotting out the merits of people follow the course of his justice, but, in the present situation, many things happen that seem to deny this judgment. With this impression in his mind he pursues the crimes of the wicked to the end of his speech. "Times are not hidden," he says, "from the Almighty," that is, in his knowledge dwells a full awareness of all our moments. It is as if he said, God does not ignore any time of our actions even as we change them constantly, yet we, who touch him with the devotion of our mind, ignore how many days of patience and deferment he hangs on our judgment.

"Others removed the landmarks." It must be noticed, in this reproof of human vices, that they are weighed more lightly or more seriously according to their effect on the virtue of soul. Thus Job and his friends are affected in different ways by different vices; the friends only accuse the acts of inhumanity, whereas Job describes the crimes of iniquity, violence, robbery, lewdness, pride and impiety. Exposition on the Book of Job 24.1-2.[1]

24:5 Like Wild Donkeys

The Looseness of the Wicked. Chrysos-

[1]CCL 88:66.

tom: "And they have departed," he says, "like asses in the field," that is, they have scorned everybody and have mocked everyone. However, nobody commits any injustice against them and does not ill-treat them. Commentary on Job 24.1-8.[2]

24:6-8 Reaping in Others' Fields

Examples of Iniquity. Isho'dad of Merv: "They reap in a field not their own" . . . as wild asses tread underfoot the fields of others and browse on their grass, so the impious, with their impudent violence, reap in fields that are not theirs and steal them from their owners. "They glean in the vineyard of the wicked." This means it is not enough for the wicked to steal from the poor, who have worked without a wage in the fields from the beginning to the end, [but also from the rich]. Commentary on Job 24.6.[3]

24:9-12b Wronging Others

Human Wickedness Spares Nobody. Olympiodorus: "They have snatched the fatherless from the breast." They have lamentably and mercilessly taken away the child who still nursed and hanged from his mother's breast. "And they have deprived the outcast," that is, they have also deprived the outcast of his properties by taking away what he had. "They have wrongfully caused others to sleep without clothing." By wrongfully stripping others, who owed them nothing, they have caused them to love rest. "They have taken away the morsel of the hungry." They have reduced them to extreme poverty and starvation. "They have unjustly laid ambush in narrow places." They have laid ambush in hidden places; in fact, in larger places and roads they wait in ambush for those who have no chance to escape.

"And they," that is, all the impious persons, "have not known the righteous way." "They have been cast forth from their cities and their houses." This refers to those who wantonly sleep without clothing. They [the fatherless] have, in fact, suffered these things from these criminals, after being driven out of their city and their houses.

"And the soul of the children has groaned aloud." From the bottom of their heart [they groaned], because they had no parents any longer who provided them with food. Commentary on Job 24.9-12.[4]

24:12c-14a God Ignores Their Prayer

God's Visitation. Olympiodorus: He says this again to his friends with a bit of hesitation, If afflictions entirely derive from sins, why did he who observes all that happens on earth allow them to go without being visited by him? "And they took no notice," that is, the iniquitous took no notice of the fact that they were not visited. Indeed it is believed and taught about divine visitation, "The Lord reproves the one he loves, as a father checks a well-loved son."[5] Commentary on Job 24.12-13.[6]

24:14b-18a Not Knowing the Light

The Unsteadiness and Constant Fear of the Wicked. Gregory the Great: And so it is well said, "If the morning suddenly appears, it is to them even as the shadow of death." For "the morning" is the mind of the righteous, which, leaving behind the darkness of sin, now breaks out into the light of eternity. As it is also said of the holy church, "Who is she that looks forth as the morning?" Therefore, in the same measure that every righteous person shining with the light of righteousness in this present life is reared to a height with honors, so the same measure of the darkness of death comes before the eyes of the wicked, in that they who remember that they have done bad things are in fear of

---

[2]PTS 35:142. [3]CSCO 229:251. [4]PTS 24:208-9. [5]Prov 3:12. [6]PTS 24:209.

being corrected. They always desire to be free in their iniquities, to live free from correction and to delight from sin. Its fatal mirth is itself appropriately described in the words that are directly introduced: "And they walk so in darkness, as in the light." For with an evil mind they delight in deeds of wickedness. Through their sin they are day by day being dragged to punishment and are full of assurance. Hence it is said by Solomon that "there are wicked people who are as secure as if they had done the deeds of righteous."[7] Concerning them it is written that they "rejoice to do evil and delight in the most wicked doings." Thus "they walk in darkness as in the light," in that they delight in the night of sin as if the light of righteousness were spread around them. . . .

"He is light on the face of the water." From the plural number he returns to the singular, because most frequently one person begins what is bad, and numbers follow after by imitating him, but the fault is primarily his, whom the bad people follow after being furnished examples of wickedness; and hence the sentence frequently returns to him who was the leader in sin. Now the surface of water is carried here and there by the breath of air. Not being steadied with any stability it is put in motion everywhere. And so the mind of the wicked is "lighter than the surface of water," in that every breath of temptation that touches it, draws it in without any retarding resistance. For if we imagine the unstable heart of any bad person, what do we discover but a surface of water set in the wind? Morals on the Book of Job 16.77-79.[8]

24:18b-20 The Wicked Cursed

Job Curses the Wicked. Philip the Priest: "May his portion of land be cursed." Indeed he who is not on the land of the saints, which is the land of the living, will be cursed; and may his portion of land, that is, his portion in the mass of humankind, be cursed. "And may he not walk in the way of the vineyard," that is, may his stay on

this earth be cursed, so that the people of God and the holy souls who are like fruitful vineyards full of fruits may not imitate him and walk in the same ways. . . . "May he pass from snow waters to the highest heat." It seems to me that the holy Job makes a reference to two kinds of hell, an icy and a fiery one, through which the devil, the heretics and the impious are led. . . . "And may his sin [pass] to hell as well." The sin of the impious and the wicked is so great and so heavy that it makes him sink into hell like a piece of lead in water. Commentary on the Book of Job 24.[9]

24:21-22a Harming the Defenseless

Further Examples of Human Cruelty. Olympiodorus: "He has not treated the barren woman well," that is, the woman who is without help because of her lack of children. And notice again how ill treatment is considered an act of impiety. "Keep away from evil," the divine psalmist says, "and practice good."[10] "And he had no pity on a feeble woman," that is, on a woman who needs help because of her feeble nature. "And in wrath he has overthrown the helpless." In fact he did not overthrow the feeble and the helpless for any rational cause, but because of the impulse of his wild soul, while being inflamed with his wrath; and he reduced them to extreme poverty. Commentary on Job 24.20-22.[11]

24:22b-24 Exalted Temporarily

Punishment Will Eventually Strike the Impious. Olympiodorus: "Therefore when he has risen, he will not feel secure of his own life." For these reasons the impious, after rising every day not really believing that he will live, remains in fear and is frightened. As the wise Solomon stated, "Fear, indeed, is nothing other than the abandonment of the supports offered by reason."[12] "When he has fallen sick, let him not hope

---

[7]Eccles 8:14. [8]LF 21:273-74**. [9]PL 26:685. [10]Ps 34:14 (33:15 LXX); 37:27 (36:27 LXX). [11]PTS 24:212. [12]Wis 17:12 (17:11 LXX).

to recover, but let him perish by disease." The diseases of the body, in fact, often occur because of sin. "Let him not hope," that is, the lack of hope is due to the consciousness of his sins. "Let him perish" by disease, that is, by the blows of calamity. "For his exaltation has hurt many."

For this reason, "let him perish," because his exaltation has hurt many. "But he has withered as mallows in the heat or as an ear of corn falling off of itself from the stalk." Other examples [from the Greek Bible] read "like grass." In a similar way, the psalmist also says, "Quick as the grass they wither, fading like the green in the field."[13] And he rightly says, "falling off of itself," indeed,

for everybody sin itself becomes a punisher. COMMENTARY ON JOB 24.22-24.[14]

24:25 Who Will Prove Me a Liar?

JOB IS CERTAIN. EPHREM THE SYRIAN: "If it is not so, may his wrath make me lie," that is, if sinners do not go into that scorn that I have mentioned before, may the wrath of God prove false what I have said. COMMENTARY ON JOB 24.25.[15]

---

[13]Ps 37:2 (36:2 LXX). [14]PTS 24:213. [15]ESOO 2:10.

25:1-6 HOW CAN A MORTAL BE RIGHTEOUS BEFORE GOD?

[1]*Then Bildad the Shuhite answered:*
  [2]*"Dominion and fear are with God;[y]*
    he makes peace in his high heaven.
  [3]*Is there any number to his armies?*
    Upon whom does his light not arise?[*]
  [4]*How then can man be righteous before*
    God?

How can he who is born of woman be
    clean?
  [5]*Behold, even the moon is not bright*
    and the stars are not clean in his
      sight;
  [6]*how much less man, who is a maggot,*
    and the son of man, who is a worm!"

y Heb *him*   *LXX *For let none think that there is a respite for robbers, and upon whom will there not come an ambush from him?*

OVERVIEW: Though Bildad rightly argues that all things are under the total control and power of God (EPHREM), he wrongly argues that Job sinned because he had dared call God to judgment (JULIAN OF ECLANUM). Bildad's reply is severely criticized by the Fathers, who read in his words new groundless accusations and wrong opinions (JULIAN OF ECLANUM, CHRYSOSTOM). In claiming that there is no respite for robbers, Bildad says the opposite of what happens, be-

cause there is respite (CHRYSOSTOM).

25:1-2 Dominion with God

A NEW ACCUSATION AGAINST JOB. JULIAN OF ECLANUM: Bildad realizes that Eliphaz's argument, which claimed holy Job was guilty because of his passions, had evidently been refuted by Job's retort demonstrating that there were many impious persons who were not exposed to any hardship. Therefore he abandons this line of debate in order to say that he who now appears to have fallen into the harshness of life is guilty. And so he insists on this argument, in order to accuse Job by declaring divine power and in order to say that he sinned, because he had dared call God to judgment. "Dominion and fear are with him." Since he is pressed by the force of the argument, he is obliged to agree with holy Job's words, so that he may, after omitting the equity of judgment for the present, declare the power of God. And since he cannot demonstrate that Job is guilty, he tries to discount him through comparison; but in this way, without noticing what this situation causes, he actually greatly praises him. Indeed it is a thing of the highest merit when man cannot be equal to the virtues of God. EXPOSITION ON THE BOOK OF JOB 25.1-2.[1]

25:3-4 How Can a Person Be Righteous?

NO RIGHTEOUS PERSON EXISTS. CHRYSOSTOM: Since he said, "You have not visited these yet,"[2] truly Bildad answers, "There is no respite

for robbers." Therefore, he says the opposite of what happens, because there is respite. But in order to play a trick on Job, he speaks in this way. "How then can a mortal be righteous before God?" Indeed, he is necessarily punished. Since Job, in fact, said, I wanted to be judged, and, even though I have not sinned, I am chastised. Bildad replied there is none that is righteous among humankind. How is it possible, he says, that any righteous person will ever exist? Therefore you desire in vain to be judged and examined. COMMENTARY ON JOB 25.2B-4B.[3]

25:5-6 The Stars Impure

THE STARS SUBJECT TO GOD'S LAWS. EPHREM THE SYRIAN: Indeed the stars themselves do not regulate the times according to their authority but know their rising and setting moments according to the [divine] law that has been fixed for them. COMMENTARY ON JOB 25.5.[4]

---

[1]CCL 88:69-70. [2]Job 24:13 LXX: Chrysostom is quoting in adapted form. [3]PTS 35:144. [4]ESOO 2:10.

26:1-14 JOB SCORNS BILDAD'S WORDS BUT RECOGNIZES GOD'S GREATNESS

[1]Then Job answered:
  [2]"How you have helped him who has no
      power!
    How you have saved the arm that has no
      strength!*
  [3]How you have counseled him who has
      no wisdom,
    and plentifully declared sound

    knowledge!†
  [4]With whose help have you uttered words,
      and whose spirit has come forth from
      you?
  [5]The shades below tremble,
      the waters and their inhabitants.
  [6]Sheol is naked before God,
      and Abaddon has no covering.‡

⁷*He stretches out the north over the void,*
    and hangs the earth upon nothing.
⁸*He binds up the waters in his thick clouds,*
    and the cloud is not rent under them.
⁹*He covers the face of the moon,^z*
    and spreads over it his cloud.[§]
¹⁰*He has described a circle upon the face*
        of the waters
    at the boundary between light and
        darkness.
¹¹*The pillars of heaven tremble,*

and are astounded at his rebuke.[#]
¹²*By his power he stilled the sea;*
    by his understanding he smote Rahab.**
¹³*By his wind the heavens were made*
        fair;
    his hand pierced the fleeing serpent.
¹⁴*Lo, these are but the outskirts of his ways;*
    and how small a whisper do we hear of
        him!
    But the thunder of his power who can
        understand?"^{††}

z Or *his throne*   *LXX *Whom do you defend, or whom are you going to succor? Is it not he that has much strength and he who has a strong arm?*   †Vg *To whom have you given counsel? Perhaps to him that has no wisdom? And you have shown your own prudence overmuch.*   ‡Vg (5-6) *Behold, the giants groan under the waters and those who live with them. The underworld is naked before him, and there is no cover to perdition.*   §LXX (7-9) *He stretches out the north wind upon nothing, and he upon nothing hangs the earth; binding water in his clouds, and the cloud is not rent under it. He keeps back the face of his throne, stretching out cloud upon it.*   #Vg *are frightened at his nod*   **Vg *his understanding struck down the proud*   ††Vg *And while we scarcely hear a little drop of his words, who will be able to look on the thunder of his majesty?*

Overview: In his reply, Job demonstrates how Bildad is falsely and groundlessly accusing him, even though he tries to appear to be prudent and wise (Chrysostom, Gregory). At the same time, Bildad's words on the divine order of the world give Job the occasion to express his comprehension and admiration for God's providential rule over the universe (Julian of Eclanum, Olympiodorus, Isho'dad, Gregory). "Excessive" prudence becomes evident when one seeks to appear more full of prudence than anyone else. To pretend to give counsel to Wisdom itself is an act of perversity (Gregory). God has ordered the light and the darkness to occupy their given times in good harmony and not to prevail over one another (Isho'dad). As usual, the Fathers also see in Job's words a prophetic message: in this speech he announces the spreading of the gospel and the destruction of the devil through the power of Christ (Philip, Ephrem).

26:1-2 Condemning the Powerless

I Am Not to Be Condemned. Chrysostom: These words mean, "I do not reprove you for

defending the role of God or to say the truth that was needed." However, you should not have condemned me, and, in fact, it is possible to plead in favor of God without allowing, at the same time, Job to be exposed to accusations. Commentary on Job 26.1-4.[1]

26:3-4 Foolish Counsel

Excess of Prudence Is Wrong. Gregory the Great: "To whom have you given counsel? Perhaps to him that has no wisdom?" To "give counsel to one who is foolish" is an act of charity. To give it to one that is wise is an act of ostentation. But to pretend to give it to Wisdom itself is an act of perversity. Those visitors, who we have said are like those today who insist on their own way, were by their mode of speech playing toward ostentation rather than usefulness. Thus it is yet further rightly added against Bildad, "And you have displayed your prudence overmuch." One who is rightly prudent does not overextend oneself because according to Paul's declaration, he seeks "not to be wise above the

[1]PTS 35:145.

degree that he ought to be wise." But to one who is excessively prudent, the result is imprudence. For when prudence is carried beyond due measure, it is made to turn off the path on one side or another. "Excessive" prudence becomes evident when one seeks to appear more full of prudence than anyone else. Those who do not have the art to be wise in moderation are prone to mouth off with foolishness. MORALS ON THE BOOK OF JOB 17.28.[2]

26:5-6 The Deep Trembles Before God

DIVINE POWER ABIDES IN THE DEEP AND IN THE UNDERWORLD. JULIAN OF ECLANUM: "Behold, giants groan under the waters." After proposing the division that he made between power and wisdom, Job puts forward his evidence. He distinguishes the deep and the underworld. Both those that live in the deep of the sea, even if they are of tremendous size (and for this reason he calls them "giants," which we understand as "wild beasts") and those in the underworld itself (which prevents the sight of viewers as if in a thick fog)—both these realms remain constantly within the realm of God's power and exposed to his eyes. "Behold, giants groan under the waters." The Greek text reads, "Will the giants receive the service of the midwife under the waters, and in their neighbor?" This must be interpreted as asking whether the dead will resurrect if they are under the waters on earth. In saying "they will resurrect," the thought is that "it will be as if they had the service of a midwife." It is interpreted according to the metaphor of a woman giving birth. The meaning is this, "The art of midwifery takes the child out of the womb." If so, is it possible to raise the dead from the underworld, when this realm belongs only to God? "The underworld is naked before him." It is impossible, he says, to hold back the dead when God wants to resurrect them. Only at his command [the earth] is forced to throw up those which it has devoured. "There is no cover to perdition." Even though

[the underworld] is covered by the thickness of darkness, it appears transparently before the eyes of the Almighty. EXPOSITION ON THE BOOK OF JOB 26.5-6.[3]

26:7-9 God Suspends the World on Nothing

RAIN USEFUL TO THE WHOLE CREATED ORDER. OLYMPIODORUS: "He stretches out the north wind upon nothing, and he upon nothing hangs the earth." Indeed the support of the earth is nothing but an understructure, but it is suspended and is sustained by divine will. "Binding water in his clouds, and the cloud is not dispersed under it." In fact, if he does not order the clouds to rain, they do not release rain on earth in the quantity that has been ordered by him. "He constrains the elements with his purposes hidden, stretching out his cloud upon them." Heaven is often called "the throne of God" in holy Scripture. Air is placed before the face of heaven. Therefore, he says that God, by containing the air and expanding the clouds, does not allow them to release rain, if not in the measure that he knows to be convenient and useful. COMMENTARY ON JOB 26.7-9.[4]

26:10 The Boundary Between Light and Darkness

THE ORDER GIVEN BY GOD. ISHO'DAD OF MERV: So God has gathered the waters that were spread on earth at the beginning and has imposed a limit on them. His command has surrounded them like a circle, so that they might not exceed it. He has set a "boundary between light and darkness." This means that he has ordered the light and the darkness to occupy their given times in good harmony and not to prevail on one another. COMMENTARY ON JOB 26.10.[5]

26:11-12 The Pillars of Heaven

[2]LF 21:297**. [3]CCL 88:71. [4]PTS 24:221-22. [5]CSCO 229:253.

THE MEANING OF PILLARS AND SEA. PHILIP THE PRIEST: "The pillars of heaven tremble and are frightened at his nod." We interpret the word *pillars* as the stability that is permanent only in the nature of angels, because they are not only constantly persistent in holiness but also splendid in the glory of eternal blessedness. Indeed about the future immobility of humanity, the Son of God said, "Those who prove victorious I will make into pillars in the sanctuary of my God."[6] But also the church, which is the congregation of all saints, is said to be the pillar and foundation of truth thanks to its eternal stability in the Lord. . . . "By his power he stilled the seas." At the beginning of Genesis we read that he did this. "And his understanding struck down the proud." We are not entirely certain whether the "proud" one is specifically the devil. He, in fact, was the first one struck down by God when he drove him out of that sublime and blessed place in heaven. This the prophet said: "You have brought down the proud as one that is slain."[7] From the spiritual point of view, we can certainly interpret "the seas" as the people of the Jews and the nations of the Gentiles. . . . Indeed from the sea, that is, from the people of the Jews, the gospel of Christ began because the new law [of Jesus] came out of Zion and reached the sea of the Gentiles. COMMENTARY ON THE BOOK OF JOB 26.[8]

26:13 God Pierced the Serpent

SYMBOLISM OF THE FLEEING SERPENT. EPHREM THE SYRIAN: These words eloquently signify the perceptible serpent that must be annihilated by Christ's death. He calls Satan a fleeing and deserting serpent in order to indicate his flight from the company of the heavenly powers, and also because he hoped to escape the punishment of his crime. COMMENTARY ON JOB 26.13.[9]

26:14 Who Can Understand God's Power?

A DROP FROM THE OCEAN OF THE SECRETS OF HEAVEN. GREGORY THE GREAT: What is meant in this place by the designation of "the ways" but the Lord's modes of acting? Hence the Lord also says by the prophet, "For my ways are not as your ways."[10] Accordingly, in telling of the advent of the Lord, he described the ways of God in part. His method of acting by which he created us was one thing; that by which he redeemed us another. Thus of those things that touch upon the Lord's way of acting and make light of by comparison with the final judgment, he says, "Lo, these things are spoken for part of his ways." He also calls this "a little drop of his words." For whatever is high, whatever is terrible within this life, these things we are brought to know by the contemplation of God, as from the vast ocean of the secrets of heaven, its refreshment wells out to us like a slight drop of the liquid element above. "And who will be able to look on the thunder of his majesty?" It is as though he expressed himself in these plain words: "If we endure the wonders of his humility and the thundering and dreadful advent of his majesty, with what courage do we meet life?" MORALS ON THE BOOK OF JOB 17.54.[11]

---

[6]Rev 3:12. [7]Ps 89:10 (88:11 Vg). [8]PL 26:689-90. [9]ESOO 2:11. [10]Is 55:8. [11]LF 21:315*.

27:1-7 JOB CONFIRMS HIS ABSOLUTE SINCERITY

¹And Job again took up his discourse, and said:
   ²"As God lives, who has taken away my right, and the Almighty, who has made my soul bitter;*
   ³as long as my breath is in me, and the spirit of God is in my nostrils;
   ⁴my lips will not speak falsehood,† and my tongue will not utter deceit.‡
   ⁵Far be it from me to say that you are right;

till I die I will not put away my integrity from me.
   ⁶I hold fast my righteousness, and will not let it go; my heart does not reproach me for any of my days.

   ⁷"Let my enemy be as the wicked, and let him that rises up against me be as the unrighteous."

*LXX (1-2) And Job further continued and said in his parable, As God lives, who has thus judged me; and the Almighty, who has embittered my soul.   †Vg iniquity   ‡Vg will not meditate falsehood

---

OVERVIEW: The Fathers interpret this part of Job's speech as a natural and further development of his previous reflections (OLYMPIODORUS). The holy man does not lie either by participation or out of set purpose, but is entirely fixed on the truth (GREGORY). Job expresses and defends his purity of heart (GREGORY), firmness and perfect innocence (EPHREM, ISHO'DAD, CHRYSOSTOM).

27:1-2 Job Speaks Again

A PROLOGUE TO HIS NEXT SPEECH. OLYMPIODORUS: While his three friends remained silent about his words, the blessed Job, by linking himself with what had been said before, adds the words that follow. Indeed he had spoken his previous words as a prologue to what follows now. COMMENTARY ON JOB 27.1.[1]

27:3-4 I Will Not Speak Falsely

NO LIE OF SET PURPOSE OR BY PARTICIPATION. GREGORY THE GREAT: What he first calls "iniquity," afterward he calls "falsehood." All "falsehood" is "iniquity," and all "iniquity" is

"falsehood." For whatever is at variance with truth is surely at odds with justice. But there is a wide difference between "to speak" and "to meditate," which he adds afterward. For sometimes it is a worse thing to "meditate" falsehood than to speak it, because speaking it is very frequently a matter of being impetuous, but to "meditate" on it shows deliberate wickedness. And who could be ignorant of the great differernce when distinguishing sin, whether one tells a lie inconsiderately or deliberately? But the holy person who perfectly adheres to the truth would neither lie deliberately, nor would he do so impetuously. MORALS ON THE BOOK OF JOB 18.5.[2]

27:5-7 I Will Not Put Away My Integrity

JOB'S FIRMNESS. EPHREM THE SYRIAN: "I hold fast my righteousness and will not let it go." That means, I will not surrender, nor will the perseverance and resolution of my soul yield, but I will patiently and bravely bear my calamity. COMMENTARY ON JOB 27.6.[3]

---

[1]PTS 24:225.   [2]LF 21:319-20*.   [3]ESOO 2:11.

A DECLARATION OF INNOCENCE. ISHO'DAD OF MERV: "My heart does not reproach me for any of my days." Job has no resentment in himself, and his conscience does not reproach him for any shameful act that he might have committed. COMMENTARY ON JOB 27.6.[4]

THE RIGHTEOUS EXPRESSES HIS INNOCENCE. CHRYSOSTOM: This is what Job means, one who is full of iniquity has neither liberty to express himself nor to say what I say now. Rather, he has been taken away and stays silent. On the contrary, I did not experience that, but I speak and answer. But the same does not happen to those who are iniquitous. COMMENTARY ON JOB 27.5B-6.[5]

---

[4]CSCO 229:253. [5]PTS 35:146.

27:8-23 JOB DECLARES HIS ABHORRENCE OF WICKEDNESS

[8]*For what is the hope of the godless when*
    God cuts him off,
  when God takes away his life?
[9]*Will God hear his cry,*
  when trouble comes upon him?
[10]*Will he take delight in the Almighty?*
  *Will he call upon God at all times?**
[11]*I will teach you concerning† the hand of*
    God;
  what is with the Almighty I will not
    conceal.‡
[12]*Behold, all of you have seen it yourselves;*
  why then have you become altogether
    vain?

[13]*This is the portion of a wicked man with*
    God,
  and the heritage which oppressors receive
    from the Almighty:
[14]*If his children are multiplied, it is for the*
    sword;

and his offspring have not enough to eat.
[15]*Those who survive him the pestilence buries,*
  and their widows make no lamentation.§
[16]*Though he heap up silver like dust,*
  and pile up clothing like clay;
[17]*he may pile it up, but the just will wear it,*
  and the innocent will divide the silver.
[18]*The house which he builds is like a*
    spider's web,ᵃ
  like a booth which a watchman makes.
[19]*He goes to bed rich, but will do so no more;ᵇ*
  he opens his eyes, and his wealth is gone.
[20]*Terrors overtake him like a flood;*
  in the night a whirlwind carries him off.
[21]*The east wind lifts him up and he is gone;*
  it sweeps him out of his place.
[22]*Itᶜ hurls at him without pity;*
  he flees from itsᵈ power in headlong
    flight.
[23]*Itᶜ claps itsᵈ hands at him,*
  *and hisses at him from itsᵈ place.**

---

a Cn Compare Gk Syr: Heb *He builds his house like the moth* **b** Gk Compare Syr: Heb *shall not be gathered* **c** Or *he (that is God* **d** Or *his* *LXX (8-10) *For what is the hope of the ungodly, that he holds to it? Will he indeed trust in the Lord and be saved? Will God hear his prayer? Or, when distress has come upon him, has he any confidence before him? Or will God* *hear him as he calls upon him?* †Vg *through* ‡LXX *I will announce to you the things that are in the hand of God, the things that are with the Almighty, and I will not lie* §LXX (14-15) *And if their children are many, they shall be for slaughter, and if they grow up, they shall beg. And they that survive of him shall utterly come to death, and no one shall pity their widows* #Vg (21-23) *The scorching wind shall carry him off and take him away and as a whirlwind shall carry him out of place. He shall let loose upon him and not spare. Fleeing he shall flee out of his hand. He shall bind up his hand over him, and he shall hiss upon him, beholding his place.*

OVERVIEW: After declaring his innocence and purity, Job expresses his scorn and absolute condemnation of wickedness. Therefore, in this part of his speech, the Fathers underline the moral aspect and edifying value of his words (OLYMPIODORUS, JULIAN OF ECLANUM, GREGORY). The righteous cohesively gather together those very testimonies of holy Scripture that the heretic piles up deductively by a dabbling employment of the written word (GREGORY). Gregory dialectically distinguishes the metaphors of scourging/sparing the offender, and binding/loosing the hands.

27:8-10 The Godless Cast Off by God

NO HOPE FOR THE GODLESS. OLYMPIODORUS: What hope, he says, does the impious have, even though he has lived so far? With what sort of assurance does he expect any salvation from God like that by which I trust to be saved? How will he confidently invoke God, after falling into misfortune, as if his prayers should be really heard? COMMENTARY ON JOB 27.8-10.[1]

27:11-13 What the Wicked Receive from God

THE AFFLICTIONS RESERVED FOR THE WICKED. JULIAN OF ECLANUM: "I will teach you through the hand of God." He says that he will describe to them with his teaching the afflictions that are given to the hypocrites through the hand of God. In order to show his full knowledge of the things that he will describe, he adds a full account of them. They cannot ignore what he is going to relate. The Greek text reads, "I will announce to you the things that are in the hand of God, the things that are with the Almighty, and I will not lie." EXPOSITION ON THE BOOK OF JOB 27.11.[2]

27:14-15 Their Children Die

THE AFFLICTIONS THAT BEFALL THE GODLESS. OLYMPIODORUS: He describes what is likely to happen to the ungodly. Admittedly, things do not always go in this manner for them. Some of them, indeed, preserve their prosperity until the end of their life, as he himself, in his quandary, has taught his friends in the previous chapters. Therefore, he calls "slaughter" the kind of death that is inflicted by enemies, and "death" the one that comes suddenly and prematurely. COMMENTARY ON JOB 27.14-15.[3]

27:16-18 Their Silver Dispersed to Others

SILVER CAN MEAN FALSE DISPLAY. GREGORY THE GREAT: Silver used to be interpreted as the clarity of sacred Scripture. As it is elsewhere said, "The words of the Lord are pure words, as silver tried in a furnace of earth." And because there are those who long to have the Word of God not inwardly in the exemplifying of it, but externally in the displaying of it, therefore it is said by the prophet, "All those who are clothed in silver are cut off," referring to those who by the word of God do not fill themselves with the interior refreshment but array themselves in the outward exhibition. Hence their "silver," that is, the word of heretics, is compared with "dust," because on matters touching the holy Scripture, there may be something that they know, but they toil and strain from the coveting of earthly applause. And these also "pile up clothing like clay," because they loosely make up testimonies of holy Scripture in a dabbling way, where they are able to defend themselves. The oppressors

---

[1]PTS 24:227. [2]CCL 88:72. [3]PTS 24:227-28.

shall "pile up" silver indeed, "but the just will wear it," because the person who is full of right faith, which used to be accounted to the saints for righteousness, cohesively gathers together those self-same testimonies of holy Scripture that the heretic piles up deductively. And from there, the just strikes home at the obstinacy of the other's error. MORALS ON THE BOOK OF JOB 18.24.[4]

27:19-23 They Awake Impoverished

THE PUNISHMENT OF THE WICKED. GREGORY THE GREAT: "The scorching wind shall carry him off and take him away." Who is it that is here called the "scorching wind"? None other than the evil spirit who stirs up the flames of diverse lusts in the heart that he may drag it to an eternity of punishments. And so "the scorching wind" is said to "carry off" the bad people, because the plotter, the evil spirit, inflames a person who is drawn toward evil and drags him when dying to torments. . . .

"And as a whirlwind shall carry him out of his place." "The place" of the wicked is the gratification of the temporal life and the enjoyment of the flesh. Therefore, every single individual is in a sense "carried out of his place by a whirlwind." He is overwhelmed with terror on the last day, severed from all gratifications. Regarding this same last day, it is immediately added, and rightly, "For he shall let loose upon him and not spare." God, as often as he chastises the sinner by smiting him, "lets loose" the scourge, precisely that he may "spare" him. But when, by punishing him, he brings his life to an end while remaining in sin, he "lets loose" the scourge and does not "spare." For the same one who "lets loose" the scourge in order that he might "spare" will one day "let it loose" with this in view—that he may not spare. For in this life the Lord is able more to spare in proportion as he scourges those who are in waiting. This is what he himself said to John by the voice of the angel, "As many as I love, I rebuke and chas-

tise;"[5] and as it is elsewhere spoken, "For whom the Lord loves, he chastises."[6] But, in reverse, it is written of the scourge of condemnation, "The wicked is trapped in the work of his own hands."[7] According to Jeremiah, when the Lord sees the multitude transgressing irreclaimably, whom he now no longer regards as sons under discipline but as enemies under unmitigated scourging, he says: "For I have wounded you with the wound of an enemy, with a cruel chastisement."[8] . . .

Then he says, "He shall bind up his hands over him." To "bind up the hands" is to establish the practices of his life in uprightness. Hence Paul also says, "Therefore lift up the loosed hands and the unstrung knees." While, then, they behold the destruction of another, they are made to turn back to the conscience. There they are to remind themselves of their own acts, by which one person is carried to torments and another is freed from torments. And so "he binds up his hands over him," because he observes in the punishment of another what to be afraid of. While he sees one living in transgression as smitten, he binds fast with the sinews of righteousness his own loose practices. And so it is brought to pass that he who, being a bad person while living, had drawn numbers into transgression by the seductiveness of sin, may in dying recover some from transgression by the terribleness of their torments. . . .

"And he shall hiss upon him, beholding his place." What is expressed in the hissing other than the wrenching of wonder? But if in the hissing there is some other meaning sought, when the sinner dies, those who witness his death draw tight the mouth in hissing, in the sense that they are converted to those spiritual words that they themselves had condemned, so that they henceforth begin to believe and to teach that which before, while they perceived the wicked person thriving, they earlier had not

---

[4]LF 21:332-33*. [5]Rev 3:19. [6]Heb 12:6. [7]Ps 9:16 (9:17 LXX). [8]Jer 30:14.

believed. For it very often happens that the mind of the weak is the more unsteadied from the hearing of the truth precisely by seeing the despisers of the truth flourishing. But when just punishment takes away the unjust, it keeps oth-ers away from wickedness. MORALS ON THE BOOK OF JOB 18.32-38.[9]

[9]LF 21:339-43*.

28:1-11 HUMAN BEINGS HAVE KNOWLEDGE OF NATURAL THINGS

[1]Surely there is a mine for silver,
    and a place for gold which they refine.
[2]Iron is taken out of the earth,
    and copper is smelted from the ore.
[3]Men put an end to darkness,
    and search out to the farthest bound
    the ore in gloom and deep darkness.*
[4]They open shafts in a valley away
        from where men live;
    they are forgotten by travelers,
    they hang afar from men, they swing to
        and fro.†
[5]As for the earth, out of it comes bread;‡
    but underneath it is turned up as by fire.
[6]Its stones are the place of sapphires,ᵉ
    and it has dust of gold.

[7]That path no bird of prey knows,
    and the falcon's eye has not seen it.
[8]The proud beasts§ have not trodden it;
    the lion# has not passed over it.

[9]Man puts his hand to the flinty rock,
    and overturns mountains by the roots.
[10]He cuts out channels in the rocks,
    and his eye sees every precious thing.
[11]He binds up the streams so that they
        do not trickle,
    and the thing that is hid he brings forth
        to light.**

e Or lapis lazuli   *LXX (2-3) For iron comes out of the earth, and brass is hewn out like stone. He has set a place for darkness and exactly determines the limit of seasons.   †Vg A stream separates from the wandering people those who are out-of-the-way and whom the foot of the needy has forgotten   ‡Peshitta They uncovered the earth, from which nourishments come.   §Vg the sons of the merchants   #Vg the lioness   **Vg (9-11) He stretches out his hand to the flint; he overturns mountains by the roots. He cuts out streams in the rocks, and his eye has seen every precious thing. The sources of the rivers he has probed; hidden things he has brought to light.

OVERVIEW: This part of Job's speech is mostly interpreted by the Fathers in a philosophic sense: the human being, who is at the center of nature, is allowed to have a limited perception and knowledge of God's power through observation of nature (CHRYSOSTOM, ISHO'DAD, JULIAN THE ARIAN, JULIAN OF ECLANUM). The elements once subsisted alone, but when humans were created, they understood what usefulness could be gained from each aspect of matter with the guidance of his reason, concerning farming, building and sailing (GREGORY). As fire takes hold of wood, so when seeds are scattered on the earth, they drive their roots in it, and thanks to the power that they receive from it, they spring up (Isho'dad). At the same time, as usual, the Fathers detect in Job's words prophetic truths and see here clear allusions to the disbelief of the Jews and the conversion of the Gentiles (Philip, Gregory). Those who are drained of excessive concern for what is below, God waters with streams from above (Gregory).

28:1-3 Silver and Gold

The Order of Nature Shows God's Power. Chrysostom: He means that if God has established an order in the realities of nature, he did even more with regard to human realities. Indeed, he foresees and takes care of events, and nothing comes from him at random. Or, on the other hand, [he means] that the whole of realities is quite visible but the plans of God are invisible; in fact, silver and copper have a place, whereas nobody has ever known the "place" of wisdom. But God only knows wisdom,[1] and he has said to mortals that "piety is wisdom,"[2] and knowledge means to do good.

"He has set a place for darkness," he says; he was right in saying "a place," because darkness knows how to give way and fade away [before the daylight]. Who drives this obscurity away? From where does such beautiful order in such a situation come? Then he discusses his power, and then his wisdom in order to persuade us that he does not want to call God to account. Why darkness, he says? Do we really know anything at all? God can do anything. He does everything with wisdom. Commentary on Job 27.14-28.3.[3]

28:4 Far from Human Dwellings

An Allusion to Those Who Refused Christ's Grace. Philip the Priest: "A stream separates from the wandering people those who are out of the way and whom the foot of the needy has forgotten." This is what holy Job says, a stream of fire separates those who are out of the way, that is, who live out of the way of

true religion and did not show mercy for the needy, that is, for the brothers of Christ, so that they are also divided from the society of the saints. The needy may also be interpreted as a reference to our Savior, who, although he was rich, became needy and poor for us.[4] So, see in his foot his dispensation, and also his assumption of the man and his entry into the world. . . . Therefore, those who did not accept the dispensation of his salvation in the gospel were given to oblivion, because they did not want to believe for the hardness of their heart. So, they are called "out of the way," because they did not receive Christ, who is the way. Commentary on the Book of Job 28.[5]

28:5 The Qualities of the Earth

Generative Power of the Earth. Isho'dad of Merv: "They have uncovered the earth, from which nourishment comes," through the art of agriculture, [the author] says; [humans] produce what is necessary for nourishment which the earth offers according to the divine precept by which it received.[6] Therefore, as the fire takes hold of the wood, so the earth acts in the same manner when the seeds are scattered on it; they drive their roots in it, and thanks to the power that they receive from it, they spring up. This is the meaning of the words "underneath it is turned up as by fire." Commentary on Job 28.5.[7]

28:6 Sapphires and Gold

The Beauties of Nature. Julian the Arian: In fact the earth itself generates the so-called precious stones and the gold; and they are the glory of the kings and the ornament of the women who love beauty. And after [Job] has shown that God has made many excellent things on the earth, he adds new details. Commentary on Job 28.6.[8]

---

[1]Cf. Job 28:23. [2]Job 28:28 LXX. [3]PTS 35:148. [4]See 2 Cor 8:9. [5]PL 26:696-97. [6]See Gen 1:11. [7]CSCO 229:254. [8]PTS 14:170.

28:7-8 A Path Unknown to Birds of Prey

KNOWLEDGE OF NATURE IS OPEN TO HUMAN BEINGS. JULIAN OF ECLANUM: Even though they sail in the air and reach paths close to heaven, they cannot approach those through which knowledge is attained. "That path no bird knows." The context of the exposition seems to demand that effects and duties follow the knowledge that he has set out to describe and that he assigns parts of it, so that people, with its guidance, may reach in the hope of their search those places that had previously been far removed from the access of mortals. And, according to his custom, he exaggeratedly says huge deserts are reached by people that are far removed from birds and other beasts while they are trodden by human foot. "The sons of the merchants have not trodden it." While he sets out to show that people penetrate the deserts, how can he now deny that wildernesses are trodden by the feet of merchants? Therefore, it seems that here he has shown the scarceness of the travelers and has denied the frequency of the merchants. "The lioness has not passed over it." No bird or reptile or quadruped ever knew those things that reason, the examiner and researcher of hidden things, has found. EXPOSITION ON THE BOOK OF JOB 28.7-8.[9]

28:9-10a Overturning Rocks and Mountains

A FORESHADOWING OF CHRIST'S CONVERSION OF THE GENTILES. GREGORY THE GREAT: "He stretches out his hand to the flint; he overturns mountains by the roots." "He stretches out his hand to the flint" means he presented the arm of his preaching to the hardness of the Gentiles. Hence the same blessed Job, forewarned of the history of his suffering being destined to be made known to the Gentiles, says, "Let these things be engraved with an iron pen in a plate of lead or hewn in the flint."[10] However, whom in this place do we understand by the "mountains" except the powerful ones of this world, who because of earthly substance puff themselves up? Concerning

them the psalmist says, "Touch the mountains, and they shall smoke"; but the mountains are overturned from the roots, because holy church, preaching the highest powers of this world, fell from their inmost thinking into the adoring of almighty God. For "the roots" of the mountains are the inmost thoughts of the proud. And "the mountains fall from the roots," because for the worshiping of God, the powers of the world are laid level with the earth from the lowest thoughts. For by a root the hidden thought is rightly denoted, because by means of that which is not seen, being within, there bursts out what should be seen without. Therefore, on the side of good it is said by the prophet, "And the remnant that is escaped of the house of Judah shall again take root downward and bear fruit upward. As though it were expressed in plain speech; "Deep down below the thought springs up, that up on high the reward may be rendered back." So then, let him say, "He stretches out his hand to the flint and overturns the mountains from the roots." While the sacred preaching sought the hardness of the Gentiles, it entirely frustrated the loftiness of the proud, however, because those it empties of earthly thoughts, it fills with heavenly gifts. Moreover, those whom it drains of interest below, it waters with streams from above. It is directly added, "He cuts out streams in the rocks," that is, in the hard hearts of the Gentiles he opened the rivers of preaching; as it is likewise spoken by the prophet of watering the dryness of the Gentiles, "He turns the wilderness into a standing water and dry ground into water springs." MORALS ON THE BOOK OF JOB 18.57-58.[11]

28:10b-11 Seeing Precious Things

THE USEFULNESS OF NATURE. JULIAN OF ECLANUM: "And his eye has seen every precious thing." That is, not only those things that were useful but also those that were convenient as an ornament, such as clothes from wool, fabrics for the rich from the threads of the Persian worms,[12]

---

[9]CCL 88:75-76. [10]Job 19:24. [11]LF 21:358-59*. [12]Silkworms.

wine from some creeping plants, ointments and other remedies from herbs. "The sources of the rivers he has probed," while his curious hand explored the stones covered by the waters. "Hidden things he has brought to light"; his reason spread the news about the previously unknown usefulness of things. In fact, since before humankind the elements subsisted alone, after he was created, he understood what usefulness could be gained from each of them with the guidance of his reason, which lands were suitable for sowing, which for plantations that benefit could be obtained from a particular plant, which wood was useful to build ships that was suitable for buildings. EXPOSITION ON THE BOOK OF JOB 28.10-11.[13]

[13]CCL 88:76.

28:12-28 WISDOM BELONGS TO GOD

[12]But where shall wisdom be found?
   And where is the place of understanding?
[13]Man does not know the way to it,[f]
   and it is not found in the land of the living.[*]
[14]The deep says, "It is not in me,"[†]
   and the sea says, "It is not with me."
[15]It cannot be gotten for gold,
   and silver cannot be weighed as its
      price.
[16]It cannot be valued in the gold of Ophir,
   in precious onyx or sapphire.[g]
[17]Gold and glass cannot equal it,
   nor can it be exchanged for jewels of fine
      gold.
[18]No mention shall be made of coral or of
      crystal;
   the price of wisdom is above pearls.[‡]
[19]The topaz of Ethiopia cannot compare
      with it,
   nor can it be valued in pure gold.

[20]Whence then comes wisdom?

And where is the place of understanding?
[21]It is hid from the eyes of all living,
   and concealed from the birds of the air.
[22]Abaddon[§] and Death say,
   "We have heard a rumor of it with our
      ears."

[23]God understands the way to it,
   and he knows its place.
[24]For he looks to the ends of the earth,
   and sees everything under the heavens.
[25]When he gave to the wind its weight,
   and meted out the waters by measure;
[26]when he made a decree for the rain,
   and a way for the lightning of the
      thunder;
[27]then he saw it and declared it;
   he established it, and searched it out.
[28]And he said to man,
   "Behold, the fear of the Lord, that is
      wisdom;
   and to depart from evil is understanding."[#]

f Gk: Heb its price   g Or lapis lazuli   *Vg of those that live sweetly   †Vg The bottomless pit says, 'It is not with me.'   ‡Vg The highest and loftier things are not worthy of mention in comparison with it; wisdom is drawn from what is hidden.   §Vg perdition   #LXX Truly piety, that is wisdom; and to abstain from evil, that is knowledge.

OVERVIEW: The final part of Job's speech is one of the most poetic passages in holy Scripture: it describes wisdom and its nature using both imaginative and philosophical language. Supreme wisdom is to worship God (CHYRSOSTOM). Wisdom surpasses majestic earthly beauty (JULIAN THE ARIAN), riches, honors and official dignity (JULIAN OF ECLANUM). Wisdom does not reside in this bottomless pit of the ungodly mind that longs to be wise in a carnal way yet shows itself foolish as to things spiritual (GREGORY). Even though Christ is here prophetically presented through a simile, his Wisdom is above any simile or figure or type (EPHREM). To souls God imparts a kind of weight in order that they should not with light motion move away from their aim at God, but settle into him with immoveable weightiness of steadfast faith (GREGORY).

28:12-14 Where Is Wisdom Found?

WISDOM CANNOT BE FOUND IN WORLDLY HEARTS. GREGORY THE GREAT: "And it is not found in the land of those that live sweetly." What is denoted in this passage by the title of the "land," except the soul of man? Concerning which the psalmist says, "My soul thirsts after you, as a land without water."[1] But this wisdom cannot "be found in the land of those that live sweetly," because the person who is still fed with the pleasures of this life is severed from the perception of eternal Wisdom. For if he were truly wise-minded, being banished from the interior delights, he would mourn over that blind estate of his exile into which he has fallen. Thus Solomon says, "He that adds knowledge, adds pain also."[2] For the more a person begins to know what he has lost, the more he begins to bewail the sentence of his corruption that he has received. For he sees how he has fallen and how that from the joys of paradise he has come to the woes of present life, from the company of the angels to caring for necessities. He considers in what a number of perils he now lies prostrate,

who before without peril disdained to stand. He bewails the exile that being accursed he undergoes. He sighs after the state of heavenly glory that he might be enjoying in security, if he had not had a mind to commit sin. . . . "The bottomless pit says, 'It is not with me.'" What does he call the "bottomless pit?" The hearts of people who by their fall are now floating in darkness and the murkiness of double dealing. Wisdom does not reside in this "bottomless pit." In this way the wicked mind, while it longs to be wise in a carnal way, shows itself foolish as to things spiritual. Which same "bottomless pit" declares that his Wisdom "is not with" it; because the wicked mind, while it longs to be wise in a carnal way, shows itself foolish as to things spiritual. Paul testifies, "The wisdom of this world is foolishness with God." Thus, so much the more completely is everyone rendered foolish within, as he endeavors to appear wise outside. . . . "And the sea says, 'It is not with me.'" For what is there denoted by the name of the sea except the bitter disquietude of worldly minds, which while they fall foul of one another in enmities by turns, dash themselves together like encountering waves? The life of worldly persons is rightly called "a sea," because, while it is agitated by the tempestuous stirrings of actions, it is parted from the tranquility and steadfastness of interior Wisdom. The opposite of this condition was well said by the prophet, "Upon whom shall my spirit rest but upon him who is humble and quiet and who trembles at my words?"[3] MORALS ON THE BOOK OF JOB 18.66-68.[4]

28:15-17 It Cannot Be Purchased

THE INCOMPARABLE NATURE OF WISDOM. JULIAN THE ARIAN: None of the most beautiful or most precious things on the earth can be compared with wisdom. Not even the great deep, or the heaped-up seas of the ocean or the glory itself of the earth can circumscribe it. . . . Wisdom sur-

---

[1]See Ps 63:1 (62:1 LXX). [2]Eccles 1:18. [3]Is 66:2. [4]LF 21:366-69**.

passes completely all these things. COMMENTARY ON JOB 28.14-19.[5]

28:18-19 Wisdom's Price Above Pearls

EXCELLENCE OF WISDOM. JULIAN OF ECLANUM: "The highest and loftier things are not worthy of mention in comparison with it." He shows that not only amassed riches but also the heights of honors and the highest peaks of official dignity become worthless in comparison with it. "Wisdom is drawn from what is hidden." Since he had depreciated all the things that delight the eyes, or entice the other senses or deceive the minds, in comparison with the honor of wisdom, he also avenges [wisdom] from that offense, in order that it may not appear to be open to everybody, that is, it may not be accused of dwelling in the desires and the actions of the crowd. EXPOSITION ON THE BOOK OF JOB 28.18.[6]

28:20-21 Where Does Wisdom Originate?

AN ALLUSION TO CHRIST. EPHREM THE SYRIAN: These words suggest that even though Christ is presented through a simile, he is, however, above any simile or figure or type and is by no means comparable to the saints. He is said to be similar to the hidden and superior powers, but it is well known that they cannot even direct their looks to him. COMMENTARY ON JOB 28.21.[7]

28:22 We Have Heard a Rumor of It

THE UNGODLY HAVE A RUMOR OF THE FEAR OF GOD. PHILIP THE PRIEST: "Perdition and Death say, 'We have heard a rumor of it with our ears.'" The devil can be called with both these names, as well as he can be defined as death, so that his bodyguards are named "perdition." Therefore, they said that they heard a rumor about the eminence of the fear of God; indeed, they cannot deny that they heard it, as they perceived it to be present in the goodness of nature, but because of the evil of their disobedience, they refused to receive it. COMMENTARY ON THE BOOK OF JOB 28.[8]

28:23-26 God Sees Everything

GOD RESTRAINED THE EVILS OF OUR LIGHTNESS. GREGORY THE GREAT: For God's "looking" is the renewing to his grace the things that were lost and undone. Hence it is written, "A king that sits in the throne of judgment scatters away all evil with his eyes."[9] For by his very glance he restrains the evils of our lightness and imparts the great value of maturity. Hence it is further added, "When he gave to the wind its weight." In the holy Scripture, by the rapidity and subtlety of the winds, souls used to be denoted, as it is spoken by the psalmist of God, "Who walks above the wings of the winds,"[10] that is, "who passes above the virtues of souls." Accordingly "He made the weight for the winds," in that while Wisdom from above fills souls, it renders them weighty with imparted maturity. This is not the same weightiness of which it is said, "You children of men, how long with a heavy heart."[11] For it is one thing to be weighty in relation to good counsel and another to be weighed down in relation to sin. It is one thing to be weighty by faithfulness, another to be weighty by wrongdoing. For this latter weightiness has the weight of burden, the other weight of merit. Therefore, souls receive weight that they should not from this day forward with light motion move away from their aim at God, but be made to settle into him with immoveable weightiness of constancy. MORALS ON THE BOOK OF JOB 19.7-8.[12]

28:27-28 Fear of the Lord Is Wisdom

WISDOM IS TO WORSHIP GOD. CHRYSOSTOM: Nothing has more value than that art, nothing is more powerful than that wisdom. "The fear of the Lord, that is the beginning of wisdom, and all

---

[5]PTS 14:173. [6]CCL 88:77. [7]ESOO 2:12. [8]PL 26:702. [9]Prov 20:8.
[10]Ps 104:3 (103:3 Vg). [11]Ps 4:2 (4:3 LXX). [12]LF 21:399**.

those who practice it have good understanding."[13] That is the greatest of all goods. Supreme wisdom is to worship God, not to take trouble to make useless notices, and especially to enquire

about events. Do not believe that you may find a different wisdom. COMMENTARY ON JOB 28.28.[14]

---

[13]Prov 1:7. [14]PTS 35:148.

29:1-25 JOB RECALLS HIS FORMER PROSPERITY

[1]And Job again took up his discourse, and said:
  [2]"Oh, that I were as in the months of old,
    as in the days when God watched over
      me;*
  [3]when his lamp shone upon my head,
    and by his light I walked through darkness;
  [4]as I was in my autumn days,
    when the friendship of God was upon my
      tent;
  [5]when the Almighty was yet with me,
    when my children were about me;
  [6]when my steps were washed with milk,
    and the rock poured out for me streams
      of oil!
  [7]When I went out to the gate of the city,†
    when I prepared my seat in the square,
  [8]the young men saw me and withdrew,‡
    and the aged rose and stood;
  [9]the princes refrained from talking,
    and laid their hand§ on their mouth;
  [10]the voice of the nobles was hushed,
    and their tongue cleaved to the roof
      of their mouth.
  [11]When the ear heard, it called me blessed,
    and when the eye saw, it approved;
  [12]because I delivered the poor who cried,#
    and the fatherless who had none
      to help him.

  [13]The blessing of him who was about to
      perish came upon me,**
    and I caused the widow's heart to sing
      for joy.*
  [14]I put on righteousness, and it clothed me;
    my justice was like a robe and a turban.††
  [15]I was eyes to the blind,
    and feet to the lame.
  [16]I was a father to the poor,
    and I searched out the cause of him
      whom I did not know.
  [17]I broke the fangs of the unrighteous,
    and made him drop his prey from his
      teeth.
  [18]Then I thought, 'I shall die in my nest,
    and I shall multiply my days as the
      sand,‡‡
  [19]my roots spread out to the waters,
    with the dew all night on my branches,
  [20]my glory fresh with me,
    and my bow ever new in my hand.'§§

  [21]"Men listened to me, and waited,
    and kept silence for my counsel.
  [22]After I spoke they did not speak again,##
    and my word dropped upon them.
  [23]They waited for me as for the rain;
    and they opened their mouths as for the

147

spring rain.***
^{24}*I smiled on them when they had no*
confidence;
and the light of my countenance they did

not cast down.†††
^{25}*I chose their way, and sat as chief,*
and I dwelt like a king among his troops,
like one who comforts mourners."

*LXX Then Job adds these words at the beginning [of his speech], Who would be able to give me back a month similar to the month of the past days? †Vg and in the street they prepared me a chair ‡Vg and hid themselves §Vg their finger #LXX I saved the poor from the hand of the powerful. **Peshitta The blessing of the one about to die will come upon me. ††LXX and I clothed myself with judgment like a double mantle ‡‡Peshitta I shall be perfected like the reeds, and I shall multiply my days like the grains of sand. §§LXX and my bow will travel in his hand ##Vg To my words they did not dare to add anything. ***Vg latter rain †††Vg (24) If I laughed on them, they did not believe it; and the light of my countenance did not fall on the earth.

OVERVIEW: At Job 29, Job begins a new speech, which is not intended as a direct reply to his friends and is usually defined as a soliloquy. It extends from Job 29 to Job 31 and represents, in a sense, the definitive sum of his reflections and opinions on his present condition. The section included in Job 29 appears to be a meditation that Job makes on the loss of his past glory. However, the Fathers do not interpret Job's words as a mere lamentation and longing for a former happiness that has now disappeared but as a proof of his piety, as an acknowledgment of divine Providence (CHRYSOSTOM), as an exhortation to goodness and benevolence (GREGORY) and as clear demonstration of Job's unblemished nature (CHRYSOSTOM, EPHREM, ISHO'DAD, JULIAN THE ARIAN). The gate of the city refers to good actions by which the soul enters the heavenly company, while the gates of death refer to bad actions that drag the soul to destruction (GREGORY).

Prophetic truths are also found in Job's words (GREGORY, CHRYSOSTOM). In the early rain he bestowed on his elect the knowledge of the law, but with the incarnation he would give "the latter rain" that waters the mouth of all who hear. The brightness of the Lord's countenance does not appear to sinners (GREGORY).

29:1-2 Oh, That I Was As Before

RECALL OF PAST GLORY. CHRYSOSTOM: What do the words "he adds at the beginning of his speech" mean? It is not that he completes his speeches, but he comes back to his starting point,

without allowing his adversaries to interrupt him or to begin new arguments. What does he say? I would like to live one month of my old happiness in order to shut your mouth and to show you who I was.

"One month comparable to a month of my past days." He calls for nothing extraordinary, only to live his past happiness for thirty days and to enjoy that prosperity with which nobody can provide him anymore. Then he describes it through his words. In fact, since it was impossible now [to live his past happiness], he shows it through his words and says what he did and how he lived before. See the piety of the man: he attributes everything to God. In fact, it is impossible that a person deprived of divine help may ever stand. COMMENTARY ON JOB 29.2A.[1]

29:3-5 Walking by God's Light

A REFERENCE TO GOD'S PROVIDENCE. CHRYSOSTOM: If he actually searched for his former happiness, that was in order to show the providence of God; this is clear when he says, "In the days when God watched over me."[2] Then he gives evidence of this godly watch. "When his lamp," he says, "shone over my head." This means, you will make the light of my lamp shine, because a lamp is really necessary, if the present darkness is deep, if the difficulties of my situation are serious, as well as the assaults of physical suffering, and the plots of the wicked and the fights and

---

[1]PTS 35:149. [2]Job 29:2.

attacks of cruel demons. All this shows that "by his light I walked through darkness." You see that darkness invades everything and that "light shines through darkness."[3] But, as natural darkness is useful to have rest, it is not useful because of its own nature but thanks to the wisdom of God, who has created everything. COMMENTARY ON JOB 29.2A-5.[4]

29:6-7 Milk and Oil

THE GATE OF THE CITY. GREGORY THE GREAT: It was the custom of the ancients that the elders should sit together in the gates and judge the cases of those entering in, so that the people of the city might be more peaceful. Now we in revering the sacred history hold it certain that this blessed Job did everything for the sake of the observance of just dealing. We are led further to investigate the mystery of the allegory.

What then is denoted by "the gate of the city"? It refers to every good action by which the soul enters into the company of the heavenly kingdom. Hence the prophet says, "You, who lifted me up from the gates of death, that I may declare all your praises in the gates of the daughter of Zion."[5] For "the gates of death" are bad actions that drag to destruction. But because Zion is the word for a viewing, "the gates of Zion" we interpret as good actions by which we enter into the country above, that we may view the glory of our King. MORALS ON THE BOOK OF JOB 19.25.[6]

29:8-9 Respected by All

A FIGURE OF THE HOLY CHURCH. GREGORY THE GREAT: Thus now "the young men see holy church and hide themselves, and the old men rise up and stand," because the youth fear its mighty righteousness, and the elderly magnify it. Those empty of mind flee. The serious and perfect do homage to [the church] by rising up in response to the merits of its life. By this discipline the mature come to love and the immature to judgment. And so "the young men see her and hide them-

selves," because they are afraid to be detected in their hidden courses of conduct. But "the elders rise up and stand," because all the perfect ones make it appear by humility how they have gained ground in good practice. But because he describes all this of his own people, let him further describe how he is feared by foreign people. . . . Who else in this place can be understood as [foreign] nobles or princes but those who promote wayward teaching? About them it is said by the psalmist, "Strife was poured out upon their princes, and they led them aside in the pathless place and not in the way."[7] For these identical persons, while they are not afraid to interpret the dispensation of God in a wrong sense, assuredly draw the common herds subject to them not into that way that is "Christ" but into "a pathless place," over whom "strife is also rightly said to be poured out," because by their statements they mutually contradict themselves. MORALS ON THE BOOK OF JOB 19.26-27.[8]

29:10-12 Princes Hushed

JOB'S GOOD REPUTATION. CHRYSOSTOM: In order to explain why they proclaimed him to be blessed, he mentions his good works. "I have saved," he says, "the poor from the hand of the powerful," but it is after attributing to God the merit of protecting and watching him that "he is glorified in the Lord."[9] COMMENTARY ON JOB 29.10-12.[10]

29:13 Blessed by the Wretched

NATURE OF THE BLESSINGS. EPHREM THE SYRIAN: "The blessing of the one about to die will come upon me," that is, the blessings of the poor, who, being without a coat, was about to die, will come upon me, as I provided him with a garment. In a different sense, you may suggest that the per-

---

[3]Jn 1:5. [4]PTS 35:149-50. [5]Ps 9:13-14 (9:14-15 LXX). [6]LF 21:416**. [7]Ps 107:40 (106:40 LXX) [8]LF 21:417-18*. [9]See 1 Cor 1:31. [10]PTS 35:151.

son about to die is he who is dead to the world and its wealth; when the world is dead together with the things that are in it, the one who said, "Whoever lost his soul for me will find it" will come to him. The blessing of this poor, Job says, will come upon me. COMMENTARY ON JOB 29.13.[11]

29:14 Clothed with Righteousness

JOB WAS A RIGHTEOUS JUDGE LIKE MOSES. CHRYSOSTOM: "I put on righteousness," he says. There are people who occupy higher positions than others but who often commit injustice. But this is not the case with Job, because he constantly lived in the greatest righteousness. So, when with regard to God you hear that "he is clothed with righteousness," do not believe that real garments clothe incorporeal beings. Job did not wear that kind of garment either. "And I clothed myself with judgment like a double mantle." That was my elegance. To be sure, others are unhappy with that activity; they find it unpleasant and heavy. But I did not, he says. As one is proud of a double mantle, so I was constantly glorified . . . in that activity. But who appointed him to be a judge? He became one by himself, thanks to his virtue, like Moses. COMMENTARY ON JOB 29.13-18.[12]

29:15-17 Eyes to the Blind

A FIGURE OF THE APOSTLES. CHRYSOSTOM: See how these miracles are worthy of the apostles.[13] Job was not able to give sight back to them, because that charisma did not yet exist, but he provided them with light, even though they remained blind, whereas now we even make blind those who are able to see.[14] He did not say, I employed my servants to do that, but I, he says, corrected the errors of nature, not only the errors that derived from the action of people but also those coming from nature itself. COMMENTARY ON JOB 29.13-18.[15]

29:18-19 Roots Spread to the Waters

JOB'S PERFECTION. ISHO'DAD OF MERV: The words "I shall be perfected like the reeds," that is, I will end my days [by becoming full] of riches, by germinating and growing like the palm tree and the reeds and the [vegetables] planted along the edge of water. Henana[16] says, "As the reeds spring up and reach a great height in a short time, so I shall be completed and perfected." COMMENTARY ON JOB 29.18.[17]

29:20 My Glory Was Fresh with Me

GOD'S JUDGMENT. JULIAN THE ARIAN: "My glory was fresh with me," that is, contrary to my expectations, this is what happened to me. Instead of lasting, I became ephemeral; instead of being happy, I became wretched, according to the judgment of God. "And my bow will travel in his hand." My means of defense was with God. If we used a hyperbaton,[18] that is, "his bow will travel in my hand," the meaning would be, all his wrath will move toward me. COMMENTARY ON JOB 29.20.[19]

29:21-24 People Listened to Job's Counsel

A METAPHOR OF CHRIST AND THE HOLY CHURCH. GREGORY THE GREAT: For this awe of those under him we unquestionably believe to have been directed toward blessed Job. But, as we have already often said, holy church, being driven to extremities by the inflictions of heretics or carnal persons, remembers the times past, in which all that is spoken by it is listened to with fear by the faithful. Lamenting the evilness of its adversaries, [the church] says, "They listened to me, and waited and kept silence for my counsel." It is as though it expressed itself in plain speech, "Not

---

[11]ESOO 2:12. [12]PTS 35:152. [13]See Acts 5:12. [14]See Jn 9:39. [15]PTS 35:152-53. [16]Henana (about 545-610), a significant figure in Syriac literature, wrote many exegetical works on the Old and New Testaments. The majority of his writings are now lost, and only fragments are preserved in the works of Isho'dad and other later Syriac authors. [17]CSCO 229:255. [18]A rhetorical figure employed to invert the elements of a sentence. [19]PTS 14:180.

like these evil and swollen ones, who while they refuse to admit the words of truth, do it as if in teaching they could forestall the sentences of my preaching." These disciples now "intent upon its counsel keep silence," because its words they dare not impugn but take on faith. For they may be able to profit by these same words; they hear them, doubtless not with a view to judge them but to follow them. Of them it is rightly added, "To my words they did not dare to add anything." The wayward teachers, free of all check, are in their freedom the most mischievous. They "dare to add something to the words [of Scripture]." They busy themselves as if to correct the rightness of [the church's] preaching. Concerning the good hearers, Job adds: "And my word dropped upon them." By this dropping of word, what else is understood but the gauge of holy preaching? Thus it is required that the boon of exhortation is bestowed to each according to the capacity of his parts. . . .

"They waited for me as for the rain; they opened their mouths as for the latter rain." Of this "latter rain" it is elsewhere written, "I will give you rain, both the early and the latter rain."[20] For he "gave the early rain," because in the former period he bestowed on his elect the knowledge of the law. He "gave the latter rain," because he caused the mystery of his incarnation to be preached in the last days. In this same mystery, holy church does not cease to tell it forth day by day. It waters the mouth of its hearers' hearts as it were by "the latter rain." . . .

"If I laughed on them, they did not believe it; and the light of my countenance did not fall on the earth." These words agree perfectly with the words of our Redeemer in the last part of the sentence where it is said, "And the light of my countenance did not fall on the earth." For what is styled "the ground" but the sinner? He is the same one to whom it was said earlier, "Earth you are, and to earth you shall return."[21] So "the light of the Lord's countenance does not fall to the earth," because the brightness of his vision does not appear to sinners. Thus it is written, "Let the ungodly man be removed away that he may not see the glory of God."[22] For light would, as it were, fall upon the earth, if when he comes in the last judgment, he manifests the brightness of his majesty to sinners. MORALS ON THE BOOK OF JOB 20.2-9.[23]

29:25 I Chose Their Way

JOB'S COMFORTING GOVERNANCE. JULIAN THE ARIAN: This is what he means: I inquired into actions, corrected them as a chief and dealt with them like the best of governors. Therefore, through me authority was pleasing to them, as if a comforter was alleviating their sufferings. COMMENTARY ON JOB 29.25.[24]

---

[20]Jer 5:24; Deut 11:14. [21]Gen 3:19. [22]Is 26:10. [23]LF 21:447-53**. [24]PTS 14.101.

30:1-13 NOW HONOR IS TURNED INTO HUMILIATION

[1]*But now they make sport of me,*
men who are younger than I,

whose fathers I would have disdained
to set with the dogs of my flock.

²*What could I gain from the strength
of their hands,
men whose vigor is gone?*
³*Through want and hard hunger
they gnaw the dry and desolate ground;*ᵇ
⁴*they pick mallow and the leaves of bushes,
and to warm themselves the roots of the
broom.**
⁵*They are driven out from among men;
they shout after them as after a thief.*
⁶*In the gullies of the torrents they must
dwell,
in holes of the earth and of the rocks.*
⁷*Among the bushes they bray;*†
under the nettles they huddle together.
⁸*A senseless, a disreputable brood,
they have been whipped out of the land.*

⁹*And now I have become their song,
I am a byword to them.*
¹⁰*They abhor me, they keep aloof from
me;
they do not hesitate to spit at the sight
of me.*‡
¹¹*Because God has loosed my cord and
humbled me,
they have cast off restraint in my
presence.*§
¹²*On my right hand the rabble rise,
they drive me*ⁱ *forth,
they cast up against me their ways of
destruction.*
¹³*They break up my path,
they promote my calamity;
no one restrains*ʲ *them.*#

h Heb *ground yesterday waste*   i Heb *my feet*   j Cn: Heb *helps*   *LXX (2-4) *What could I gan from the strength of their hands? For them the full term of life was lost. One is childless in want and famine, such as they that fled but lately the distress and misery of drought, who compass the salt places on the sounding shore, who had salt herbs for their food and were dishonorable and of no repute, in want of every good thing; who also ate roots of trees by reason of great hunger.*   †Peshitta *under the rocks and the thorny bushes*   ‡Vg *they flee away from me; they do not hesitate to spit at my face.*   §Vg *He has opened his quiver and afflicted me and put a bridle into my mouth.*   #LXX (12-13) *They have risen up against me on the right hand of their offspring; they have stretched out their foot and directed against me the ways of their destruction. My paths are ruined; for they have stripped off my raiment; he has shot at me with his weapons.*

OVERVIEW: The second part of Job's soliloquy is more focused on the inward aspect of his sufferings. The Fathers emphasize how Job is vexed by unworthy detractors and consequently suffers (JULIAN OF ECLANUM, JULIAN THE ARIAN, ISHO'DAD, CHRYSOSTOM). Job's affliction is also a symbol and a figure of the church in the time of its tribulations being spat upon, insulted and bridled (GREGORY). The righteous are most hurt when mocked by those who reproach them for evil actions they themselves have committed (CHRYSOSTOM, GREGORY).

30:1 They Jeer at Me

JOB'S FORMER AUTHORITY AND PRESENT MISERY. JULIAN OF ECLANUM: "But now they make sport of me, those who are younger than I." These words testify to the authority, power and grace that, as he has asserted, he used to own in his previous days. The more favorable his state of former happiness had been, the more bitter now it makes his feeling of pain after turning into misfortune.

"Whose fathers I would have disdained to set with the dogs of my flock." He now refers to an evidence of extreme poverty, through which also the vileness of his condition appears, not only the fact that he lives on charity but also that he is appointed to take care of the food of dogs. EXPOSITION ON THE BOOK OF JOB 30.1.[1]

30:2-4 They Lack Vigor

NATURE OF JOB'S DETRACTORS. JULIAN THE

[1]CCL 88:81.

ARIAN: Without intelligence, strength is ruin rather than advantage. And death is over them, because they are useless; neither hunger nor their solicitude causes their soul to become sane again. They are so inept that, because of their foolishness, they cannot defend themselves but can only devour the result of their useless vanity and the reciprocal pains of their worthlessness. COMMENTARY ON JOB 30.2-4.[2]

30:5-8 They Live in the Ground

THEIR ABSOLUTE INEPTITUDE. ISHO'DAD OF MERV: The words "under the rocks and the thorny bushes," that is, those, who are on the prowl in the mountains and the deserts, live on the fruits of thorny bushes because of their destitution. COMMENTARY ON JOB 30.6-7.[3]

30:9-11 They Mock Me

THE CHURCH IN ITS TIME OF AFFLICTION. GREGORY THE GREAT: By these same words the time of holy church is set forth, when it is openly derided by the lost; when the wicked are gaining ground, faith becomes a reproach. Truth becomes a ground of accusation. So much the more contemptible shall each individual be in proportion to his righteousness. The worse object of abhorrence, the more worthy object of praise. Therefore the holy church of the elect in the time of calamity "becomes a proverb" to the wicked. . . . "They abhor me, they flee away from me; they do not hesitate to spit at my face." All the wicked "flee away" from holy church, not by the paces of footsteps but by the characters of their practices. They fly far not in place but desert, whereas, pride gaining ground, they condemn the church with open upbraiding. For "to spit at his face" implies not only to speak evil of the good in their absence but also to openly defy the just in their presence. And these then while the wicked by openly deriding put them down, they let out insults upon them in loose words, like streams of spittle running down. . . .

"He has opened his quiver and afflicted me." What is denoted by the "quiver" of God but secret counsel? Now the Lord casts the arrow from the quiver, when from his secret counsel he sends forth an open sentence. Any one can suffer, but the cause of the suffering is obscure. After the scourge, amendment of life follows and the actual power of counsel is itself disclosed as well. So the quiver shut is hidden counsel. But we are chastised by an open quiver when by that which follows after the scourge, we see with what counsel we are stricken. . . .

"And he put a bridle into my mouth." Therefore because holy church, who ever gives forth its words in a spirit of charity, let it say, "He has put a bridle into my mouth." It is as though he confessed openly, saying, "Because in some I did not see any progress from preaching, I refrained assault that through the events of life they might be taught with patience. With words of preaching only they would never consent to receive counsel." But this grieves us especially in troubles that occur with kinfolk, where we have trusted them with love. MORALS ON THE BOOK OF JOB 20.44-47.[4]

30:12-13 The Rabble Rise

JOB'S MAIN AFFLICTION. CHRYSOSTOM. You see what especially afflicts him is to be mocked by those who reproach him for the evil actions that they commit. Some "thieves," he says, some wicked, some criminals, some robbers have made us the subject of their proposals and conversations. COMMENTARY ON JOB 30.12A-13.[5]

---

[2]PTS 14:181-82. [3]CSCO 229:256. [4]LF 21:483-85**. [5]PTS 35:156.

30:14-31 JOB'S PRESENT AFFLICTIONS

^{14}As through a wide breach they come;
   amid the crash they roll on.
^{15}Terrors are turned upon me;
   my honor is pursued as by the wind,
   and my prosperity has passed away like
      a cloud.*

^{16}And now my soul is poured out within
      me;
   days of affliction have taken hold of me.
^{17}The night racks my bones,
   and the pain that gnaws me takes
      no rest.†
^{18}With violence it seizes my garment;^{l}
   it binds me about like the collar of my
      tunic.
^{19}God has cast me into the mire,
   and I have become like dust and ashes.
^{20}I cry to thee and thou dost not answer me;
   I stand, and thou dost not^m heed me.
^{21}Thou hast turned cruel to me;
   with the might of thy hand thou dost
      persecute me.
^{22}Thou liftest me up on the wind, thou
      makest me ride on it,
   and thou tossest me about in the roar

of the storm.‡
^{23}Yea, I know that thou wilt bring me
      to death,
   and to the house appointed for all living.

^{24}Yet does not one in a heap of ruins
      stretch out his hand,
   and in his disaster cry for help?"^{n}§
^{25}Did not I weep for him whose day was
      hard?
   Was not my soul grieved for the poor?#
^{26}But when I looked for good, evil came;
   and when I waited for light, darkness
      came.
^{27}My heart is in turmoil, and is never still;
   days of affliction come to meet me.
^{28}I go about blackened, but not by the sun;
   I stand up in the assembly, and cry for
      help.
^{29}I am a brother of jackals,
   and a companion of ostriches.
^{30}My skin turns black and falls from me,
   and my bones burn with heat.
^{31}My lyre is turned to mourning,
   and my pipe to the voice of those
      who weep.**

k Cn: Heb like l Gk: Heb my garment is disfigured m One Heb Ms and Vg: Heb lacks not n Cn: Heb obscure *Vg I am reduced to nothing, you took away my desire like a wind, and my welfare has passed like clouds. †LXX and my sinews are disjointed ‡LXX (21-22) You attacked me without mercy, you have scourged me with a strong hand. And you have put me to grief and have cast me away from safety. §Vg However you do not put forth your hand for their destruction; and if they are brought to the ground, you will save them. #Vg I wept for those who were in trouble; my soul suffered with the poor. **LXX (29-31) I have become a brother of sirens and a companion of ostriches. And my skin has been greatly blackened, and my bones are burned with heat. My harp also has been turned into mourning, and my song into weeping.

OVERVIEW: The Fathers note how Job's condition would be virtually unbearable for any human being. He is subject to intense physical and psychological pain but has no comfort from any friend or relative (JULIAN OF ECLANUM, JULIAN THE ARIAN, GREGORY, CHRYSOSTOM). His welfare has disappeared—not his life—which was placed in the comforts of his home and bodily safety (JULIAN OF ECLANUM). He feels pain in every limb (JULIAN THE ARIAN).

His present affliction is a foreshadowing of Christ's passion and a figure of the future salvation through the grace of the Redeemer (EPHREM, GREGORY). Job prefigures Emmanuel who, even though he was God, was thoughtlessly considered to be unworthy when clothed with flesh (EPHREM). The Lord does not destroy those who sin if by striking he reforms them from sin. The compassionate give something even to one who does not give thought to compassion. The faithful who look for good but receive evil hope, by the hidden grace of recompense, to already be admitted to the joys of the angels however long they are exposed to persecution (GREGORY).

30:14-15 Times of Terrors

NO COMFORT LEFT. JULIAN OF ECLANUM: After those things that used to or could move my affections in themselves have dispersed, that is, after I have been deprived of both comforts and occupations, I know that no hope is left for me through which I may be supported. "And my welfare has passed like clouds." He said that his welfare has passed—not his life—which was placed in the comforts of his home and in his body for his safety. EXPOSITION ON THE BOOK OF JOB 30.15.[1]

30:16-17 Days of Affliction

SPIRITUAL AND PHYSICAL DISCOMFORT. JULIAN THE ARIAN: After I swiftly passed like a cloud, I became familiar to the evildoers, and for this reason they took courage and rebelled against me. Consequently I will unload all my reflections on myself and my days of affliction, and I will feel pain at night, not in one limb but everywhere, as when sinews are disjointed from their natural connections. COMMENTARY ON JOB 30.16-17.[2]

30:18-20 Like Dust and Ashes

A PARALLEL WITH CHRIST. EPHREM THE SYRIAN: "I have become like dust and ashes," that is, I have been rendered contemptible to them as if I were dust, and I appear to be similar to vile mud. Emmanuel too, even though he was God, was thoughtlessly considered to be unworthy when he was clothed with flesh, so that the impure Jews said, "Even though you are a man, you make yourself God." COMMENTARY ON JOB 30.19.[3]

30:21-22 Cruelty and Persecution

HELPLESSNESS IN SUFFERING. JULIAN THE ARIAN: "You attacked me without mercy." He attributes to God his affliction, as if he finally accepted that, and he says that his pains are beyond his human power. "You have scourged me with a strong hand. And you have put me to grief, and have cast me away from safety." You tormented me with great power; as in nature you made everything according to humid and dry essence, so you made me according to your will, in order that I might suffer as much as possible. COMMENTARY ON JOB 30.21-22.[4]

30:23-24 Brought to Death

SALVATION FROM DEATH. GREGORY THE GREAT: It is said, "I know that you will bring me to death, and to the house appointed for all living." . . . Before the grace of the Redeemer even the just were carried to the caverns of hell. For the mere entering of "hell" is itself called "the house of all living," because no one came there who before the advent of the Mediator did not enter by the simple constitution of his own state of corruption. No one came there who did not go on to the death of the flesh, by the steps of that same corruption belonging to him. . . . The same judgment pertains to the accents of the holy church in which there are weak persons who hold the faith to the extent of the word of the lips but contrary to the precepts of faith act the slave to their desires. For [the church] says, "I know that you will deliver me to death, where the house appointed for all living is." For because it sees

---

[1]CCL 88:82. [2]PTS 14:184. [3]ESOO 2:13. [4]PTS 14:184-85.

multitudes in it devoted to pleasures and already foresees their destruction, [the church] reflects that in the course of the present life they serve their desires indeed, yet all are brought to the house of death who in the same way live carnally. But there are some who are brought down into the pit of their gratifications, yet by the tears of repentance quickly recover the foot from below. For them the strokes of smiting from above cut rather for instruction than destruction.

"However you do not put forth your hand for their destruction; and if they are brought to the ground, you will save them." So, while speaking of himself in arguing, [Job] subjoins cases applying to others, and he shows how many he represents in the person of himself. Accordingly, the Lord "does not put forth his hand for the destruction" of those who sin if by striking he reforms from sins. "He saves those that are falling to the ground" when those falling into transgression are brought to health of the body through their wounds. Being brought low outwardly, they arise inwardly. Those who lie prostrate in body are brought back to inward standing, while those who are standing outwardly are brought low in soul. MORALS ON THE BOOK OF JOB 20.66-67.[5]

30:25-26 Evil Comes Rather Than Good

THE RIGHTEOUS SUFFER PERSECUTION. GREGORY THE GREAT: With almighty God greater sometimes is the gift of the mind than of the [outward] benefit. For this reason the holy man says: "One day I wept for him who was in trouble, and my soul had compassion on the poor man." For in bestowing outward things, he granted an object apart from himself. But one who bestows upon his neighbor weeping and compassion gives him something even from his very self. On this account we say that compassion is more than the gift. One who is compassionate gives something even to the one who does not give thought to compassion. One who feels true compassion never withholds that which he deems to be necessary for his neighbor. . . .

"But when I looked for good, evil came; and when I waited for light, darkness came." For the faithful person who "looks for good" but receives evil, "waits for light" and meets with darkness, because by the grace of recompense one hopes to now already be admitted to the joys of the angels. Yet being delayed for a longer time here below, one is exposed to the hands of those that persecute. And he who expects to enjoy as quickly as possible the recompensing of the eternal light is still forced to suffer here the darkness of his persecutors. The same ills of those persecuting them would grieve them the less if they arose from unbelievers and adversaries. But they torture the mind of the elect the worse in equal proportion to those from which they proceed, upon whom they were promising good. MORALS ON THE BOOK OF JOB 20.70-72.[6]

30:27-31 I Cry for Help

AFFLICTIONS OBLIGE JOB TO CRY FOR HELP. CHRYSOSTOM: The excess of misfortunes that have befallen him force him to groan and to wail. Even if I wanted it, I could not stay silent, he says. "I stand up in the assembly and cry for help" without being ashamed before any of those present and without blushing before the multitude of the assembly. This attitude is due to the greatness of his misfortunes. I have fallen, he says, into the animal condition of birds. I have not recognized my real nature anymore; my situation is not better than theirs. COMMENTARY ON JOB 30.26-29.[7]

---

[5]LF 21:500-502*. [6]LF 21:503-4**. [7]PTS 35:157.

31:1-40 JOB DECLARES THAT
HIS CONDUCT IS BLAMELESS

¹"I have made a covenant with my eyes;
    how then could I look upon a virgin?*
²What would be my portion from God
      above,
    and my heritage from the Almighty on
      high?
³Does not calamity befall the unrighteous,
    and disaster the workers of iniquity?
⁴Does not he see my ways,
    and number all my steps?

⁵"If I have walked with falsehood,
    and my foot has hastened to deceit;
⁶(Let me be weighed in a just balance,
    and let God know my integrity!)
⁷if my step has turned aside from the
      way,
    and my heart has gone after my eyes,
    and if any spot has cleaved to my hands;¹
⁸then let me sow, and another eat;
    and let what grows for me be rooted out.

⁹"If my heart has been enticed to a woman,
    and I have lain in wait at my neighbor's
      door;
¹⁰then let my wife grind for another,
    and let others bow down upon her.
¹¹For that would be a heinous crime;
    that would be an iniquity to be punished
      by the judges;
¹²for that would be a fire which consumes
      unto Abaddon,
    and it would burn to the root all my
      increase.‡

¹³"If I have rejected the cause of my
      manservant or my maidservant,
    when they brought a complaint against
      me;
¹⁴what then shall I do when God rises up?§
    When he makes inquiry, what shall I
      answer him?
¹⁵Did not he who made me in the womb
      make him?
    And did not one fashion us in the womb?

¹⁶If I have withheld anything that the poor
      desired,
    or have caused the eyes of the widow to
      fail,
¹⁷or have eaten my morsel alone,
    and the fatherless has not eaten of it
¹⁸(for from his youth I reared him as a
      father,
    and from his mother's womb I guided
      him°);
¹⁹if I have seen any one perish# for lack of
      clothing,
    or a poor man without covering;
²⁰if his loins have not blessed me,
    and if he was not warmed with the fleece
      of my sheep;
²¹if I have raised my hand against the
      fatherless,
    because I saw help in the gate;**
²²then let my shoulder blade fall from my
      shoulder,
    and let my arm be broken from its socket.
²³For I was in terror of calamity from God,

and I could not have faced his majesty.[††]
[24]"If I have made gold my trust,

or called fine gold my confidence;
[25]if I have rejoiced because my wealth was
        great,
    or because my hand had gotten much;
[26]if I have looked at the sun[p] when it shone,
    or the moon moving in splendor,
[27]and my heart has been secretly enticed,
    and my mouth has kissed my hand;
[28]this also would be an iniquity to be
        punished by the judges,
    for I should have been false to God above.

[29]"If I have rejoiced at the ruin of him that
        hated me,
    or exulted when evil overtook him
[30](I have not let my mouth sin
    by asking for his life with a curse);[‡‡]
[31]if the men of my tent have not said,
    'Who is there that has not been filled
        with his meat?'
[32](the sojourner has not lodged in the street;
    I have opened my doors to the wayfarer);[§§]

[33]if I have concealed my transgressions from
        men,[q]
    by hiding my iniquity in my bosom,
[34]because I stood in great fear of the
        multitude,
    and the contempt of families[##] terrified me,
    so that I kept silence, and did not go out
        of doors—
[35]Oh, that I had one to hear me!
    (Here is my signature! let the Almighty
        answer me!)[***]
    Oh, that I had the indictment written by
        my adversary!
[36]Surely I would carry it on my shoulder;
    I would bind it on me as a crown;
[37]I would give him an account of all my steps;
    like a prince I would approach him.[†††]
[38]"If my land has cried out against me,
    and its furrows have wept together;
[39]if I have eaten its yield without payment,
    and caused the death of its owners;
[40]let thorns grow instead of wheat,
    and foul weeds instead of barley."

The words of Job are ended.

---

o Cn: Heb for from my youth he grew up to me as a father, and from my mother's womb I guided her   p Heb the light   q Cn: Heb like men or like Adam   *Vg so that I might not think about a virgin   †LXX (6-7) I stay on a just balance, and the Lord knows my innocence; if my foot has turned aside out of the way, or if my heart has followed my eye, and if I have also touched gifts with my hands.   ‡Vg (11-12) For this is a heinous crime and the greatest iniquity. For it is a fire that consumes to destruction and that roots out all increase.   §LXX when God tries me?   #Vg If I despised any passing by   **LXX trusting that my strength was far superior to his   ††Vg (23) For I always feared God like waves swelling over me, and I could not endure the weight of him.   ‡‡LXX (29-30) And if too I was glad at the fall of my enemies and my heart said, 'Aha! Let then my ear hear my curse, and let me be a byword among my people in my affliction.   §§LXX (31-32) And if too my handmaids have often said, 'Oh, that we might be satisfied with his flesh'; whereas I was very kind, for the stranger did not lodge without, and my door was opened to everyone that came.   ##Vg of neighbors   ***Vg Who will give me a hearer, so that the Almighty may listen to my desire?   †††LXX (33-37) Or if also having sinned unintentionally, I hid my sin (for I did not turn away from the great multitude of my people, so as not to declare boldly before them) and if also I permitted a poor man to go out of my door with an empty bosom (Oh that I had a hearer) and if I had not feared the hand of the Lord; and as to the written charge that I had against any one, I would place it as a chaplet on my shoulders and encircle myself with it like a crown. And if I did not tear it and return it, having taken nothing from the debtor.

OVERVIEW: Job 31 constitutes the final part of Job's soliloquy, in which he openly declares his mercifulness, devotion and love. The Fathers clearly see in Job's sincere words a figure and a foreshadowing of the Christian life and piety. Job appears as a template of all those values and virtues that will be asserted in the Gospels and the preaching of Christ (JULIAN OF ECLANUM, PHILIP, CHRYSOSTOM, GREGORY, JULIAN THE ARIAN, EPHREM, ISHO'DAD).

though in things they execute the office of pity, yet in words lose the grace of humility, so that for the most part it seems they are now paying satisfaction for an injury inflicted when after abuse they bestow gifts. Nor is it a thing of high practice that they give the things that are begged for, because of the very boon of their giving they scarcely cover over that transgression of speech. MORALS ON THE BOOK OF JOB 21.19.29.[12]

31:21-23 Consequences of Neglecting the Poor

GOD'S LOVE FOR THE NEEDY. JULIAN THE ARIAN: I have said that God can protect the orphans, destroy those who offend them and break their arms, because he hates the wicked. I certainly know this. COMMENTARY ON JOB 31.21-22.[13]

BENEFITING FROM FEAR OF GOD'S STRICTNESS. GREGORY THE GREAT: "For I always feared God like waves swelling over me, and I could not endure the weight of him." Consider here that blessed Job says these things concerning himself after having been pained and smitten. If he had been stricken in order to increase his moral excellences by one he so feared, one need not despise the one who disciplines. How shall the judgments of God weigh down for a time [those] who always dread these things in humility? How shall he be able to endure the weight of God, who condemns, if this same weight even he underwent under the rod who foresaw it in fear. Hence, with the utmost earnestness, we ought to dread that inquest of so great strictness. Now it is plain that in this life, when he smites, if amendment follows the stroke, it is the discipline of a father, not the wrath of a judge, the love of one correcting, not the strictness of one punishing. And so by that very present scourge itself, the eternal judgments ought to be weighed. And we ought with the greatest pains to reflect how that anger may be borne that casts away, if that anger of his that purifies may scarcely now be borne. MORALS ON THE BOOK OF JOB 21.22.36.[14]

31:24-25 No Rejoicing in Wealth

DESPISE OF MATERIAL WEALTH. CHRYSOSTOM: Now what kind of fault can be detected there? You see that he is not keen on riches. Observe him, while he reflects and considers in truth the accidental, transitory, ephemeral and negligible character of human realities. COMMENTARY ON JOB 31.17-25.[15]

31:26 No Idolatry

JOB DECLARES HIS REFUTATION OF IDOLATRY. EPHREM THE SYRIAN: "If I had looked at the sun when it shone or the moon moving in splendor," that is, if I had seen the rising sun and worshiped it or had embraced the moon and kneeled down before it, I would have certainly erred in worshiping them. COMMENTARY ON JOB 31.26.[16]

31:27-28 No Secret Enticement

A GESTURE OF AFFECTION. ISHO'DAD OF MERV: "My mouth has kissed my hand" . . . is said in analogy with those who have the habit to bring their hands [to their mouth] and to kiss [them] when they meet people who are dear to them. COMMENTARY ON JOB 31.27.[17]

31:29-30 Not Seeking Revenge

DEVOID OF DESIRE FOR REVENGE. PHILIP THE PRIEST: It is certainly admirable that one, even though he can, does not take revenge upon his enemies. But when he does not even rejoice in his heart for their ruin that is even more pleasing to God. COMMENTARY ON THE BOOK OF JOB 31.[18]

31:31-32 A Model of Philanthropy

JOB'S GENEROSITY. JULIAN THE ARIAN: With my wisdom I loved to practice philanthropy

---

[12]LF 21:538*. [13]PTS 14:192. [14]LF 21:544-45**. [15]PTS 35:162. [16]ESOO 2:14. [17]CSCO 229:257. [18]PL 26:720.

above all, he says that he did that. And so his handmaids practiced it as well, and when they led a stranger, after receiving him kindly, to their rejoicing master, they considered that opportunity a great benefit. He was a model of godly philanthropy not only outside but also in his own house, like the holy Abraham. Commentary on Job 31.31-32.[19]

31:33-34a Recognizing One's Faults

Job Honestly Recognizes His Faults. Chrysostom: "Because I did not turn away," he says, "from the great multitude of my people," that is, away from my subjects, from those who were aware, who knew even the character itself of my fault. This is real wisdom. "First of all confess spontaneously your sins in order to be justified."[20] So I took nobody as a witness of my good works, because I wanted everybody to be aware of my faults and errors. That is the summit of wisdom, that is the rule of virtue: to hide one's good work and to expose one's faults in public. But the people of today just do the opposite. Commentary on Job 31.32-34a.[21]

31:34b-35b Oh, That I Had One to Hear Me!

Job Invokes the Testimony of God. Julian of Eclanum: Since he had been driven to the confession of his virtues both by the accusations of his friends and his pious devotion to God [and from the fear of God his virtues had proceeded],

he now chooses to add the testimony of the sentence of the Judge in support of his words, so that, after God had declared that he had said the truth, no one among his opponents may deny it. Exposition on the Book of Job 31.35.[22]

31:35c-37 More Proof of Giving

Another Proof of Job's Philanthropy. Chrysostom: "I have torn all that was received unjustly."[23] Without boasting, I have torn what I had received. And the expression "on my shoulders" suggests that some [of his friends] gloried in the afflictions of the others; and I did not content myself with giving it back simply, but I nullified it by tearing it. "I have torn all that was received unjustly." Commentary on Job 31.35-40.[24]

31:38-40 Perceiving Injustice

Job's Honest Use of Earthly Goods. Chrysostom: "If my land has ever cried out against me, or if its furrows have wept together." Therefore, neither the land cries out nor weeps. What does he mean? Certainly the land does not really groan, but inanimate beings perceive injustices. As the prophet asserts, "The earth stood up and shuddered."[25] Now the earth moans every time we make an unjust use of its fruits. Commentary on Job 31.35-40.[26]

---

[19]PTS 14:194-95. [20]Is 43:26. [21]PTS 35:164-65. [22]CCL 88:87. [23]Is 58:6. [24]PTS 35:166. [25]Jer 2:12. [26]PTS 35:166.

32:1-14 ELIHU'S SPEECH ABOUT WISDOM

[1]So these three men ceased to answer Job, because he was righteous in his own eyes. [2]Then Elihu the son of Barachel the Buzite, of the family of Ram, became angry. He was angry at Job because

he justified himself rather than God;* ³he was angry also at Job's three friends because they had found no answer, although they had declared Job to be in the wrong. ⁴Now Elihu had waited to speak to Job because they were older than he. ⁵And when Elihu saw that there was no answer in the mouth of these three men, he became angry.

⁶And Elihu the son of Barachel the Buzite answered:

"I am young in years,
and you are aged;
therefore I was timid and afraid
to declare my opinion to you.
⁷I said, 'Let days speak,
and many years teach wisdom.'
⁸But it is the spirit in a man,†
the breath of the Almighty, that makes
him understand.‡
⁹It is not the oldʳ that are wise,
nor the aged that understand what is
right.
¹⁰Therefore I say, 'Listen to me;

let me also declare my opinion.'

¹¹"Behold, I waited for your words,
I listened for your wise sayings,
while you searched out what to say.§
¹²I gave you my attention,
and, behold, there was none that
confuted Job,
or that answered his words, among you.
¹³Beware lest you say, 'We have found
wisdom;
God may vanquish# him, not man.'
¹⁴He has not directed his words against me,
and I will not answer him with your
speeches."

r Gk Syr Vg: Heb *many* *LXX (1-2) *for Job was righteous before them. Then Elius the son of Barachiel, the Buzite, of the kindred of Ram, of the country of Ausis, was angered; and he was angry with Job, because he had justified himself before the Lord.* †Peshitta *mortals* ‡Peshitta *that makes them intelligent* §Vg *while you were disputing in words* #Vg *held out*

OVERVIEW: Elihu's intervention, which brings to an end the series of speeches of Job's friends, is interpreted by the Fathers according to their usual line: they recognize a certain arrogance and misunderstanding on the part of Elihu (CHRYSOSTOM, GREGORY) but notice in his words some correctness and morality that can be discussed and developed for the edification of the faithful (CHRYSOSTOM, ISHO'DAD, JULIAN OF ECLANUM). Job did not reproach God for any injustice; it is the younger Elihu who understood it so (CHRYSOSTOM). While some may think correctly concerning God, they yet seek not God's glory but their own. Elihu remained silent while the aged were speaking not with the desire to learn from them but to judge them (GREGORY).

32:1-3 Elihu's Anger at Job

ELIHU MISUNDERSTANDS JOB'S WORDS.
CHRYSOSTOM: Elihu is inflamed not because [Job] declared himself to be righteous but because he did that before the Lord, as he invoked him as his witness; or because he thought that [Job] brought an action against God. In fact, to justify oneself has no great importance in itself, but to do that with the intention of bringing an action against God is absolutely inopportune.... Now, if this is true, what an extreme act of impiety on the part of Job if he believed himself to be more righteous than God [and to be authorized to bring action against him]. What really happened? This was not Job's thought at all. It is Elihu who believed so. Job did not speak with the idea that he was more righteous than God but with the idea that God was responsible for his afflictions. Therefore he did not reproach God for any injustice: it is

Elihu who understood it so. COMMENTARY ON JOB 32.2-3.[1]

32:4-5 Elihu's Anger at the Three Friends

THE ARROGANCE OF THE HERETICS. GREGORY THE GREAT: Though holy church is unquestionably older than its adversaries (for they went forth from it, not it from them, as is said of them by John, "They went out from us, but they were not of us"),[2] yet Elihu is properly described as having been younger than these same adversaries. Because in truth after the contests that arose with the heretics, haughty people began to have place in the church, puffed up with the pride of learning. For when more grievous contests commenced with the enemy, there were certainly required some subtle dart points of thought, opposition of arguments and a more involved research of words. And while people of glowing genius invent these weapons to suit the circumstances, they are frequently puffed up with pride, and (as is generally the case in the sin of pride) they are themselves made to fall by the same subtle meanings with which they assail the foe, while in what they think correctly concerning God, they seek not God's glory but their own. Thus, while Elihu says many things correctly, he is yet reproved by the divine voice, as though he had stated errors. MORALS ON THE BOOK OF JOB 23.11.[3]

32:6 Afraid to Give My Opinion

ELIHU IS COMPELLED TO SPEAK. CHRYSOSTOM: Why is it not said, But then, why did you not fight from the start together with us in order to defend God? He answers, I withdrew into my age, while I expected, he says, to hear you pronounce a beautiful and wonderful speech. Notice how he did not look for honors, how he conceded them the first rank, how he showed that even now he would not have spoken if they had not compelled him to do so. COMMENTARY ON JOB 32.6.[4]

32:7-9 The Spirit in a Mortal

THE WISDOM OF HUMAN BEINGS. ISHO'DAD OF MERV: The words "but truly it is the spirit in mortals," [indicate] a rational soul. The words "the breath of the Almighty that makes them intelligent," [indicate] that if we need to find a superior wisdom in human beings, we will recognize it in those who have received the virtue from God. COMMENTARY ON JOB 32.8.[5]

32:10-11 Listen to Me

THE CONDUCT OF PROUD PEOPLE. GREGORY THE GREAT: As far as regards the literal meaning, Elihu proves to us, when he speaks, how proudly he remained silent. For when he says, "For I waited for your words, and I was thinking that you would say something," he plainly shows that he remained silent, while the aged were speaking, with the desire of judging rather than with the wish of learning from them. Though these expressions are even a better description of the conduct of proud people, who, when at length brought within holy church, are accustomed to looking at its opponents to consider not so much the years of their age as the intention of their words. Regardless of how much older the heretics may be than these same haughty people, they boldly overbear those persons in whose words they reprove false doctrine. MORALS ON THE BOOK OF JOB 23.14.[6]

32:12-14 No One Confuted Job

THE FUTILITY OF THE SPEECHES. JULIAN OF ECLANUM: Since your speech has ceased, and you have not been able to reply to the words spoken to you, now you think you can be supported by this argument, so that you can say, what we tried to demonstrate with our points is confirmed by the judgment of God, that is, that he is guilty of a crime. In fact, divine revenge would have not had any right against him if it had not found any evil

[1]PTS 35:167-68. [2]1 Jn 2:19. [3]LF 23:11*. [4]PTS 35:168. [5]CSCO 229:257-58. [6]LF 23:14*.

action in him. "He has not directed his words against me, and I will not answer him with your speeches." I was not involved, as you know, in his debate, nor did he provoke me to bitterness after assuming the intention to speak against me.

Therefore, the words that I speak are not suggested by indignation but by reason. EXPOSITION ON THE BOOK OF JOB 32.13-14.[7]

---

[7]CCL 88:88.

32:15-22 ELIHU'S ZEAL TO SPEAK

15They are discomfited, they answer no
   more;
  they have not a word to say.
16And shall I wait, because they do not
   speak,
  because they stand there, and answer no
   more?*
17I also will give my answer;
  I also will declare my opinion.
18For I am full of words,
  the spirit within me constrains me.

19Behold, my heart is like wine that has
   no vent;
  like new wineskins, it is ready to
   burst.†
20I must speak, that I may find relief;
  I must open my lips and answer.
21I will not show partiality to any person
  or use flattery toward any man.
22For I do not know how to flatter,
  else would my Maker soon put an end
   to me.‡

Vg *Because therefore I have waited, and they have not spoken, they have stood, and have answered no more* † Peshitta *my belly is in pain and does not open; like a fruit of the season, it is cut off* ‡ LXX (20-22) *I will speak, that I may open my lips and relieve myself. For truly I will not be awed because of man, nor indeed will I be confounded before a mortal. For I do not know how to admire persons, and if otherwise, even the moths would eat me.*

OVERVIEW: Elihu shows genuine honesty in his desire to speak and wisdom in his capacity to check his ardor (CHRYSOSTOM, EPHREM, JULIAN THE ARIAN), but he appears to be led by arrogance. He is too much in haste not merely to refute the arguments of his opponents but to display his own wisdom (GREGORY). The gifts of those who try to please by premature agreement are as dangerous for those who give them as for those who receive them (CHRYSOSTOM).

32:15-16 Should I Wait to Speak?

OSTENTATION OF FALSE WISDOM. GREGORY

THE GREAT: The friends of Job are said to have been afraid of the words of Elihu, since frequently proud defenders of the church, though they do not observe due order in what they say, confound the adversaries by the very virtue of their words. It follows, "Because therefore I have waited, and they have not spoken, they have stood and have answered no more." Wise people are accustomed to make it the limit of their speaking, to speak as far as silence to their adversaries, for they do not wish to display their own powers but to put down the false teachers. But after, it is said of the friends of Job, "They are dismayed, they answer no more; they have not a word to say," Elihu sub-

165

joins and says, "Because therefore I have waited, and they have not spoken, they have stood and have answered no more." Even when they are already silent, he yet multiplies his words, because, being an arrogant man and representing the character of the arrogant, he is in haste not merely to refute the arguments of his opponents but to display his own wisdom. MORALS ON THE BOOK OF JOB 23.16-17.[1]

32:17-19 I Will Answer

ELIHU'S PATIENCE. CHRYSOSTOM: He wants to show that he suffered for a long time and waited to speak and that he contained himself and could burst. Therefore, he needed a large amount of patience. To be able to control one's words is the greatest proof of wisdom, and [Elihu's] ardor for God has enabled him to bear such an interior fire. COMMENTARY ON JOB 31.18-19.[2]

32:20-22 Speaking to Find Relief

ELIHU'S PHYSICAL NEED TO SPEAK. EPHREM THE SYRIAN: "I must speak so that I may find relief," like a woman in labor, who, after bringing forth her offspring, is relieved from the pain of giving birth. And again, "my belly is in pain and does not open," that is, I was in pain and could

not find any respite, because I strongly desired to speak, but I abstained from it. Now I will break my voice and will make a revelation. COMMENTARY ON JOB 32.20.[3]

ELIHU ASSERTS HIS FRANKNESS AND VERACITY. JULIAN THE ARIAN: "I will speak that I may open my lips and relieve myself." I do not conceal who I am anymore by turning my thoughts away from your betrayal. You do not keep silent because of your wisdom but for lack of truthful words. "For truly I will not be awed because of man, nor indeed will I be confounded before a mortal, for I do not know how to admire persons." Truth is dear to me and of all things the most precious. In fact, I do not admire its mere appearance, after neglecting it, like you do. Nor do I become the betrayer of the righteous, after uselessly feeling ashamed of my ignominy. I am not accustomed to being pleasing to my friends; these sorts of gifts, in fact, are dangerous for those who give them and for those who receive them. "And unless otherwise, even the moths would eat me." I would certainly demand this kind of punishment if I honored the mortals instead of the truth. COMMENTARY ON JOB 32.20-22.[4]

---

[1]LF 23:15-16*. [2]PTS 35:169. [3]ESOO 2:14. [4]PTS 14: 204-5.

33:1-13 ELIHU INVITES JOB NOT TO CONTEND WITH GOD

[1]*But now, hear my speech, O Job,*
   and listen to all my words.
[2]*Behold, I open my mouth;*
   the tongue in my mouth speaks.
[3]*My words declare the uprightness of*

   my heart,
   and what my lips know they speak
      *sincerely.**
[4]*The spirit of God has made me,*
   and the breath of the Almighty gives

me life.
⁵Answer me, if you can;
    set your words in order before me; take
        your stand.
⁶Behold, I am toward God as you are;
    I too was formed from a piece of clay.
⁷Behold, no fear of me need terrify you;
    my pressure will not be heavy upon you.†

⁸Surely, you have spoken in my hearing,
    and I have heard the sound of your words.
⁹You say, "I am clean, without transgression;

I am pure, and there is no iniquity in me.
¹⁰Behold, he finds occasions against me,
    he counts me as his enemy;
¹¹he puts my feet in the stocks,
    and watches all my paths."

¹²Behold, in this you are not right. I
        will answer you.
    God is greater than man.
¹³Why do you contend against him,
    saying, "He will answer none of
        myˢ words"?‡

ˢ Compare Gk: Heb *his*   *LXX *My heart shall be found pure by my words, and the understanding of my lips shall meditate purity.*   †Vg *yet let not my wonder terrify you, nor my eloquence be burdensome to you*   ‡LXX (12-13) *For how did you say, I am righteous, yet he has not hearkened to me? For he that is above mortals is eternal. But you said, Why has he not heard every word of my cause?*

OVERVIEW: In the second part of Elihu's speech, which covers Job 33, the Fathers continue to notice a certain intellectual honesty on his part that leads him to accurate assertions about the justice of God (CHRYSOSTOM, JULIAN OF ECLANUM) but also self-admiration and arrogance, which cause him to accuse and reprove Job groundlessly and falsely (GREGORY, JULIAN OF ECLANUM). Chrysostom thinks more highly of Elihu's motives than Gregory. It is typical of the arrogant that they believe, even before they speak, that they are going to say some wonderful thing, just before they fall on their face (GREGORY).

33:1-3 Sincerity of Heart

ELIHU'S SINCERE MIND. CHRYSOSTOM: These words mean, I do not speak so out of envy or jealousy. Even though the three friends said the same things as him, they did not do so in the same spirit or in order to defend God. Indeed also Judas and the eleven disciples expressed the same opinion about the vase of perfume, but not in the same spirit. Therefore, let us not examine the words but the intention with which each expresses himself. How the first wanted to over-

throw him, whereas the latter wanted the opposite. Take heed: Elihu, who speaks last, expresses the thoughts that God is about to express, so that God may justify himself even better, once Job has heard the same remarks from his companions in bondage that he will afterwards hear from the Master. COMMENTARY ON JOB 33.1-3.[1]

33:4-5 Impelled by the Spirit of God

ANSWERING GOD IS FAR HARDER THAN ANSWERING A MAN. JULIAN OF ECLANUM: [Elihu] believes that with the aid of a comparison he can make some effective assertions against Job. "If you," he says, "cannot reply to me, a creation of God, be certain that you will be much less able to reply to God, the Maker of everything." EXPOSITION ON THE BOOK OF JOB 33.4-5.[2]

33:6-7 The Same Before God

ELIHU'S FOOLISH SELF-ADMIRATION. GREGORY THE GREAT: For it is peculiar to the arrogant that they always believe, even before they speak,

---

[1]PTS 35:170.   [2]CCL 88:89.

that they are going to say some wonderful thing. And they anticipate their own words by their own admiration, because, with all their acuteness, they are not sensible to how great a folly is their very pride. We must observe also that Paul, when he was giving the Hebrews some striking warnings, subjoined, "I beseech you, brethren, suffer the word of consolation, for I have written to you in few words."[3] But Elihu uttered empty words and afterwards added, as if for consolation, "Yet let not my wonder terrify you or my eloquence be burdensome to you." The one called his sayings the words of consolation; the other called them eloquence and a marvel. Behold, how different in taste are the fruits that spring forth from diverse roots of thought. The one thinks humbly of his high qualities; the other exalts himself without reason on his scanty endowments. What then is specially to be observed in all this, but that those who are about to rise think themselves low, and that they who are soon to fall ever stand on high ground? As Solomon bears witness, "The heart is exalted before destruction and is brought low before honor."[4] MORALS OF THE BOOK OF JOB 23.29.[5]

33:8-11 *Clean and Pure*

DID JOB COMMIT SIN IN HIS YOUTH? JULIAN OF ECLANUM: This is what holy Job had said above, "Do you want me to reap the iniquities of my youth?"[6] Therefore, [Elihu] refutes this as a blasphemy, that is, the fact that holy Job had believed that no fault could be found in him; he was blameless in his mature age but was punished severely for the errors committed in his youth. EXPOSITION ON BOOK OF JOB 33.8-10.[7]

33:12-13 *Why Do You Contend Against God?*

GOD'S BLAMELESSNESS. JULIAN OF ECLANUM: If you believe that you must also show this to those who are ungrateful, you will nonetheless consent that God is undoubtedly superior to all. Therefore, since he is also the first in justice and wisdom, he cannot appear to have done something that may incur your note of reproof. EXPOSITION ON THE BOOK OF JOB 33.12.[8]

---

[3]Heb 13:22. [4]Prov 16:18. [5]LF 23:25-26*. [6]Job 13:26 Vg. [7]CCL 88:89. [8]CCL 88:89.

33:14-33 GOD CALLS MORTALS TO REPENTANCE IN DIFFERENT WAYS

[14]For God speaks in one way,
 and in two,* though man does not
  perceive it.
[15]In a dream, in a vision of the night,
 when deep sleep falls upon men,
  while they slumber on their beds,
[16]then he opens the ears of men,
 and terrifies them with warnings,
[17]that he may turn man aside from his deed,

 and cut off[t] pride from man;[t]
[18]he keeps back his soul from the Pit,
 his life from perishing by the sword.

[19]Man is also chastened with pain upon
  his bed,
 and with continual strife in his bones;
[20]so that his life loathes bread,
 and his appetite dainty food.

^{21}His flesh is so wasted away that it
    cannot be seen;
  and his bones which were not seen stick
    out.
^{22}His soul draws near the Pit,
  and his life to those who bring death.
^{23}If there be for him an angel,
  a mediator, one of the thousand,
  to declare to man what is right for him;‡
^{24}and he is gracious to him, and says,
  "Deliver him from going down into the
    Pit,
  I have found a ransom;
^{25}let his flesh become fresh with youth;
  let him return to the days of his youthful
    vigor";§
^{26}then man prays to God, and he accepts
  him,

he comes into his presence with joy.
He recounts^{u} to men his salvation,
^{27}and he sings before men, and says:
"I sinned, and perverted what was right,
  and it was not requited to me.
^{28}He has redeemed my soul from going down
    into the Pit,
  and my life shall see the light."
^{29}Behold, God does all these things,
  twice, three times, with a man,
^{30}to bring back his soul from the Pit,
  that he may see the light of life.$^{v#}$
^{31}Give heed, O Job, listen to me;
  be silent, and I will speak.
^{32}If you have anything to say, answer me;
  speak, for I desire to justify you.
^{33}If not, listen to me;
  be silent, and I will teach you wisdom.

t Cn: Heb *hide* u Cn: Heb *returns* v Syr: Heb *to be lighted with the light of life* *LXX *once or a second time* †Peshitta *that he may turn them aside from their deeds, he covers the body of man* ‡Vg *If there should be an angel, speaking for him one of like things to show the righteousness of man.* §LXX (24-25) *He will support him, that he should not perish, and will restore his body as fresh plaster upon a wall; and he will fill his bones with marrow. And he will make his flesh tender as that of a babe, and he will restore him among men in his full strength.* #Vg (29-30) *All these things God works three times in every man, so that he may recall their souls from corruption and enlighten them with the light of the living.*

OVERVIEW: This section of Elihu's speech (Job 33:14-33), which concerns repentance, enables the Fathers to develop different arguments all pointing to Christian doctrine and life. Elihu's words become a clear figure of Christian faith, which has two of its main fundamentals in repentance and conversion (JULIAN THE ARIAN, ISHO'DAD, EPHREM, GREGORY, PHILIP). Through dreams and visions, God guards people from shameful actions (ISHO'DAD, JULIAN THE ARIAN). God comes to us as a Physician from above, and finding us oppressed with such great disease, applies to our case something of a like and something of contrary nature, coming to our humanity as a man, and to our sin as the incomparably just One (GREGORY). It is an admirable thing, and very pleasing to God, that humans do not feel ashamed to confess their sins (PHILIP). Though the mind of the elect suffers in each of three stages—the pain of conversion, the trial of probation and the dread of dissolution—they are purified and set free from this very suffering (GREGORY).

33:14-16 God Speaks in Different Ways

GOD'S PROVIDENCE. JULIAN THE ARIAN: God has established everything once, and in his creation he travels through the regions that have been limited by him. He has also established the visions in sleep through which he warns people. And since he loves humans, in the circumstances of life he provides them with the means to solve problems, and succors those who committed no offense against justice and gives perception to those who did good works. COMMENTARY ON JOB 33.14-18.[1]

---

[1]PTS 14:208.

33:17-18 *Kept from Pride*

EXPRESSIONS OF GOD'S MERCY. ISHO'DAD OF
MERV: The words "that he may turn them aside
from their deeds" means this: by way of those
[dreams and visions] God keeps people from
shameful actions. The words "he covers the body
of man" [mean] sometimes he brings on righteous diseases and pains as well, in order to preserve him in this manner from the punishment of
perdition. COMMENTARY ON JOB 33.17.[2]

33:19-22 *Chastened with Pain*

NO ENJOYMENT FOR THE WICKED. EPHREM
THE SYRIAN: These words mean that the soul of
the wicked will never rejoice in the sins that it
has committed or in the justice that it has never
reached. COMMENTARY ON JOB 33.20.[3]

33:23 *One Who Can Make Humanity Upright*

A FIGURE OF CHRIST THE SAVIOR. GREGORY
THE GREAT: Who is this angel but the one the
prophet calls "the angel of mighty counsel"?[4]
To declare is called "evangelize" in Greek,
and the Lord in announcing himself to us is
called "angel." And he well says, "If there should
be a messenger [or angel] speaking for him
one of like things to show the righteousness of
man." For, as the apostle says, he even intercedes
for us. But let us hear what he says for us,
"One of like things." It is the way with medicine
to cure disease sometimes by similar, some
times by contrary remedies. For it has frequently been wont to cure the hot by warm
and the cold by cold applications; and on the
contrary, the cold by warmth, hot by cold. Our
Physician then, on coming to us from above
and finding us oppressed with such great disease, applied to our case something of a like
and something of a contrary nature, for he came
to us as Man to humanity, as well as a just
One to those who were in sin. He agreed with

us in the truth of his nature; he differed from
us in the power of his righteousness. For
sinful humankind could not be amended except by God. MORALS ON THE BOOK OF JOB
24.2.[5]

33:24-25 *Deliverance from the Pit*

REGENERATION THROUGH REPENTANCE.
JULIAN THE ARIAN: This is what he says, if he,
who must pay for his sins, is able, with his love,
to convince God, he will make him favorable and
accommodating and inclined to mercy, so that he
does not only leave behind the sins which surround him, but he also regenerates his dead body
as through a rebirth, and so will appear to be as
beautiful as new plaster on an old wall. COMMEN-
TARY ON JOB 33.24-25.[6]

33:26 *Repaid for Righteousness*

HAPPINESS IN GOD'S GRACE. PHILIP THE
PRIEST: This is what happens in human hearts
when mortals possess a good conscience through
the agency of God. They will see the face of God,
feeling that his countenance is benevolent to
them, and they will return justice to him with a
convenient satisfaction. COMMENTARY ON THE
BOOK OF JOB 33.[7]

33:27-28 *Redeeming the Soul*

REPENTANCE IS PLEASING TO GOD. PHILIP
THE PRIEST: It is an admirable thing, and very
pleasing to God, that humans do not feel
ashamed to confess their sins, especially if they
understand that they are punished because of
them, so that they may humiliate themselves to
endure their chastisement and may realize that
they will gain an equal prize for their merits.
COMMENTARY ON THE BOOK OF JOB 33.[8]

---

[2]CSCO 229:258.   [3]ESOO 2:15.   [4]Is 9:6 LXX.   [5]LF 23:50-51**.
[6]PTS 14:210.   [7]PL 26:726.   [8]PL 26:726.

33:29-30 *God Does All These Things*

EARTHLY SUFFERINGS, ETERNAL LIFE. GREGORY THE GREAT: Elihu therefore, because he first spoke of the bitterness of sorrow and afterwards of the joy of consolation, fitly added of this person thus afflicted and thus delivered, "All these things God works three times in every man," that is to say, in conversion, in probation and in death. For in these three states, a person first suffers under sharp pangs of sorrow and afterward is comforted by great pleasures of security. But because the mind of each of the elect suffers in each of these three stages [in the pain of conversion, the trial of probation or the dread of dissolution] and is purified and set free from this very suffering, it is appropriately added, "So that he may recall their souls from corruption and enlighten them with the light of the living." This is the light of the dying that we behold with our bodily eyes. They who still live for this world are in darkness in the light of the dying. But they are enlightened with the light of the living, who, despising the light of the world, return to the splendor of the inward brightness, so that they may live in that place where they may see, by feeling it, the true light, where light and life are not different from each other but where the light itself is life also. The light so encircles us from without as to fill us within; and so it fills us within, as, being itself not circumscribed, to circumscribe us without. They are enlightened therefore with this light of the living that they will behold at that time the more clearly. They now live the more purely by its aid. MORALS ON THE BOOK OF JOB 24.34-35.[9]

33:31-33 *Teaching Wisdom*

ELIHU RECEIVES NO ANSWER. JULIAN THE ARIAN: Again he addresses his words to the blessed Job and says, "I was the one who honored you and respected you, if you had something to say. Be confident and speak; you openly assert that your good actions have shown you to be righteous in the favor and testimony of God but not among your intimates. If you have nothing to say, listen to what I tell you and learn the works of wisdom. Now the wisdom of any fact is said, the wisdom of words and actions." After he had said these things, he was silent waiting for an answer; when he saw that nobody said anything, he spoke again. COMMENTARY ON JOB 33.31-33.[10]

---

[9]LF 23:76-77*.   [10]PTS 14:212-13

34:1-30 GOD THE ALMIGHTY NEVER ACTS UNJUSTLY

[1] Then Elihu said:
  [2]"Hear my words, you wise men,
    and give ear to me, you who know;
  [3]for the ear tests words
    as the palate tastes food.*
  [4]Let us choose what is right;
    let us determine among ourselves

    what is good.
  [5]For Job has said, 'I am innocent,†
    and God has taken away my right;
  [6]in spite of my right I am counted a liar;
    my wound is incurable, though I
      am without transgression.'
  [7]What man is like Job,

who drinks up scoffing like water,
⁸who goes in company with evildoers
    and walks with wicked men?
⁹For he has said, 'It profits a man nothing
    that he should take delight in God.'[‡]

¹⁰"Therefore, hear me, you men of
        understanding,
    far be it from God that he should do
        wickedness,
    and from the Almighty that he should do
        wrong.
¹¹For according to the work of a man he will
        requite him,
    and according to his ways he will make it
        befall him.
¹²Of a truth, God will not do wickedly,
    and the Almighty will not pervert justice.
¹³Who gave him charge over the earth
    and who laid on him^w the whole world?[§]
¹⁴If he should take back his spirit^{x#} to
        himself,
    and gather to himself his breath,
¹⁵all flesh would perish together,
    and man would return to dust.

¹⁶"If you have understanding, hear this;
    listen to what I say.
¹⁷Shall one who hates justice govern?
    Will you condemn him who is righteous
        and mighty,^{**}
¹⁸who says to a king, 'Worthless one,'
    and to nobles, 'Wicked man';
¹⁹who shows no partiality to princes,
    nor regards the rich more than the poor,

for they are all the work of his
        hands?
²⁰In a moment they die;
    at midnight the people are shaken and
        pass away,
    and the mighty are taken away by no
        human hand.^{††}

²¹"For his eyes are upon the ways of a man,
    and he sees all his steps.
²²There is no gloom or deep darkness
    where evildoers may hide themselves.
²³For he has not appointed a time^y for any
        man
    to go before God in judgment.
²⁴He shatters the mighty without investi-
        gation,
    and sets others in their place.
²⁵Thus, knowing their works,
    he overturns them in the night, and
        they are crushed.
²⁶He strikes them for their wickedness
    in the sight of men,
²⁷because they turned aside from following
        him,
    and had no regard for any of his ways,
²⁸so that they caused the cry of the poor to
        come to him,
    and he heard the cry of the afflicted—
²⁹When he is quiet, who can condemn?
    When he hides his face, who can behold
        him,
    whether it be a nation or a man?—
³⁰that a godless man should not reign,
    that he should not ensnare the people."

---

w Heb lacks *on him*   x Heb *his heart his spirit*   y Cn: Heb *yet*   *LXX *as the mouth tastes meat*   †Vg *righteous*   ‡Vg *A man will not please God, even though he runs with him.*
§Vg (12-13) *For truly God will not condemn without cause, nor will the Almighty subvert judgment. Whom else has he appointed over the earth, or whom has he placed over the world that he has made?*   #Vg *if he should direct his heart to him*   **LXX *Do you not believe that he, who hates injustice and makes the wicked perish, and is eternal, is just?*   ††LXX *But it shall turn out vanity to them, to cry and beseech a man; for they dealt unlawfully, the poor being turned aside from their right.*

OVERVIEW: In the third part of Elihu's speech, the Fathers notice three main aspects: in the first place, a certain understanding on his part of the ways of God's justice toward human beings (OLYMPIODORUS, JULIAN OF ECLANUM, GREGORY, CHRYSOSTOM, EPHREM, JULIAN THE ARIAN, ISHO'DAD, PHILIP); in the second, a wrong reproachful and accusatory attitude toward Job, which is constant throughout his speech (PHILIP, JULIAN OF ECLANUM, GREGORY); in the third, a certain prophetic value of his words that announce the advent and revelation of Christ and peace in the church (PHILIP). Though they speak against each other, in a sense both the arguments of Job and Elihu bear a certain truth (JULIAN OF ECLANUM).

Do not try to understand the judgment of God before everything has been completed, because you will get no profit from your hurriedness. God is not required everyday to give explanations about what happened. God manages a matter whose fulfillment must extend over a long period (CHRYSOSTOM). God governs himself the world he created by himself. The One who provided for our being before we were made does not forsake us after our creation. Although our sufferings seem to be unjust, yet they are rightly inflicted in his secret judgment (GREGORY). Those who approach a king with rudeness have already proven their fault by their very approach (JULIAN THE ARIAN). The ungodly show contempt for God by rebelling against their own conscience and the precepts of God engraved in their hearts. The phrase "If he should take back his spirit to himself, and gather to himself his breath, all flesh would perish" is best interpreted in a Trinitarian manner through the spirit of prophecy, in light of the New Testament teaching that God the Father assumed flesh in the Son that he might gather to himself the spirit and breath of the afflicted world (PHILIP).

34:1-3 Hear Me, Wise Men

A MORE ACCOMMODATING ATTITUDE. OLYM-

PIODORUS: Because of the former accusations that he had brought against his hearers, Elihu soothes them now with softer words by calling them wise men who know righteousness and honesty. COMMENTARY ON JOB 34.1-6.[1]

34:4-6 Job Had Proclaimed His Innocence

ELIHU EXAGGERATES JOB'S WORDS. PHILIP THE PRIEST: "Let us choose what is right; let us determine among ourselves what is good," that is, let us discuss before condemning the man. "For Job has said, 'I am righteous.'" Job never pronounced such words, but while he exposed the virtues of his justice, he demonstrated himself to be undoubtedly righteous, and God had already called him righteous. "God has taken away my right; in spite of being right I am counted a liar; my wound is incurable, though I am without transgression." . . . We must believe that Job's words were mostly spoken incautiously and without really knowing God's justice. Therefore, God rightly says to him, "Anyone who argues with God must respond";[2] and in these divine words [Job] is reproached. COMMENTARY ON THE BOOK OF JOB 34.[3]

34:7-8 Job a Companion of Evildoers

ACCUSATIONS OF IMPIETY. JULIAN OF ECLANUM: "Who is there like Job, who drinks up scoffing like water?" [Job is compared with one] who reproves God's judgments, despises them and thinks that they must be considered vile. "Who goes in company with evildoers"; since he has an ill feeling against the judgments of God, he does not differ at all from those who are proven to be impious by the injustice of their actions. EXPOSITION ON THE BOOK OF JOB 34.7-8.[4]

34:9 No Profit from Delighting in God

AN INVENTION TO FIND FAULT IN JOB. GREG-

[1]PG 93:356. [2]Job 40:2. [3]PL 26:727. [4]CCL 88:91.

ory the Great: "For he has said, 'A man will not please God even though he runs with him.'" But that he never said so, everyone acknowledges who reads the words of blessed Job. Is it not a wonder that he, who speaks for the sole purpose of proudly setting himself off, invents something to find fault within another person? How can he adhere to truth in his words of reproof, whom pride of mind within removes far away from the same truth? MORALS ON THE BOOK OF JOB 24.43.[5]

34:10-11 God Will Not Act Wickedly

JOB AND ELIHU SAY THE TRUTH. JULIAN OF ECLANUM: "Therefore, hear me, you who have sense, far be it from God that he should do wickedness. For according to their deeds he will repay them." Since, according to the rules of debating, it is easier, in general, that they both lie rather than saying the truth. Here, as they speak against each other, it is nonetheless proven that the arguments of both are true. In fact, what Elihu says cannot be completely proved by holy Job to be false, and what Job asserts cannot be proven to be untrue. Therefore the fact that God repays according to the deeds of each one, though not in everybody, can be proven in many; on the other hand, Job is convinced by testimonies that God does not repay [many]. So, in a sense, it is evident that what both say is true: according to Elihu, [God] does not repay everybody; according to Job, he did not repay many. EXPOSITION ON THE BOOK OF JOB 34.10-11.[6]

34:12-13 God Will Not Pervert Justice

THE PERFECTION OF GOD'S PROVIDENCE. GREGORY THE GREAT: The Lord said to the devil, "You have moved me against him to afflict him without cause."[7] But Elihu says, "That the Lord will not condemn without cause." A statement that is believed to be at variance with the words of Truth, unless weighed with careful consideration. To condemn is one thing, to afflict another.

He afflicts therefore in some respect without cause but does not condemn without cause. Had he not afflicted Job in some respect without cause; since sin was not blotted out, how could his merit be increased by it? For he cannot condemn without reason, inasmuch as condemnation cannot partly take place for a certain purpose, since it punishes at the end all the ungodliness that anyone has here committed. Nor does almighty God subvert judgment, because, although our sufferings seem to be unjust, yet they are rightly inflicted in his secret judgment. It follows, "Whom else has he appointed over the earth, or whom has he placed over the world which he has made?" In order, namely, that you may understand, "No one." For he governs indeed by himself the world that he created by himself, nor does he need the aid of others in governing, who needed it not for creating. These points are brought together in order that he might plainly point out that if almighty God does not neglect to govern by himself the world which he created, he most certainly governs correctly that which he created correctly. He does not order in heartlessness that which he fashioned in mercy. And he who provided for their being before they were made does not forsake them after their creation. He who was the first cause at their creation is present to rule. He, therefore, does not omit to take care of us. MORALS ON THE BOOK OF JOB 24.45-46.[8]

34:14-15 Life Comes from God's Spirit

A PROPHECY ABOUT CHRIST. PHILIP THE PRIEST: These places can be interpreted through the spirit of prophecy as figures, because they are now fulfilled in Christ after the dispensation of the assumed flesh. The Father directed his own Son—the one through whom he created everything—as an expression of his heart to this world. He did this so that he might gather to himself its spirit and breath, that is, he did this in

---

[5]LF 23:84. [6]CCL 88:91. [7]Job 2:3. [8]LF 23:85-86.

order to take away the world's spirit through the humility of the cross. In other words, he came to take away its arrogant, worldly spirit and the breath of its puffed-up eloquence in which it boasted. And so, once a person becomes weakened by the repressive tumor of pride swelling in his own head and returns to himself, he will recognize himself that he is only dust and ashes. COMMENTARY ON THE BOOK OF JOB 34.[9]

34:16-17 Righteous and Mighty

GOD'S JUDGMENT NOT UNDERSTOOD BEFORE EVERYTHING COMPLETED. CHRYSOSTOM: Did you see? He did not dare come to the conclusion that he is [just]; with great discretion he avoided asserting it plainly. Not only by participating in the universe, or in the creation or in his power, we must realize his justice, but also by participating in his own nature and acts. He hates the wicked and loves human beings. He is not like us, who keep away from sin not because of our aversion to vice but because of the fear of punishment. Where does [this fear] come from? From the fact that he "hates injustice and makes the wicked perish." "He, who is eternal," he adds. Elihu is right in introducing the concept of eternity because God is not required every day and for every action to give explanations about what happened; it is usual that God manages a matter whose fulfillment must extend over a long period. Therefore, do not anticipate the conclusion of a fact, and do not try to understand the judgment of God before everything has been completed, because you will get no profit from your hurriedness. That is why he says, eternal and just. All past testifies to him. Is it possible that he has changed now? COMMENTARY ON JOB 34.12-17.[10]

34:18-19 Showing No Partiality

GOD'S IMPARTIALITY. EPHREM THE SYRIAN: "Who says to a king, 'You scoundrel!'" These words are referred to God, who is the King of kings and rulers, and exercises his power on everyone, so that no rich or poor is privileged. COMMENTARY ON JOB 34.18-19.[11]

34:20 Dying in a Moment

PUNISHMENT AND REDEMPTION. JULIAN THE ARIAN: "But it shall turn out vanity for them to cry and beseech a man; for they dealt unlawfully, the poor being turned aside from their right." Those who approach a king with rudeness and speak more freely than required, after having a proof of his strength, kneel down as suppliants and suffer also those things of which they believed to be superior. Without needing anything, they will have a benefit through their rudeness. In fact, even though they used their license to afflict those wronged by them, they had a proof of their faults by approaching the king.[12] COMMENTARY ON JOB 34.20.[13]

34:21-26 God Sees the Ways of People

DIVINE JUSTICE OF GOD. ISHO'DAD OF MERV: "For he has not appointed a time for anyone to go before God in judgment," that is, recognize the power of God and do not consider him as a man, and do not desire to be with him in judgment, as he brings afflictions to many criminals as their punishment but makes the righteous prosper and increase instead of them. COMMENTARY ON JOB 34.23.[14]

34:27-28 Disregard for God's Ways

THE IDOLATROUS ORIGIN OF CONTEMPT FOR GOD. PHILIP THE PRIEST: All sinners and impious act against the goodness of nature conceded to them, as also the apostle confirms, "But in spite of their knowledge of God, they did not pay the homage due to him as

---

[9]PL 26:728. [10]PTS 35:174. [11]ESOO 2:15. [12]In the LXX version of the Bible, which is used by all Greek Fathers, Job 34:16-30 differs significantly from the Hebrew text and Vg. See the variants listed at the foot of this pericope. [13]PTS 14:218. [14]CSCO 229:258-59.

God."[15] How did they know God but through the inspiration and the judgment of the mind? And they nonetheless showed contempt for his glory, and withdrew from it against their own conscience, and they refused to know and understand all the ways of the precepts of God that were engraved in their hearts, while they acted so unjustly and impiously against people that the cries of the oppressed poor reached God. COMMENTARY ON THE BOOK OF JOB 34.[16]

34:29-30 Who Can Condemn?

FIGURES OF PEACE IN THE CHURCH AND THE

REVELATION OF CHRIST. PHILIP THE PRIEST: "When he is quiet, who can condemn?" . . . He grants peace to the church and quiet, when the fights of persecution do not rise against it and when the arguments and the scandals of the heretics stand still. "When he hides his face, who can behold him, whether a nation or an individual?" This means, who but he deigned to reveal himself to humans? Who was ever able to look at him with his own strength or to reach his majesty through his contemplation? COMMENTARY ON THE BOOK OF JOB 34.[17]

---

[15]Rom 1:21.   [16]PL 26:730.   [17]PL 26:730.

34:31-37 JOB'S CRITICISM IS DUE TO IGNORANCE

[31]For has any one said to God,
   "I have borne chastisement; I will not
      offend any more;
[32]teach me what I do not see;
   if I have done iniquity, I will do it
      no more"?
[33]Will he then make requital to suit you,
   because you reject it?
For you must choose, and not I;
   therefore declare what you know.[z]*

[34]Men of understanding will say to me,
   and the wise man who hears me will
      say:
[35]"Job speaks without knowledge,
   his words are without insight."
[36]Would that Job were tried to the end,
   because he answers like wicked men.
[37]For he adds rebellion to his sin;
   he claps his hands among us,
      and multiplies his words against God.†

z The Hebrew of verses 29-33 is obscure   *Vg (31-33) Because I have spoken to God, I will not hinder you also. If I have sinned, teach me; if I have spoken iniquity, I will add no more. Does God require it of you, because it has displeased you? For you did begin to speak, not I. But if you know anything better, say on.   †LXX (36-37) Instruct yourself, Job, no longer make answer like the foolish, because iniquity will be reckoned against us if we speak for a long time before the Lord.

OVERVIEW: Elihu continues to show contradictory elements in his speech: on the one hand, he appears to be hypocritical and disloyal in his accusations and reproofs against Job (GREGORY); on the other, he asserts his submission to God's justice (CHRYSOSTOM), while the argument between Job and his friends finds no solution (JULIAN OF ECLANUM).

It is very difficult for a pride that reigns in the heart not to break through into the voice. Everything in the doings of the proud that is concealed by a covering of words will be brought to light.

The ungodly imitate the words of the just while forsaking the life of the just (GREGORY). Those who argue with a king do well not to argue for a long time (CHRYSOSTOM).

34:31-33 Enduring Punishment

EVIDENCE OF HYPOCRISY IN ELIHU'S WORDS. GREGORY THE GREAT: For, as I said, it is a craft peculiar to the boastful to be eager to enquire about their erring when they know that they have not erred. And again, they disdain to make this enquiry and to be convicted of error whenever they plainly foresee that they have done wrong. They do not seek to be but to appear humble. They assume an appearance of humility by making the inquiry when they are praised the more from the very inquiry itself. But because it is very difficult for pride, which reigns in the heart, not to break in the voice, if the hearers of these haughty people wait for a while and consider their sayings in silence, the words that follow too soon manifest in their hearts. They cannot continue long in that guise of humility that they assume in appearance only. . . . "Does God require it of you, because it has displeased you?" As though he were saying, I am about to give reasons, in the sight of God, why my iniquity is now blamed by you, though it is plain that it is not required of you in judgment. When good people are unjustly assailed by the world, they appeal to the judgment of heaven. Hence also it is said by the same blessed Job, "Behold, my witness is in heaven, and he who knows me is on high."[1] And because they especially desire to please him, they seek for the witness of him only. Wicked people also, who forsake the life of the just, sometimes imitate their words when reproved for their misdeeds and adopt that as a ground of defense which the righteous urge as an evidence of their purity. Hence it has become already a custom with them, when anyone blames them for their doings, to seek the judgment of God rather than of people even when they are not afraid of being judged by him and

are ashamed of being judged by people. . . . But since those who speak first in a dispute are usually more to blame than those who reply, he subjoins, "For you did begin to speak, not I." He believed himself to be so innocent, inasmuch as he burst forth only on being struck, being doubtless ignorant that innocence is not defended on the score of time but on that of reason. What support does it give to his defense that, though he did not revile him when silent, when he began properly, he replied to him insultingly? But after he displays himself in words of pride, behold, he again conceals himself under the pretext of a demand and proceeds to say, "But if you know anything better, say on." Yet he does not say, "because you know better," but "if you know anything better, say on." It was itself too arrogant that he had doubted the knowledge of his superior. But he showed that he had exhibited his humility in having given blessed Job an opportunity for speaking. As was before stated, everything in the doings of the proud that is concealed by a covering of words is brought to light. When the boastful purpose again breaks forth, Elihu speedily made it known with what purpose he required blessed Job to speak. MORALS ON THE BOOK OF JOB 26.2-4.[2]

34:34-35 Those with Sense

OPPOSING ARGUMENTS. JULIAN OF ECLANUM: "Those who have sense will say to me." It seems that, as his friends, with the silence that they have observed, approve and ascribe to their praise the fact that they have endured those arguments that were said by him, so holy Job praises himself for what he has demonstrated with his words. EXPOSITION ON THE BOOK OF JOB 34.34.[3]

34:36-37 The Answers of the Wicked

SUBMISSION TO GOD'S MAJESTY. CHRYSOSTOM: He did not say, in an iniquitous and impi-

---

[1]Job 16:19. [2]LF 23:133-35*. [3]CCL 88:93.

ous manner, but "for a long time," showing that we must not argue with God for a long time. If, when we are in the presence of a king, we do not dare argue with him for a long time, even more so we must behave before God. COMMENTARY ON JOB 34.36-37.[4]

[4]PTS 35:176.

35:1-8 IT IS WRONG TO SAY THAT RIGHTEOUSNESS IS UNAVAILING

[1] And Elihu said:
   [2]"Do you think this to be just?
      Do you say, 'It is my right before God,'*
   [3]that you ask, 'What advantage have I?
      How am I better off than if I had
         sinned?'[†]
   [4]I will answer you
      and your friends with you.
   [5]Look at the heavens, and see;
      and behold the clouds, which are higher
         than you.
   [6]If you have sinned, what do you accomplish
         against him?
      And if your transgressions are multiplied,
         what do you do to him?
   [7]If you are righteous, what do you give to
         him;
      or what does he receive from your
         hand?
   [8]Your wickedness concerns a man like
         yourself,
      and your righteousness a son of man."

*Vg Elihu therefore spoke these words again, "Does your thought seem right to you, that you said, I am more righteous than God?"   †Vg You said that you do not like what is virtuous, or [asked] what advantage you get if I have sinned.

OVERVIEW: In the fourth part of Elihu's speech, the Fathers mostly emphasize how this character is led in his reflections and consequent accusations against Job by a confused and partly wrong opinion concerning the ways of God's justice. In this section of the text, it is evident again how the speeches of Job's friends are necessarily interpreted by the Fathers according to two different points of view: on the one hand, the friends' speeches contain some general truths that can be discussed and developed for a moral comment. On the other, the friends appear to be narrowminded and blind in many respects when they comment on the justice of God, and especially on the way it is applied to the case of Job (GREGORY, JULIAN OF ECLANUM, ORIGEN, CHRYSOSTOM, ISHO'DAD). Since Job believed that he was scourged for the sake of washing away his sins and not for the increasing of his merits, he was confident that his judgment would come to victory (GREGORY). Elihu accuses Job of impudence because he had said that he desired to have a trial with God on an equal level (JULIAN OF ECLANUM). A donkey can look to heaven with physical eyes, but only a human being with spiritual eyes can look to heaven in the proper sense, by looking away from earth (ORIGEN).

35:1-2 What Is Just?

ELIHU'S RHETORIC MISREPRESENTS JOB.
GREGORY THE GREAT: "Elihu therefore spoke
these words again." Everyone who says many
things is always anxious to begin his speech once
again, in order . . . to keep his hearers in suspense,
so that they may be the more attentively silent, the
more they expect, as it were, to hear some new
thing. But Elihu, finishing one subject, begins
another without delay, in order that his loquacity
may be continued without limit by beginnings
being constantly joined. It follows, "Does your
thought seem right to you, that you said, I am
more righteous than God?" Everyone observes,
who reads the text of the history, that blessed Job
did not say that he was more righteous than God.
But he says, "Let him put forth equity against me,
and my judgment shall come to victory."[1] Examining his life without knowing the reasons of his
smiting, as has been often observed, Job believed
that he was scourged for the sake of washing away
his sins and not the increasing of his merits. He
was therefore confident that his judgment would
come to victory, because he found in himself no
fault for which he deserved to be smitten. This
indeed the Lord also said of him to the devil, "You
have moved me against him, to afflict him without
cause." What had Job sinned then, by speaking in
this way, who unknowingly agreed in these words
with the divine and secret sentence on himself?
Or what harm is there, if, in the judgment of people, our words differ on the surface from the exact-
ness of truth, when, in that on which they turn
in the heart, they are closely joined to and agree
with it? The ears of people consider our words to
be such as they sound outwardly, but the divine
judgments hear them as they are uttered from
our inmost heart. MORALS ON THE BOOK OF JOB
26.14-15.[2]

35:3-4 What Advantage Have I?

AN ANSWER TO JOB'S WRONG OPINIONS.
JULIAN OF ECLANUM: "He said, you do not like

what is virtuous." Elihu says that holy Job had a
wrong opinion about God, and these words are
gathered from his reflections, because God is
offended by this fact, as Job ascribes to him the
errors of others. "What advantage will you get if I
sin?" This concept is even more evident in
another passage, "What advantage did I get from
not committing sin?" That is, What else would I
have suffered because of the iniquity of my
actions, if I received such misfortunes after my
dedication to virtue? "I will answer you and your
friends with you." Since your friends taught you
to agree with a wrong opinion about the judgments of God, so that you think to be righteous.
Whereas God is unjust, now I will take care to
answer in order to confute you and them. EXPO-
SITION ON THE BOOK OF JOB 35.3-4.[3]

35:5 Look and Observe

**ELIHU UNDERLINES JOB'S NOTHINGNESS
BEFORE GOD.** JULIAN OF ECLANUM: The immensity itself of the unbounded separation [between
God and humanity] can teach you that God may
neither be offended by your evil actions, nor be
benefited by your good deeds. "Look at the heavens and see; observe the clouds, which are higher
than you." Through the testimony of divine Providence he wants to accuse him of an impudent
action, because he had said that he desired to
have a trial with God on an equal level, and then
he applies himself to approve the eminence of
[God's] works and benefits. EXPOSITION ON THE
BOOK OF JOB 35.5.[4]

**ONLY THE RIGHTEOUS CAN LOOK AT THE
HEAVENS.** ORIGEN: The one who looks at the
heavens is not he who raises his physical eyes and
observes the heavens. Indeed, also dogs and donkeys look at the heavens in this manner. No one
who loves the world looks at the heavens, but
only he who does not love the world and the
things which are in it. If we love the things that

---

[1]Job 23:7. [2]LF 23:142*. [3]CCL 88:93. [4]CCL 88:93-94.

are here, we do not look to the heavens. The clouds are not so high and so removed from us that, if I follow the life and conduct of Moses, through which he was pleasing to God, and recognize my weakness and humility, I will not be able to gain a higher and even more removed cloud. If I imitate Jesus, son of Nun, and the life of the blessed prophets and carefully examine their actions, I will fulfill what was written. FRAGMENTS ON JOB 24.11-12.[5]

35:6-7 What Did You Accomplish Against God?

GOD'S IMPERTURBABILITY. CHRYSOSTOM: These words mean, you will do no wrong to him, and you will not be more useful to him by being righteous. In fact, he said, "If I have sinned, what shall I be able to do?"[6] What shall I do to you? Elihu says, Why did you say that? Does God care about the fact that you sinned, as if he is the victim of an injustice or as if he is suffering damage? COMMENTARY ON JOB 35.6.[7]

CHRIST IS OUR ADVOCATE. ORIGEN: If you look at the heavens and contemplate the clouds, you will understand that you sinned. And what do you need to do? It is necessary that you approach the high priest and implore him to offer a victim for you. "If any one does sin, we have an advocate with the Father, Jesus Christ the righteous; and he is the expiation of our sins."[8] If you will do this, you will dissolve your numerous sins. And for those irremediable sins from which we cannot be cured, Jesus Christ came from heaven to cure what was irremediable, and so that it might happen that "blessed are they whose transgressions are forgiven and whose sins are covered."[9] FRAGMENTS ON JOB 24.15-16.[10]

35:8 Deeds Affect Others

REASONS FOR PUNISHMENT OF THE WICKED. ISHO'DAD OF MERV: "Your wickedness affects others like you." If one asks, "Why does God judge [the wicked] if their sin does not harm him personally?" [the author] brings forward the reason and says, "Because of the multitude of oppressions people cry out; they call for help."[11] It is not for him, he says, that the [impious] are punished, but because of those who are oppressed and robbed and cry out to him, so that he may take revenge on those who compel them to suffer afflictions. COMMENTARY ON JOB 35.8.[12]

---

[5]PTS 53:199-200. [6]Job 7:20. [7]PTS 35:176. [8]1 Jn 2:1-2. [9]Ps 32:1 (31:1 LXX). [10]PTS 53:201. [11]Job 35:9. [12]CSCO 229:259.

35:9-16 MANY ARE NOT HEARD BECAUSE OF THEIR INFIDELITY

[9]*Because of the multitude of oppressions*
people cry out;
they call for help because of the arm of
the mighty.

[10]*But none says, "Where is God my Maker,*
who gives songs in the night,
[11]*who teaches us more than the beasts of the*
earth,

and makes us wiser than the birds of the
air?"*

^{12}There they cry out, but he does not
answer,

because of the pride of evil men.

^{13}Surely God does not hear an empty
cry,

nor does the Almighty regard it.

^{14}How much less when you say that you do

not see him,

that the case is before him, and you are
waiting for him!†

^{15}And now, because his anger does not
punish,

and he does not greatly heed
transgression,^{a}

^{16}Job opens his mouth in empty talk,

he multiplies words without knowledge.

a Theodotion Symmachus Compare Vg: The meaning of the Hebrew word is uncertain *LXX (9-11) They that are oppressed by a multitude will be ready to cry out; they will call for help in order to avoid the arm of the multitude. But no one said, "Where is God that made me, who appoints the night watches, who makes me to differ from the four-footed beasts of the earth, and from the birds of the sky?" †LXX For he, the Almighty, observes all those who commit impieties. But plead before him, if you can praise him conveniently.

OVERVIEW: In the second part of Job 35, Elihu is able to express correctly some general views on the divine order set by God in the world (CHRYSOSTOM): on the brutality and degradation of sin (ORIGEN, EPHREM), on the absolute devotion due to God (CHRYSOSTOM) and on the afflictions that await the righteous in this world (GREGORY). No creature exceeds its own limit within the divine order (CHRYSOSTOM). The licentious are like four-footed beasts (ORIGEN). God does not hearken to the proud (EPHREM). To be unable to praise God as he deserves is serious, but to be unable to do so while we are pleading to him—that is really serious (CHRYSOSTOM). Suffering is here the portion of the elect so they may be trained for the rewards of their heavenly inheritance (GREGORY).

35:9-11 Where Is God?

DIVINE ORDER. CHRYSOSTOM: These words mean, do you not see that everything is set in good order, as in a field, and that with an even greater precision each object is in the most convenient place? [Do you not see] that no object exceeds its own limit or steps on the area reserved to another? It is as if the night watches control everything; during the sleep of mortals nobody tries to attack. Observe wild animals. When they move around, that is the time when human beings sleep. They must not invade cities; people must not perish, because they sleep being conquered by sleep. COMMENTARY ON JOB 35.10B.[1]

THE ANIMALS SYMBOLIZE THOSE WHO SIN. ORIGEN: "Who makes me different from the four-footed beasts of the earth?"[2] If you are a sinner, you were not distinguished from the four-footed beasts of the earth. "Man that has honor does not understand, he is compared to the senseless cattle, and is like them."[3] If you are a sinner, you were not distinguished from the four-footed beasts of the earth, but it is said to you, "So that you might not be like horses and mules that have no understanding."[4] If you are a sinner, if you are licentious, if you are reckless, you are not distinguished from the four-footed beasts. "They became like wanton horses."[5] For this reason he audaciously said that he was segregated. "Who makes me different from the four-footed beasts of the earth?" FRAGMENTS ON JOB 24.25.[6]

35:12-13 The Pride of the Wicked

A REPROACH AGAINST PRIDE. EPHREM THE SYRIAN: "Because of the pride of humanity," that

---

[1]PTS 35:177. [2]Job 35:11 LXX. See the apparatus at the foot of the pericope. [3]Ps 49:20 (48:21 LXX). [4]Ps 32:9 (31:9 LXX). [5]Jer 5:8. [6]PTS 53:204.

is, they are reproved for the pride and arrogance that they show before their neighbors. And God will not hear the vain cries of proud people. COMMENTARY ON JOB 35.12-13.[7]

35:14 You Say You Do Not See God

PRAISE IS ALWAYS DUE TO GOD. CHRYSOSTOM: "For he, the Almighty, observes all those who commit impieties. But plead before him, if you can praise him conveniently." If he had established a court and had published its decisions, you would have not praised him, you would have not glorified him, as he deserves, with regard to what happened to you, because you think you have been unjustly punished. Not to be able to praise God as he deserves, that is not too serious; but not to be able to praise him as he deserves when we plead before him, that is really serious. COMMENTARY ON JOB 35.11-16.[8]

35:15-16 Job's Talk Is Empty

SUFFERING IN THIS WORLD. GREGORY THE GREAT: For God in truth bears a long while with him whom he condemns forever; and forebears now to bring on his wrath, because he reserves it to be poured forth, hereafter, without end. For suffering is here the portion of the elect, so they may be trained for the rewards of their heavenly inheritance. It is our portion to receive stripes here, for whom an eternity of joy is reserved. Hence it is written, "He scourges every son whom he receives."[9] It is also said to John, "I rebuke and chastise those whom I love."[10] Peter says, "It is time that judgment must begin at the house of God."[11] And then Peter immediately adds with astonishment, "But if it first begin at us, what shall be the end of them that believe not the gospel of God?"[12] For the severity of God does not permit sins to remain unpunished; but the wrath of judgment commences with our punishment here, in order that it may cease to rage at the damnation of the reprobate. Let the reprobate proceed then and accomplish the desires of their pleasures, with unpunished iniquity, and let them feel no temporal scourges, since eternal punishments await them.... "Job opens his mouth in empty talk, he multiplies words without knowledge." But this seems also to be a peculiar fault of the arrogant, that they believe much that they have said, to be little, and the little which is said to them, to be much. Because they always wish to speak their own words, they cannot hear the words of others. And they think that they suffer violence if they do not pour forth their own immoderate opinions more immoderately. Although blessed Job was silent at his words, Elihu finds cause for invective in the speech in which he had replied to his friends. In order to get himself a larger space of his silence, and that he himself might answer many things, he asserts that he had multiplied words. For he immediately begins the commencement of a tedious speech and endeavors to commence, as though he had as yet said nothing at all. MORALS ON THE BOOK OF JOB 26.21.37-22.40.[13]

---

[7]ESOO 2:15. [8]PTS 35:178. [9]Heb 12:6. [10]Rev 3:19. [11]1 Pet 4:17. [12]1 Pet 4:17. [13]LF 23:161-63*.

36:1-21 GOD'S JUST DESIGNS IN HUMAN AFFLICTION

And Elihu continued, and said:
²"Bear with me a little, and I will show you,
for I have yet something to say on God's
behalf.
³I will fetch my knowledge from afar,
and ascribe righteousness to my Maker.
⁴For truly my words are not false;
one who is perfect in knowledge is with you.

⁵"Behold, God is mighty, and does not
despise any;
he is mighty in strength of understanding.
⁶He does not keep the wicked alive,
but gives the afflicted their right.
⁷He does not withdraw his eyes from the
righteous,
but with kings upon the throne
he sets them for ever, and they are
exalted.*
⁸And if they are bound in fetters
and caught in the cords of affliction,
⁹then he declares to them their work
and their transgressions, that they are
behaving arrogantly.
¹⁰He opens their ears to instruction,†
and commands that they return from
iniquity.
¹¹If they hearken and serve him,
they complete their days in prosperity,
and their years in pleasantness.

¹²But if they do not hearken, they perish by
the sword,
and die without knowledge.‡

¹³"The godless in heart cherish anger;§
they do not cry for help when he binds
them.
¹⁴They die in youth,
and their life ends in shame.ᵇ
¹⁵He delivers the afflicted by their affliction,
and opens their ear by adversity.#
¹⁶He also allured you out of distress
into a broad place where there was no
cramping,**
and what was set on your table was full
of fatness.

¹⁷"But you are full of the judgment on the
wicked;
judgment and justice seize you.
¹⁸Beware lest wrath entice you into scoffing;
and let not the greatness of the ransom
turn you aside.
¹⁹Will your cry avail to keep you from distress,
or all the force of your strength?
²⁰Do not long for the night,
when peoples are cut off in their place.
²¹Take heed, do not turn to iniquity,
for this you have chosen rather than
affliction."††

b Heb *among the cult prostitutes*   *Vg (5-7) *God does not reject the mighty, though he himself is mighty. But he does not save the wicked, and he gives judgment to the poor. He will not withdraw his eyes from the righteous but establishes kings on the throne forever, and there they are exalted.*   †LXX *he will hearken to the righteous*   ‡Vg (11-12) *If they hear and observe him, they shall fulfill their days in good and their years in glory; but if they do not hear, they shall pass away by the sword and shall be consumed with folly.*   §Vg *The simulators and the cunning cause God's wrath.*   #Vg *They will die in the tempest of their soul and their life among the effeminate. He will take the poor away from his anguish and will reveal his ear in tribulation.*

**Vg He will also save you largely from the narrow mouth that has no foundation, and the rest of your table will be full of fatness.   ††Vg (19-21) Lay down your greatness without tribulation, and all the mighty in strength. Do not prolong the night, so that people should go up for them. Take heed that you do not decline to iniquity, for you have begun to follow this after misery.

OVERVIEW: The fifth part of Elihu's speech, covering Job 36, attracts more favorable comments on the part of the Fathers. In this section, Elihu, whose words are introduced by the biblical author with an allusion to the previous parts of his long speech (JULIAN OF ECLANUM), demonstrates that he is able to hold correct, general views on the ways of God's justice (GREGORY, JULIAN THE ARIAN, JULIAN OF ECLANUM, PHILIP). However, the Fathers also notice how Elihu's attitude toward Job is arrogant, unjust and false (PHILIP, GREGORY). The faithful are like kings because they have learned not to yield to temptations by consenting to them, but to gain mastery by ruling over them. There are some whom not even punishment keeps back from loose habits. They sometimes become worse by scourge because, when attacked by pain, they are hardened in their obstinacy (GREGORY). To "die among the effeminate" suggests that one is deprived of his strength by misfortunes that happen to him (JULIAN OF ECLANUM). "The place of no restraint" is the mouth of hell that is ironically defined as "narrow" because it is large in receiving and very narrow in releasing (PHILIP).

36:1-4 *Asking for Patience*

AN INVITATION TO PATIENCE. JULIAN OF ECLANUM: The author of the book, while distributing the chapters of the different speeches to us, connects the words that follow to the beginning. Since he had stirred the attention of the listeners by discussing the providence of God, he also asks their patience for the things that he is about to say. EXPOSITION ON THE BOOK OF JOB 36.1-2.[1]

36:5-7 *God's Understanding*

HUMILITY IS REWARDED, PRIDE IS CONDEMNED. GREGORY THE GREAT: "God does not reject the mighty, though he himself is mighty." ... Great is that temporal power that, from being well administered, has its special reward from God, and yet sometimes, from being preeminent over others, it swells with pride of thought. All things for its use are at its service, while its commands are speedily fulfilled according to its wish and while all its subjects praise its good deeds. If there are any who do not oppose its evil doings with any authority, then they too will commonly praise them, even that which they ought to blame. The mind, being led astray by those things that are beneath it, is raised above itself, and while it is encircled with unbounded applause outside, it is bereft of truth inside. . . . "But he does not save the wicked and gives judgment to the poor." Holy Scripture is frequently prone to call the humble, "poor." Hence they are mentioned in the Gospel with the addition "spirit" when it is said, "Blessed are the poor in spirit, for theirs is the kingdom of heaven."[2] Riches visibly manifest the powerful; those are poor in their own sight, who are not puffed up in their minds. But he calls those "wicked" who are either cut off from the piety of the faith or who contradict themselves by their wicked habits, in that which they faithfully believe. . . .

"He will not withdraw his eyes from the righteous but establishes kings on the throne forever, and there they are exalted." But holy people are properly termed "kings," in the language of Scripture, because having been raised above all the motions of flesh, at one time they control the appetite of lust; at another they moderate the heat of avarice; at one time they bow down the boastfulness of pride; at another they crush the suggestions of envy; at another they extinguish the fire of passion. They are "kings" then, because they have learned not to give way to the motions of their temptations by consenting to them but to gain mastery by ruling over them. Since, therefore, they pass from

---

[1]CCL 88:95.   [2]Mt 5:3.

this power of authority to the power of retribution, let it be rightly said, "He establishes kings on the throne forever." They are wearied for a time by ruling themselves, but they are placed forever on the throne of the kingdom of eternal elevation; and there they receive the power of justly judging others, just as they are here unskilled in unjustly sparing themselves. Morals on the Book of Job 26.44-53.[3]

36:8-10 Openness to Instruction

GOD'S MERCY TOWARD THE REPENTANT.
JULIAN THE ARIAN: But after accusing those who are bound in fetters, he will deliver them from their chains through his benevolence and will bring them back to his doctrine. And when the impious think that they are at the climax of their greatness, he declares to them their works and gives their fruits to the righteous as recompense. If they turn to God and serve him, they will not only earn a punishment but also eternal life and a good reputation. COMMENTARY ON JOB 36.5-11.[4]

36:11-12 Dying Without Knowledge

PUNISHMENT OF OBSTINATE WICKEDNESS.
GREGORY THE GREAT: "If they hear and observe him, they shall fulfill their days in good and their years in glory; but if they do not hear, they shall pass away by the sword and shall be consumed with folly." By "good" is designated right conduct, but by "glory" heavenly recompense. They, then, who study to obey the divine commands fulfill their days in good and their years in glory. Because they pass the course of this life in right deeds, they perfect their consummation by a blessed retribution. "But if they do not hear, they shall pass away by the sword and shall be consumed with folly." Vengeance smites them in tribulation, and the end shuts them up in folly. For there are some whom not even torments keep back from their loose habits. Of them it is said by the prophet, "You have stricken them, but they have not grieved; you have scourged them, and

they have refused to receive correction."[5] And of them it is said under the figure of Babylon, "We have cured Babylon, and she is not healed."[6] Of them it is said again, "I have slain and destroyed my people, and yet they have not returned from their ways."[7] These sometimes become worse by the scourge, because, when attacked by pain, they are either more hardened in their contumacious obstinacy or, what is worse, launch out into even the exasperation of blasphemy. It is well said then that they pass away by the sword and are consumed with folly; for through their scourges, they increase those sins that they ought, in consequence of them, to correct. And they both feel even here the punishment of the blow and do not escape there the sufferings of righteous retribution. It is the infatuation of folly that iniquity so fetters them and that not even punishment keeps them from offending. MORALS ON THE BOOK OF JOB 26.57.[8]

36:13 The Godless Do Not Seek God's Help

A REPROACHFUL REFERENCE TO ELIHU.
PHILIP THE PRIEST: "The simulators and the cunning cause God's wrath; they do not cry for help when he binds them." It seems that through these words holy Job is obliquely hinting at Elihu himself, because he is acting, in a sense, in a cunning and unjust way: he also pretends to be an excellent man. COMMENTARY ON THE BOOK OF JOB 36.[9]

36:14-15 Ending in Shame

A RIGHT RETRIBUTION. JULIAN OF ECLANUM: "They will die in the tempest of their soul, and their life among the effeminate." Since he had said above, "God will not be humble before the powerful," here he has rightly said that the one who through his scorn inflames the wrath of the avenger will die among the effeminate, that is, he

---

[3]LF 23:165-75. [4]PTS 14: 228. [5]Jer 5:3. [6]Jer 51:9. [7]Jer 15:7. [8]LF 23:177*. [9]PL 26:735.

deserves to be deprived of all his strength by the misfortunes that will happen to him. "He will take the poor away from his anguish and will reveal his ear in tribulation." Through the voices of the facts themselves he will teach them that he has not forgotten the cry of the poor. EXPOSITION ON THE BOOK OF JOB 36.14-15.[10]

36:16 A Place of No Constraint

A DESCRIPTION OF HEAVEN AND HELL. PHILIP THE PRIEST: "He will also save you largely from the narrow mouth that has no foundation." Through these words Elihu describes the dwellings of hell, which have no foundation for their immense capacity. . . . And the mouth of hell is appropriately defined as "narrow," because it is large in receiving and very narrow in releasing, as it keeps in itself the dead and does not suffer that they come back to life. . . . "And the rest of your table will be full of fatness." By mentioning "the rest" he refers to the pleasantness and joy of paradise. COMMENTARY ON THE BOOK OF JOB 36.[11]

36:17-21 Judgment and Justice

THE WISH OF THE ARROGANT. GREGORY THE GREAT: ["Lay down your greatness without tribulation, and all the mighty in strength. Do not prolong the night, so that people should go up for them. Take heed that you do not decline to iniquity, for you have begun to follow this after misery."] . . . What is this that, while he forbids him to decline iniquity, he condemns him for it at once, as if he had already declined it? Does this suggest that arrogant people wish rather to appear as judges rather than consolers? Hence also, they sometimes smite with severe sentences those faults that they suspect have arisen in the heart. And before the fault of the offenders is certain, severe invective of words is brought forward; and a person is struck by their sentence before anything appears to be smitten. Even just people commonly oppose, by reproof, wicked and secret thoughts, but when any preceding doings make plain these thoughts, they frequently root out from the hearts of their hearers, by the hand of reproof, those sins that have not shown themselves. But then they perceive that they are already following from others that proceed. For as physicians of the body discern that some diseases have already appeared but heal others, that they may not appear, so do holy teachers sometimes restore to health the wounds they have discovered, and sometimes so deal with people's minds that they are not wounded. MORALS ON THE BOOK OF JOB 26.86-87.[12]

---

[10]CCL 88:95-96.   [11]PL 26:735-36.   [12]LF 23:197-98*.

36:22-33 GOD'S GREATNESS AND INFINITE WISDOM

[22]Behold, God is exalted in his power;
    who is a teacher like him?
[23]Who has prescribed for him his way,
    or who can say, "Thou hast done wrong"?
[24]"Remember to extol his work,
    of which men have sung.*
[25]All men have looked on it; †
    man beholds it from afar.
[26]Behold, God is great,‡ and we know him
    not;

the number of his years is unsearchable.
²⁷For he draws up the drops of water,
*   heᶜ distils his mist in rain*
²⁸which the skies pour down,
*   and drop upon man abundantly.*
²⁹Can any one understand the spreading of
*   the clouds,*
*   the thunderings of his pavilion?*
³⁰Behold, he scatters his lightning about

him,
*   and covers the roots of the sea.§*
³¹For by these he judges peoples;
*   he gives food in abundance.*
³²He covers his hands with the lightning,
*   and commands it to strike the mark.#*
³³Its crashing declares concerning him,
*   who is jealous with anger against*
*   iniquity.*

c Cn: I Ieb *they distil* *Vg *Remember that you do not know the works of him whom men have sung.* †Vg *him* ‡Vg *See, God is great* §LXX (29-30) *And though one should under-stand the outspreading of the clouds or the measure of his tabernacle, behold, he will stretch his bow against him, and he covers the bottom of the sea;* Vg (30) *He will also cover the hinges of the sea.* #Peshitta *He will cover the light with his hands and will go toward them so that they may come to meet him.*

OVERVIEW: Elihu shows again all his sensibility and accurateness in his general statements on God's justice (EPHREM), on the limitations of human knowledge (GREGORY) and on the omnipresence of God (GREGORY, JULIAN THE ARIAN, ISHO'DAD). He is also able to prophesy the conversion of the Gentiles (GREGORY).

36:22-23 Who Is a Teacher Like God?

GOD'S POWER IS JUSTICE. EPHREM THE SYRIAN: And you certainly, he says, were tested so far in the furnace of correction. But God will indeed restore you and will bring you back to your former wealth and dignity. COMMENTARY ON JOB 36.22.[1]

36:24-25 Looking at God

MORTALS CANNOT REACH A FULL KNOWLEDGE OF GOD. GREGORY THE GREAT: "Remember that you do not know the works of him whom men have sung." . . . Therefore people sing to the Lord when the angelic spirits or the perfect doctors teach us his power. But they do not know his works, because they, who are now preaching, worship his judgments without understanding them. And so they know him whom they are preaching but ignore his works, because they know him through grace who cre-

ated them, but [they] cannot understand his judgments, which occur through his agency even above them. . . . "All people have looked on him; everyone watches him from far away." Every person, because he is endowed with reason, must infer from his own reason that God created him. To observe through reasoning his dominion undoubtedly is like seeing him already. After saying, "All people looked on him," he rightly adds, "everyone watches him from far away." To watch him from far away is not like seeing him directly yet, but it is like considering him by simply admiring his works. MORALS ON THE BOOK OF JOB 27.6-8.[2]

36:26-28 We Do Not Know God

GOD IS PRESENT EVERYWHERE. GREGORY THE GREAT: He had said above, "See, God is exalted in his power"; now he repeats, "See, God is great." What does "see" mean when speaking about God, and why does he repeat "see," but for the reason that we are speaking of what we indicate in the present? And since God is present everywhere, when we say, "see" with regard to him we recall the fact that he is present also with those who do not see him. MORALS ON THE BOOK OF JOB 27.9.[3]

---

[1]ESOO 2:15-16. [2]CCL 143b:1334-35. [3]CCL 143b:1336.

36:29-30a Who Can Understand Clouds and Thunder?

We Learn God's Power. Julian the Arian: "And though one should understand the outspreading of the clouds or the measure of his tabernacle." If you understood the measure and uniformity and harmony of clouds, would you guess who is the Maker of the clouds? With what plane did he produce such uniformity? With what paint did he make such wonderful, harmonious and laudable pictures? "Behold, he will stretch his bow against him, and he covers the bottom of the sea." He calls "bow" the rainbow which others call "belt." Moses calls it "bow," while Daniel calls it "rainbow." The former says, "I lay my bow on the clouds";[4] the latter, "And lo a rainbow and a saint from heaven,"[5] and the mere divinity of it can really strike the viewer. By casting the arrows of light in a certain way, it announces the wisdom of God to those who contemplate the universe, its immense dimension and the ineffable Owner of the circle of the heavenly dome. By inciting us to gratefulness toward God, it exhorts us to cry, "How magnificent are your works, O Lord, you made all them in wisdom."[6] Commentary on Job 36.29-30a.[7]

36:30b-31 Covering the Roots of the Sea

A Prophecy Fulfilled. Gregory the Great: "And he will also cover the hinges of the sea." From Elihu's voice we hear that this will happen, but we see that through the agency of God, it has happened already. The almighty Lord, in fact, has covered the limits of the sea with glowing clouds, because, through the fulminating miracles performed by his preachers, he has led to faith even the most extreme lands of the world.... "For by these he governs peoples; he gives food in abundance." By these words of his preachers, that is, by these drops of the clouds and by the lightning of miracles, God judges people. He calls to repentance their frightened hearts. Indeed, as soon as they hear the heavenly words, as soon as they see the wondrous works, they come back to their heart and, repenting of their past iniquities, fear the eternal chastisements. Morals on the Book of Job 27.21-22.[8]

36:32-33 God's Way of Acting

Performance Follows Command. Isho'dad of Merv: The words, "He will cover the light with his hands" [mean] that when he wants to make the rain fall for the sake of earth, he condenses the air as if with his hands and covers the sun with clouds. And the words "he will go toward them so that they may come to meet him" [mean] that in the same instant in which his command goes to his works, they promptly come to meet him, that is, the performance instantly follows the command. Commentary on Job 36.32.[9]

---

[4]Gen 9:13. [5]Dan 4:13 (4:10 Vg). [6]Ps 104:24 (103:24 LXX). [7]PTS 14:237. [8]CCL 143b:1345-46. [9]CSCO 229:259.

37:1-13 THE EFFECTS OF GOD'S VOICE ON NATURE

¹At this also my heart trembles,
    and leaps out of its place.
²Hearken to the thunder of his voice
    and the rumbling that comes from his
        mouth.*
³Under the whole heaven he lets it go,†
    and his lightning to the corners of the earth.
⁴After it his voice roars;
    he thunders with his majestic voice
    and he does not restrain the lightnings^d
        when his voice is heard.‡
⁵God thunders wondrously with his voice;
    he does great things which we cannot
        comprehend.
⁶For to the snow he says, "Fall on the earth";
    and to the shower and the rain,^e "Be
        strong."

⁷He seals up the hand of every man,
    that all men may know his work.^f§
⁸Then the beasts go into their lairs,
    and remain in their dens.
⁹From its chamber comes the whirlwind,
    and cold from the scattering winds.
¹⁰By the breath of God ice is given,
    and the broad waters are frozen
        fast.#
¹¹He loads the thick cloud with moisture;
    the clouds scatter his lightning.**
¹²They turn round and round by his
        guidance,
    to accomplish all that he commands them
    on the face of the habitable world.
¹³Whether for correction, or for his land,
    or for love, he causes it to happen.††

d Heb *them*   e Cn Compare Syr: Heb *shower of rain* and *shower of rains*   f Vg Compare Syr Tg: Heb *that all men whom he has made may know it*   *Peshitta *the judgment that comes from his mouth*   †Peshitta *Under the whole heaven he will be praised*.   ‡Vg *Behind him the thunder will roar; he will thunder with the voice of his greatness, and after hearing his voice nobody will be able to investigate*.   §LXX (7) *He seals up the hand of everyone, so that everyone may know his own weakness*.   #Vg (9-10) *A tempest will come forth from the inner parts and cold from Arcturus. When God blows, the ice congeals, and the waters are again poured forth abundantly*.   **Vg *Wheat desires the clouds; and the clouds spread their light*.   ††Vg *They traverse all things in a circuit, wherever the will of their Ruler shall lead them, to everything which he shall command them upon the face of the earth. Whether in one tribe or in his own land or in whatsoever place of his mercy he shall order them to be found*.

OVERVIEW: The sixth and final part of Elihu's speech is mostly interpreted by the Fathers under a favorable light. They notice how he condemns human iniquity (JULIAN THE ARIAN) and how he invites humankind to repentance and humility through the thunder of punishment and the observation of nature (ISHO'DAD, GREGORY, CHRYSOSTOM). They also underline how his words have a prophetic meaning and announce the persecutions of the Jews and the Gentiles, as well as the preaching and spreading of the gospel (GREGORY).

37:1 A Trembling Heart

ELIHU'S ASTONISHMENT. JULIAN THE ARIAN: Indeed, he says, creation belongs to God. Therefore when I see that people commit iniquities against each other, my heart is troubled and fades away, while I am astonished at their wickedness, and, on the other hand, at their resignation. COMMENTARY ON JOB 36.33B-37.1.[1]

37:2-4 The Thunder of God's Voice

THE THUNDER OF PUNISHMENT. ISHO'DAD OF MERV: [By] the words "the judgment that comes

[1]PTS 14:239.

from his mouth; under the whole heaven he will be praised," [the author] speaks about the thunder that is produced in the instant itself, in which punishment is inflicted on sinners; it is heard everywhere and everyone who hears it praises God. COMMENTARY ON JOB 37.2.[2]

REPENTANCE THROUGH GRACE AND THE VOICE OF GOD. GREGORY THE GREAT: "Behind him the thunder will roar." Certainly God transforms into tears the life of him whom he filled with his illumination, and the more he reminds the illuminated soul of eternal punishments, the harder he submits it to the groans for its past wickedness; and so a person feels the pain for what he has been, because he begins by now to see the good he did not do, he hates himself for what he has been, and he loves himself for what he should have been. . . . "He will thunder with the voice of his greatness." God thunders with the voice of his greatness when he suggests to us, who are now well disposed through our tears, how great he is there on high. . . . "And after hearing his voice, nobody will be able to investigate." The voice of God is heard when the soul perceives the inspiration of his grace. . . . But not even the soul illuminated by it can investigate this voice of the Spirit, which reaches and penetrates the ear of the heart. MORALS ON THE BOOK OF JOB 27.39-41.[3]

37:5-8 Commanding the Snow

CREATION INVITES US TO HUMILITY. CHRYSOSTOM: This is the reason, he says, for the grandiosity of his creations, the reason for the cold and the heat, the reason for the irregularity of the winds. Was it impossible to produce a harmonious blend? [If God did not do that], it is because he wants to prevent by any means the pride and arrogance of thought. It is "so that everyone may know his own weakness." "Who can resist," Scripture says, "before his cold?"[4] The entire universe has been created for this purpose, and everything exists for it. Since [pride] first of all drove away from us our trust in God, for this rea-

son God has organized everything in view of its contrary, either the creation, or the fashioning of our body or the course of our life, so that all this exists for humility in order that we may learn to act with moderation and recognize our own weakness. COMMENTARY ON JOB 37.7B.[5]

37:9-10 Winds and Whirlwind

A FIGURE OF PERSECUTIONS. GREGORY THE GREAT: "A tempest will come forth from the inner parts, and cold from Arcturus." When holy Scripture mentions the inner parts, in opposition to Arcturus, it designates the quarter of the south, opposite to the parts of the north. Hence it is written in this same book, "Who makes Arcturus and the Orions and the inner parts of the south?"[6] Because then the sun pervades with greater warmth the inner parts of the south, but it does not pursue its course at all in the north, by the word "inner parts" in this place is expressed the Jewish people, and by the term "Arcturus" the Gentile people. For they who had known the one and invisible God and obeyed his law, at least carnally, were kept, as it were, in the warmth of faith, under the glow of the midday sun. But because the Gentiles had not attained to any knowledge of heavenly wisdom, they were remaining, as it were, in the cold without the sun under the north. Moreover, a tempest impels, but cold oppresses with torpor. It is now rightly said, "A tempest will come forth from the inner parts, and cold from Arcturus." As if it were plainly said, From the Jews there arises persecuting malice, and from the Gentiles oppressing power. MORALS ON THE BOOK OF JOB 27.51.[7]

37:11 Clouds and Lightning

A FIGURE OF CHRISTIAN PREACHING. GREGORY THE GREAT: "Wheat desires the clouds."

---

[2]CSCO 229:260. [3]CCL 143b:1360-61. [4]Ps 147:17 (147:6 LXX).
[5]PTS 35:179. [6]Job 9:9. [7]LF 23:239*.

What else are the elected but God's wheat destined to be stored in the heavenly barn? . . . But this wheat, up until it reaches the perfection of fruits, waits for the rain of the clouds in order to grow. The souls of the righteous are watered by the words of the preachers, in order that the sun of carnal desires may not dry the lymph of charity. . . .

"And the clouds spread their light." The clouds spread their light in the sense that the holy preachers, by speaking and living, divulge models of life. Even though they diffuse the light of the call to salvation, they cannot convert all the hearts that they would like to convert. MORALS ON THE BOOK OF JOB 27.54-55.[8]

37:12-13 Accomplishing God's Commands

ELIHU'S PROPHETIC WORDS. GREGORY THE GREAT: ["They traverse all things in a circuit wherever the will of their Ruler shall lead them. To everything that he shall command them upon the face of the earth, whether in one tribe, or in his own land, or in whatsoever place of his mercy, he shall order them to be found."] . . . God therefore leads his clouds, either in one tribe, or in his own land or in whatever place of his mercy, and shall order them to be found. In earlier times he conferred preachers of the Old Testament on the tribe of Judah only and rejected nearly the whole of Israel because of the wicked governing of their kings. At another time, he made these clouds to rain, even in his own land, because he recalled this same people of Israel to his former favor after correction in captivity. Then at another he wished them to shine forth from the place of his mercy when he made known even to the Gentiles, by holy preachers of the New Testament, the miracles of his power. By his sole mercy he thus freed those from the yoke of error who his wrath was weighing down in their innate unbelief.

But see, because Elihu has perceived future events by the spirit of prophecy, because he has uttered many sublime truths, the haughty man, wearied with the weight of his pride, is unable to bear the burden of what he says. MORALS ON THE BOOK OF JOB 27.58.[9]

---

[8]CCL 143b:1373-74. [9]LF 23:243-44**.

37:14-24 JOB IS INVITED TO LEARN FROM NATURE

[14]*Hear this, O Job;*
stop* and consider the wondrous works
of God.
[15]*Do you know how God lays his command*
upon them,
and causes the lightning of his cloud to
shine?[†]
[16]*Do you know the balancings of the clouds,*
the wondrous works of him who is perfect
in knowledge,
[17]*you whose garments are hot*
when the earth is still because of the
south wind?[‡]
[18]*Can you, like him, spread out the skies,*
hard as a molten mirror?
[19]*Teach us what we shall say to him;*
we cannot draw up our case because of
darkness.[§]
[20]*Shall it be told him that I would*
speak?

Did a man ever wish that he would be
swallowed up?

[21] And now men cannot look on the light
when it is bright in the skies,
when the wind has passed and cleared
them.
[22] Out of the north comes golden splendor;

God is clothed with terrible majesty.*
[23] The Almighty—we cannot find him;
he is great in power and justice,
and abundant righteousness he will not
violate.
[24] Therefore men fear him;
he does not regard any who are wise in
their own conceit.**

*Vg stand   †Vg Do you know when God commanded the rains to show forth the light of his clouds?   ‡LXX (17) Your robe is hot, and there is quiet upon the land.   §Peshitta Teach us what we shall say to him, so that we may not rejoice at the sight of darkness.   #Vg (21-22) But now they do not see the light; suddenly the sky is covered with clouds, and the passing wind will drive them away. From Aquilon gold and the timorous praise of God come.   **Vg The Almighty—we cannot find him adequately; he is so great in power, discernment and justice that he cannot be described. Therefore people will fear him, and all those who think to be wise will not dare contemplate him.

OVERVIEW: The sincere admiration of God's works (GREGORY) enables humankind to praise God with an open heart (EPHREM, JULIAN OF ECLANUM), and with the full consciousness of human limitation (PHILIP). According to Chrysostom, Elihu is suggesting to Job that he will soon be delivered from his afflictions through death, but he may also mean that Job is now kept away from fights and war as a sort of punishment (CHRYSOSTOM).

37:14-16 Consider the Works of God

ABSOLUTE SINCERITY AND LOVE. GREGORY THE GREAT: There are some who consider the wondrous works of God, but then they lie down, rather than standing up by acting rightly. They do not follow and respect the power of his doings. This is why Paul also said, "Let him who thinks he stands take heed lest he falls."[1] They often indeed admire the judgments of heaven. They love the announcements of their heavenly country when they hear them and are astounded at the wondrous operations of his inward ordaining. But [they] still neglect to attain to these words by their love and their lives. They then become idle. Even while considering in their understanding the wondrous works of God, they do not love it in their lives.

They indeed turn the eye of their minds to thinking on these things, but yet do not manifest their intentions by lifting themselves up from the earthly. . . .

Elihu therefore, who did not believe that blessed Job had maintained the life that he professed, says, as if advising him, "Stand, and consider the wondrous works of God." He still further examines him as to future events and adds, as if humbling him for his ignorance, "Do you know when God commanded the rains to show forth the light of his clouds?" If "clouds" are holy preachers, then the rain from the clouds are the words of their preaching. When clouds fly through the air, unless rain descends from above, we do not know what an immensity of water they carry. Unless the glittering sun breaks forth amid the rain, we cannot understand what brightness also is concealed within them. Doubtless, if holy preachers are silent and do not show by their words how great is the brightness of heavenly hope that they bear in their hearts, they seem to be like other people or far more despicable. MORALS ON THE BOOK OF JOB 27.59-60.[2]

37:17-18 When the Earth Is Still

REST OR PUNISHMENT? CHRYSOSTOM: Here he

[1] 1 Cor 10:12.   [2] LF 23:244-45**.

may mean, You are now in the midst of afflictions, but later you will have rest—and there is also the proof given by divine wisdom, which has foreseen death as a solution and end to human tribulations. Or perhaps [he means], even in the midst of your trials, you remain out of the fight of the war and the troubles, and he punishes you in this manner.[3] COMMENTARY ON JOB 37.17.[4]

37:19 Teach Us

NOTHING MUST BE HIDDEN. EPHREM THE SYRIAN: "Teach us what we shall say to him, so that we may not rejoice at the sight of darkness," that is, take heed that you do not hide anything from us. COMMENTARY ON JOB 37.19.[5]

37:20-22 Bright Light in the Sky

CONTEMPLATION AND PRAISE OF GOD'S MAJESTY. JULIAN OF ECLANUM: "But now they do not see the light; suddenly the sky is covered with clouds; and the passing wind will drive them away." With his words he demonstrates how they do not see the light he demonstrates with his words by saying, "Suddenly the sky is covered with clouds"; the splendor of the sun is hidden by thick clouds and a darkened sky, but it is called back for the use of mortals through the repelling

of the clouds. "From Aquilon comes gold."[6] "From Aquilon the golden-colored clouds [come], the great glory and honor of God is in them." "From Aquilon gold comes." He said "Aquilon" for the east[7] and "gold" for dawn, which imitates the appearance of the shining metal with its glowing color. "And the timorous praise of God"; certainly the service of praising him is not taken without fear because of the immensity of his fame. EXPOSITION ON THE BOOK OF JOB 37.21-22.[8]

37:23-24 We Cannot Find the Almighty

HUMAN WEAKNESS. PHILIP THE PRIEST: Certainly, he says, as God is great in power and strength, so he is true in discernment and justice and cannot be described. Therefore, since this is his nature, he cannot be found by his creature that is so weak and feeble. As a consequence great and wise people must not assume that the incomprehensible [God] can be investigated. They must not try to observe his invisible nature. COMMENTARY ON THE BOOK OF JOB 37.[9]

---

[3]Chrysostom suggests that God prevents humans from dying in order to punish them. See also Job 33:18. [4]PTS 35:180. [5]ESOO 2:16. [6]LXX. [7]Aquilon is the north wind, or simply a way to indicate the north, but here Julian interprets it as a name for the east. [8]CCL 88:98. [9]PL 26:745.

38:1-41 GOD INTERVENES AND SHOWS HOW JOB IS IGNORANT

[1]Then the LORD answered Job out of the whirlwind:*
    [2]"Who is this that darkens counsel† by words without knowledge?
    [3]Gird up your loins like a man,
    I will question you, and you shall declare to me.

    [4]"Where were you when I laid the foundation of the earth?

Tell me, if you have understanding.
⁵Who determined its measurements—surely
        you know!
    Or who stretched the line upon it?
⁶On what were its bases sunk,
    or who laid its cornerstone,
⁷when the morning stars sang together,‡
    and all the sons of God shouted for joy?

⁸"Or who shut in the sea with doors,
    when it burst forth from the womb;
⁹when I made clouds its garment,
    and thick darkness its swaddling band,
¹⁰and prescribed bounds for it,
    and set bars and doors,
¹¹and said, 'Thus far shall you come, and no
        farther,
    and here shall your proud waves be
        stayed'?

¹²"Have you commanded the morning since
        your days began,
    and caused the dawn to know its place,
¹³that it might take hold of the skirts of
        the earth,
    and the wicked be shaken out of it?§
¹⁴It is changed like clay under the seal,
    and it is dyedᵍ like a garment.
¹⁵From the wicked their light is withheld,
    and their uplifted arm is broken.#

¹⁶"Have you entered into the springs** of
        the sea,
    or walked in the recesses of the deep?
¹⁷Have the gates of death been revealed
        to you,
    or have you seen the gates of deep
        darkness?††
¹⁸Have you comprehended the expanse
        of the earth?
    Declare, if you know all this.

¹⁹"Where is the way to the dwelling of light,
    and where is the place of darkness,
²⁰that you may take it to its territory
    and that you may discern the paths to its
        home?
²¹You know, for you were born then,
    and the number of your days is great!‡‡

²²"Have you entered the storehouses of the
        snow,
    or have you seen the storehouses of
        the hail,§§
²³which I have reserved for the time of
        trouble,
    for the day of battle and war?##
²⁴What is the way to the place where the
        light is distributed,
    or where the east wind is scattered upon
        the earth?

²⁵"Who has cleft a channel for the torrents
        of rain,
    and a way for the thunderbolt,
²⁶to bring rain on a land where no man is,
    on the desert in which there is no
        man;
²⁷to satisfy the waste and desolate land,
    and to make the ground put forth grass?***

²⁸"Has the rain a father,
    or who has begotten the drops of dew?
²⁹From whose womb did the ice come forth,
    and who has given birth to the hoarfrost
        of heaven?
³⁰The waters become hard like stone,
    and the face of the deep is frozen.

³¹"Can you bind the chains of the Pleiades,
    or loose the cords of Orion?
³²Can you lead forth the Mazzaroth in their
    season,
    or can you guide the Bear with its
    children?
³³Do you know the ordinances of the
    heavens?
    Can you establish their rule on
    the earth?ᵗᵗᵗ
³⁴"Can you lift up your voice to the clouds,
    that a flood of waters may cover you?
³⁵Can you send forth lightnings, that
    they may go
    and say to you, 'Here we are'?ᵗᵗᵗ

³⁶Who has put wisdom in the clouds,ᵇ
    or given understanding to the mists?ᵇ
³⁷Who can number the clouds by wisdom?
    Or who can tilt the waterskins of
    the heavens,
³⁸when the dust runs into a mass
    and the clods cleave fast together?§§§

³⁹"Can you hunt the prey for the lion,
    or satisfy the appetite of the young lions,
⁴⁰when they crouch in their dens,
    or lie in wait in their covert?###
⁴¹Who provides for the raven its prey,
    when its young ones cry to God,
    and wander about for lack of food?"

g Cn: Heb *they stand forth.* h The meaning of the Hebrew word is uncertain. *LXX *And after Elihu had ceased from speaking, the Lord spoke to Job through the whirlwind and the cloud.* †Vg *my sentences* ‡Peshitta *and who created at the same time the morning stars?* §Vg *Did you take hold of and did you shake the extremities of the earth, and did you remove the wicked from it?* #Vg *(14-15) The seal shall be restored as clay and shall stand as a garment. The light shall be taken away from the wicked, and their high arm shall be broken.* **Vg *depth* ††Vg *Have the gates of death been opened to you, and have you seen the gloomy doors?* ‡‡Vg *Did you know that you would have been born? And you knew the number of your days?* §§The text of the LXX employed by Chrysostom reads *of the sea.* ##LXX *And is there a store of them for you against the time of your enemies, for the day of wars and battles?* ***Vg *(25-27) Who has given a course for the most violent shower and a way for the sounding thunder, that it should rain upon the earth without man, in the desert, where no mortal dwells, that it should fill the pathless and desolate land and should produce green herbs?* †††Vg *Do you know the course of heaven, and will you set down its reason on the earth?* ‡‡‡LXX *What do you want?* §§§Vg *Who can describe the reason of heaven, and who can make the concert of heaven sleep, when the dust spreads on the earth and the clods cling together?* ###LXX *(39-40) And will you hunt a prey for the lions and satisfy the desires of the dragons? For they fear in their lairs and lying in wait crouch in the woods.*

OVERVIEW: The first part of God's speech, which brings the book of Job to its logical and natural conclusion, is commented upon by the Fathers along three main lines of interpretation: theological limitation, pastoral encouragement and prophetic expectation. First, the intervention of God in his role as Creator is an image and concrete representation of his divine power, which is presented in this manner to the imperfect and limited senses of humans (CHRYSOSTOM, ISHO'DAD, JULIAN OF ECLANUM, PHILIP). Or, by addressing Job directly with his words of encouragement, God demonstrates his benevolence toward the righteous and all those who want to repent, and his scorn for the hypocrite and the proud (GREGORY, CHRYSOSTOM, JULIAN OF ECLANUM, ISHO'DAD, JULIAN THE ARIAN). Or, in God's words there is the prophetic procla-mation of Christ, the church and the redemption of humankind (GREGORY, EPHREM, PHILIP).

The Lord speaks in the form of questions, which are the best means to convince (CHRYSOSTOM). The single foundation of all things is the Lord himself (GREGORY). The restlessness of the sea proclaims his power (CHRYSOSTOM). Formed from clay and adorned with the likeness of the divine image, having received the gift of reason, humanity forgets, when swelling with pride of heart, that it was formed of the basest materials. The human mind is unable to comprehend itself, like an obscure deep, hidden from itself (GREGORY). The course of human life is regulated by the alternation of times (JULIAN OF ECLANUM). Many who are counted as faithful hear the words of life with their ears but do not permit them to pass through to the inward places of their heart (GREGORY).

38:1 Out of the Whirlwind

THE CLOUD REPRESENTS HEAVEN. CHRYSOS-
TOM: In my opinion, he has placed at this stage a
cloud over this righteous man in order to raise his
thoughts and to persuade him that "that voice"
came "from above," as [in the case] of the "mercy
seat placed upon the ark of alliance."[1] Since the
cloud is a symbol of heaven, it is as if God wanted
to place heaven itself over Job, as if he had moved
his throne near him. This is what also happened, it
seems to me, "on the mountain," when "the cloud"[2]
settled on it, so that we might learn that "the voice
came from above." Let us listen carefully, because it
is the common Master of the universe who speaks.
Let us see how he exhorts Job. Does he do it with
the same vehemence of humankind? Not at all.
Now we find a very clear solution to all the previous, disquieting questions, dear friends, which Job
asked and to which we have tried to find a solution. COMMENTARY ON JOB 38.1.[3]

38:2 Words Without Knowledge

ELIHU IS A MODEL OF ARROGANCE. GREGORY
THE GREAT: As often happens with one who
incorrectly says right words and correctly bad
words, so Elihu, in his arrogance, does not speak
right words correctly, because in his defense of
God he speaks humble sentences with an arrogant tone. So he is the perfect example of those
who, in the universal church, look for vainglory.
While they believe themselves to be more expert
than anybody else, they are accused of being ignorant by the judgment of God, because, as the
apostle says, "If one believes to know something,
he still has to learn how to know."[4] MORALS ON
THE BOOK OF JOB 28.11.[5]

38:3 I Will Question, and You Will Answer

WORDS TO ENCOURAGE. CHRYSOSTOM: Since
Job was overwhelmed by his dejection, God

encourages him with his words, so that he may pay
attention to what is said now, and he introduces
his speech in the form of questions, which is the
best means to convince. Above all, he shows that
he does everything with wisdom and intelligence,
and therefore it would have been inconsistent with
God, who did so many things with wisdom and
intelligence, to neglect the human beings for whom
he has created everything, even when they are
wretched, as in this case. "What do you say?" God
asks. COMMENTARY ON JOB 38.3.[6]

38:4-5 The Foundation of the Earth

**AN ALLEGORICAL REFERENCE TO THE
CHURCH.** GREGORY THE GREAT: In the holy
Scriptures the foundations represent the preachers. The Lord first put them in the church, and
on them the structure of the building was developed. That is the reason why the priest, by entering the tabernacle, had to wear twelve stones on
his breast, because our high priest, who offers
himself for us, giving us from the beginning firm
preachers, wore twelve stones under his head in
the upper part of his body. And so the holy apostles are the stones that constitute the main ornament of the breast and are the foundations that
make the building firm on the ground. . . . When
holy Scripture does not speak of different foundations but of a single foundation, it refers to the
Lord himself, who supports our weak and fickle
hearts with the power of his divinity. MORALS ON
THE BOOK OF JOB 28.14.[7]

38:6-7 The Morning Stars

SYMBOLISM OF THE MORNING STARS. EPHREM
THE SYRIAN: "And who created at the same time
the morning stars?" that is, those stars that also
rise and appear in the evening. But in a different
sense [we may intend], when we refer to these
stars to the substances that are separated from

---

[1]Num 7:89. [2]See Ex 19:16. [3]PTS 35:181. [4]1 Cor 8:2. [5]CCL
143b:1402. [6]PTS 35:182. [7]CCL 143b:1405-6.

our senses, their generation does not agree with the nature of angels. Therefore, we say that Christ is signified through the term *morning* and the apostles through *stars*; and the teachers, sons of the angels, are defined as participants in the angelic nature. COMMENTARY ON JOB 38.7.[8]

38:8-9 Delimiting the Sea

CREATION OF THE SEA. ISHO'DAD OF MERV: The sea is like a baby who gets out after being fashioned in the womb and is wrapped in clothes of wool. After bringing it into existence from nothing, God gathers the sea together from the place where it was and delimits, shuts and encircles it in the womb of the earth. COMMENTARY ON JOB 38.8.[9]

38:10-11 Stopping the Waves

THE RESTLESSNESS OF THE SEA. CHRYSOSTOM: He keeps [the sea] firmly within a sort of barrier, and in some perfect prescriptions of docility, as if he had given it precise commands. I have spoken, he says, and it did not reply, because that happens not only when no constraint forces it but also if the violence of an unchained power whips it quite hard. God has not allowed the sea to stand still and calm, in order that it may proclaim his power, because its nature fights against his commandments, and his commandment rules it everywhere. If water stood still, many people would have attributed its tranquility to the nature of the water; but since, in reality, it is restless and rises from inside, but without the strength to exceed its limits, its restlessness proclaims the power of God. COMMENTARY ON JOB 38.11.[10]

38:12-13 Commanding the Morning

A FORESHADOWING OF THE CHURCH. PHILIP THE PRIEST: This morning is our Savior, who is also called Sun of justice.[11] He illuminates the church, that is, the rational world, with the heat of faith and the splendor of his grace.... "Did you

take hold of and did you shake the extremities of the earth, and did you remove the wicked from it?" This earth can be interpreted as the church, about whose foundations the Lord has spoken above. In the extremities of the earth, that is, at the end of the world, sinners are destined to be removed from it. COMMENTARY ON THE BOOK OF JOB 38.[12]

38:14-15 Like Clay or a Garment

PUNISHMENT OF THE PROUD. GREGORY THE GREAT: "The seal shall be restored as clay and shall stand as a garment." The Lord made humankind, whom he fashioned after his own likeness, as a kind of seal of his power. But it shall be restored as clay, because, though he may by conversion escape eternal sufferings, yet he is condemned by the death of the flesh in punishment for the pride he has committed. Humankind, who has been formed from clay and adorned with the likeness of the divine image, having received the gift of reason, forgets, when swelling with pride of heart, that it was formed of the basest materials. Hence it has been ordered by the marvelous justice of the Creator that because he [humanity] became proud in consequence of that reasonable sense which he received, he should again by death become earth which he was unwilling humbly to regard himself. And when the spirit is summoned from the body, it is stripped, as it were, of its kind of covering of flesh; it is fitly subjoined of the same clay. "The seal shall be restored as clay." ... He subjoins what is the special punishment of the proud by saying, "The light shall be taken away from the wicked, and their high arm shall be broken," for the death of the flesh that restores the elect to their light takes away their light from the reprobate. The light of the proud is the glory of this present life, and that light is then withdrawn from it when it is called by the death of the flesh to the darkness of it own retributions. Then the high arm is there broken, because of the loftiness of the heart that has

[8]ESOO 2:16. [9]CSCO 229:261. [10]PTS 35:186. [11]See Mal 4:2. [12]PL 26:750.

been violently seized upon beyond the order of nature, and it is scattered by the weight of divine justice, which overwhelms it. MORALS ON THE BOOK OF JOB 29.21-22.[13]

38:16-17 The Springs of the Sea

A SYMBOLISM OF SIN AND REDEMPTION. GREGORY THE GREAT: "Have you entered into the depth of the sea?" The "sea" is the mind of humankind, and God enters its depths when it is roused from its inmost thoughts to lamentations of penitence through its knowledge of itself, and when he calls to its memory the wickedness of its former life and rouses the mind, which is agitated by its own confusion. God penetrates the depth of the sea when he changes hearts that are in despair. For he goes into the sea when he humbles a worldly heart. He enters the depth of the sea when he does not disdain to visit minds that are even overwhelmed with sins. Hence it is rightly added in a question, "And have you walked in the recesses of the deep?" What deep is there but the human mind, which while unable to comprehend itself is like an obscure deep, hid from itself, in everything that it is. . . . "Have the gates of death been opened to you?" From the gates of death are wicked thoughts that we open to God when we confess them with weeping in penitence. He beholds them even when not confessed, but he enters into them when confessed. He then in truth opens a way for himself in the gates of death when we have put aside evil thoughts, and he comes to us after confession. They are called the gates of death for this reason, because the way to death is always opened through evil thoughts. Which is again repeated when it is subjoined, "And have you seen the gloomy doors?" For the gloomy doors are the lurking evils of the mind that can exist within and yet not be observed by another; the Lord beholds when he destroys them by the secret look of grace. MORALS ON THE BOOK OF JOB 29.27-30.[14]

38:18-21 The Expanse of the Earth

PROOFS OF GOD'S BENEVOLENCE. JULIAN OF ECLANUM: "Where is the way to the dwelling of light, and where is the place of darkness?" He says what he had said before but more clearly, that is, that the course of human life is regulated by the alternation of times, so that at one time people dedicate themselves to work; in another time, the vigor of the body, which exhaustion had taken away, is returned to them.

"Did you know then that you would be born?"[15] These words are not said without purpose but to demonstrate that God's benevolence is the reason for everything. If you owe the fact that you exist to my benevolence, since you did not exist before, he says, how can you think that [benevolence] is denied to you, now that you live and are able to function? EXPOSITION ON THE BOOK OF JOB 38.18-21.[16]

38:22-24 The Storehouses of Snow

POWER AND PROVIDENCE OF GOD. CHRYSOSTOM: Obviously this does not mean that there exist such storehouses, but he simply shows that these elements are at his complete disposal when he wants, as if he took them from his own reserves. "And is there a store of them for you against the time of your enemies, for the day of wars and battles?" You certainly understand that he wants to emphasize their opportunity, the fact that they come at the right moment and never at random. Then he equally speaks about all the rest, that is, about rain, hail and, on the other hand, about the Notus.[17] COMMENTARY ON JOB 38.22-23.[18]

38:25-27 A Channel for Rain

THE POWER OF COMPUNCTION AND REPENTANCE. GREGORY THE GREAT: But these things that have been stated generally of the Gentile world, we see taking place, if we carefully exam-

---

[13]LF 23:316-17*. [14]LF 23:320-21*. [15]RSV, "Surely you know, for you were born then." [16]CCL 88:101. [17]The Notus is the south wind, which brings rain; hail is produced by the north wind. [18]PTS 35:188-89.

ine them, in individuals within the bosom of holy church. For there are many, grievously insensible to the words of God, who are counted under the name of faith, who hear the words of life with their ears but do not permit them to pass through to the inward places of their heart. What else are these than desert land? And that land in truth has no human vitality, because their mind is void of the sense of reason. And no mortal dwells in this land, because if thoughts of reasonable meanings ever spring up in their conscience, they do not remain there. For evil desires find a resting place in their hearts, but if good desires have ever come there, they pass away, as if urged on. But when the merciful God deigns to give a course to his shower and a way to the sounding thunder, being stung with grace within, they open the ears of their heart to the words of life. And the pathless land is filled, for while it grants a hearing to the world, it is overwhelmed with mystery. And it brings forth green herbs, because when watered by the grace of compunction, it not only willingly receives the words of preaching but also returns them with abundant increase; so that it is now eager to speak what it could not hear, and that which had become dry, even within, through not listening, feeds with its verdure as many as are hungry. MORALS ON THE BOOK OF JOB 29.53.[19]

38:28-30 Who Begets the Dew?

AN ALLUSION TO GOD AS THE FIRST CAUSE. CHRYSOSTOM: God does not want to say that it comes out from his womb, God forbid! But then what do the words about "begetting" and "womb" mean in this context? As when the author said about the sea, "When its mother begot it,"[20] he did not mean that it has a mother; so here he does not mean that [ice] came forth [literally] from God's womb, but he wants to speak about its formation and origin. . . . Why then did he constantly use here the words about "begetting"? In my opinion he wants to allude to the One who is the first and only cause of everything and to the fact that creatures were shaped even before being

completely perfected. COMMENTARY ON JOB 38.28A-29A.[21]

38:31-32 Binding or Loosing the Constellations

IMMUTABILITY OF DIVINE ORDER. JULIAN OF ECLANUM: Since in ordering the complexity of the world, Providence did not lack the collaboration of [divine] power, Job now enumerates those things that evidently are an integral part of the power of the Creator. Another interpretation: even though the amount of space between them [i.e., the stars of Pleiades] might be small, your strength will never be able to accomplish this, that is, to force them together into a single place and location, after removing whatever it is that makes them distinct. Neither will you be able to change the turning about of Arctuaus (i.e., Ursa Minor) and move it to a location or region different from the one that I have set. EXPOSITION ON THE BOOK OF JOB 38.31.[22]

38:33 Can You Establish Ordinances?

INSCRUTABILITY OF DIVINE JUDGMENTS. GREGORY THE GREAT: "Do you know the course of heaven, and will you set down its reason on the earth?" To know the course of heaven is to see the secret predestinations of the heavenly disposals. But to set down its reason on the earth is to lay open before the hearts of people the causes of such secrets. To set down, namely, the reason of heaven on the earth is either to examine the mysteries of the heavenly judgments, by consideration, or to make them manifest in words. And this certainly no one can do who is located in this [finite] life. To pass from little to greater things, who can understand what is the secret reason that a just person frequently returns from a trial not only without being revenged but even punished besides, and that his wicked adversary escapes not only without punishment but even

---

[19]LF 23:339*. [20]Job 38:8 LXX. [21]PTS 35:189. [22]CCL 88:101-2.

victorious? MORALS ON THE BOOK OF JOB 29.77.[23]

38:34-35 Can You Control the Lightning?[24]

GOD'S DIVINE ART. CHRYSOSTOM: Up to this point God divides the heavenly realities in terms of those through which he punishes us, as distinguished from those through which he benefits us. Notice how the lightnings answer. They do not really mean, "What do you want?" The text wants to signify that all creatures, as though they were living creatures, bend their ear to God. Every time he wants to show the difference in their formation, God talks about "begetting" and "maternal womb." Every time, on the other hand, he wants to show their docility and perfection, he depicts them as if they bent their ear to his call. Why did he present himself not only as a craftsman but as a father as well? This is because the art that presides over nature is quite superior to any manual art, for it is, so to speak, divine. COMMENTARY ON JOB 38.35A-B.[25]

38:36 Wisdom in the Inner Parts

WISDOM COMES FROM GOD. ISHO'DAD OF MERV: The words "Who has put wisdom in the inwards parts?" means who else [but God] has secretly put the wisdom of reason in the souls of mortals? COMMENTARY ON JOB 38.36.[26]

38:37-38 Numbering the Clouds

THE CONCERT OF THE ANGELS. PHILIP THE PRIEST: "Who can describe the reason of heaven?" It is certain that nobody can describe with words or conceive in his mind the reason of heaven or the course of stars. . . . "Who can make the concert of heaven sleep?" We can interpret the "concert of heaven" as the holy angels. They are called "heaven" because of their heavenly residency by the prophet. "Heaven of heaven for the Lord."[27] Who will make this concert of heaven sleep? the Lord says. That is, who will be able to stop and to prevent them, as if they were sleeping, from their constant praises and from singing and blessing [the Lord]? COMMENTARY ON THE BOOK OF JOB 38.[28]

38:39-41 Giving Food to the Lions

GOD'S PERFECT PROVIDENCE. JULIAN THE ARIAN: "And will you hunt a prey for the lions and satisfy the desires of the dragons? For they fear in their lairs, even as they lie in wait, couch in the woods." I do not only provide people with food, and those animals who deserve help with fodder, but I also give meat to the carnivorous and nourishment to the reptiles. I certainly do not hesitate in doing these things, nor do I consider anything unworthy of my attention. And I have placed fear in them as well, so that they may not harm other living creatures. COMMENTARY ON JOB 38.39-40.[29]

---

[23]LF 23:358*. [24]In the LXX version employed by Chrysostom: "What do you want?" [25]PTS 35:190. [26]CSCO 229:262. [27]See Ps 113:4 (112:4 LXX). [28]PL 26:763-64. [29]PTS 14:274.

39:1-30 FURTHER DEMONSTRATIONS OF JOB'S IGNORANCE

¹Do you know when the mountain goats
    bring forth?
  Do you observe the calving of the hinds?
²Can you number the months that they
    fulfil,
  and do you know the time when they
    bring forth,
³when they crouch, bring forth their
    offspring,
  and are delivered of their young?*
⁴Their young ones become strong, they grow
    up in the open;†
  they go forth, and do not return to them.

⁵Who has let the wild ass go free?
  Who has loosed the bonds of the swift
    ass,
⁶to whom I have given the steppe for his
    home,
  and the salt land for his dwelling place?
⁷He scorns the tumult of the city;
  he hears not the shouts of the driver.‡
⁸He ranges the mountains as his pasture,
  and he searches after every green thing.

⁹Is the wild ox§ willing to serve you?
  Will he spend the night at your crib?
¹⁰Can you bind him in the furrow with
    ropes,
  or will he harrow the valleys after you?
¹¹Will you depend on him because his
    strength is great,
  and will you leave to him your labor?
¹²Do you have faith in him that he will
    return,
  and bring your grain to your threshing
    floor?ⁱ

¹³The wings of the ostrich wave proudly;
  but are they the pinions and plumage of
    love?ʲ
¹⁴For she leaves her eggs to the earth,
  and lets them be warmed on the ground,
¹⁵forgetting that a foot may crush them,
  and that the wild beast may trample
    them.
¹⁶She deals cruelly with her young, as if they
    were not hers;
  though her labor be in vain, yet she has
    no fear;
¹⁷because God has made her forget wisdom,
  and given her no share in understanding.#
¹⁸When she rouses herself to flee,ᵏ
  she laughs at the horse and his rider.

¹⁹Do you give the horse his might?
  Do you clothe his neck with strength?ˡ
²⁰Do you make him leap like the locust?
  His majestic snorting is terrible.
²¹He pawsᵐ in the valley, and exults in his
    strength;
  he goes out to meet the weapons.
²²He laughs at fear, and is not dismayed;
  he does not turn back from the sword.
²³Upon him rattle the quiver,
  the flashing spear and the javelin.
²⁴With fierceness and rage he swallows
    the ground;

he cannot stand still at the sound of
    the trumpet.**
²⁵When the trumpet sounds, he says "Aha!"
    He smells the battle from afar,
    the thunder of the captains, and
    the shouting.††

²⁶Is it by your wisdom that the hawk soars,
    and spreads his wings toward the south?‡‡

²⁷Is it at your command that the eagle
    mounts up
    and makes his nest on high?
²⁸On the rock he dwells and makes his home
    in the fastness of the rocky crag.
²⁹Thence he spies out the prey;
    his eyes behold it afar off.
³⁰His young ones suck up blood;
    and where the slain are, there is he.

i Heb *your grain and your threshing floor* j Heb obscure k Heb obscure l Tg: The meaning of the Hebrew word is obscure m Gk Syr Vg: Heb *they dig* *LXX (1-3) *Say if you know the time of the bringing forth of the wild goats of the rock, and if you have protected the calving of the hinds, and if you have numbered the full months of their being with young, and if you have relieved their pangs and have reared their young without fear; and will you loosen their pangs?* †Vg *Their young ones leave and go to pasture.* ‡Vg *of the tax collector* §LXX and Peshitta *unicorn*; Vg *rhinoceros* #Vg (16-17) *It is hardened against its young ones, as though they were not its, it has labored in vain; no fear compelling it. God has deprived it of wisdom, neither has he given it understanding.* **LXX (19-24) *Have you invested the horse with strength and clothed his neck with terror? And have you clad him in perfect armor and made his breast glorious with courage? He paws exulting in the plain and goes forth in strength into the plain. He laughs to scorn a king as he meets him and will by no means turn back from the sword. The bow and sword resound against him; and his rage will swallow up the ground, and he will not believe until the trumpet sounds.* ††Vg *When he hears the trumpet, he says, 'Vah.' He smells the battle afar off, the exhortation of the captains and howling of the army.* ‡‡LXX *And does the hawk remain steady by your wisdom, having spread out its wings unmoved, looking toward the region of the south?*

OVERVIEW: In the second part of God's speech, the Fathers especially notice an instructive and edifying content that appears to be a sort of preparation for the full Christian doctrine of the New Testament. In the pastures of eternal life the faithful do not need doctors and doctrine (GREGORY). God has left things out of our reach in order that we may not admire our own wisdom when we reach our limits (CHRYSOSTOM).

The references to real or legendary animals assume essentially symbolic meanings (CHRYSOSTOM, GREGORY, PHILIP THE PRIEST, EPHREM, JULIAN THE ARIAN). The faithful soul is like the unicorn endowed with a single horn, symbolizing the ascent up the mountain with singleness of mind (EPHREM). The hypocrite is like the ostrich who so lacks affection that its young are abandoned (GREGORY, EPHREM). Even in birds of prey there is a certain reasonable wisdom that derives from the natural instinct living in each of them (CHRYSOSTOM). The eagle on the high rock prefigures Christ (EPHREM). The soul of the hypocrite never stays in the place where it fell, because, after falling voluntarily, the weight of its evilness leads it to worse and worse actions. For when pride, the queen of sins, has fully possessed a conquered heart, she surrenders it immediately to the seven principal sins, as if to some of her generals, to lay it waste (GREGORY).

39:1-4 The Mountain Goats and Their Young

NATURAL PROVIDENCE. CHRYSOSTOM: He is right in saying, "Have you protected the calving of the hinds?" Since flight, fear and anxiety are usual in this kind of animal, which never ceases from leaping and galloping, how, he says, can it not abort, so do you know how its young can be given birth at the right time? "Say if you have numbered the full months of their being with young, and if you have relieved their pangs. [Speak out if you] have reared their young without fear. Will you loosen their pangs?" This animal is timorous. How may its young ones, which cannot count on the speed of their legs, be devoid of fear? Who watches them? You see that nature never abandons them, neither the lion rules through its strength, nor is the hind abandoned. COMMENTARY ON JOB 39.1B-3B.[1]

THE HEAVENLY PEACE OF THE RIGHTEOUS. GREGORY THE GREAT: "Their young ones leave and go to pasture." Holy Scripture calls "pasture" that green place of eternity where our nourishment will never be spoiled by any drought. About this pasture the psalmist says, "The Lord is my shepherd, and I will never lack anything. In a green place, there he gave me rest."[2] And again, "We are his people and herd of his pasture."[3] And the Truth himself says about these pastures, "If one enters through me, he will be saved and will get out and will find pasture."[4] They go to pasture because, after going out of their body, they find the eternal green pastures. They go out and do not go back to them, because, after being received in that joyful contemplation, they do not need to hear the words of those who teach. And so, after going out they do not go back to them, because after escaping the afflictions of life, they do not seek to receive any longer from the doctors the doctrine of life. MORALS ON THE BOOK OF JOB 30.49.[5]

39:5-8 The Wild Donkey

REGULATED BY GOD'S WILL. CHRYSOSTOM: Then he adds, "Who has let the wild ass go free?" "Who has disposed things in this manner?" he says. "Who has established the laws of nature?" These are, he says, permanent laws that never change. This animal is strong and untamed. Even if you multiply your efforts, you will never have it under your control. "Who will destroy the decisions that God has taken?"[6] You see that according to Providence and because God wants that, everything yields and obeys us. But if he does not want us to obtain obedience, we can use every means, and it will be of no use. We will gain nothing. Therefore, why is our effort useless, even though we want to get results? That is because when we see a domesticated animal we can admire the docility in which it has been established. But God has left things out of our

reach in order that, before those things that are subjected to you, you may not admire your own wisdom and may not attribute to your capability the obedience of that animal. COMMENTARY ON JOB 39.5A.[7]

A FIGURE OF THE UNFAITHFUL. PHILIP THE PRIEST: The church is this city which is constituted by a multitude of countless nations and about which the Lord says, "The city that is on a mountain cannot be hidden."[8] Therefore, some of the Jews, by scorning and refusing it, despised the shouts of all those who announced the word of God, and when they demanded the obedience of faith, they did not listen, that is, they refused to obey. COMMENTARY ON THE BOOK OF JOB 39.[9]

39:9-12 The Wild Ox

SYMBOLIC MEANING OF THE UNICORN. EPHREM THE SYRIAN: "Is the unicorn willing to serve you?"[10] This animal, as is reported, is similar to an ox and is found in the austral regions, armed with a single horn. In the unicorn, whoever is not subjected at all to the bondage of the world is covertly represented. It is said to be provided with a single horn, because there is only one truth for the righteous. Again the human soul is compared with the unicorn, and it must be defined as endowed with a single horn if it is led by a single movement to the top. Moreover, it is said that the unicorn cannot be caught as its strength and dangerousness are extreme. However, the virgin hunter can win it, after being captured by the pleasure of beauty. So the soul is caught by the things that it has loved. COMMENTARY ON JOB 39.9.[11]

39:13-18 The Ostrich and Its Young

A REFERENCE TO THE SYNAGOGUE. EPHREM

---

[1]PTS 35:192. [2]Ps 23:1-2 (22:1-2 Vg). [3]Ps 95:7 (94:7 Vg). [4]Jn 10:9. [5]CCL 143b:1524-25. [6]Is 14:27. [7]PTS 35:192-93. [8]Mt 5:14. [9]PL 26:770. [10]See LXX and Peshitta. [11]ESOO 2:17.

THE SYRIAN: The sort of wings described here appears to signify the synagogue of those who led Christ to the cross. Indeed, who is that mother who generated many children but whose children are not hers? It can only be the one who gave birth to the prophets and brought up the apostles, who are not hers though. Indeed both prophets and apostles, after being adopted into the church, abandoned it. COMMENTARY ON JOB 39.13.[12]

AN ALLEGORICAL DESCRIPTION OF THE HYPOCRITE. GREGORY THE GREAT: For he whom the grace of charity does not fall upon looks upon his neighbor as a stranger, even though he has himself begotten him to God. Doubtless all are hypocrites whose minds in truth, while ever aiming at outward objects, become insensible within. While they are ever seeking their own, in everything they do they are not softened by any compassion of charity for the feelings of the neighbor. . . . But hypocrites do not know these gut level feelings of charity. Because the more their mind is let loose on outward subjects by worldly concupiscence, the more it is hardened inside by its lack of affection. And it is frozen by a benumbing torpor within, because it is softened by fatal love outside. It is unable to reflect upon itself, because it does not strive to think of itself. A mind cannot think on itself which is not entirely at home in itself. It is unable to be entirely at home in itself, because by as many lusts as it is hurried away, by as many objects as it is distracted from itself and scattered, it lies below, though with collected strength it may rise, if it willed, to the greatest heights. . . .

"God has deprived it of its wisdom, nor has he given it understanding." Although to deprive is one thing and "not to give" is another, yet his first expression, "deprived," he repeated by subjoining "has not given." As if he were saying, My expression "deprived" means not that he has unjustly taken away wisdom but that he has justly not given it. Hence the Lord is described as having hardened the heart of Pharaoh, not because

he himself inflicted hardness or, in accord with the demands of his deserts, because he softened it by a sensibility of heavenly infused fear. But now, because the hypocrite pretends that he is holy and conceals himself under the semblance of good works, he keeps down peace of the holy church and is therefore, before our eyes, arrayed with the appearance of religion. But if any temptation of his faith springs up, the rabid mind of the wolf strips itself of its garb of sheep's skin and shows by persecution how greatly it rages against the holy. MORALS ON THE BOOK OF JOB 31.17-26.[13]

ALL THE HYPOCRITE'S FAULTS WILL BE PUNISHED. GREGORY THE GREAT: In every step of the fall, the beginning is represented by the lighter faults that later, with the increase of guilt, become more and more serious. Here the evilness of this hypocrite is analyzed through his progressive iniquities. First, he presents himself as a righteous person, which he is not at all. Then, he scorns the righteous. Finally, he even insults the Creator. Indeed, the soul never stays in the place where it fell, because, after falling voluntarily, the weight of its evilness leads it to worse and worse actions. And so, by precipitating [the fall], it is submerged more and more deeply. Let the hypocrite then go now and seek for his own praises. Later he will oppress the life of his neighbor, and one day he will even scorn his own Creator. The more he devises arrogant attitudes, the more he sinks into atrocious punishments as a result. MORALS ON THE BOOK OF JOB 31.28.[14]

39:19-25 The Might of the Horse

A GIFT OF GOD'S PROVIDENCE. JULIAN THE ARIAN: In this passage, by exalting the horse, he shows that also this animal has been generated by his command and authority. It has been clothed with such a power that it alleviates human slowness with its speed, gives people rescue through

---

[12]ESOO 2:17. [13]LF 31:438-46*. [14]CCL 143b:1570.

flight, fights the enemies with its strength and courage and appears splendid in its armor. COMMENTARY ON JOB 39.19-25.[15]

AN ALLEGORY OF HUMAN FIGHT AGAINST SIN. GREGORY THE GREAT: Concerning "the exhortation of the captains and the howling of the army," the tempting vices that fight against us in invisible contest in behalf of the pride that reigns over them, some of them go first, like captains, others follow, after the manner of an army. For all faults do not occupy the heart with equal access. But while the greater and the few surprise a neglected mind, the smaller and the numberless pour themselves upon it in a whole body. For when pride, the queen of sins, has fully possessed a conquered heart, she surrenders it immediately to the seven principal sins, as if to some of her generals, to lay it waste. And an army in truth follows these generals, because doubtless there spring up from them importunate hosts of sins. MORALS ON THE BOOK OF JOB 31.87.[16]

39:26 The Soaring Hawk

INSTINCT DIVINELY INSPIRED. CHRYSOSTOM: How does God keep hawks hovering in the air?

How does he provide them with nourishment? You can figure out all that he said from a small number of examples! Why did he not mention beefs or rams or other animals of this kind, but only those that are useless for us and seem to exist without reason? This is in order to show that if wisdom and providence appear in useful animals, they appear even more in those that seem to be useless, because you see that carnivorous birds of prey possess a certain reasonable wisdom that derives from the natural instinct living in each of them. So . . . some of them are inclined to fight, others scent the corpses, and the vulture remains still in the air. COMMENTARY ON JOB 39.26-30.[17]

39:27-30 The Eagle

THE EAGLE IS CHRIST. EPHREM THE SYRIAN: The eagle is Christ. The high rock is the cross. The young ones licking the blood are the souls of the saints, who feed on Christ's blood flowing from his side, that blood that also the nations of the believers enjoy like young ones of the heavenly eagle. COMMENTARY ON JOB 39.27.[18]

---

[15]PTS 14:278. [16]LF 31:489*. [17]PTS 35:194. [18]ESOO 2:18.

40:1-14 GOD INVITES JOB TO SHOW HIS POWER

*[1]And the LORD said to Job:
[2]"Shall a faultfinder contend with the Almighty?
He who argues with God, let him answer it."†

[3]Then Job answered the LORD:
[4]"Behold, I am of small account; what shall I answer thee?

I lay my hand on my mouth.
[5]I have spoken once, and I will not answer; twice, but I will proceed no further."‡

[6]Then the LORD answered Job out of the whirlwind:
[7]"Gird up your loins like a man;
I will question you, and you declare to me.
[8]Will you even put me in the wrong?

Will you condemn me that you may be
justified?[§]
[9]Have you an arm like God,
and can you thunder with a voice like
his?

[10]"Deck yourself with majesty and dignity;
clothe yourself with glory and splendor.
[11]Pour forth the overflowings of your anger,
and look on every one that is proud, and

abase him.
[12]Look on every one that is proud, and bring
him low;
and tread down the wicked where they
stand.
[13]Hide them all in the dust together;
bind their faces in the world below."[n]
[14]Then will I also acknowledge to you,
that your own right hand can give you
victory."

n Heb *hidden place*   *In the Vg Job 40:1-5 is numbered 39:31-35.   †Vg *Does he who contends with God so easily remain quiet? He that reproves God ought certainly also to answer him.*   ‡LXX (4-5) *Why do I yet plead? Being rebuked even while reproving the Lord, hearing such things, whereas I am nothing, and what shall I answer to these arguments? I will lay my hand upon my mouth. I have spoken once; but I will not do so a second time.*   §LXX *Do not set aside my judgment, and do you think that I have dealt with you in any other way, than that you might appear to be righteous?*

OVERVIEW: The third part of God's speech, which covers Job 40, is mostly interpreted by the Fathers in a moral sense. The edifying and instructive purpose of the divine words is now essentially referred to in the sphere of the personal and ethical behavior of each individual. God expects humility from human beings, and his benevolence is the support of the humble and the righteous (GREGORY, JULIAN THE ARIAN, CHRYSOSTOM, ORIGEN, JULIAN OF ECLANUM).

Job did not speak as he did in order to condemn others but to show God's righteousness (CHRYSOSTOM). Even while losing his riches, Job praised the One who gave him afflictions (ORIGEN). One who carefully weighs the good qualities of others illumines his own deeds by a powerful ray of humility (GREGORY). It is necessary to kneel down instead of looking at the face of One so powerful as the Lord (JULIAN THE ARIAN). The "arm" of God does not refer to a corporeal feature, but as a figure that the almighty God humbles himself to our context to suggest to us sublime truths (GREGORY).

40:1-2 A Faultfinder Must Answer God

AN INVITATION TO HUMILITY. GREGORY THE

GREAT: But we know that one who, even when acting rightly, forgets to see the virtues of his betters, extinguishes the eye of his heart by the darkness of pride. But, on the other hand, one who carefully weighs the good qualities of others enlightens his own deeds by a powerful ray of humility, because when he sees the things he has done himself done by others also, and he keeps down that swelling of pride that strives to break forth from within from singularity. Hence it is said by the voice of God to Elijah, when thinking that he was solitary, "I have left me seven thousand men who have not bent their knees before Baal."[1] This was said so that by learning he did not remain solitary, that he might avoid the boasting of pride that might arise in him from his personal uniqueness. Blessed Job, therefore, is not blamed for having done anything perversely, but he is informed of the good deeds of others besides, in order that while he considers that he has others also equal to him, he may humbly submit himself to him who is specially the Highest. MORALS ON THE BOOK OF JOB 31.107.[2]

40:3-5 What Shall I Answer You?

[1] 1 Kings 19:18.   [2] LF 31:504-5*.

JOB'S HUMILITY. JULIAN THE ARIAN: I have continued to look for the reason that caused my misfortune but have not put the blame on creation. Now I have nothing to reply about what was said. I will keep silent, and after speaking once, I will not speak a second time. Indeed, it is necessary to kneel down instead of looking at the face of such a powerful Lord. COMMENTARY ON JOB 40.3-5.[3]

40:6-8 I Will Question You

PURPOSE OF JOB'S TRIALS. CHRYSOSTOM: Either he speaks here about his present intervention, as if to say, "I do not speak so in order to condemn you but to show that you are righteous"; or he wants to speak about his trial by calling intervention his approval. This means, "Do not think that I managed things in this manner for any other reason." He did not say, "In order that you might be righteous" but "that you might appear to be righteous," as you actually were, so that you might teach others. Finally, he may want to speak about his present intervention, as if to say, "If I said it, it is in order that you might appear to be righteous after the words that I had expressed, not in order to condemn you." Then he places again before him his power and his hatred for the wicked, because I am not only powerful, he says, but I act and use my power against the wicked. COMMENTARY ON JOB 40.8.[4]

THE PERFECT BENEVOLENCE OF GOD. ORIGEN: "I will question you, and you answer me." The perfect rewards of the struggles are reserved after this life to those who fought bravely. The grace of God nevertheless offers a sort of pledge to the athletes. For this reason, Job faced the hardest fights; while losing his riches, he praised him who gave him these afflictions. After losing his children, he glorified him who had taken them away. While realizing that worms grew out of his body, he was not defeated by his diseases. God gave him the firstlings and the pledge of his fights by speaking to him out of the clouds and the whirlwind. After he had listened to the former speeches, when it was necessary to speak to God, he was silent, as if he had no faculty to speak to him. In fact, he did not know yet what would have been written by Moses, "Moses spoke, and God answered him with a voice."[5] Therefore, he was like someone who did not know that he did not want to answer God. But God conceded him forgiveness to speak. The benevolence of God is such that he does not play the role of the judge but that of the lawyer, who discusses the case with a man. FRAGMENTS ON JOB 28.7.[6]

40:9 Are You Like God?

CONCRETE WORDS LEADING TO SUBLIME TRUTHS. GREGORY THE GREAT: When there is a reference to the voice or the "arm" [power] of God, we must be very careful not to attribute to him any corporeal feature. To enclose into corporeal dimensions him who cannot be circumscribed and fills and embraces everything would mean to fall into the heresy of the Anthropomorphites.[7] But the almighty God, drawing us toward his condition, humiliates himself to our context, and in order to suggest to us sublime truths, he lowers himself to the humble ones. Therefore the soul of the little ones, being led by well-known models, rises to look for what is unknown, and moves with firm steps towards the Most High. MORALS ON THE BOOK OF JOB 32.7.[8]

40:10-11 Pour Out Your Anger

SMALLNESS OF HUMAN NATURE. CHRYSOSTOM: The thunder and all the rest exist not in order to impress but so that God may be known. See with how many arguments he convinces him that his nature is small. He does not say to him, "You are small, but, I am great, and you cannot do what I do." COMMENTARY ON JOB 40.11-12.[9]

---

[3]PTS 14:280. [4]PTS 35:195. [5]Ex 19:19. [6]PTS 53:321. [7]The Anthropomorphites or Audians (from Audius, their founder) were a heretical sect that originated in Syria and Mesopotamia in the fourth century. After being condemned by Constantine, they survived until the end of the fifth century. [8]CCL 143b:1631. [9]PTS 35:195.

AN EXHORTATION TO FIGHT AND DEFEAT THE DEVIL. ORIGEN: A slanderer conspired against you. Sometimes he said to me, "Stretch out your hand now."[10] He said to me, "Touch all that he has,"[11] and he added about you that "you would have cursed me to my face."[12] But, on the contrary, you were victorious. Therefore I say to you, "Clothe yourself with glory. Abase the slanderer completely. Humiliate his angels. He was arrogant against you, but you destroy the arrogant. He was impious against you, but you strike him by lightning." FRAGMENTS ON JOB 28.21.[13]

WORDS SPOKEN WITH AFFECTION. JULIAN OF ECLANUM: These words are not spoken with an offended mind but with zealous affection, so that they may be useful in consoling and instructing him and that he may understand that to perform such a great judgment is beyond human strength. "Then I will also acknowledge you that your own right hand can give you victory." If you could play the role of such a judge, as I described it in my speech, evidently you would not need any further help. EXPOSITION ON THE BOOK OF JOB 40.6-9.[14]

40:12-14 Tread on the Wicked

---

[10]Job 1:11. [11]Job 1:11. [12]Job 1:11. [13]PTS 53:327. [14]CCL 88:104.

40:15-24 THE BEHEMOTH

[15]Behold, Behemoth,°
  which I made as I made you;*
  he eats grass like an ox.
[16]Behold, his strength in his loins,†
  and his power in the muscles‡ of his belly.
[17]He makes his tail stiff like a cedar;
  the sinews of his thighs are knit together.
[18]His bones are tubes of bronze,
  his limbs like bars of iron.§

[19]He is the first of the works^p of God;
  let him who made him bring near
  his sword!^#

[20]For the mountains yield food for him
  where all the wild beasts play.
[21]Under the lotus plants he lies,
  in the covert of the reeds and in
  the marsh.**
[22]For his shade the lotus trees cover him;
  the willows of the brook surround him.††
[23]Behold, if the river is turbulent he is not
  frightened;
  he is confident though Jordan rushes
  against his mouth.
[24]Can one take him with hooks,^q
  or pierce his nose with a snare?

o Or the hippopotamus p Heb ways q Cn: Heb in his eyes *LXX But now look at the wild beasts with you †Peshitta in its cover ‡LXX in the navel §Vg its cartilage like iron foils #Vg It is the beginning of the ways of God. He who made him provided him with his sword. **LXX (20-21) And when he has gone up to a steep mountain, he causes joy to the quadrupeds in the deep. He lies under trees of every kind, by the papyrus and reed and bulrush. ††Peshitta The shadows surround it, and the crows of the torrent surround it.

OVERVIEW: The section of God's speech that covers Job 40:15-24 is a lively depiction of the Behemoth. Most of the Fathers accept the idea of the real existence of this animal (EPHREM, ISHO'DAD, ORIGEN) but especially underline, in their comments on its nature, the symbolic meaning that such an animal assumes. The Behemoth is for some a monster created to inspire the fear of God (JULIAN OF ECLANUM, CHRYSOSTOM) or a representation of devil, who must be opposed and defeated by the righteous (ISHO'DAD, PHILIP, GREGORY). The mercy of the Creator has set a limit to the power of the Behemoth (GREGORY). God has not created such enormous beasts to show what is useful for us, but what is done according to his will (CHRYSOSTOM).

40:15 Look at Behemoth

NATURE OF THE BEHEMOTH. EPHREM THE SYRIAN: The Behemoth is a dragon, that is, a land animal, just as the Leviathan is an aquatic sea animal. COMMENTARY ON JOB 40.15.[1]

IS THE BEHEMOTH REAL OR IMAGINARY? ISHO'DAD OF MERV: The Behemoth is a dragon without equal. The Interpreter[2] calls it "an imaginary dragon" that the author [of the book of Job] has poetically invented by himself. He has reported many statements in the name of Job, of his friends and in the name of God himself that are not appropriate to them, that appear to be unlikely. In the whole creation, he says, there is no animal that is unique and not male or female, because all animals have been created in pairs. On the other hand, those who assert that this book was written by the divine Moses maintain the reality of the Behemoth.[3] It is a figure of Satan, they say, and as this animal destroys everything it sees, so Satan does the same thing secretly, and therefore it has been made Satan's accomplice in crime. Both in its name and in its action it is the figure of Satan, because, according to the sense of the word, Behemoth means "through it death," that is, death has entered among people through it. But the Jews assert that it is an ox, and, some day they will eat it and the Leviathan as well when they come back.[4] COMMENTARY ON JOB 40.10(15).[5]

CREATED FOR THE EDIFICATION OF HUMANKIND. JULIAN OF ECLANUM: Through the cre-

ation of such a hateful and tremendous beast people are given three opportunities of edification. They can recognize that the power of the Creator did not only make those beasts that would have served human beings but also fashioned those who frighten them; they can understand the goodness of Providence, because it removed those beasts that would have been deadly from the midst [of humans] and placed them in the wilderness. There they can learn how severe he is against vices. These [beasts] that are troublesome to mortals according to their size and strength are also subject to his regulation. EXPOSITION ON THE BOOK OF JOB 40.10.[6]

40:16-19 Its Strength and Power

STRENGTH OF THE BEHEMOTH. ISHO'DAD OF MERV: The words "its strength is in its cover" [mean] its strength and vigor are precisely in the animal itself. Animals usually take shelter in different places, but [the author] says this animal does not need a shelter at all. COMMENTARY ON JOB 40.16.[7]

AN ALLEGORY OF THE DEVIL ENSLAVING CARNAL PEOPLE. PHILIP THE PRIEST: "It makes its tail stiff like a cedar." It seems to me that this is said because not even in the end—which is signified by "its tail"—will it return to God. On the contrary, being arrogant and impious in its tyranny, it will never repent. Therefore, since it is exalted like a high cedar, it is destined to be destroyed and annihilated by the voice of the Lord, who judges righteously. . . . "The sinews of its thighs are knit together." I believe that through the image of the sinews, which are very strong and insoluble, he describes the pleasures through which it enchains carnal per-

---

[1]ESOO 2:18. [2]That is, Theodore of Mopsuestia. Isho'dad is referring to a lost work by Theodore. [3]Henana is among these authors. See page 150, footnote 16. [4]That is, when they rise from the dead, according to the Talmud. [5]CSCO 229:265. [6]CCL 88:104-5. [7]CSCO 229:263. See also Origen Fragments on Job 28.40 (PTS 53:332).

sons. Commentary on the Book of Job 40.[8]

The Absolute Evilness of the Devil.
Philip the Priest: "Its bones are tubes of
bronze, its cartilage like iron foils." Through
these names of limbs it is signified that the devil
is hard, harsh and inflexible with his subjects.
Indeed, in the bones and the cartilage, that is,
inside and outside, in words and actions, his
absolute malice is clearly displayed. Commentary on the Book of Job 40.[9]

Limited by God's Providence. Gregory
the Great: "This is the beginning of the ways of
God. He who made him provided him with his
sword." The sword of this Behemoth is his own
malice in inflicting harm. But he who made him
good in his nature[10] provided him with his sword,
because, according to divine will, his malice is
limited, so that he is not allowed to strike human
beings as much as he would like to. Now, if our
enemy can do much but strikes less, this is due to
the fact that the mercy of our Creator sets a limit
to his sword. Therefore, [the devil] hides inside
his conscience, and his malice, through which he
makes people die, does not exceed the proper limits set by God. Morals on the Book of Job
32.50.[11]

40:20-24 Under the Lotus Plants

Monsters That Lead to the Knowledge

of God. Chrysostom: "And when he has gone
up to a steep mountain, he causes joy to the quadrupeds in the deep." This means the wild animals
have raised their heads only when this animal has
withdrawn to the mountains. If [God] has created these two enormous beasts,[12] he did so in
order that you might know that he may create all
of them according to their own type. But God
does not do so because his creation is oriented to
provide what is useful to you. Notice how these
beasts observe their proper laws: they haunt that
part of the sea which is not navigable. But one
may ask, What is their use? We ignore what is the
mysterious utility of these monsters, but, if we
want to take the risk of an explanation, we may
say that they lead toward the knowledge of God.
Commentary on Job 40.20.[13]

An Extraordinary Size. Isho'dad of Merv:
The words "the shadows surround it." Because of
the size of the animal, [the author says], anywhere it goes, it casts shadows around it. The
words "the crows like a torrent surround it."
[This is said] because the habit of these birds is
to approach and croak anytime they see something terrifying. Commentary on Job 40.22.[14]

---

[8]PL 26:783. [9]PL 26:783. [10]Gregory refers to the fact that the devil
was good at the beginning and was the prince of the angels. [11]CCL
143b:1668. [12]Gregory refers to the Behemoth and the Leviathan,
which is described in Job 41. [13]PTS 35:196. [14]CSCO 229:263.

41:1-34 GOD'S POWER RULES THE LEVIATHAN AND ALL CREATURES

[1r]*Can you draw out Leviathan[s] with a
fishhook,
or press down* his tongue with a cord?*
[2]*Can you put a rope in his nose,
or pierce his jaw with a hook?[†]*
[3]*Will he make many supplications to you?*

Will he speak to you soft words?[‡]
[4]Will he make a covenant with you
    to take him for your servant for ever?
[5]Will you play with him as with a bird,
    or will you put him on leash for your
      maidens?
[6]Will traders bargain over him?
    Will they divide him up among the
      merchants?
[7]Can you fill his skin with harpoons,
    or his head with fishing spears?[§]
[8]Lay hands on him;
    think of the battle; you will not do
      it again![#]
[9t]Behold, the hope of a man is disappointed;
    he is laid low even at the sight of him.[**]
[10]No one is so fierce that he dares to stir
      him up.
    Who then is he that can stand before me?
[11]Who has given to me,[u] that I should repay
      him?
    Whatever is under the whole heaven
      is mine.

[12]I will not keep silence concerning
      his limbs,
    or his mighty strength, or his goodly
      frame.
[13]Who can strip off his outer garment?
    Who can penetrate his double coat of
      mail?[v†]
[14]Who can open the doors of his face?
    Round about his teeth is terror.
[15]His back[w] is made of rows of shields,
    shut up closely as with a seal.
[16]One is so near to another
    that no air can come between them.
[17]They are joined one to another;
    they clasp each other and cannot be

separated.
[18]His sneezings flash forth light,
    and his eyes are like the eyelids of
      the dawn.
[19]Out of his mouth go flaming torches;
    sparks of fire leap forth.
[20]Out of his nostrils comes forth smoke,
    as from a boiling pot and burning rushes.
[21]His breath kindles coals,
    and a flame comes forth from his mouth.
[22]In his neck abides strength,
    and terror dances before him.
[23]The folds of his flesh cleave together,
    firmly cast upon him and immovable.
[24]His heart is hard as a stone,
    hard as the nether millstone.
[25]When he raises himself up the mighty[x]
      are afraid;
    at the crashing they are beside themselves.
[26]Though the sword reaches him, it does
      not avail;
    nor the spear, the dart, or the javelin.[‡‡]
[27]He counts iron as straw,
    and bronze as rotten wood.
[28]The arrow cannot make him flee;
    for him slingstones are turned to stubble.
[29]Clubs are counted as stubble;
    he laughs at the rattle of javelins.
[30]His underparts are like sharp potsherds;
    he spreads himself like a threshing sledge
      on the mire.
[31]He makes the deep boil like a pot;
    he makes the sea like a pot of ointment.
[32]Behind him he leaves a shining wake;
    one would think the deep to be hoary.[§§]
[33]Upon earth there is not his like,
    a creature without fear.[##]
[34]He beholds everything that is high;
    he is king over all the sons of pride.

r Ch 40.25 in Heb   s Or the crocodile   t Ch 41.1 in Heb   u The meaning of the Hebrew is uncertain   v Gk: Heb bridle   w Cn Compare Gk Vg: Heb pride   x Or gods   *Vg bind   †Vg a ring in his nostrils, or pierce his jaw with a bracelet?   ‡In the text of the LXX, Vg and Peshitta the first eight verses of Job 41 are attached to Job 40. In the text of the Peshitta, the passage at Job 41:2 and Job 41:3 reads And who will prevent me from giving my retribution? For all that is under heaven belongs to me. And I will not be silent.   §Vg Will you fill nets with its skin and the cabin of fish with its head? LXX And all the ships come together would not be able to bear the mere skin of his tail; neither shall they carry his head in fishing-vessels.   #LXX But you shall lay your hand upon him once, remembering the war that is waged by his mouth; and let it not be done any more.   **Vg Behold, his hope will be disappointed, and before everybody's eyes he will fall down.   ††Vg Who will uncover the face of its garment, and who will enter into the midst of its mouth?   ‡‡Vg (25-26) When it is taken away, the angels will fear and, being frightened, will be purified. When the sword reaches it, neither a spear nor a shield will succor him.   §§LXX (31-32) He makes the deep boil like a brazen caldron; and he regards the sea as a pot of ointment, and the lowest part of the deep as a captive, he reckons the deep as his range.   ##Vg A path will shine after it, and it will esteem the deep as growing old. There is no power on earth that can be compared to it which was made to fear no one.

OVERVIEW: Job 41 is constituted by a long, detailed depiction of the Leviathan. All the Fathers agree in seeing in this monstrous animal a symbolic representation of the devil. They analyze this depiction along three main lines of interpretation: in the first place, the Leviathan reveals in its physical features all the spiritual characters of malice and evilness of the devil (GREGORY, ORIGEN, OLYMPIODORUS); in the second, the Leviathan appears to represent evilness in its different manifestations among humankind (GREGORY, ORIGEN, OLYMPIODORUS, JULIAN OF ECLANUM); in the third, the Leviathan, which is subject to the power of God and destined to be defeated by Christ, symbolizes victory over evil through the grace of Christ (GREGORY, OLYMPIODORUS, ORIGEN, JULIAN THE ARIAN, EPHREM, PHILIP).

A ring is put into the Leviathan's nostrils when its cunning is restrained so as not to prevail against the weakness of humanity (GREGORY).

It is pictured as a quadruped (Behemoth) deprived of reason because of the foolishness of its impure behavior, a dragon (Leviathan) because of the malice through which it causes harm, a bird because of the agility of its spiritual nature (GREGORY).

People using bodies or ships cannot by themselves lift a single piece of the skin of the Leviathan's tail, but with divine favor they can bear not only a piece of the skin of his tail but also his entire body, and mortify it (ORIGEN). In the end this cruel beast will in eternity be brought among the faithful in chains (EPHREM), and together with its body, all the wicked will be condemned (JULIAN THE ARIAN). Meanwhile it presents itself to some as more manifestly wicked, as though they were its friends; but to others it covers itself with a cloak of attractiveness, as if they were strangers, to conceal beneath the cover of a good action the evil that it cannot actually accomplish (GREGORY). Those whom a similar guilt associates with one another, the same perverse defensiveness crowds them together in obstinate agreement, that they may protect each other with mutual defense for their sins (GREGORY, OLYMPIODORUS).

The dragon wears a mask of virtue for any vice (ORIGEN). But the demonic always overestimates itself (OLYMPIODORUS). This ancient deceiver, therefore, in the minds of the wicked that it binds up, makes light of future punishments, as if they were bound by a terminal limit (GREGORY).

41:1-2 Can You Control Leviathan?

GOD'S POWER OVER THE DEVIL. GREGORY THE GREAT: "Can you put a ring in its nose?" As stratagems are signified by "nostrils," so by a "ring" is designated the omnipotence of divine power. For when it keeps us from being seized by temptations, it encircles around and holds firm in wondrous ways the snares of the ancient enemy. A ring is therefore put into its nostrils when by the strength of heavenly protection drawn around us, its cunning is restrained so as not to prevail against the weakness of humanity, as far as it secretly searches out its fatal arguments. . . . "Or can you pierce its jaw with a bracelet?" . . . The Lord therefore bores through the jaw of this Leviathan with a bracelet, because by the ineffable power of his mercy he so thwarts the malice of the ancient enemy that he sometimes loses even those whom it has seized, and they, as it were, fall from its mouth, who, after the commission of sin, return to innocence. Who, once seized by its mouth, would escape his jaw, if it were not bored through? Did it not seize Peter in his mouth when he denied? Did it not seize David in its mouth when he plunged himself into such a gulf of lust? But when they returned, each of them through penitence to life, this Leviathan let them escape, as it were, through the holes of his jaws. Those therefore are withdrawn from its mouth through the hole of its jaw who after the perpetration of such great wickedness have come back with penitence. MORALS ON THE BOOK OF JOB 33.21-22.[1]

41:3-4 Will It Speak Gently to You?

THE DEVIL'S HUMILIATION. OLYMPIODORUS: He said this because the demons asked the Lord not to cast them into the abyss,[2] or because Satan said to Christ, "I will give you all these things."[3] Will he now, he says, implore you with a soft speech? Will he make a covenant with you, and will he stop fighting his war against you? COMMENTARY ON JOB 40.22-23.[4]

41:5-6 Will You Treat It As a Pet?

THE CHARACTERS OF THE DEVIL. GREGORY THE GREAT: Why is our enemy first called Behemoth, then Leviathan and finally is compared to a bird that God plays with in order to destroy it? Behemoth, as we have said, means "a huge beast," a quadruped that eats grass like an ox. The Leviathan appears to be a serpent of the sea, because it is caught by hook. But now it takes on the guise of a bird, when God says, "Will you play with it as with a bird?" Let us see why it is called huge beast, dragon and bird. We can immediately understand the meaning of these names by examining the malice of his schemes. From heaven he descended on earth and cannot rise anymore on high as he has no aspiration to the hope of getting heavenly goods.

Therefore, it is a quadruped deprived of reason because of the foolishness of its impure behavior, a dragon because of the malice through which it causes harm, a bird because of the agility of its spiritual nature. MORALS ON THE BOOK OF JOB 33.30.[5]

41:7-9 Can You Capture It?

A FIGURE OF THE CHURCH OF CHRIST. GREGORY THE GREAT: "Will you fill nets with its skin and the cabin of fish with its head?" What is designated by "nets" or a "cabin of fish" except the churches of the faithful that make one universal church? Hence it is written in the Gospel, "The kingdom of heaven is like a net cast into the sea and gathering of every kind of fish."[6] "Will you fill nets with its skin and the cabin of fish with its head?" What is designated by "nets" or a "cabin of fish" except the churches of the faithful that make one universal church? Hence it is written in the Gospel, "The kingdom of heaven is like a net cast into the sea and gathering of every kind of fish."[7] The church is in truth called the kingdom of heaven, for while the Lord exalts its conduct to things above, it already reigns herself in toward the Lord by heavenly conversation. And the church is also rightly compared with a net cast into the sea, gathering every kind of fish, because when cast into this Gentile world, it rejected no one but caught the wicked with the good, the proud with the humble, the angry with the gentle and the foolish with the wise. By the "skin" of this Leviathan, we understand the foolish, and by "its head," the wise ones of its body. Or certainly by the "skin," which is outermost, are designated those who serve it as inferiors in these lowest offices, but by the "head" those placed over them. And the Lord observing the proper order rightly declares that he will fill these "nets" or "cabin of fish," that is, his church, and the wishes of the faithful with its "skin" first and then with its

---

[1]LF 31:575-77*. [2]See Lk 8:31. [3]Mt 4:9. [4]PG 93:433. [5]CCL 143b:1699. [6]Mt 13:47. [7]Mt 13:47.

"head." MORALS ON THE BOOK OF JOB 33.34.[8]

DEFEATING LEVIATHAN THROUGH THE VIRTUE OF GOD. ORIGEN: ["And all the ships come together would not be able to bear the mere skin of his tail."] All the ships come together are not capable to mortify the extreme and main parts of the dragon. People using bodies or ships cannot by themselves lift a single piece of the skin of his tail. But with the favor of divine virtue, they can bear not only a piece of the skin of his tail but also his entire body, and [they can] mortify it. Each of us mortifies what is in him, that is, the devil, according to the words of the apostle, "Then God will soon crush Satan under your feet."[9] FRAGMENTS ON JOB 28.85.[10]

JOB'S FORTHCOMING GLORY. JULIAN THE ARIAN: He alludes through these words to the afflictions that befell Job and to the glory that he obtains through his afflictions, and he forces the devil to liquidate his debt with humankind. COMMENTARY ON JOB 40.32.[11]

AN ETERNAL PUNISHMENT. GREGORY THE GREAT: He will fall down before everybody's eyes, because, when the Judge appears in his awesome aspect, before the eyes of the angelic legions, before the eyes of the entire court of the heavenly powers and before the eyes of all the elect summoned to this spectacle, this cruel and strong beast will be brought among them in chains, and together with its body, that is, all the wicked, will be condemned to the eternal fire of Gehenna. MORALS ON THE BOOK OF JOB 33.37.[12]

41:10-12 Who Can Stand Before It?

THE DEVIL'S FINAL DEFEAT. EPHREM THE SYRIAN: "All that is under heaven belongs to me. And I will not be silent." These words indicate the devil, whose prodigious nature is described in these two beasts, who is destined to be conquered by the power of Christ when the fullness of time will come. COMMENTARY ON JOB 41.2-3.[13]

41:13 Leviathan's Double Coat of Mail?

THE FALSE WORDS OF THE DEVIL. GREGORY THE GREAT: "Who will uncover the face of its garment?" This Leviathan tempts in one way the minds of people who are religious, and in another those who are devoted to this world. It presents openly to the wicked the evil things they desire, but it secretly lays snares for the good and deceives them under a show of sanctity. It presents itself to the one as more manifestly wicked, as though they were its friends, but to the others it covers itself, as it were, with a cloak of comeliness, as if they were strangers, in order to introduce secretly, concealed beneath the cover of a good action, the evil that it cannot actually accomplish. Hence its members, when they are unable to injure by open wickedness, often assume the guise of a good action and display themselves to be wicked in conduct, but yet they deceive by their appearance of sanctity. For if the wicked were openly evil, they would not be received at all by the good. But they assume something of the look of good, in order that while good people receive in them the appearance that they love, they may also take the poison blended with it that they avoid. . . .

"And who will enter into the midst of its mouth?" You only listen to me, who, by the discreet minds of the elect, examine the words of its suggestions and prove that they are not such as they sound. For they seem to promise what is good, but they lead to a fatal end. To enter, therefore, into the middle of his mouth is so to penetrate its words of cunning, as to consider not their sound but their meaning. MORALS ON THE BOOK OF JOB 33.44-45.[14]

41:14-15 The Doors of Its Face

THE DEVIL WEARS MASKS. ORIGEN: Why did he not say, "Who can disclose his face?" What is the purpose of these doors? "Who can open," he

---

[8]LF 31:590*. [9]Rom 16:20. [10]PTS 53:349. [11]PTS 14:289. [12]CCL 143:1707. [13]ESOO 2:18. [14]LF 31:598-99.

says, "the doors of his face?" In order to understand what is said here, let us take the example of
the actors, who wear masks not in order to show
what they are but in order to show what they want
to look like. Indeed, those who play a certain character on the scene wear masks, so that they sometimes play the role of a general or a king, and often
of a woman. Therefore, their real face is concealed,
and they do not show what they are, while only
what they want to look like is seen. The dragon
acts in the same way. He never shows his face, but
by assuming a mask in order to deceive humankind, he takes advantage of it. The enemy has
many masks and wears a mask of virtue for any
vice. And who can detect the mask that he wears?
Who can disclose and show how the dragon is
inside? Such are also his other followers, "who
come to you in sheep's clothing but inwardly are
ravenous wolves."[15] FRAGMENTS ON JOB 28.95.[16]

WE MUST FEAR GOD ONLY. OLYMPIODORUS.
This is not the fear of God but the fear that is all
around [the Leviathan's] teeth. But if you have
Christ in you, you must not be worried by this
fear. Indeed, you will fear the Lord God and will
fear no one else. COMMENTARY ON JOB 41.5.[17]

41:16-17 What Cannot Be Separated

THE OBSTINACY OF THE WICKED. GREGORY
THE GREAT: These scales of sinners are both
hardened and joined together, so as not to be penetrated by any breath of life from the mouth of
preachers. For those whom a similar guilt associates with one another, the same perverse defensiveness crowds them together in obstinate
agreement, in order that they may protect each
other with mutual defense for their sins. For
everyone fears for himself when he beholds
another admonished or corrected. Therefore, he
arises with similar defensiveness against the
words of those who reprove, because, in protecting another, he protects himself. It is thus well
said, "One is so near to another that no air can
come between them," because while they mutu-

ally shield each other in their iniquities by their
proud defense, they do not permit the breath of
holy exhortation to reach them in any way. He
added more plainly to their deadly agreement by
saying, "They are joined one to another; they
clasp each other and cannot be separated." For
they who might be corrected if divided, persevere
when united in the obstinacy of their iniquity.
They are day by day the more easily separable
from the knowledge of righteousness, the more
they are not mutually separated from each other
by any reproach. MORALS ON THE BOOK OF JOB
33.54-55.[18]

41:18-21 Light Flashes from Its Sneezes

THE DEVIL'S CUNNING DEVICES. OLYMPI-
ODORUS: Others believe that here he alludes to
the fact that sneezing has the power to purify the
brain; therefore, [the devil] transfigures himself
into light, and even pretends to be able to purify.
So [faithless] Gentiles and wizards use the devil's
power in certain rites of purification, pretending
that they have the power of the light, whereas
they are entirely full of filth. COMMENTARY ON
JOB 41.9.[19]

**THE IMPIOUS DOCTRINES OF FALSE TEACH-
ERS.** ORIGEN: I believe that all the impious teachers of immoral doctrines are properly the limbs of
the dragon. What are the names, if you want to
listen, of the limbs of the dragon? The mouth of
the dragon can be metaphorically interpreted as
the main limb, because all the dangerous speeches
come from it. "From his mouth go flaming
torches." From it you hear the insulting speech
under the guise of Christianity, the speech vilify-
ing the Creator, or on the other hand that openly
supports the theories of Marcion, Basilides and
Valentinus.[20] Whenever they speak about the

---

[15]Mt 7:15. [16]PTS 53:353. [17]PG 93:440. [18]LF 31:606-7*. [19]PG
93:441. [20]Marcion, Basilides and Valentinus were the founders of
three distinct Gnostic schools in the second century. Marcion asserted
that the God of the Old Testament was a demiurge and quite different
from the God of the New Testament.

Founder of heaven and earth, whenever they assert that he does not exist and has no spiritual essence—there you will see flaming torches coming out of their mouths and sparks of fire leaping up. Therefore, let us preserve ourselves without deliberating those impious theories, so that those flaming torches may never burn us and sparks of fire may never touch us. FRAGMENTS ON JOB 28.114.[21]

41:22-24 Producing Terror

THE DEVIL'S POWER. OLYMPIODORUS: "In its neck" means in arrogant self-estimation; "its strength abides," because it does not stand still but always overestimates itself. The souls that advance with a high neck (as is confirmed by Isaiah)[22] are [like the devil's] neck, because they have the power to deceive. But such a power is vain; indeed, the weakness that my Savior and Lord assumed for me, which is called the weakness of God, completely defeated that power. COMMENTARY ON JOB 41.13.[23]

41:25-26 Raising Itself Up

THE PURIFICATION OF SOULS. PHILIP THE PRIEST: "When it is taken away, the angels will fear and, being frightened, will be purified." These words can be interpreted as a reference to the time of the beginning of the world. Already at that time, the angels could know how great was the evilness of pride, when the usurper, who tried to establish a tyranny in heaven, was cast out of his fortress, and the angels stayed in the truth, where the devil did not stay. . . . Concerning the words "when the [devil] is taken away, the angels will fear and, being frightened, will be purified"—they must not be interpreted in the sense that the angels, by keeping away from the sin of pride, will become purer . . . but I think that they must refer to people, who will come into the society of angels as new angels, and after the condemnation of the devil will be purified. COMMENTARY ON THE BOOK OF JOB 41.[24]

41:27-30 Iron as Straw

ONLY GOD CAN FATALLY WOUND THE DEVIL. OLYMPIODORUS: The spiritual weapons [of humans], he says, are unable to kill him, and [the devil] considers as straw and rotten wood those weapons that cannot inflict a lethal wound on him. COMMENTARY ON JOB 41.18.[25]

41:31-33 The Deep Boils

AN ALLEGORICAL DESCRIPTION OF THE WORLD. PHILIP THE PRIEST: We infer that this sea is our world, according to an allegorical interpretation, because it is dark due to its obscurity and the excessive blindness of its foolishness. The devil inflames [the world] with carnal concupiscence, so that it may boil in its love of earthly pleasures. COMMENTARY ON THE BOOK OF JOB 41.[26]

NATURE OF THE POWER AND FEARLESSNESS OF THE DEVIL. GREGORY THE GREAT: "It will esteem the deep as growing old." . . . This Leviathan, therefore, will look on the deep as growing old [white-haired], because it so infatuates the hearts of the reprobate as to infuse in them a suspicion that the approaching [eternal] judgment may come to an end. For it imagines that the abyss is growing old in thinking that the heavenly infliction of punishment will ever be brought to a close. This ancient deceiver, therefore, in the minds of the wicked that it binds up, makes light of future punishments, as if they were bound by a terminal limit. This only prolongs their faults without any limit from reproof, and that they may not put here an end to their sins the more they imagine the punishments of sins will be there brought to a close. . . .

[In these ways] "there is no power on earth that can be compared with it." . . . For though it has lost the happiness of eternal felicity, yet it

---

[21]PTS 53:361. [22]See Is 3:16. [23]PG 93:444. [24]PL 26:793. [25]PG 93:445. [26]PL 26:795.

has not lost the greatness of its nature. By this strength it still surpasses all human things, though it is inferior to holy people, by the baseness of its deserts. Hence the meritorious recompense of the saints, who are contending against [the devil], is the more increased, the more it is defeated by [the saints] when it boasts that by the power of its nature, it has a right to rule over people. It follows, "Which was made to fear no one" [*a creature without fear*]. The Leviathan was so indeed made by nature as to be bound to feel a chaste fear for its Creator; that is to say, with a subdued and fearless fear, not with the fear that love casts out, but with fear that remains for ever and ever. . . . Even the Leviathan had thus been so created, as with joyful dread to fear its Maker with love and to love him with fear. But by its own perversity, [the Leviathan] was made such as to fear no creature. MORALS ON THE BOOK OF JOB 34.34-40.[27]

41:34 *King over the Proud*

ALLEGORICAL REFERENCES TO SPIRITUAL INIQUITY. JULIAN OF ECLANUM: This is the true description of the beast according to the faithful [understanding] of the story. There must be no doubt about their great size because of the power of the Creator. However, [these words] are also addressed to a plane of higher intellect, so that we may believe through them that something else is signified as well, and therefore the strength of spiritual iniquity may be perceived more easily in the image of the bodies. As these [beasts] are deadly for the body, so they are for human morality, and as the sin of pride must be imputed to them, so it must be punished. EXPOSITION ON THE BOOK OF JOB 41.25.[28]

---

[27]LF 31:645-48*. [28]CCL 88:108.

42:1-6 JOB REPENTS BEFORE GOD

[1]Then Job answered the LORD:
[2]"I know that thou canst do all things,
    and that no purpose of thine can be
        thwarted.
[3]'Who is this that hides counsel without
        knowledge?'
Therefore I have uttered what I did not
        understand,
    things too wonderful for me, which I did

    not know.*
[4]'Hear, and I will speak;
    I will question you, and you declare to
        me.'
[5]I had heard of thee by the hearing of
        the ear,
    but now my eye sees thee;
[6]therefore I despise myself,
    and repent in dust and ashes."†

*LXX (2-3) I know that you can do all things, and nothing is impossible with you. For who is he that hides counsel from thee? Or who keeps back his words, and thinks to hide them from you? And who will tell me what I did not know, great and wonderful things which I did not understand? †LXX Therefore I have counted myself vile and have been consumed by chagrin, and I have esteemed myself dust and ashes.

OVERVIEW: According to the Fathers, Job finally obtains justification from God when he openly recognizes God's omniscience and control over every event in human life (OLYMPIODORUS) and shows his sincere humility (Gregory) and the fullest repentance (Chrysostom). A person asks a question in order to be able to learn that of which he is ignorant; for a person to question God is to acknowledge that he is ignorant in his sight (Gregory). It is evident that the Fathers see in Job an anticipation of the fundamental virtues of Christian life. Job had not been delivered yet from his trial when he repented, but still was in the midst of his torments when he spoke so. Job now becomes priest while the visitors bring offerings. He had made sacrifices for his children; now he makes them for his friends. One who accuses the righteous will have to expiate a serious fault (Chrysostom).

42:1-3 God's Purpose Cannot Be Thwarted

Job Recognizes God's Omniscience. Olympiodorus: [Job] openly declares that he had not learned these things before but had come to know the unconquered power of God. And since God penetrates the decisions of people and understands the thoughts of all, there is nobody who can hide from his eye, which sees everything. Who is he, he says, who being sparing of words, can hide the secrets of his mind in silence, because they have not been expressed in words? Commentary on Job 42.1-3.[1]

42:4-5 Hear, and I Will Speak

The Human Senses. Gregory the Great: To hear is, with us, to adapt our ear, which is in one place, to a sound that comes from another. But with God, on the other hand, to whom nothing is external, hearing is properly for him to perceive our longings that are rising up beneath him. For us then to speak to God, who is acquainted with the hearts even of those that hold their peace, is not for us to utter what we think with the words of our throat but to long for him with eager desires. A person asks a question in order to be able to learn that of which he is ignorant; for a person to question God is to acknowledge that he is ignorant in his sight. But for God, to reply is for him to instruct with his secret inspirations the one who humbly acknowledges his ignorance. Morals on the Book of Job 35.4.[2]

42:6 I Repent in Dust and Ashes

Job Is Justified When He Condemns Himself. Chrysostom: God clearly said to him, "Do you think that I have dealt with you in any other way than that you might appear to be righteous?"[3] That was in order, he says, to make you speak as you are speaking now, and not in order to condemn you. This is a justification for all that happened before. Actually he has not been delivered yet from his trial when he speaks so, but he is still in the midst of his torments when he makes his retraction. I attach no importance to myself, he says; I am only going to present the justification of God with regard to what has happened before. I was not even worthy of that. It is when Job has condemned himself that God justifies him. And what does he say? He has said to his friends that they must expiate their guilt and constantly calls Job his servant. Commentary on Job 42.6.[4]

---

[1]PG 93:452. [2]LF 31:664*. [3]Job 40:8. [4]PTS 35:197-98.

42:7-10 GOD REBUKES JOB'S FRIENDS

⁷After the LORD had spoken these words to Job, the LORD said to Eliphaz the Temanite: "My wrath is kindled against you and against your two friends; for you have not spoken of me what is right, as my servant Job has. ⁸Now therefore take seven bulls and seven rams, and go to my servant Job, and offer up for yourselves a burnt offering; and my servant Job shall pray for you, for I will accept his prayer not to deal with you according to your folly; for you have not spoken of me what is right, as my servant Job has."* ⁹So Eliphaz the Temanite and Bildad the Shuhite and Zophar the Naamathite went and did what the LORD had told them; and the LORD accepted Job's prayer.

¹⁰And the LORD restored the fortunes of Job,† when he had prayed for his friends; and the LORD gave Job twice as much as he had before.

*LXX *Now therefore take seven bulls and seven rams, and go to my servant Job, and he shall offer a sacrifice for you. And my servant Job shall pray for you, for I will only accept him. If it were not for him, I would have destroyed you, for you have not spoken the truth against my servant Job.*   †Vg *And the Lord turned to the penitence of Job.*

OVERVIEW: In this section of Job 42 the main issue is the contrast between the figure of Job and that of his friends. Job represents the righteous in full possession of the knowledge and comprehension that is conceded by God to human beings, while his friends appear to have an imperfect knowledge and comprehension due to their pride and hypocrisy. It is evident that the Fathers see in this contrast a foreshadowing of the arguments and controversies between the Christians, the Jews and the Gentiles (GREGORY, CHRYSOSTOM).

42:7 God's Anger Against the Three Friends

JOB'S JUSTICE AND INNOCENCE. GREGORY THE GREAT: For in a holy person sojourning in this temporary state, the rule of the divine judgment has still something to judge, though in comparison with the rest of people it has, even now, something to praise. Blessed Job therefore believed that he was scourged for his fault and not as a favor. He considered that his sins were lopped off, not that his merits were increased. He is blamed for imagining that the intention of the scourging was different. Yet this intent is preferred, as seen in the decision of the inward judg-

ment of his friends who opposed him. Hence it is plainly evident how great was his justice in establishing the innocence of his doings against the arguments of his friends, since he is preferred in the divine judgment even to those very persons who defended the divine judgment. MORALS ON THE BOOK OF JOB 35.9.[1]

42:8 A Sacrifice

THE FRIENDS EXPIATE. CHRYSOSTOM: He would have not ordered that if there had been the law, but now he becomes priest, while they bring offerings. Job had made sacrifices for his children; now he makes them for his friends. See how the text shows that Job is devoid of resentment. God takes [Job's friends] as witnesses of the virtue of the man, and equally he shows the gravity of their fault through the extraordinary importance of the offering. He would have not needed such great victims if the faults to be expiated had not been so serious. He also shows that the sacrifice was not sufficient,

---

[1]LF 31:667-68*.

"for," he says, "but for his sake," I would have not healed you from your guilt. In this manner he shows that he has forgiven them as well. "I would have destroyed you," he says, "for but for his sake," "because you have not spoken the truth against my servant Job." Notice that even though they could speak with zeal as much as they wanted, they were accused just the same of saying nothing true, or rather, they did not speak with the zeal that is fitting to God. In that case, they would have been forgiven. This is also the reason why Job attacked them. Through this we learn that the one who accuses the righteous will have to expiate a serious fault. COMMENTARY ON JOB 42.8.[2]

42:9-10 God Accepts Job's Prayer

PRAYER PLEASING TO GOD. GREGORY THE GREAT: But when the text immediately adds, "And the Lord turned to the penitence of Job, when he had prayed for his friends," it clearly shows that through penitence he deserved to have his prayers fulfilled promptly, because he had interceded for others. He held that his prayers were effective for him, as he had offered them for others. The merciful Judge more favorably receives the sacrifice of prayer when it is accompanied by the love of neighbor, and one enriches it even more truthfully when he offers it for his enemies as well. MORALS ON THE BOOK OF JOB 35.21.[3]

[2]PTS 35:198-99.   [3]CCL 143b:1787.

42:11-17 JOB IS FINALLY REHABILITATED

[11]*Then came to him all his brothers and sisters and all who had known him before, and ate bread with him in his house; and they showed him sympathy and comforted him for all the evil that the LORD had brought upon him; and each of them gave him a piece of money[y] and a ring of gold.* [12]*And the LORD blessed the latter days of Job more than his beginning; and he had fourteen thousand sheep, six thousand camels, a thousand yoke of oxen, and a thousand she-asses.* [13]*He had also seven sons and three daughters.* [14]*And he called the name of the first Jemimah; and the name of the second Keziah; and the name of the third Keren-happuch.** [15]*And in all the land there were no women so fair as Job's daughters; and their father gave them inheritance among their brothers.* [16]*And after this Job lived a hundred and forty years, and saw his sons, and his sons' sons, four generations.* [17]*And Job died, an old man, and full of days.*

y Heb *qesitah*   *LXX *He called the first [daughter] Day, the second Cinnamon and the third Amalthea's horn.*

OVERVIEW: The final part of Job 42 is mostly interpreted by the Fathers in a prophetic sense. They read in the last events of Job's life a foreshadowing of the future church of Christ, and the beauty of those who are elected in Christ (PHILIP, GREGORY). It is said that Job lived before Moses (ISHO'DAD). In addition to prefigurative references, the Fathers believed that the incidents reported in Job's story were actual events of history, but hoped that the story's meaning would also happen mystically (GREGORY, CHRYSOSTOM, EPHREM, ISHO'DAD). In reporting the years of Job's life, the seven years of his temptation were not counted, since they appear to belong to a period of death more than life (EPHREM).

42:11 Job's Siblings Eat with Him

ALLEGORICAL MEANING OF "BROTHERS AND SISTERS." PHILIP THE PRIEST: When the text says "they came," this means that they were incorporated with him through faith, so that they might be gathered into the church in a single spirit, as all those who believe in God are the limbs of the church. "Brothers and sisters" denote that entire family of Jews, from whom Christ was born. But we can also interpret "brothers and sisters" as the multitudes of all nations, because [Christ] assumed the flesh from the mass of humankind and through it deigned to make all human beings his brothers and sisters. COMMENTARY ON THE BOOK OF JOB 42.[1]

42:12 Job Blessed More Than at the Beginning of His Life

THE GATHERING OF SOULS. GREGORY THE GREAT: We believe that this happened in history, but we hope that this may also happen mystically. The Lord blesses the new condition of Job more than the former, because, with regard to the receiving of the people of Israel into faith—while the present world progressively moves toward its end—the Lord comforts the pain of the holy church with an abundant gathering of souls. The more clearly it appears that the time of the present life approaches its end, the more the church will be enriched with the souls [of Jews]. MORALS ON THE BOOK OF JOB 35.35.[2]

42:13-15 Job's Daughters

THE NAMES OF JOB'S DAUGHTERS. CHRYSOSTOM: "He also had," the text says, "seven sons and three daughters." Later he gives them names that

seem to be inspired by the circumstances. He calls them "Day, Cinnamon and Amalthea's horn." COMMENTARY ON JOB 42.13.[3]

THE SPIRITUAL BEAUTY OF THE ELECT. GREGORY THE GREAT: For the souls of the elect surpass, by the comeliness of their beauty, all the human race that lives after the fashion of men on the earth. The more they humble themselves by outward affliction, the more truly do they array themselves within. Hence this is said by the psalmist to the holy church, which is adorned with the beauty of the elect, "The King has greatly desired your beauty."[4] And of him it is added a little after, "All the glory of this daughter of kings is from within,"[5] for if [the church] sought glory outside, it would have no beauty within for the king greatly to desire. And although many shine therein with the beauty of virtues and surpass the merits of others by the very perfection of their conduct, yet some, because they are not able to attain to higher things being conscious of their own weakness, are embraced in the bosom of its gentleness. These, as far as they possess strength, avoid sins, although they do not fulfill higher excellencies as far as thy desire. Yet God graciously receives them and admits them to himself in proportion to the recompense they deserve. MORALS ON THE BOOK OF JOB 35.45.[6]

42:16-17 And Job Died

JOB'S AGE AT THE TIME OF HIS DEATH. EPHREM THE SYRIAN: Scripture reports God increased by half all of Job's things, except for the children.[7] It is evident, therefore, that the length of his life was also increased by a half. If he had lived 170 years when he was delivered from that calamity, it appears that he lived for 85 years

---

[1]PL 26:798-99. [2]CCL 143b:1797. [3]PTS 35:199. [4]Ps 45:11 (44:12 LXX). [5]Ps 45:13 (44:14 LXX). [6]LF 31:696*. [7]The Syriac text says that Job's things were doubled, but from the calculations made by Ephrem it is evident that he considers an increase of a half in comparison to what he owned before.

more to the end of his life, that is, for the number of years that is the half of 170. Now, if you add 85 years to the 170 years he had lived before, you have a sum of 255. Actually Scripture declares that Job lived 248 years, therefore those 7 years that are not included in the sum were the years of his temptation. And with good reason they were not counted, because they appear to belong to a period of death more than life. COMMENTARY ON JOB 42.16.[8]

JOB LIVED BEFORE MOSES. ISHO'DAD OF MERV: If it is true that Moses knew Job, why did he never mention him in any of his works? It is evident that [Job] lived before the law, because we know that in every time, in every place and in every person, the knowledge of God exists without the need of a human instruction, as is attested by [Job's] friends, who composed a high doctrine on God. Evagrius[9] says, . . . There is no time in which virtue did not exist, nor a time in which it will not exist. COMMENTARY ON JOB 42.16.[10]

---

[8]*ESOO* 2:19.   [9]See Evagrius Ponticus *Les Six Centuries*, 1.40.   [10]CSCO 229:268.

APPENDIX
Early Christian Writers and the Documents Cited

The following table lists all the early Christian documents cited in this volume by author, if known, or by the title of the work. The English title used in this commentary is followed in parentheses with the Latin designation and, where available, the Thesaurus Linguae Graecae (=TLG) digital references or Cetedoc Clavis numbers. Printed sources of original language version may be found in the bibliography of work in original languages.

Augustine
City of God (*De civitate Dei*)   Cetedoc 0313

Basil the Great
Letters (*Epistulae*)   TLG 2040.004

Clement of Alexandria
Catena, Fragment (*see* Chrysostom *Ad eos qui magni aestimant opes* [Spurious])   TLG 2062.364

Didymus the Blind
Commentary on Job (*Commentarii in Job*)   TLG 2102.001-4

Ephrem the Syrian
Commentary on Job (*Commentarii in Job*)

Gregory the Great
Morals on the Book of Job (*Moralia in Job*)   Cetedoc 1708

Hesychius of Jerusalem
Homilies on Job (*Homiliae in Job*)

Isho'dad of Merv
Commentary on Job (*Commentarius in Job*)

John Chrysostom
Commentary on Job (*Commentarius in Job*)   TLG 2062.505

Julian of Eclanum
Exposition on the Book of Job (*Expositio libri Job*)   Cetedoc 0777

Julian the Arian
Commentary on Job (*Commentarius in Job*)

Olympiodorus
Commentary on Job (*Commentarii in Job*)   TLG 2865.001

Origen
Fragments on Job
  Enarrationes in Job   TLG 2042.073
  Homiliae in Job (fragmenta in catenis)   TLG 2042.086
  Selecta in Job   TLG 2042.057

Philip the Priest
Commentary on the Book of Job (*Commentarii in librum Job*)

BIOGRAPHICAL SKETCHES & SHORT DESCRIPTIONS OF SELECT ANONYMOUS WORKS

This listing is cumulative, including all the authors and works cited in this series to date.

Acacius of Beroea (c. 340-c. 436). Syrian monk known for his ascetic life. He became bishop of Beroea in 378, participated in the council of Constantinople in 381, and played an important role in mediating between Cyril of Alexandria and John of Antioch; however, he did not take part in the clash between Cyril and Nestorius.

Acacius of Caesarea (d. c. 365). Pro-Arian bishop of Caesarea in Palestine, disciple and biographer of Eusebius of Caesarea, the historian. He was a man of great learning and authored a treatise on Ecclesiastes.

Adamnan (c. 624-704). Abbot of Iona, Ireland, and author of the life of St. Columba. He was influential in the process of assimilating the Celtic church into Roman liturgy and church order. He also wrote *On the Holy Sites*, which influenced Bede.

Alexander of Alexandria (fl. 312-328). Bishop of Alexandria and predecessor of Athanasius, on whom he exerted considerable theological influence during the rise of Arianism. Alexander excommunicated Arius, whom he had appointed to the parish of Baucalis, in 319. His teaching regarding the eternal generation and divine substantial union of the Son with the Father was eventually confirmed at the Council of Nicaea (325).

Ambrose of Milan (c. 333-397; fl. 374-397). Bishop of Milan and teacher of Augustine who defended the divinity of the Holy Spirit and the perpetual virginity of Mary.

Ambrosiaster (fl. c. 366-384). Name given by Erasmus to the author of a work once thought to have been composed by Ambrose.

Ammonius (c. fifth century). An Aristotelian commentator and teacher in Alexandria, where he was born and of whose school he became head. Also an exegete of Plato, he enjoyed fame among his contemporaries and successors, although modern critics accuse him of pedantry and banality.

Amphilochius of Iconium (b. c. 340-345, d.c. 398-404). An orator at Constantinople before becoming bishop of Iconium in 373. He was a cousin of Gregory of Nazianzus and active in debates against the Macedonians and Messalians.

Andreas (c. seventh century). Monk who collected commentary from earlier writers to form a catena on various biblical books.

Andrew of Caesarea (early sixth century). Bishop of Caesarea in Cappadocia. He produced one of the earliest Greek commentaries on Revelation and defended the divine inspiration of its author.

Antony (or Anthony) the Great (c. 251-c. 356).

225

An anchorite of the Egyptian desert and founder of Egyptian monasticism. Athanasius regarded him as the ideal of monastic life, and he has become a model for Christian hagiography.

Aphrahat (c. 270-350; fl. 337-345). "The Persian Sage" and first major Syriac writer whose work survives. He is also known by his Greek name Aphraates.

Apollinaris of Laodicea (310-c. 392). Bishop of Laodicea who was attacked by Gregory of Nazianzus, Gregory of Nyssa and Theodore for denying that Christ had a human mind.

Aponius/Apponius (fourth–fifth century). Author of a remarkable commentary on Song of Solomon (c. 405-415), an important work in the history of exegesis. The work, which was influenced by the commentaries of Origen and Pseudo-Hippolytus, is of theological significance, especially in the area of Christology.

Apostolic Constitutions (c. 381-394). Also known as *Constitutions of the Holy Apostles* and thought to be redacted by Julian of Neapolis. The work is divided into eight books, and is primarily a collection of and expansion on previous works such as the *Didache* (c. 140) and the *Apostolic Traditions*. Book 8 ends with eighty-five canons from various sources and is elsewhere known as the *Apostolic Canons*.

Apringius of Beja (middle sixth century). Iberian bishop and exegete. Heavily influenced by Tyconius, he wrote a commentary on Revelation in Latin, of which two large fragments survive.

Arethas of Caesarea (c. 860-940) Byzantine scholar and disciple of Photius. He was a deacon in Constantinople, then archbishop of Caesarea from 901.

Arius (fl. c. 320). Heretic condemned at the Council of Nicaea (325) for refusing to accept that the Son was not a creature but was God by nature like the Father.

Arnobius the Younger (fifth century). A participant in christological controversies of the fifth century. He composed *Conflictus cum Serapione*, an account of a debate with a monophysite monk in which he attempts to demonstrate harmony between Roman and Alexandrian theology. Some scholars attribute to him a few more works, such as *Commentaries on Psalms*.

Athanasius of Alexandria (c. 295-373; fl. 325-373). Bishop of Alexandria from 328, though often in exile. He wrote his classic polemics against the Arians while most of the eastern bishops were against him.

Athenagoras (fl. 176-180). Early Christian philosopher and apologist from Athens, whose only authenticated writing, *A Plea Regarding Christians*, is addressed to the emperors Marcus Aurelius and Commodius, and defends Christians from the common accusations of atheism, incest and cannibalism.

Augustine of Hippo (354-430). Bishop of Hippo and a voluminous writer on philosophical, exegetical, theological and ecclesiological topics. He formulated the Western doctrines of predestination and original sin in his writings against the Pelagians.

Babai (c. early sixth century). Author of the Letter to Cyriacus. He should not be confused with either Babai of Nisibis (d. 484), or Babai the Great (d. 628).

Babai the Great (d. 628). Syriac monk who founded a monastery and school in his region of Beth Zabday and later served as third superior at the Great Convent of Mount Izla during a period of crisis in the Nestorian church.

Basil of Seleucia (fl. 444-468). Bishop of Seleucia in Isauria and ecclesiastical writer. He took part in the Synod of Constantinople in 448 for the condemnation of the Eutychian errors and the deposition of their great champion, Dioscurus of Alexandria.

Basil the Great (b. c. 330; fl. 357-379). One of the Cappadocian fathers, bishop of Caesarea and champion of the teaching on the Trinity propounded at Nicaea in 325. He was a great administrator and founded a monastic rule.

Basilides (fl. second century). Alexandrian heretic of the early second century who is said to have believed that souls migrate from body to body and that we do not sin if we lie to protect the body from martyrdom.

Bede the Venerable (c. 672/673-735). Born in Northumbria, at the age of seven, he was put under the care of the Benedictine monks of Saints Peter and Paul at Jarrow and given a broad classical education in the monastic tradition. Considered one of the most learned men of his age, he is the author of *An Ecclesiastical History of the English People*.

Benedict of Nursia (c. 480-547). Considered the most important figure in the history of Western monasticism. Benedict founded many monasteries, the most notable found at Montecassino, but his lasting influence lay in his famous Rule. The Rule outlines the theological and inspirational foundation of the monastic ideal while also legislating the shape and organization of the cenobitic life.

Besa the Copt (5th century). Coptic monk, disciple of Shenoute, whom he succeeded as head of the monastery. He wrote numerous letters, monastic catecheses and a biography of Shenoute.

Book of Steps (c. 400). Written by an anonymous Syriac author, this work consists of thirty homilies or discourses which specifically deal with the more advanced stages of growth in the spiritual life.

Braulio of Saragossa (c. 585-651). Bishop of Saragossa (631-651) and noted writer of the Visigothic renaissance. His *Life* of St. Aemilianus is his crowning literary achievement.

Caesarius of Arles (c. 470-543). Bishop of Arles renowned for his attention to his pastoral duties. Among his surviving works the most important is a collection of some 238 sermons that display an ability to preach Christian doctrine to a variety of audiences.

Callistus of Rome (d. 222). Pope (217-222) who excommunicated Sabellius for heresy. It is very probable that he suffered martyrdom.

Cassia (b. c. 805, d. between 848 and 867). Nun, poet and hymnographer who founded a convent in Constantinople.

Cassian, John (360-432). Author of the *Institutes* and the *Conferences*, works purporting to relay the teachings of the Egyptian monastic fathers on the nature of the spiritual life which were highly influential in the development of Western monasticism.

Cassiodorus (c. 485-c. 580). Founder of the monastery of Vivarium, Calabria, where monks transcribed classic sacred and profane texts, Greek and Latin, preserving them for the Western tradition.

Chromatius (fl. 400). Bishop of Aquileia, friend of Rufinus and Jerome and author of tracts and sermons.

Clement of Alexandria (c. 150-215). A highly educated Christian convert from paganism, head of the catechetical school in Alexandria and pioneer of Christian scholarship. His major works, *Protrepticus, Paedagogus* and the *Stromata*, bring Christian doctrine face to face with the ideas and achievements of his time.

Clement of Rome (fl. c. 92-101). Pope whose *Epistle to the Corinthians* is one of the most important documents of subapostolic times.

Commodian (probably third or possibly fifth century). Latin poet of unknown origin (possibly Syrian?) whose two surviving works suggest chiliast and patripassionist tendencies.

Constitutions of the Holy Apostles. See Apostolic Constitutions.

Cyprian of Carthage (fl. 248-258). Martyred bishop of Carthage who maintained that those baptized by schismatics and heretics had no share in the blessings of the church.

Cyril of Alexandria (375-444; fl. 412-444). Patriarch of Alexandria whose extensive exegesis, characterized especially by a strong espousal of the unity of Christ, led to the condemnation of Nestorius in 431.

Cyril of Jerusalem (c. 315-386; fl. c. 348). Bishop of Jerusalem after 350 and author of *Catechetical Homilies*.

Cyril of Scythopolis (b. c. 525; d. after 557). Palestinian monk and author of biographies of famous Palestinian monks. Because of him we have precise knowledge of monastic life in the fifth and sixth centuries and a description of the Origenist crisis and its suppression in the mid-sixth century.

Diadochus of Photice (c. 400-474). Antimonophysite bishop of Epirus Vetus whose work *Discourse on the Ascension of Our Lord Jesus Christ* exerted influence in both the East and West through its Chalcedonian Christology. He is also the subject of the mystical *Vision of St. Diadochus Bishop of Photice in Epirus.*

Didache (c. 140). Of unknown authorship, this text intertwines Jewish ethics with Christian liturgical practice to form a whole discourse on the "way of life." It exerted an enormous amount of influence in the patristic period and was especially used in the training of catechumen.

Didymus the Blind (c. 313-398). Alexandrian exegete who was much influenced by Origen and admired by Jerome.

Diodore of Tarsus (d. c. 394). Bishop of Tarsus and Antiochene theologian. He authored a great scope of exegetical, doctrinal and apologetic works, which come to us mostly in fragments because of his condemnation as the predecessor of Nestorianism. Diodore was a teacher of John Chrysostom and Theodore of Mopsuestia.

Dionysius of Alexandria (d. c. 264). Bishop of Alexandria and student of Origen. Dionysius actively engaged in the theological disputes of his day, opposed Sabellianism, defended himself against accusations of tritheism and wrote the earliest extant Christian refutation of Epicureanism. His writings have survived mainly in extracts preserved by other early Christian authors.

Dorotheus of Gaza (fl. c. 525-540). Member of Abbot Seridos's monastery and later leader of a monastery where he wrote *Spiritual Instructions.* He also wrote a work on traditions of Palestinian monasticism.

Ennodius (474-521). Bishop of Pavia, a prolific writer of various genre, including letters, poems and biographies. He sought reconciliation in the schism between Rome and Acacius of Constantinope, and also upheld papal autonomy in the face of challenges from secular authorities.

Ephrem the Syrian (b. c. 306; fl. 363-373). Syrian writer of commentaries and devotional hymns which are sometimes regarded as the greatest specimens of Christian poetry prior to Dante.

Epiphanius of Salamis (c. 315-403). Bishop of Salamis in Cyprus, author of a refutation of eighty heresies (the *Panarion*) and instrumental in the condemnation of Origen.

Epiphanius the Latin. Author of the late fifth-century or early sixth century Latin text *Interpretation of the Gospels,* with constant references to early patristic commentators. He was possibly a bishop of Benevento or Seville.

Epistle of Barnabas. *See Letter of Barnabas.*

Eucherius of Lyons (fl. 420-449). Bishop of Lyons c. 435-449. Born into an aristocratic family, he, along with his wife and sons, joined the monastery at Lérins soon after its founding. He explained difficult Scripture passages by means of a threefold reading of the text: literal, moral and spiritual.

Eugippius (b. 460). Disciple of Severinus and third abbot of the monastic community at Castrum Lucullanum, which was made up of those fleeing from Noricum during the barbarian invasions.

Eunomius (d. 393). Bishop of Cyzicyus who was attacked by Basil and Gregory of Nyssa for maintaining that the Father and the Son were of different natures, one ingenerate, one generate.

Eusebius of Caesarea (c. 260/263-340). Bishop of Caesarea, partisan of the Emperor Constantine and first historian of the Christian church. He argued that the truth of the gospel had been foreshadowed in pagan writings but had to defend his own doctrine against suspicion of Arian sympathies.

Eusebius of Emesa (c. 300-c. 359). Bishop of Emesa from c. 339. A biblical exegete and writer on doctrinal subjects, he displays some semi-Arian tendencies of his mentor Eusebius of Caesarea.

Eusebius of Gaul, or Eusebius Gallicanus (c. fifth century). A conventional name for a collection of seventy-six sermons produced in Gaul and revised in the seventh century. It contains material from different patristic authors and focuses on ethical teaching in the context of the liturgical cycle (days of saints and other feasts).

Eusebius of Vercelli (fl. c. 360). Bishop of Vercelli who supported the trinitarian teaching of Nicaea (325) when it was being undermined by compromise in the West.

Eustathius of Antioch (fl. 325). First bishop of Beroea, then of Antioch, one of the leaders of the anti-Arians at the council of Nicaea. Later, he was banished from his seat and exiled to Thrace for his support of Nicene theology.

Euthymius (377-473). A native of Melitene and influential monk. He was educated by Bishop Otreius of Melitene, who ordained him priest and placed him in charge of all the monasteries in his diocese. When the Council of Chalcedon (451) condemned the errors of Eutyches, it was greatly due to the authority of Euthymius that most of the Eastern recluses accepted its decrees. The empress Eudoxia returned to Chalcedonian orthodoxy through his efforts.

Evagrius of Pontus (c. 345-399). Disciple and teacher of ascetic life who astutely absorbed and creatively transmitted the spirituality of Egyptian and Palestinian monasticism of the late fourth century. Although Origenist elements of his writings were formally condemned by the Fifth Ecumenical Council (Constantinople II, A.D. 553), his literary corpus continued to influence the tradition of the church.

Eznik of Kolb (early fifth century). A disciple of Mesrob who translated Greek Scriptures into Armenian, so as to become the model of the classical Armenian language. As bishop, he participated in the synod of Astisat (449).

Facundus of Hermiane (fl. 546-568). African bishop who opposed Emperor Justinian's *post mortem* condemnation of Theodore of Mopsuestia, Theodoret of Cyr and Ibas of Ebessa at the fifth ecumenical council. His written defense, known as "To Justinian" or "In Defense of the Three Chapters," avers that ancient theologians should not be blamed for errors that became obvious only upon later theological reflection. He continued in the tradition of Chalcedon, although his Christology was supplemented, according to Justinian's decisions, by the theopaschite formula *Unus ex Trinitate passus est*

("Only one of the three suffered").

Fastidius (c. fourth-fifth centuries). British author of *On the Christian Life*. He is believed to have written some works attributed to Pelagius.

Faustinus (fl. 380). A priest in Rome and supporter of Lucifer and author of a treatise on the Trinity.

Faustus of Riez (c. 400-490). A prestigious British monk at Lérins; abbot, then bishop of Riez from 457 to his death. His works include *On the Holy Spirit*, in which he argued against the Macedonians for the divinity of the Holy Spirit, and *On Grace*, in which he argued for a position on salvation that lay between more categorical views of free-will and predestination. Various letters and (pseudonymous) sermons are extant.

The Festal Menaion. Orthodox liturgical text containing the variable parts of the service, including hymns, for fixed days of celebration of the life of Jesus and Mary.

Filastrius (fl. 380). Bishop of Brescia and author of a compilation against all heresies.

Firmicus Maternus (fourth century). An anti-Pagan apologist. Before his conversion to Christianity he wrote a work on astrology (334-337). After his conversion, however, he criticized paganism in *On the Errors of the Profane Religion*.

Fructuosus of Braga (d. c. 665). Son of a Gothic general and member of a noble military family. He became a monk at an early age, then abbot-bishop of Dumium before 650 and metropolitan of Braga in 656. He was influential in setting up monastic communities in Lusitania, Asturia, Galicia and the island of Gades.

Fulgentius of Ruspe (c. 467-532). Bishop of Ruspe and author of many orthodox sermons and tracts under the influence of Augustine.

Gaudentius of Brescia (fl. 395). Successor of Filastrius as bishop of Brescia and author of twenty-one Eucharistic sermons.

Gennadius of Constantinople (d. 471). Patriarch of Constantinople, author of numerous commentaries and an opponent of the Christology of Cyril of Alexandria.

Gerontius (c. 395-c.480). Palestinian monk, later

archimandrite of the cenobites of Palestine. He led the resistance to the council of Chalcedon.

Gnostics. Name now given generally to followers of Basilides, Marcion, Valentinus, Mani and others. The characteristic belief is that matter is a prison made for the spirit by an evil or ignorant creator, and that redemption depends on fate, not on free will.

Gregory of Elvira (fl. 359-385). Bishop of Elvira who wrote allegorical treatises in the style of Origen and defended the Nicene faith against the Arians.

Gregory of Nazianzus (b. 329/330; fl. 372-389). Cappadocian father, bishop of Constantinople, friend of Basil the Great and Gregory of Nyssa, and author of theological orations, sermons and poetry.

Gregory of Nyssa (c. 335-394). Bishop of Nyssa and brother of Basil the Great. A Cappadocian father and author of catechetical orations, he was a philosophical theologian of great originality.

Gregory Thaumaturgus (fl. c. 248-264). Bishop of Neocaesarea and a disciple of Origen. There are at least five legendary *Lives* that recount the events and miracles which led to his being called "the wonder worker." His most important work was the *Address of Thanks to Origen*, which is a rhetorically structured panegyric to Origen and an outline of his teaching.

Gregory the Great (c. 540-604). Pope from 590, the fourth and last of the Latin "Doctors of the Church." He was a prolific author and a powerful unifying force within the Latin Church, initiating the liturgical reform that brought about the Gregorian Sacramentary and Gregorian chant.

Hesychius of Jerusalem (fl. 412-450). Presbyter and exegete, thought to have commented on the whole of Scripture.

Hilary of Arles (c. 401-449). Archbishop of Arles and leader of the Semi-Pelagian party. Hilary incurred the wrath of Pope Leo I when he removed a bishop from his see and appointed a new bishop. Leo demoted Arles from a metropolitan see to a bishopric to assert papal power over the church in Gaul.

Hilary of Poitiers (c. 315-367). Bishop of Poitiers and called the "Athanasius of the West" because of his defense (against the Arians) of the common nature of Father and Son.

Hippolytus (fl. 222-245). Recent scholarship places Hippolytus in a Palestinian context, personally familiar with Origen. Though he is known chiefly for *The Refutation of All Heresies,* he was primarily a commentator on Scripture (especially the Old Testament) employing typological exegesis.

Horsiesi (c. 305-c. 390). Pachomius's second successor, after Petronius, as a leader of cenobitic monasticism in Southern Egypt.

Ignatius of Antioch (c. 35-107/112). Bishop of Antioch who wrote several letters to local churches while being taken from Antioch to Rome to be martyred. In the letters, which warn against heresy, he stresses orthodox Christology, the centrality of the Eucharist and unique role of the bishop in preserving the unity of the church.

Irenaeus of Lyons (c. 135-c. 202). Bishop of Lyons who published the most famous and influential refutation of Gnostic thought.

Isaac of Nineveh (d. c. 700). Also known as Isaac the Syrian or Isaac Syrus, this monastic writer served for a short while as bishop of Nineveh before retiring to live a secluded monastic life. His writings on ascetic subjects survive in the form of numerous homilies.

Isho'dad of Merv (fl. c. 850). Nestorian bishop of Hedatta. He wrote commentaries on parts of the Old Testament and all of the New Testament, frequently quoting Syriac fathers.

Isidore of Seville (c. 560-636). Youngest of a family of monks and clerics, including sister Florentina and brothers Leander and Fulgentius. He was an erudite author of comprehensive scale in matters both religious and sacred, including his encyclopedic *Etymologies.*

Jacob of Nisibis (d. 338). Bishop of Nisibis. He was present at the council of Nicaea in 325 and took an active part in the opposition to Arius.

Jacob of Sarug (c. 450-c. 520). Syriac ecclesiastical writer. Jacob received his education at Edessa. At the end of his life he was ordained bishop of

Sarug. His principal writing was a long series of metrical homilies, earning him the title "The Flute of the Holy Spirit."

Jerome (c. 347-420). Gifted exegete and exponent of a classical Latin style, now best known as the translator of the Latin Vulgate. He defended the perpetual virginity of Mary, attacked Origen and Pelagius and supported extreme ascetic practices.

John Chrysostom (344/354-407; fl. 386-407). Bishop of Constantinople who was noted for his orthodoxy, his eloquence and his attacks on Christian laxity in high places.

John of Antioch (d. 441/42). Bishop of Antioch, commencing in 428. He received his education together with Nestorius and Theodore of Mopsuestia in a monastery near Antioch. A supporter of Nestorius, he condemned Cyril of Alexandria, but later reached a compromise with him.

John of Apamea (fifth century). Syriac author of the early church who wrote on various aspects of the spiritual life, also known as John the Solitary. Some of his writings are in the form of dialogues. Other writings include letters, a treatise on baptism, and shorter works on prayer and silence.

John of Damascus (c. 650-750). Arab monastic and theologian whose writings enjoyed great influence in both the Eastern and Western Churches. His most influential writing was the *Orthodox Faith*.

John the Elder (c. eighth century). A Syriac author who belonged to monastic circles of the Church of the East and lived in the region of Mount Qardu (northern Iraq). His most important writings are twenty-two homilies and a collection of fifty-one short letters in which he describes the mystical life as an anticipatory experience of the resurrection life, the fruit of the sacraments of baptism and the Eucharist.

John the Monk. Traditional name found in *The Festal Menaion*, believed to refer to John of Damascus. *See* John of Damascus.

Josephus, Flavius (c. 37-c. 101). Jewish historian from a distinguished priestly family. Acquainted with the Essenes and Sadducees, he himself became a Pharisee. He joined the great Jewish revolt that broke out in 66 and was chosen by the Sanhedrin at Jerusalem to be commander-in-chief in Galilee. Showing great shrewdness to ingratiate himself with Vespasian by foretelling his elevation and that of his son Titus to the imperial dignity, Josephus was restored his liberty after 69 when Vespasian became emperor.

Julian of Eclanum (c. 385-450). Bishop of Eclanum in 416/417 who was removed from office and exiled in 419 for not officially opposing Pelagianism. In exile, he was accepted by Theodore of Mopsuestia, whose Antiochene exegetical style he followed. Although he was never able to regain his ecclesiastical position, Julian taught in Sicily until his death. His works include commentaries on Job and parts of the Minor Prophets, a translation of Theodore of Mopsuestia's commentary on the Psalms, and various letters. Sympathetic to Pelagius, Julian applied his intellectual acumen and rhetorical training to argue against Augustine on matters such as free will, desire and the locus of evil.

Julian the Arian (c. fourth century) Antiochene, Arian author of *Commentary on Job,* and probably a follower of Aetius and Eunomius. The 85 *Apostolic Canons*, once part of the *Apostolic Constitutions*, and the Pseudo-Ignatian writings are also attributed to him.

Justin Martyr (c. 100/110-165; fl. c. 148-161). Palestinian philosopher who was converted to Christianity, "the only sure and worthy philosophy." He traveled to Rome where he wrote several apologies against both pagans and Jews, combining Greek philosophy and Christian theology; he was eventually martyred.

Lactantius (c. 260-c. 330). Christian apologist removed from his post as teacher of rhetoric at Nicomedia upon his conversion to Christianity. He was tutor to the son of Constantine and author of *The Divine Institutes*.

Leander (c. 545-c. 600). Latin ecclesiastical writer, of whose works only two survive. He was instrumental in spreading Christianity among the Visigoths, gaining significant historical influence in Spain in his time.

Leo the Great (regn. 440-461). Bishop of Rome whose *Tome to Flavian* helped to strike a balance between Nestorian and Cyrilline positions at the Council of Chalcedon in 451.

Letter of Barnabas (c. 130). An allegorical and typological interpretation of the Old Testament with a decidedly anti-Jewish tone. It was included with other New Testament works as a "Catholic epistle" at least until Eusebius of Caesarea (c. 260/263-340) questioned its authenticity.

Letter to Diognetus (c. third century). A refutation of paganism and an exposition of the Christian life and faith. The author of this letter is unknown, and the exact identity of its recipient, Diognetus, continues to elude patristic scholars.

Lucifer (d. 370/371). Bishop of Cagliari and vigorous supporter of Athanasius and the Nicene Creed. In conflict with the emperor Constantius, he was banished to Palestine and later to Thebaid (Egypt).

Luculentius (fifth century). Unknown author of a group of short commentaries on the New Testament, especially Pauline passages. His exegesis is mainly literal and relies mostly on earlier authors such as Jerome and Augustine. The content of his writing may place it in the fifth century.

Macarius of Egypt (c. 300-c. 390). One of the Desert Fathers. Accused of supporting Athanasius, Macarius was exiled c. 374 to an island in the Nile by Lucius, the Arian successor of Athanasius. Macarius continued his teaching of monastic theology at Wadi Natrun.

Macrina the Younger (c. 327-379). The elder sister of Basil the Great and Gregory of Nyssa, she is known as "the Younger" to distinguish her from her paternal grandmother. She had a powerful influence on her younger brothers, especially on Gregory, who called her his teacher and relates her teaching in *On the Soul and the Resurrection*.

Manichaeans. A religious movement that originated circa 241 in Persia under the leadership of Mani but was apparently of complex Christian origin. It is said to have denied free will and the universal sovereignty of God, teaching that kingdoms of light and darkness are coeternal and that the re-deemed are particles of a spiritual man of light held captive in the darkness of matter (*see* Gnostics).

Marcellus of Ancyra (d. c. 375). Wrote a refutation of Arianism. Later, he was accused of Sabellianism, especially by Eusebius of Caesarea. While the Western church declared him orthodox, the Eastern church excommunicated him. Some scholars have attributed to him certain works of Athanasius.

Marcion (fl. 144). Heretic of the mid-second century who rejected the Old Testament and much of the New Testament, claiming that the Father of Jesus Christ was other than the Old Testament God (*see* Gnostics).

Marius Victorinus (b. c. 280/285; fl. c. 355-363). Grammarian of African origin who taught rhetoric at Rome and translated works of Platonists. After his conversion (c. 355), he wrote against the Arians and commentaries on Paul's letters.

Mark the Hermit (c. sixth century). Monk who lived near Tarsus and produced works on ascetic practices as well as christological issues.

Martin of Braga (fl. c. 568-579). Anti-Arian metropolitan of Braga on the Iberian peninsula. He was highly educated and presided over the provincial council of Braga in 572.

Martyrius. *See* Sahdona.

Maximus of Turin (d. 408/423). Bishop of Turin. Over one hundred of his sermons survive on Christian festivals, saints and martyrs.

Maximus the Confessor (c. 580-662). Palestinian-born theologian and ascetic writer. Fleeing the Arab invasion of Jerusalem in 614, he took refuge in Constantinople and later Africa. He died near the Black Sea after imprisonment and severe suffering, having his tongue cut off and his right hand mutilated. He taught total preference for God and detachment from all things.

Methodius of Olympus (d. 311). Bishop of Olympus who celebrated virginity in a *Symposium* partly modeled on Plato's dialogue of that name.

Minucius Felix (second or third century). Christian apologist who was an advocate in Rome. His *Octavius* agrees at numerous points with the *Apologeticum* of Tertullian. His birthplace is believed to be in Africa.

Montanist Oracles. Montanism was an apocalyptic and strictly ascetic movement begun in the latter half of the second century by a certain Montanus in Phrygia, who, along with certain of his followers, uttered oracles they claimed were inspired by the Holy Spirit. Little of the authentic oracles remains and most of what is known of Montanism comes from the authors who wrote against the movement. Montanism was formally condemned as a heresy before by Asiatic synods.

Nemesius of Emesa (fl. late fourth century). Bishop of Emesa in Syria whose most important work, *Of the Nature of Man*, draws on several theological and philosophical sources and is the first exposition of a Christian anthropology.

Nestorius (c. 381-c. 451). Patriarch of Constantinople (428-431) who founded the heresy which says that there are two persons, divine and human, rather than one person truly united in the incarnate Christ. He resisted the teaching of *theotokos*, causing Nestorian churches to separate from Constantinople.

Nicetas of Remesiana (fl. second half of fourth century). Bishop of Remesiana in Serbia, whose works affirm the consubstantiality of the Son and the deity of the Holy Spirit.

Nilus of Ancyra (d. c. 430). Prolific ascetic writer and disciple of John Chrysostom. Sometimes erroneously known as Nilus of Sinai, he was a native of Ancyra and studied at Constantinople.

Novatian of Rome (fl. 235-258). Roman theologian, otherwise orthodox, who formed a schismatic church after failing to become pope. His treatise on the Trinity states the classic western doctrine.

Oecumenius (sixth century). Called the Rhetor or the Philosopher, Oecumenius wrote the earliest extant Greek commentary on Revelation. Scholia by Oecumenius on some of John Chrysostom's commentaries on the Pauline Epistles are still extant.

Olympiodorus (early sixth century). Exegete and deacon of Alexandria, known for his commentaries that come to us mostly in catenae.

Origen of Alexandria (b. 185; fl. c. 200-254). Influential exegete and systematic theologian. He was condemned (perhaps unfairly) for maintaining the preexistence of souls while purportedly denying the resurrection of the body. His extensive works of exegesis focus on the spiritual meaning of the text.

Pachomius (c. 292-347). Founder of cenobitic monasticism. A gifted group leader and author of a set of rules, he was defended after his death by Athanasius of Alexandria.

Pacian of Barcelona (c. fourth century). Bishop of Barcelona whose writings polemicize against popular pagan festivals as well as Novatian schismatics.

Palladius of Helenopolis (c. 363/364-c. 431). Bishop of Helenopolis in Bithynia (400-417) and then Aspuna in Galatia. A disciple of Evagrius of Pontus and admirer of Origen, Palladius became a zealous adherent of John Chrysostom and shared his troubles in 403. His *Lausaic History* is the leading source for the history of early monasticism, stressing the spiritual value of the life of the desert.

Paschasius of Dumium (c. 515-c. 580). Translator of sentences of the Desert Fathers from Greek into Latin while a monk in Dumium.

Paterius (c. sixth-seventh century). Disciple of Gregory the Great who is primarily responsible for the transmission of Gregory's works to many later medieval authors.

Paulinus of Milan (late 4th-early 5th century). Personal secretary and biographer of Ambrose of Milan. He took part in the Pelagian controversy.

Paulinus of Nola (355-431). Roman senator and distinguished Latin poet whose frequent encounters with Ambrose of Milan (c. 333-397) led to his eventual conversion and baptism in 389. He eventually renounced his wealth and influential position and took up his pen to write poetry in service of Christ. He also wrote many letters to, among others, Augustine, Jerome and Rufinus.

Paulus Orosius (b. c. 380). An outspoken critic of Pelagius, mentored by Augustine. His *Seven Books of History Against the Pagans* was perhaps the first history of Christianity.

Pelagius (c. 354-c. 420). Contemporary of Augustine whose followers were condemned in 418 and 431 for maintaining that even before Christ there were people who lived wholly without sin and that salvation depended on free will.

Peter Chrysologus (c. 380-450). Latin archbishop of Ravenna whose teachings included arguments for adherence in matters of faith to the Roman see, and the relationship between grace and Christian living.

Peter of Alexandria (d. c. 311). Bishop of Alexandria. He marked (and very probably initiated) the reaction at Alexandria against extreme doctrines of Origen. During the persecution of Christians in Alexandria, Peter was arrested and beheaded by Roman officials. Eusebius of Caesarea described him as "a model bishop, remarkable for his virtuous life and his ardent study of the Scriptures."

Philip the Priest (d. 455/56) Acknowledged by Gennadius as a disciple of Jerome. In his *Commentary on the Book of Job*, Philip utilizes Jerome's Vulgate, providing an important witness to the transmission of that translation. A few of his letters are extant.

Philo of Alexandria (c. 20 B.C.-c. A.D. 50). Jewish-born exegete who greatly influenced Christian patristic interpretation of the Old Testament. Born to a rich family in Alexandria, Philo was a contemporary of Jesus and lived an ascetic and contemplative life that makes some believe he was a rabbi. His interpretation of Scripture based the spiritual sense on the literal. Although influenced by Hellenism, Philo's theology remains thoroughly Jewish.

Philoxenus of Mabbug (c. 440-523). Bishop of Mabbug (Hierapolis) and a leading thinker in the early Syrian Orthodox Church. His extensive writings in Syriac include a set of thirteen *Discourses on the Christian Life*, several works on the incarnation and a number of exegetical works.

Photius (c. 820-891). An important Byzantine churchman and university professor of philosophy, mathematics and theology. He was twice the patriarch of Constantinople. First he succeeded Ignatius in 858, but was deposed in 863 when Ignatius was reinstated. Again he followed Ignatius in 878 and remained the patriarch until 886, at which time he was removed by Leo VI. His most important theological work is Address on the Mystagogy of the Holy Spirit, in which he articulates his opposition to the Western filioque, i.e., the procession of the Holy Spirit from the Father and the Son. He is also known for his Amphilochia and Library (Bibliotheca).

Poemen (c. fifth century). One-seventh of the sayings in the *Sayings of the Desert Fathers* are attributed to Poemen, which is Greek for shepherd. Poemen was a common title among early Egyptian desert ascetics, and it is unknown whether all of the sayings come from one person.

Polycarp of Smyrna (c. 69-155). Bishop of Smyrna who vigorously fought heretics such as the Marcionites and Valentinians. He was the leading Christian figure in Roman Asia in the middle of the second century.

Potamius of Lisbon (fl. c. 350-360). Bishop of Lisbon who joined the Arian party in 357, but later returned to the Catholic faith (c. 359?). His works from both periods are concerned with the larger Trinitarian debates of his time.

Primasius (fl. 550-560). Bishop of Hadrumetum in North Africa (modern Tunisia) and one of the few Africans to support the condemnation of the Three Chapters. Drawing on Augustine and Tyconius, he wrote a commentary on the Apocalypse, which in allegorizing fashion views the work as referring to the history of the church.

Procopius of Gaza (c. 465-c. 530). A Christian exegete educated in Alexandria. He wrote numerous theological works and commentaries on Scripture (particularly the Hebrew Bible), the latter marked by the allegorical exegesis for which the Alexandrian school was known.

Prosper of Aquitaine (c. 390-c. 463). Probably a lay monk and supporter of the theology of Augustine on grace and predestination. He collaborated closely with Pope Leo I in his doctrinal statements.

Prudentius (c. 348-c. 410). Latin poet and hymn-writer who devoted his later life to Christian writing. He wrote didactic poems on the theology of the incarnation, against the heretic Marcion and against the resurgence of paganism.

Pseudo-Clementines (third-fourth century). A series of apocryphal writings pertaining to a conjured life of Clement of Rome. Written in a form of popular legend, the stories from Clement's life, including his opposition to Simon Magus, illustrate and promote articles of Christian teaching. It is likely that the corpus is a derivative of a number of Gnostic and Judeo-Christian writings. Dating the corpus is a complicated issue.

Pseudo-Dionysius the Areopagite (fl. c. 500). Author who assumed the name of Dionysius the Areopagite mentioned in Acts 17:34, and who composed the works known as the *Corpus Areopagiticum* (or *Dionysiacum*). These writings were the foundation of the apophatic school of mysticism in their denial that anything can be truly predicated of God.

Pseudo-Macarius (fl. c. 390). An anonymous writer and ascetic (from Mesopotamia?) active in Antioch whose badly edited works were attributed to Macarius of Egypt. He had keen insight into human nature, prayer and the inner life. His work includes some one hundred discourses and homilies.

Quodvultdeus (fl. 430). Carthaginian bishop and friend of Augustine who endeavored to show at length how the New Testament fulfilled the Old Testament.

Rufinus of Aquileia (c. 345-411). Orthodox Christian thinker and historian who nonetheless translated and preserved the works of Origen, and defended him against the strictures of Jerome and Epiphanius. He lived the ascetic life in Rome, Egypt and Jerusalem (the Mount of Olives).

Sabellius (fl. 200). Allegedly the author of the heresy which maintains that the Father and Son are a single person. The patripassian variant of this heresy states that the Father suffered on the cross.

Sahdona (fl. 635-640). Known in Greek as Martyrius, this Syriac author was bishop of Beth Garmai. He studied in Nisibis and was exiled for his christological ideas. His most important work is the deeply scriptural *Book of Perfection* which ranks as one of the masterpieces of Syriac monastic literature.

Salvian the Presbyter of Marseilles (c. 400-c. 480). An important author for the history of his own time. He saw the fall of Roman civilization to the barbarians as a consequence of the reprehensible conduct of Roman Christians. In *The Governance of God* he developed the theme of divine providence.

Second Letter of Clement (c. 150). The so-called *Second Letter of Clement* is an early Christian sermon probably written by a Corinthian author, though some scholars have assigned it to a Roman or Alexandrian author.

Severian of Gabala (fl. c. 400). A contemporary of John Chrysostom, he was a highly regarded preacher in Constantinople, particularly at the imperial court, and ultimately sided with Chrysostom's accusers. He wrote homilies on Genesis.

Severus of Antioch (fl. 488-538). A monophysite theologian, consecrated bishop of Antioch in 522. Born in Pisidia, he studied in Alexandria and Beirut, taught in Constantinople and was exiled to Egypt.

Shenoute (c. 350-466). Abbot of Athribis in Egypt. His large monastic community was known for very strict rules. He accompanied Cyril of Alexandria to the Council of Ephesus in 431, where he played an important role in deposing Nestorius. He knew Greek but wrote in Coptic, and his literary activity includes homilies, catecheses on monastic subjects, letters, and a couple of theological treatises.

Shepherd of Hermas (second century). Divided into five *Visions*, twelve *Mandates* and ten *Similitudes*, this Christian apocalypse was written by a former slave and named for the form of the second angel said to have granted him his visions. This work was highly esteemed for its moral value and was used as a textbook for catechumens in the early church.

Sulpicius Severus (c. 360-c. 420). An ecclesiastical writer from Bordeaux born of noble parents. Devoting himself to monastic retirement, he became a personal friend and enthusiastic disciple of St. Martin of Tours.

Symeon the New Theologian (c. 949-1022). Compassionate spiritual leader known for his strict rule. He believed that the divine light could be perceived and received through the practice of mental prayer.

Tertullian of Carthage (c. 155/160-225/250; fl. c. 197-222). Brilliant Carthaginian apologist and polemicist who laid the foundations of Christology and trinitarian orthodoxy in the West, though he himself was later estranged from the catholic tradition due to its laxity.

Theodore of Heraclea (d. c. 355). An anti-Nicene bishop of Thrace. He was part of a team seeking reconciliation between Eastern and Western Christianity. In 343 he was excommunicated at the council of Sardica. His writings focus on a literal interpretation of Scripture.

Theodore of Mopsuestia (c. 350-428). Bishop of Mopsuestia, founder of the Antiochene, or literalistic, school of exegesis. A great man in his day, he was later condemned as a precursor of Nestorius.

Theodore of Tabennesi (d. 368) Vice general of the Pachomian monasteries (c. 350-368) under Horsiesi. Several of his letters are known.

Theodoret of Cyr (c. 393-466). Bishop of Cyr (Cyrrhus), he was an opponent of Cyril who commented extensively on Old Testament texts as a lucid exponent of Antiochene exegesis.

Theodotus the Valentinian (second century). Likely a Montanist who may have been related to the Alexandrian school. Extracts of his work are known through writings of Clement of Alexandria.

Theophanes (775-845). Hymnographer and bishop of Nicaea (842-845). He was persecuted during the second iconoclastic period for his support of the Seventh Council (Second Council of Nicaea, 787). He wrote many hymns in the tradition of the monastery of Mar Sabbas that were used in the *Paraklitiki*.

Theophilus of Antioch (late second century). Bishop of Antioch. His only surviving work is *Ad Autholycum*, where we find the first Christian commentary on Genesis and the first use of the term *Trinity*. Theophilus's apologetic literary heritage had influence on Irenaeus and possibly Tertullian.

Theophylact of Ohrid (c. 1050-c. 1108). Byzantine archbishop of Ohrid (or Achrida) in what is now Bulgaria. Drawing on earlier works, he wrote commentaries on several Old Testament books and all of the New Testament except for Revelation.

Tyconius (c. 330-390). A lay theologian and exegete of the Donatist church in North Africa who influenced Augustine. His *Book of Rules* is the first manual of scriptural interpretation in the Latin West. In 380 he was excommunicated by the Donatist council at Carthage.

Valentinus (fl. c. 140). Alexandrian heretic of the mid-second century who taught that the material world was created by the transgression of God's Wisdom, or Sophia (*see* Gnostics).

Valerian of Cimiez (fl. c. 422-439). Bishop of Cimiez. He participated in the councils of Riez (439) and Vaison (422) with a view to strengthening church discipline. He supported Hilary of Arles in quarrels with Pope Leo I.

Verecundus (d. 552). An African Christian writer, who took an active part in the christological controversies of the sixth century, especially in the debate on Three Chapters. He also wrote allegorical commentaries on the nine liturgical church canticles.

Victorinus of Petovium (d. c. 304). Latin biblical exegete. With multiple works attributed to him, his sole surviving work is the *Commentary on the Apocalypse* and perhaps some fragments from *Commentary on Matthew*. Victorinus expressed strong millenarianism in his writing, though his was less materialistic than the millenarianism of Papias or Irenaeus. In his allegorical approach he could be called a spiritual disciple of Origen. Victorinus died during the first year of Diocletian's persecution, probably in 304.

Vincent of Lérins (d. before 450). Monk who has exerted considerable influence through his writings on orthodox dogmatic theological method, as contrasted with the theological methodologies of the heresies.

Timeline of Writers of the Patristic Period

Location Period	British Isles	Gaul	Spain, Portugal	Rome* and Italy	Carthage and Northern Africa
2nd century				Clement of Rome, fl. c. 92-101 (Greek)	
				Shepherd of Hermas, c. 140 (Greek)	
				Justin Martyr (Ephesus, Rome), c. 100/110-165 (Greek)	
		Irenaeus of Lyons, c. 135-c. 202 (Greek)		Valentinus the Gnostic (Rome), fl. c. 140 (Greek)	
				Marcion (Rome), fl. 144 (Greek)	
3rd century				Callistus of Rome, regn. 217-222 (Latin)	Tertullian of Carthage, c. 155/160- c. 225 (Latin)
				Minucius Felix of Rome, fl. 218-235 (Latin)	
				Hippolytus (Rome, Palestine?), fl. 222-235/245 (Greek)	Cyprian of Carthage, fl. 248-258 (Latin)
				Novatian of Rome, fl. 235-258 (Latin)	
				Victorinus of Petovium, 230-304 (Latin)	

*One of the five ancient patriarchates

Alexandria* and Egypt	Constantinople* and Asia Minor, Greece	Antioch* and Syria	Mesopotamia, Persia	Jerusalem* and Palestine	Location Unknown
Philo of Alexandria, c. 20 B.C. – c. A.D. 50 (Greek)				Flavius Josephus (Rome), c. 37-c. 101 (Greek)	
Basilides (Alexandria), 2nd cent. (Greek)	Polycarp of Smyrna, c. 69-155 (Greek)	*Didache* (Egypt?), c. 100 (Greek)			
Letter of Barnabas (Syria?), c. 130 (Greek)		Ignatius of Antioch, c. 35–107/112 (Greek)			
Theodotus the Valentinian, 2nd cent. (Greek)	Athenagoras (Greece), fl. 176-180 (Greek)	Theophilus of Antioch, c. late 2nd cent. (Greek)			*Second Letter of Clement* (spurious; Corinth, Rome, Alexandria?) (Greek), c. 150
Clement of Alexandria, c. 150-215 (Greek)	*Montanist Oracles*, late 2nd cent. (Greek)				
Sabellius (Egypt), 2nd–3rd cent. (Greek)					Pseudo-Clementines 3rd cent. (Greek)
			Mani (Manichaeans), c. 216-276		
Letter to Diognetus, 3rd cent. (Greek)	Gregory Thaumaturgus (Neocaesarea), fl. c. 248-264 (Greek)				
Origen (Alexandria, Caesarea of Palestine), 185-254 (Greek)					
Dionysius of Alexandria, d. 264/5 (Greek)					
	Methodius of Olympus (Lycia), d. c. 311 (Greek)				

Timeline of Writers of the Patristic Period

Location	British Isles	Gaul	Spain, Portugal	Rome* and Italy	Carthage and Northern Africa
Period					
4th century				Firmicus Maternus (Sicily), fl. c. 335 (Latin)	
		Lactantius, c. 260-330 (Latin)		Marius Victorinus (Rome), fl. 355-363 (Latin)	
				Eusebius of Vercelli, fl. c. 360 (Latin)	
			Hosius of Cordova, d. 357 (Latin)	Lucifer of Cagliari (Sardinia), d. 370/371 (Latin)	
		Hilary of Poitiers, c. 315-367 (Latin)	Potamius of Lisbon, fl. c. 350-360 (Latin)	Faustinus (Rome), fl. 380 (Latin)	
				Filastrius of Brescia, fl. 380 (Latin)	
			Gregory of Elvira, fl. 359-385 (Latin)	Ambrosiaster (Italy?), fl. c. 366-384 (Latin)	
			Prudentius, c. 348-c. 410 (Latin)	Faustus of Riez, fl. c. 380 (Latin)	
			Pacian of Barcelona, 4th cent. (Latin)	Gaudentius of Brescia, fl. 395 (Latin)	Paulus Orosius, b. c. 380 (Latin)
				Ambrose of Milan, c. 333-397; fl. 374-397 (Latin)	
				Paulinus of Milan, late 4th early 5th cent. (Latin)	
5th century				Rufinus (Aquileia, Rome), c. 345-411 (Latin)	
	Fastidius (Britain), c. 4th-5th cent. (Latin)	Sulpicius Severus (Bordeaux), c. 360-c. 420/425 (Latin)		Aponius, fl. 405-415 (Latin)	Quodvultdeus (Carthage), fl. 430 (Latin)
				Chromatius (Aquileia), fl. 400 (Latin)	
		John Cassian (Palestine, Egypt, Constantinople, Rome, Marseilles), 360-432 (Latin)		Pelagius (Britain, Rome), c. 354-c. 420 (Greek)	Augustine of Hippo, 354-430 (Latin)
				Maximus of Turin, d. 408/423 (Latin)	Luculentius, 5th cent. (Latin)
		Vincent of Lérins, d. 435 (Latin)		Paulinus of Nola, 355-431 (Latin)	
		Valerian of Cimiez, fl. c. 422-449 (Latin)		Peter Chrysologus (Ravenna), c. 380-450 (Latin)	
		Eucherius of Lyons, fl. 420-449 (Latin)		Julian of Eclanum, 386-454 (Latin)	

*One of the five ancient patriarchates

Alexandria* and Egypt	Constantinople* and Asia Minor, Greece	Antioch* and Syria	Mesopotamia, Persia	Jerusalem* and Palestine	Location Unknown
Antony, c. 251-355 (Coptic /Greek)	Theodore of Heraclea (Thrace), fl. c. 330-355 (Greek)	Eustathius of Antioch, fl. 325 (Greek)	Aphrahat (Persia) c. 270-350; fl. 337-345 (Syriac)	Eusebius of Caesarea (Palestine), c. 260/263-340 (Greek)	Commodius, c. 3rd or 5th cent. (Latin)
Peter of Alexandria, d. c. 311 (Greek)	Marcellus of Ancyra, d.c. 375 (Greek)	Eusebius of Emesa, c. 300-c. 359 (Greek)			
Arius (Alexandria), fl. c. 320 (Greek)	Epiphanius of Salamis (Cyprus), c. 315-403 (Greek)	Ephrem the Syrian, c. 306-373 (Syriac)	Jacob of Nisibis, fl. 308-325 (Syriac)		
Alexander of Alexandria, fl. 312-328 (Greek)	Basil (the Great) of Caesarea, b. c. 330; fl. 357-379 (Greek)	Julian the Arian (c fourth century)			
Pachomius, c. 292-347 (Coptic/Greek?)	Macrina the Younger, c. 327-379 (Greek)				
Theodore of Tabennesi, d. 368 (Coptic/Greek)	Apollinaris of Laodicea, 310-c. 392 (Greek)				
Horsiesi, c. 305-390 (Coptic/Greek)	Gregory of Nazianzus, b. 329/330; fl. 372-389 (Greek)	Nemesius of Emesa (Syria), fl. late 4th cent. (Greek)			
		Diodore of Tarsus, d. c. 394 (Greek)		Acacius of Caesarea (Palestine), d. c. 365 (Greek)	
Athanasius of Alexandria, c. 295-373; fl. 325-373 (Greek)	Gregory of Nyssa, c. 335-394 (Greek)	John Chrysostom (Constantinople), 344/354-407 (Greek)		Cyril of Jerusalem, c. 315-386 (Greek)	
Macarius of Egypt, c. 300-c. 390 (Greek)	Amphilochius of Iconium, c. 340/345-c. 398/404 (Greek)	Apostolic Constitutions, c. 375-400 (Greek)			
Didymus (the Blind) of Alexandria, 313-398 (Greek)	Evagrius of Pontus, 345-399 (Greek)	Didascalia, 4th cent. (Syriac)			
Tyconius, c. 330-390 (Latin)	Eunomius of Cyzicus, fl. 360-394 (Greek)	Theodore of Mopsuestia, c. 350-428 (Greek)		Diodore of Tarsus, d. c. 394 (Greek)	
	Pseudo-Macarius (Mesopotamia?), late 4th cent. (Greek)	Acacius of Beroea, c. 340-c. 436 (Greek)		Jerome (Rome, Antioch, Bethlehem), c. 347-420 (Latin)	
	Nicetas of Remesiana, d. c. 414 (Latin)				
Palladius of Helenopolis (Egypt), c. 365-425 (Greek)	Nestorius (Constantinople), c. 381-c. 451 (Greek)	Book of Steps, c. 400 (Syriac)	Eznik of Kolb, fl. 430-450 (Armenian)	Jerome (Rome, Antioch, Bethlehem), c. 347-419 (Latin)	
		Severian of Gabala, fl. c. 400 (Greek)			
Cyril of Alexandria, 375-444 (Greek)	Basil of Seleucia, fl. 440-468 (Greek)	Nilus of Ancyra, d.c. 430 (Greek)		Philip the Priest (d. 455/56)	
	Diadochus of Photice (Macedonia), 400-474 (Greek)			Hesychius of Jerusalem, fl. 412-450 (Greek)	
				Euthymius (Palestine), 377-473 (Greek)	

Timeline of Writers of the Patristic Period

Location / Period	British Isles	Gaul	Spain, Portugal	Rome* and Italy	Carthage and Northern Africa
5th century (cont.)		Hilary of Arles, c. 401-449 (Latin)			
		Eusebius of Gaul, 5th cent. (Latin)		Leo the Great (Rome), regn. 440-461 (Latin)	
		Prosper of Aquitaine, c. 390-c. 463 (Latin)		Arnobius the Younger (Rome), fl. c. 450 (Latin)	
		Salvian the Presbyter of Marseilles, c. 400-c. 480 (Latin)		Ennodius (Arles, Milan, Pavia) c. 473-521 (Latin)	
		Gennadius of Marseilles, d. after 496 (Latin)			
6th century		Caesarius of Arles, c. 470-543 (Latin)	Paschasius of Dumium (Portugal), c. 515-c. 580 (Latin)	Epiphanius the Latin, late 5th–early 6th cent. (Latin)	Fulgentius of Ruspe, c. 467-532 (Latin)
			Apringius of Beja, mid-6th cent. (Latin)		Verecundus, d. 552 (Latin)
			Leander of Seville, c. 545-c. 600 (Latin)	Eugippius, c. 460- c. 533 (Latin)	Primasius, fl. 550-560 (Latin)
				Benedict of Nursia, c. 480-547 (Latin)	
			Martin of Braga, fl. 568-579 (Latin)		Facundus of Hermiane, fl. 546-568 (Latin)
				Cassiodorus (Calabria), c. 485-c. 540 (Latin)	
7th century				Gregory the Great (Rome), c. 540-604 (Latin)	
				Gregory of Agrigentium, d. 592 (Greek)	
			Isidore of Seville, c. 560-636 (Latin)	Paterius, 6th/7th cent. (Latin)	
			Braulio of Saragossa, c. 585-651 (Latin)		
	Adamnan, c. 624-704 (Latin)		Fructuosus of Braga, d.c. 665 (Latin)		
8th-12th century	Bede the Venerable, c. 672/673-735 (Latin)				

*One of the five ancient patriarchates

Alexandria* and Egypt	Constantinople* and Asia Minor, Greece	Antioch* and Syria	Mesopotamia, Persia	Jerusalem* and Palestine	Location Unknown
Ammonius of Alexandria, c. 460 (Greek)	Gennadius of Constantinople, d. 471 (Greek)	John of Antioch, d. 441/2 (Greek)		Gerontius of Petra c. 395-c.480 (Syriac)	
Poemen, 5th cent. (Greek)		Theodoret of Cyr, c. 393-466 (Greek)			
Besa the Copt, 5th cent.		Pseudo-Victor of Antioch, 5th cent. (Greek)			
Shenoute, c. 350-466 (Coptic)		John of Apamea, 5th cent. (Syriac)			
	Andrew of Caesarea (Cappadocia), early-6th cent. (Greek)				
Olympiodorus, early 6th cent.	Oecumenius (Isauria), 6th cent. (Greek)	Philoxenus of Mabbug (Syria), c. 440-523 (Syriac)	Jacob of Sarug, c. 450-520 (Syriac)	Procopius of Gaza (Palestine), c. 465-530 (Greek)	Pseudo-Dionysius the Areopagite, fl. c. 500 (Greek)
		Severus of Antioch, c. 465-538 (Greek)	Babai the Great, c. 550-628 (Syriac)	Dorotheus of Gaza, fl. 525-540 (Greek)	
		Mark the Hermit (Tarsus), c. 6th cent. (4th cent.?) (Greek)	Babai, early 6th cent. (Syriac)	Cyril of Scythopolis, b. c. 525; d. after 557 (Greek)	
	Maximus the Confessor (Constantinople), c. 580-662 (Greek)	Sahdona/Martyrius, fl. 635-640 (Syriac)	Isaac of Nineveh, d. c. 700 (Syriac)		(Pseudo-) Constantius, before 7th cent.? (Greek)
					Andreas, c. 7th cent. (Greek)
		John of Damascus (John the Monk), c. 650-750 (Greek)			
	Theophanes (Nicaea), 775-845 (Greek)		John the Elder of Qardu (north Iraq), 8th cent. (Syriac)		
	Cassia (Constantinople), c. 805-c. 848/867 (Greek)		Isho'dad of Merv, d. after 852 (Syriac)		
	Arethas of Caesarea (Constantinople/Caesarea), c. 860-940 (Greek)				
	Photius (Constantinople), c. 820-891 (Greek)				
	Symeon the New Theologian (Constantinople), 949-1022 (Greek)				
	Theophylact of Ohrid (Bulgaria), 1050-1126 (Greek)				

Bibliography of Works
in Original Languages

This bibliography refers readers to original language sources and supplies Thesaurus Linguae Graecae (=TLG) or Cetedoc Clavis (=Cl.) numbers where available. The edition listed in this bibliography may in some cases differ from the edition found in TLG or Cetedoc databases.

Augustine. *De civitate Dei.* In *Aurelii Augustini opera.* Edited by Bernhard Dombart and Alphons Kalb. CCL 47, 48. Turnhout, Belgium: Brepols, 1955. Cl. 0313.

Basil the Great. "Epistulae." In *Saint Basil: Lettres.* Edited by Yves Courtonne. Vol. 2, pp. 101-218; vol. 3, pp. 1-229. Paris: Les Belles Lettres, 1961-1966. TLG 2040.004.

Clement of Alexandria. "Ex Nicetae Catena in Job." In *Clementis Alexandrini opera quae exstant omnia.* PG 9, cols.740-41. Edited by J.-P. Migne. Paris: Migne, 1857. For a similar text, see Pseudo-Chrysostom, PG 64, cols. 456-57, also found in TLG 2062.364.

Didymus the Blind. *Kommentar zu Hiob.* PTA 1 and 2. Edited by Albert Henrichs; PTA 3 and 33.1. Edited by Dieter Hagedorn, Ursula Hagedorn and L. Koenen. Bonn: R. Habelt 1968-1985. TLG 2102.001-4.

Ephrem the Syrian. *Commentarii in Job.* In *ESOO 2.* Edited by J. S. Assemani. Rome, 1740.

Gregory the Great. *Moralia in Job.* Edited by Mark Adriaen. CCL 143, 143A, 143B. Turnhout, Belgium: Brepols, 1979-1985. Cetedoc 1708.

Hesychius of Jerusalem. *Homélies sur Job.* Edited by Charles Renoux and Charles Mercier. PO 42, Fasc.1-2. Turnhout, Belgium: Brepols, 1983.

[Isho'dad of Merv]. *Commentaire d'Iso'dad de Merv sur l'Ancien Testament: III. Livres des Sessions.* CSCO 229 (Scriptores Syri 96). Edited by Ceslas van den Eynde. Louvain, Belgium: Secretariat du Corpus, 1962.

John Chrysostom. *Kommentar zu Hiob.* PTS 35, pp. 1-200. Edited by Ursula and Dieter Hagedorn. Berlin; New York: de Gruyter, 1990. TLG 2062.505.

Julian of Eclanum. "Expositio libri Job." In *Juliani Aeclanensis Expositio libri Job, Tractatus prophetarum Osee Johel et Amos, Operum deperditorum fragmenta.* Edited by Lucas de Coninck. CCL 88, pp. 1-109. Turnhout, Belgium: Brepols, 1977. Cetedoc 0777.

[Julian the Arian]. *Der Hiobkommentar des arianers Julian.* Edited by Dieter Hagedorn. PTS 14. Berlin; New York: de Gruyter, 1973.

Olympiodorus. "Commentarium in Beatum Job." In *Hesychii hierosolymitani presbyteri, Olympiodor Alexandrini, Leontii Neapoleos in Cyro Episcopi, Opera omnia.* PG 93, cols. 11-470. Edited by J.-P. Migne. Paris: Migne, 1860. TLG 2865.001.

———. *Kommentar zu Hiob.* Edited by Ursula and Dieter Hagedorn. PTS 24. Berlin and New York: de Gruyter, 1984. TLG 2865.001.

Origen. *Die älteren griechischen Katenen zum Buch Hiob.* Vols. 2 and 3. PTS 48 and 53. Edited by Ursula and Dieter Hagedorn. Berlin and New York: de Gruyter, 1997-2000.

Philip the Priest. See "Commentarii in librum Job." In *S. Eusebii Hieronymi, Opera omnia.* PL 26, cols. 619-802. Edited by J.-P. Migne. Paris: Migne, 1845.

Bibliography of Works in English Translation

Augustine. *City of God, Christian Doctrine*. Translated by Marcus Dods and J. F. Shaw. NPNF 2. Series 1. Edited by Philip Schaff. 14 vols. 1886-1889. Reprint, Peabody, Mass.: Hendrickson, 1994.

Basil the Great. "The Letters." In *Letters and Select Works*, pp. 109-327. Translated by Blomfield Jackson. NPNF 8. Series 2. Edited by Philip Schaff. 14 vols. 1886-1889. Reprint, Peabody, Mass.: Hendrickson, 1994.

[Clement of Alexandria]. "Fragments of Clemens Alexandrinus" in *Fathers of the Second Century: Hermas, Tatian, Athenagoras, Theophilus and Clement of Alexandria*, pp. 569-87. Translated by William Wilson. ANF 2. Edited by Alexander Roberts and James Donaldson. 10 vols. 1885-1887. Reprint, Peabody, Mass.: Hendrickson, 1994.

Gregory the Great. *Morals on the Book of Job*. Translated by Members of the English Church. LF 18, 21 and 23. Oxford: John Henry Parker, 1844-1850.

Authors/Writings Index

Subject Index